Two's a Crew

One of the world's greatest adventures - Following Flinders wake around Australia - 9000 nautical miles across six climatic zones, Jack and Jude explore their adopted homeland. An ancient country, one filled with beauty, yet harsh, remote, and containing mysteries that still baffle the greatest minds.

Jack and Jude have travelled the remoter parts of Earth for more than forty years. Land trips across America and Europe were followed by a honeymoon trek from England to South Africa. Travelling to Australia in 1969, they homebuilt a ferrocement yacht while starting a family. That took three years of arduous work and their sons Jason and Jerome were walking by the time it was completed, so they grabbed the dream of sharing nature and adventure before what seemed mandatory school years. Miraculously their journey lasted not the one-year imagined, but the next fifteen. In ever increasing circles, the *Four J's* explored Earth, touching 80 countries while they boat-schooled their sons to the final year of high school.

Jack and Jude are grandparents now, and still aboard the same vessel have just circumnavigated Australia. In their lifetime, mankind has dominated the wild kingdom, taking what's wanted, leaving less for every creature. In doing this, the balance of Nature has been upset. And while no one would deny the improvements enjoyed today, Jack and Jude often wonder if such a growing impact isn't robbing all Earth's creatures of a better life.

Comparing today's world with what they had seen on previous travels their stories are peppered with historical notes woven into the adventurous fabric of two grandparents alone, manning a powerful sailing craft through some of the world's most dangerous waters.

Man's heart away from nature becomes hard. ~ Standing Bear

Two's a Crew
A circumnavigation of Australia

Following the wakes of Flinders and King,
The BANYANDAH searches for knowledge and discovers adventure

Jack and Judith Binder

Our story, above all, is a personal journey that we dedicate to our grandchildren and to all young ones around the world who will one day direct the course of mankind. To those who helped us achieve our dreams and who made the journey that much more full and fun, to name each would take a separate volume, so, to you, we say thank you. Your kindness has shown yet again the beautiful qualities that reside in most of us.

Copyright © Jack and Judith Binder 2010, 2011, 2020

All photographs and diagrams by Jack and Judith Binder

All rights reserved. No part of this book may be reproduced or transmitted in any form or by any means electronic or mechanical, including photocopying, recording or by any information storage and retrieval system, without prior permission in writing from the publishers or authors.

First edition published in Australia 2010
Second edition published in 2011
Third edition published Worldwide 2020

Tujays Publishing
Empire Vale P.O., NSW
Australia 2478
Email: capjack2j@gmail.com
Web: www.jackandjude.com

Papers used in the production of this book are natural, renewable and recyclable products sourced from sustainable forests.

Two's a Crew

Biography
ISBN 978-0-9808720-1-9 (pbk.)
ISBN 978-0-9808720-2-6 (hbk.)

Note:
Both imperial and metric measurements used throughout.
1 nautical mile (nm) = 1.15 land miles (m) = 1.852 kilometres (km)
Australian dollars are shown
Australian spelling is used

Contents

Beyond the Four J's	1
First Departure	7
Jayden Comes to Play	15
Lucky, Lucky, Lucky	21
Le Top	25
Sailing Off the Edge	29
The Giant's Pool	42
Visiting Ancient Folk	50
Twin Falls	58
Careening Bay	63
Lost Dreams	68
Spiritual Place	73
Making Our Escape	79
Pristine Oasis – The Journey	85
Pristine Oasis – The Island	95
Pristine Oasis – The Lagoon	105
Pristine Oasis – The Reality	117
Paying the Piper	127
Export Inc	133
Setting the Night on Fire	144
Giant Mutant Lobster	151
Stormy Weather	158
Have Sails – Will Travel	166
Carnarvon Dreaming	177
Beginning of Life	189
Travels South	199
Adventure Bound	203
Moonlight Across the Southern Ocean	207
They Called It Meebberlee	215
On Pain and Sorrow	226
Here Comes Dessert	234
Licking Our Lips	239
Digestive Anyone	244
Lost Hideaway	251
Ochre Red	259
Hunter Gatherer	268
Melaleuca Visions	281
Turning Home	289
Hello from Coffs	291
Start	295
Bibliography	
Glossary	

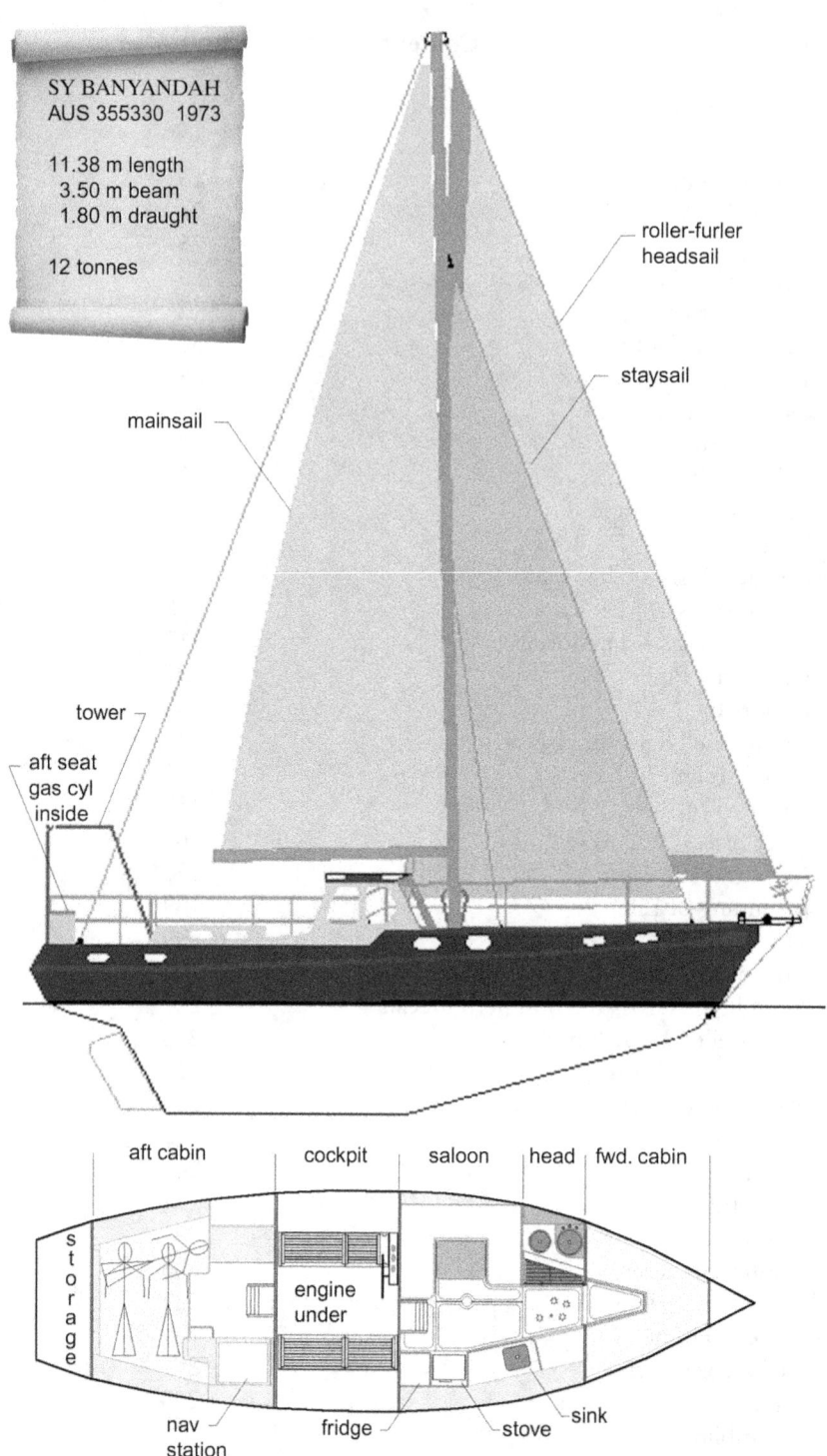

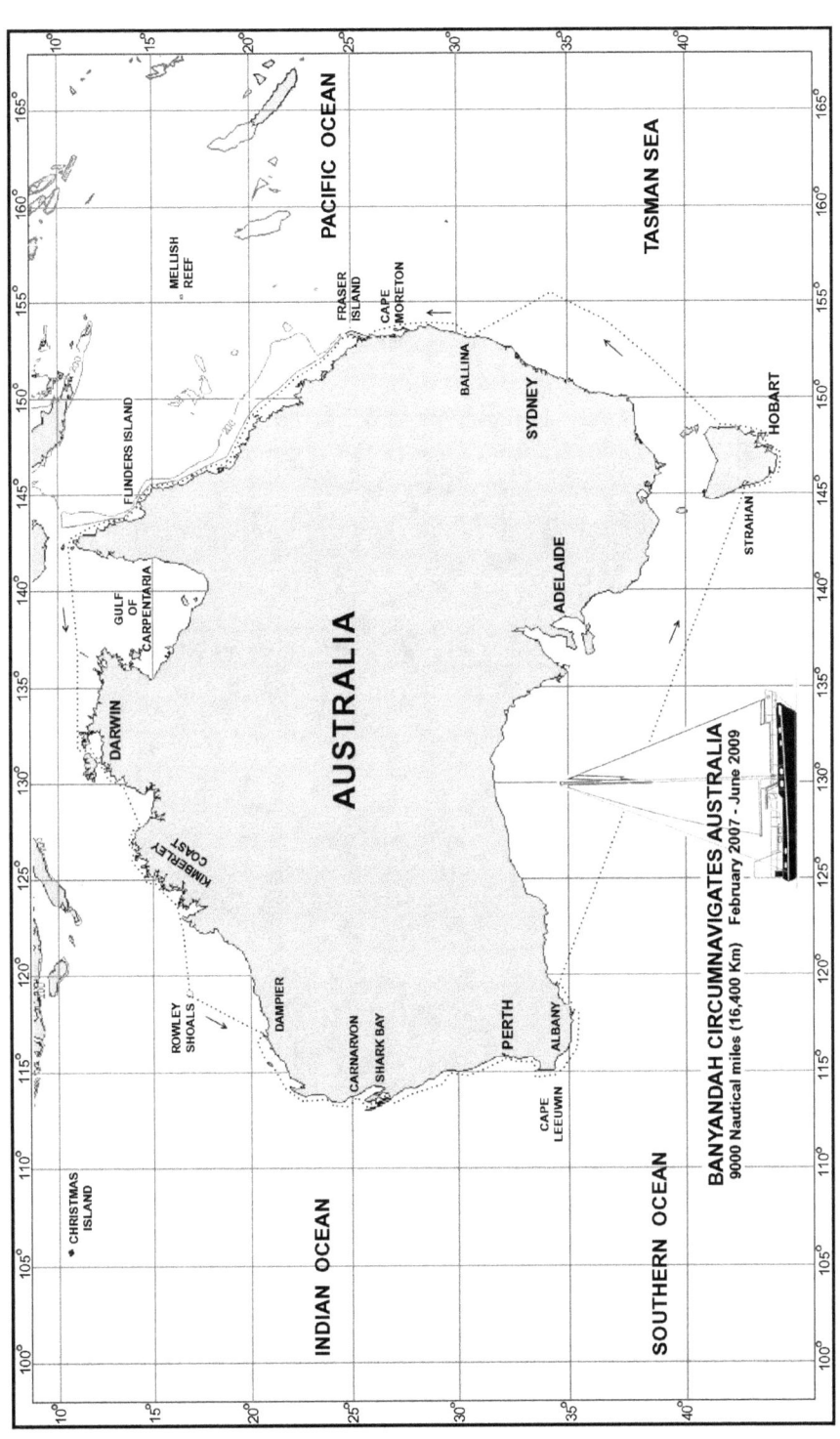

BEYOND THE FOUR J's

Storm clouds race above The Hazards casting dark shadows across the same pink granite mountains that the great French explorer Freycinet sketched from *Le Naturaliste* more than two hundred years earlier. Across Wineglass Bay, cold wetness is falling to an open horizon flecked white that calls our spirits to run free, close the last link, and complete the circle around Earth's largest inhabited island. So far, every link has needed courage and strength. Each has been as different as the colours in a rainbow.

To not lose the weather edge, we must commit to the south wind's fury and sail north knowing we will be alone at sea, not for hours, but days exceeding a week. Why is it Judith and I gamble our lives trekking the wild places? Why do we sally forth without thought of assistance, with few comforts, and fewer companions?

We go where there are no rules - except Nature's - survive. No marked lanes. No stoplights. As if wandering through the Garden of Eden, Earth and her creatures provide wonder, adventure, and entertainment. They reveal mysteries beyond our wisdom, offer knowledge by simply observing life.

In 1803, Captain Matthew Flinders became the first to circumnavigate the fifth continent, producing a map of remarkable accuracy on which for the first time, "Australia" was provocatively inscribed. Flinders would have found Terra Australis little different from when man first wandered its vastness. However, his map would dramatically change that.

When the Industrial Revolution called our people from the land, our growth began to dominate the wild kingdom, taking what's wanted, leaving less for every creature. And while no one would deny the improvements we enjoy, we have upset Nature and have become more trapped by systems we've developed. Jude and I have long wondered if man's growing impact isn't robbing all Earth's creatures of a better life.

So we set off on one of the world's greatest adventures - Following Flinders wake around Australia - 9000 nautical miles across six climatic zones to explore more closely our adopted homeland. An ancient country, one filled with beauty, yet harsh, remote, and containing mysteries that still baffle the greatest minds.

We wanted to compare today's world with what we had seen on previous travels and write to our grandchildren, encouraging them to have a full life, one connected to Earth, with a positive influence on the course of mankind. During our odyssey, we posted many anecdotes home. Meant to educate as well as entertain, we peppered our stories with historical notes woven into the adventurous fabric of two grandparents alone, manning a powerful sailing craft through some of the world's most dangerous waters.

Our story begins many years earlier when two young people first met and found in the other a strength of character so strong each entrusted their life in the hands of the other. Coming from entirely different backgrounds, instead of clashing, it added to our strength as a team. But this wasn't evident when we first embarked on our journey through life together.

We met while hitchhiking around Europe, in the Frankfurt Youth Hostel, where I tried to talk Judith and her girlfriend Beth into travelling back to Berlin with me. They didn't have enough time for that, so we ended up challenging the other to a race to Paris using only our charm and wits. I won - but Jude says, "Doesn't matter." She and Beth had a really gay time sampling wine with two French hunks they met along the way.

Jude and I were married in a quaint north England church then set off in a dilapidated VW van we had rescued from a farmer's field. Mechanically fixing it up in her mother's driveway, then adding a bed and stove after replacing the Volkswagen's hard bench seat with two comfy Mercedes red bucket seats, that van became our first home as man and wife. From England, we journeyed down the war-torn continent of Africa, crying for Biafrans and fearing remnants of Simba and Mau-Mau. That year-long journey opened our young eyes and sharpened our survival skills.

When we came to the sunburnt country of Australia in 1969, we found space everywhere with a feeling of "she'll be right" that encouraged us to not only start a family but also to start the construction of a 12-metre sailing vessel. That arduous project took three years of strenuous work and our two sons were walking by the time it was completed. That's when we grabbed hold of our dream to share adventure and Nature with them before what seemed mandatory school years. Leaving our rented digs, we moved aboard our new yacht, naming her *Banyandah*, which means "home on the water." We then boldly cast adrift our small business and friends.

Jason 11 months inside propellor aperture & Jerome inside Jude

In 1974, with sons aged two and three, we began a journey into the unknown. Starting with no sailing experience, frightened and unsure, we overcame many obstacles while our sea roving life eventually took us around the world touching eighty countries in an odyssey that lasted not the one year imagined, but the next fifteen. When our sons were toddlers, they frolicked with dusky natives on sugar-white beaches. When others their age were just starting school, they played and stayed with the Muslims and Hindus of Asia. And when nine and ten, our sons soaked up the culture of Japan before enjoying the good life in Hawaii and the South Pacific as they entered puberty. And when still a bit wild, but now reliable sailing hands, we shared long night watches during a three-year circumnavigation of the world on "voyages of education." First stop, Africa to see the remaining wild beasts and gaze upon Egyptian mummies. Then we travelled through Europe teaching early civilisations to our sons. South America came next, to witness what remained of the wild Amazon and study Inca ruins, and that's where we talked the Ecuadorian Navy into letting us tour all of the Galapagos. We told them their unique creatures belonged to every child of the world. Coming home to Australia, we stopped at Easter Island where the boys stayed with Orlando, a living legend mentioned in *Aku-Aku*. When we departed that mysterious isle, his son was on board, so he too could experience an ocean adventure just as his father had.

While travelling Earth, the reward for our dedication and hard work was meeting a diverse cross-section of people and seeing history's most significant monuments, and of course, witnessing Earth's magnificent beauty. All while boat-schooling our children to their final year of high school.

But that was then. Life has moved on, and The *Four J's* have matured. We have grandchildren now, so it was just mom and pop who were free to continue exploring Earth. Our physical forms have weakened, our confidence has been tempered, but Jude and I have always heard the call of the wild beckoning us to witness Nature in all her glory again. So we unleashed our spirits to journey forth once again.

But before lines could be cast free, *Banyandah* needed repair. Her years of service had taken their toll. Home built by amateurs, which is what we were, she had a few inherent faults that needed to be put right. Plus with advancing age came a desire for more comfort. A desire for full headroom, a want for a shower with hot water on tap, and a need to make her more easy and safe to manage. So, the wrecking hammers came out. And once the first blow was struck, it became impossible to stop until only a shell remained, as bare and empty as when first concreted back in 1971.

Plans and dreams often melt away in the heat of execution. At best, they just take much longer. Life's that way. Family, work, recreation, all nibble away at project time and it is easy to lose focus. We had a five-year plan that stretched to ten, then another five years drifted by so swiftly that when celebrating our thirty-eighth year of marriage, with three grandchildren and more on the way, alarm bells began ringing when we looked in the mirror and saw grey hair and wrinkled faces looking back. Judith and I knew we had to go or never realise the dream we had kept alive since moving from the sea to the land. With that realisation, a pang of doubt hardened in our guts and fear of failure stole into our hearts. We could have easily stayed onshore as most seniors would, to enjoy family and friends, but while we still had our good health, we knew we must go.

The best way to make sure something gets done is to set a deadline, so the very next morning we booked a crane to relaunch *Banyandah* in three months. Once committed, renewed energy flowed. And gosh, was it needed to finish the many tasks that always seem to be forgotten when setting deadlines.

After sixteen years afloat, followed by sixteen years sitting on our front lawn, a massive crane entered our drive, and a new page in *Banyandah's* life began. To be honest, we were astounded to see that she indeed still floated. But to our immense pleasure, our dear lady took to the water like a beautiful black swan, and a new adventure began. After so many years on the land, Judith and I had to re-hone old skills, and we had to test every one of *Banyandah's* new systems. Her machinery had been totally rebuilt, as had her electrics, plumbing, anchoring system; everything was new, including a new rig and new rudder. Confidence in her, and ourselves, had to be created anew by putting both to trial.

There were blunders and failures, and we made errors, but overall, once again, *Banyandah* became a superbly comfortable craft, easy to handle, and really great to live aboard.

Jason (1) & Jerome (4 months)
The *FOUR J's* 1972

Jason, just a bub, on boat scaffolding, 1971

Backyard built, a happy Jack looks down from the deck of his new ship

Our first cruise complete with a pool

First sail for homemade BANYANDAH

Bath time on board >

Our first BIG fish - big exitement for all

After 16 years afloat, Banyandah rests on our front lawn while we built our land house and helped our sons set off on their own path of life. At the same time, we started securing our future by creating timber furniture, and in our free time, we gutted our lady then totally rebuilt her from bare hull.

After 16 years on the land, completely rebuilt, Banyandah is relaunched, re-rigged, and sets off on her journey around Australia with the family wishing us Bon Voyage.

FIRST DEPARTURE

This is where our journey starts. We had taken all we wanted from the house and left it empty. That it had sustained our growth through a long and vital period was in our thoughts as we took one last look around then turned the key. Unstoppable like the hands of a clock we were next in our fully-loaded station wagon driving the few hundred metres to Gary's jetty to move fulltime on board *Banyandah*.

It was Friday, the day before our much-touted departure and the tradesmen had been tooting their horns wishing us good luck as they drove home from work. Up forward, bags of sails hid the bunk, and opposite the toilet, medical gear lay in piles on the seat, while in the saloon Jude sorted food and culinary items into one of three lockers, or into her new galley drawers, which she loved. Back aft, a stack of dog-eared charts had to be sorted, but first, a mess of clothes covering the bed needed a home. Between us, the cockpit had spare parts and tools strewn about. Back and forth, our chatter filled the air.

"Hey Jude, where should I put…" And I would mention a book, article of clothing, or a packet of medicines.

"Jack, did you remember to bring the…" And she would ask about the waterproof torch, extra batteries, or some bit of safety gear.

Some of our conversation centred on how the next few days might go, but a lot toyed with more distant horizons.

"Wonder if we'll find any more of the wreck on Herald's Beacon," Jude mused.

"Dunno," I replied, picking up the basic metal detector we were taking. Touching it released a cherished memory of a bare sand islet darkened by seabirds roosting in the open and I exclaimed, "Hope when we arrive, the seabirds will be in the same numbers. And with babies like before."

"April, you think?" Jude asked. But not always waiting for a reply, she then blurted out, "If there are heaps, it'll be grand on video. Maybe we could make a documentary on mid-ocean seabirds."

The packing lasted late and not having slept afloat for many years, filled with apprehension and excitement, the tinkling of water and gentle motion, while exotic at first, were reasons we slept lightly.

Arising out the aft cabin at daybreak, the smooth river reflected an explosion of reds that set fire to the Alstonville escarpment still darkly streaked by forested gullies. Nearer at hand in the mangroves, birdsong competed against distant traffic. And further gladdening our hearts, we heard no sound of surf on the nearby beach.

Naturally anxious to see the shallow sandbank barring the river entrance, Jude drove us ten minutes up South Ballina Road to the break-wall where we joined a small troop of black-suited surfies carrying their boards towards beautiful sets sweeping around the breakwater. Perfect for them, but between the two rock groynes, the outgoing tide was causing havoc. The sea was piling up, breaking steeply in several patches across the river mouth. And on the outer bar, it was even more vicious. I'm not sure how Jude felt, she said not a word, but this made me feel a tad nervous.

In our youth, we had safely crossed many scary sandbars; primarily because our Hartley designed *Banyandah* has a long keel that tracks straight and true through just about anything. Watching these breakers, I was thinking they would significantly ease with the change to an incoming tide and then be dictated more by the wind, which at that early hour touched our cheeks only lightly.

Our vessel was ready, the flat horizon beckoned, and keen to go a decision was taken to get underway in two hours, at 9 am if conditions improved as expected.

Jude dropped me back at the boat for final checks then sped off for last-minute fresh veggies. I cast my eye around the engine room; all ready there. Then while taking down the sun awning, my gaze settled again on the river. I paused and reflected on the path taken to that moment. Like that shiny river, we had survived many storms and calms to move point by point until now we were able to sail away and explore new destinations.

The "what ifs" then started drifting in. I knew them well, as Jude did, having had them in our heads or discussed so many times over the many years rebuilding *Banyandah*. I am a humble man and had to admit there were parts of this vessel I could not remember making, although I did. And there were other bits that I thought about all too often, and these would remain foremost in my thoughts until we survived our first storm. Nevertheless, Jude and I were tracking on a course set down many years ago, and we were determined that these aged bodies would take this rebuilt veteran out across the river bar to the open sea once again.

Jude returned, and just as the ship's bells struck nine, our ancient diesel roared into life. A few minutes later, the lines holding *Banyandah* to our neighbour's jetty were released, and with a wave from Gary and Lyn, we moved off feeling dumbstruck to be actually underway. Thick in a mental fog, we passed our house then snapped awake to share a fond farewell with good neighbours George and Judy on the riverbank shouting a hearty bon voyage as *Banyandah* left behind the riverside address she'd known for nearly two decades.

Excitement grew with each text message we sent announcing our imminent departure. My tension also increased. I tried diverting it, with limited success, using an old habit of moving about checking every detail like a nervous drake checking his brood.

Where the Richmond bends east towards the sea, the Burns Point car ferry was crossing on cables that have kept us connected to Ballina for so many years. With a big cheerio to coxswain Brock, we shouted, "see you when we get back," then raised the mainsail even though there was not a skerrick of breeze. It just made us look a proper sailing ship.

We thumped past the trawler harbour then gave a wave to those enjoying breakfast on the League Club's veranda. Then as we passed the sailing club opposite Mobbs Bay, the first ocean swells rocked *Banyandah*. Minutes later, the Coast Guard tower was nearly abeam, and that brought in view our first ocean white. Now we could see a few curly ones still breaking on the outer bar, and my heart nearly missed a beat when a sweet one formed right across the river mouth. But it was nothing the old girl wouldn't have taken in her stride, so we just kept going.

As we came up the north wall, we could see the tide had slackened, but it was still assisting us out whether we wanted to go or not. Then Jude spotted our grandchildren on the break-wall and began waving and calling out while still driving the boat.

Quite suddenly, all our preparations were being tested. The river took us out into the oncoming swells, Jude responding to my instructions while still madly blowing kisses to the grandkids. While I, very business-like, hopped about surveying the horizon for any unexpected nasties. In this fashion, we crabbed across the river towards the deeper south passage, riding up and over a few big ocean swells.

And then we were out, the first time in decades. The river mouth behind us, open sea in front, sandy shores like silver ribbons, we turned north for Fraser Island under power from our grand old thumper. That ancient piece of machinery, originally rescued from a truck built in the '50s and then re-built, had served us well around the world. When refitting *Banyandah*, instead of retiring her, we rebuilt her again. And now she didn't miss a beat while our grandchildren became minuscule blips on the rocky break-wall that was fast being eaten by the sea. Elation mixed with the tears down Jude's cheeks while I stood numb as a statue. Talked about for so many years, we had finally departed. And all the perfect day lacked was a bit of wind in our new sailing rig.

During her refit, we had ditched *Banyandah's* original ketch rig that had carried sail on two masts; the foremast thirteen metres tall, the aft eight metres. She had also flown a single headsail from the tip of her bow to the top of her mainmast. During her previous sixteen years of service, six different sized sails fitting that fore-triangle had been accumulated. But during her stint on the land, yacht equipment had greatly improved, so today's vessels frequently use a roller furler to reduce sail area. They work much like a Venetian blind, rolling up sail from the safety of the cockpit - You beauty! Too many times, I'd been a wild bull rider being whipped about by wild forces when pulling down a flogging sail. Dangerous many times, but because *Banyandah's* solid railing gave such great support, and a catching hand, whenever I was sent flying, changing headsails, was more often just hard, difficult, wet work.

For our new rig, a roller furler was a must. We put it out on a short bowsprit; because they look so pretty and would keep the anchor away from the hull when raised in choppy conditions. Bowsprits are also a great place to take pictures of your ship parting the waves.

Here's an anecdote illustrating our fetish for this fantastic craft and our long-standing lust to continue sailing. Our new single-mast rig is centred on a mainsail we purchased from Egyptian fishermen met when we were the *Four J's* circumnavigating the world. These threadbare fishermen had salvaged it off a French yacht that had ripped itself open on a Red Sea reef when on its maiden voyage. Stuck fast after gashing a hole and sinking, the Frenchies had abandoned her. Appearing brand new, their mainsail was about the same area as ours although much taller. Stowed aboard, it continued the voyage around the world with us, and then sat in our storage locker until our new mast went up. The higher aspect sail made us build a taller mast by another 2.5 metres, and now we have two sets of spreaders instead of one.

Getting rid of the short mizzenmast that had cluttered our aft deck, we installed a pipe tower across the stern to mount solar cells, the GPS, and radio antennas. It also became somewhere to stretch our awning to, with the other end attaching to the wires supporting the mast. They're also new, stainless this time instead of galvanised. All in all, it's a much more powerful rig that should be easier to handle.

The old "B" was the colour of sunshine, and we called her the Yellow Submarine when she was naughty, or the Banana when rowing home from a tropical isle. This time, she's a moody blue, so we have affectionately dubbed her Big Blue because she's a bit sassy and her new rig should power us through the sea very nicely.

Our home river the Richmond is scenic and peaceful, but far too restrictive to sail the cheeky Big Blue seriously. Therefore we ended up sailing her only once on the river before deciding to head for the open sea. Our master plan called for us to get physically fit during a couple months shakedown cruise in Hervey Bay behind World Heritage Fraser Island. That seemed a pleasant way of deciding whether we can and still wanted to go off adventuring again. If we did, we would bus home, rent the house, kiss the kids goodbye, and then set sail across the Coral Sea to a faraway coral reef we once visited back in 1982. There's a French frigate sunk somewhere along its outer edge. We found a bronze bolt from it when there on a charter and have often dreamt of searching for her hull and treasure. You see how easy it is to have exotic dreams with a vessel capable of going anywhere.

On this sparkling day motor sailing away from our home, we studied a shoreline intimately known from the land and reminisced. The beautiful bluff headland at Lennox Point fell astern, and not being used to time lingering, both Jude and I withdrew into our own thoughts as the bold vertical face of Cape Byron quickly approached, helped by a north going counter current. Lunch we ate standing up, still hand steering the ship until a late afternoon sea breeze prompted us to unroll the new second-hand headsail that we'd tried only once. Now we had enough headway to shut down the engine, engage the windvane steering device and have Big Blue take us north under sail power alone. Quietly admiring the green hills backing golden beaches, we once again experienced the sublime peace of slipping through the sea, with land distant enough not to be a concern, yet close enough to inspire.

Light breezes usually increase or fade after dark. Ours faded as the night deepened, and by the end of my first watch at midnight, we were dead in the water. Wanting an easy first night, as I climbed into bed, I told Jude, "Just let the old girl drift."

But in the wee hours, the GPS warned Jude that a current shift was taking us backwards. So I got up, started the engine, and set Jude steering a course for Southport, thinking we might call in there if the morning light didn't bring more puff.

I arose again with the sun to find no wind, only Gold Coast high-rises reflecting the morning's golden light across a calm silver sea. But now that we were going, Jude didn't want to stop. She felt more wind was coming, so we saluted the Southport breakwater then kept motoring north.

That proved a wise decision because a sailable breeze arose from the east shortly after. With the engine once again secured, our second day became bliss as we scooted along Stradbroke Island, in close to catch the counter current and sail past a rock that had caused us considerable grief some thirty years earlier - just at the end of our very first ocean passage.

This story does not paint my navigational skills in good light, but I was a newbie then and even more prone to human error. In a nutshell, after two years away we had sailed from the Solomon Islands heading back to Australia. Crossing the Coral Sea, we had had two weeks of easy fair winds with my sextant sights plotting a very neat line going straight for Brisbane, a 1200 nautical mile passage. But when approaching land with 300 nm to go, our fair wind turned into a nasty black nor'easter.

There was no GPS then; sextant sights were the primary navigational tool. And without a view of the sun, we were going by dead reckoning; that is, we were plotting the compass course we thought we had steered then correcting that by whatever factors might be acting upon us, such as leeway and current. Well, after three horrible days and nights working the ship in strong winds and total cloud cover, land appeared just ahead through heavy showers, and a lighthouse was seen. As I had been aiming for the lighthouse at Double Island Point, I loudly congratulated myself for a job well done, even though the light flashed differently from what it had two years earlier.

Shrugging that off with, "Well, light characteristics are sometimes changed," I turned our ship south towards Brisbane as planned. That day we flew, barely in control, the sky exploding and the sea an odd shade of green. Then, just when expected, another lighthouse appeared on a headland.

"Perfect," I proclaimed, "there'll be hot showers in a marina tonight."

But not more than a minute after making this statement, a huge flat rock whooshed out the sea barely a boat length away from *Banyandah*.

"What the hell was that," roared out my mouth as I madly turned the rudder.

Re-examining the chart, in a less assured voice, I remarked that they must have missed that rock... Yeah, sure. That was my second mistake. The first was to forget the East Australian Current, which every good Aussie sailor knows sets south at up to four knots.

Well, we were not anywhere near Brisbane that night. In fact, we had already passed that destination long before sighting land but didn't discover this until after a frightening night of trying to escape the sandbanks fronting Brisbane - which is where I thought we were, but we were not.

After the storm blew out, Gold Coast high-rises appearing at first light set the cat amongst the pigeons, and that blunder taught me not to bend facts to suit what I wanted. And so, just for old time's sake, we thought we'd take another look at that rock. It made good video passing close with the afternoon sun glinting off its horrible sharp edges.

Oh what a beautiful life basking in a warm breeze, all our cares just a blur on the horizon, and an exciting destination ahead. *Banyandah* was closing in on Cape Moreton as our second night began, and this time the easy wind continued after the heavens turned on the stars. Jude went to bed a little earlier because at our present speed I'd be waking her sometime before midnight to help us round the cape. Three rocks lie just off it with a deep channel between. We had gone inside on another occasion and wanted to experience the thrill of watching the sandy shore slip past in bright moonlight again.

Conditions were perfect for doing just that, so I fashioned a course to take us through the channel using our new GPS navigational system that locates us within a boat length on a digital chart. It all went so swimmingly I almost didn't wake Judith but knew she'd be hopping mad if I didn't. So, warmed by mugs of Milo, we watched the sweeps of the lighthouse race along the shore break and twinkle off the band of silver sand. And in less time than finishing our drink, we raced through, and the lighthouse began dwindling into the dark night.

With Jude now fully awake, I took her place in bed. And in what seemed an eye blink, first light had me yawning and rubbing away sleepy heads. Arising, Cape Moreton was just a vague smudge behind, and an easy sea rolled shoreward, taking the last of our breeze with it.

After Jude went for a mini-sleep, I fired up the iron topsail to make an anchorage before nightfall. Motor-sailing most of that third day, we pulled in behind Double Island Point with just an hour of light to spare.

Of course, we started cheering as soon as the anchor went down. In plain view across a span of open water was our destination, the sandy shores of Fraser Island. Hallelujah! Our first thought was to take the following day off. But the small ships weather forecast changed that. A strong onshore wind bringing rain was forecast, and that would make the sandbar we had to cross even more dangerous, and worse, make our present anchorage untenable.

After consulting the tide tables, we needed to cross the Wide Bay Bar at first light to have the full tide and slack water required for safety. That meant a 4 am start.

The alarm rang at the appointed hour. Groggy from too little sleep and too much rocking, I climbed out my bunk to be confronted by absolute blackness and pouring rain. Crikey! You've got to be dedicated to be a sailor.

"C'mon sweetie. Time to get up." I gently rocked my lover. She took some coaxing but started moving once I put a hot cup of tea by her bed.

In ritual fashion, we donned oilskins, started the engine, turned on the red compass light then raised the anchor. Pulling up the mainsail in pouring rain and darkness was not a whole lot of fun, but it had to be done. And soon Jude had us groping out the bay into thundery blackness; lead by the compass that said we were going northeast and our depth sounder showing it getting deeper.

Two hours later, after several torrential downpours, the rain stopped long enough for a bit of fuzzy grey to appear where the sun should have been. Within half an hour, we could see a hundred metres around a rolling sea clothed in spooky mist. Supposedly, our GPS had taken us close to the channel crossing the Wide Bay Bar, so we stopped.

As the light slowly improved, a trawler appeared within hailing distance. And when it started moving towards the land, we followed as if it had been sent to lead us in. Very soon a line of breakers appeared ahead. When the trawler went through a gap between tumbling white water, all looked good, so we continued to follow. But then, shock horror, a big sneaky one reared up behind the trawler.

Jude and I had just enough time to give each other a look of alarm, when next we looked ahead he was lost from sight then a big one started rising out the ocean behind us. Unstoppable once on their way, *Banyandah* scampered along the foaming wave top, Jude at the helm owning a big smile and me keeping a lookout from the bow as we surged atop the boiling water.

I love this boat. She tracks so straight and true, she makes dicey situations like this one just lots of big-time fun. Yahooing to the heavens with my arms thrust high, I tried to out blast the noise of Nature. Probably a good thing no one could see us, but hey, who cares when you're master of a vessel capable of going just about anywhere.

As if travelling down a bunny hole, by crossing that bar, we entered a magical kingdom. Everywhere calm water, shores of sugar sand, a hinterland of green forests and not one sign of habitation. Now in a stronghold of Nature just given a good wash, there were safe anchorages everywhere. So picking a spot for a celebratory big breakfast was a mighty tough ask. We chose a cute little nick and parked close to lush green palms overhanging another sugar-white beach. And that brought out our hunger. We were ready for a good feed and Jude's at her best in these conditions, so I was pampered in what is a unique part of Earth.

While celebrating our good fortune, somewhat awed, we noted it had taken only two nights and three days to move from one world to a completely different one. And by so doing, declared ourselves truly on our way.

JAYDEN COMES TO PLAY

After gaining entry to Nature's wonderland, a world of extraordinary beauty enveloped our home on the water. Lush tall forests on the mainland and islands were separated by enchanting waterways. Smooth, wide, and vacant they tantalisingly narrowed then disappeared in the distance inviting all gypsies to explore. But its beauty hid dangers. Unseen below turbid waters lurked the shifting sandbanks of the notorious Great Sandy Strait, and immediately before us, an almost endless collection of red and green markers restricted its broad expanse. Further on, this drunken line of markers disappeared where that gypsy road was devoured by two lands coming together.

We knew this passage from our previous travels, remembering that we had come to grief more than once when weaving through on the tides. So for the moment, further sail training was put on hold. Instead, we fired up the diesel to cautiously enter this enchanting yet scary world with darting eyes and fast-beating hearts, and once again immerse ourselves into cruising.

For many, the word cruising conjures up images of lolling about surrounded by grand vistas while doing no more than holding up a good book and dining well under glorious sunsets. But it's much more than that. Isolation for one. It's not possible to run to the shops or drop in to see friends. Our world became only what we could see. And by an invisible cord, we became attached to our ship. As parents with a new child, we began worrying whenever *Banyandah* was not in sight, imagining all the bad things that could happen. If a zephyr suddenly stole across the calm, we would worry the anchor might drag. If a chop developed, we'd think a through-hull fitting might suddenly break, flooding our baby. And if everything stayed perfect, some baddy might steal our things.

Amongst the cruising fraternity, some never leave their ship when at anchor, even though they may travel around the world. Contrary to this, when we were the *Four J's*, though we built our own craft, *Banyandah* was always the means to travel, and we often left her in strange places while we went exploring. And now it was essential to re-establish that mindset again, and we started by wandering faraway from our anchorage, putting *Banyandah* out our thoughts. Fortunately, this came rather quickly as there was so much attracting our attention.

Fraser Island stretches over 123 kilometres in a nearly north-south direction and is 22 kilometres at its widest point making it the largest sand island in the world. It's the only place in the world where tall rainforests grow on sand dunes, where the low wallum heaths are of particular evolutionary and ecological significance, besides growing magnificent wildflowers. Also, the immense sand blows and cliffs of coloured sands are still evolving and are part of the longest and most complete coastal dune system in the world. The highest reach 240 m above sea level.

The indigenous people of Fraser Island are the Butchulla clan whose name for the island is K'gari, meaning paradise. According to legend, a beautiful spirit created an idyllic island with trees, flowers and lakes, and then put birds, animals, and people on it to keep them company.

It is uncertain how long the Butchulla people occupied the island, but evidence suggests it was more than 6000 years, maybe upwards of 20,000. Population numbers are also unknown, although it's thought that during times of plentiful resources up to 2000 people may have lived on the island. We do know that in 1770, Captain Cook sighted the Butchulla people when the *Endeavour* sailed close along Fraser Island's eastern beaches, naming the next headland after sighting them, *Indian Head*. Captain Matthew Flinders was possibly the first white man to have direct contact with the islanders. He held peaceful meetings with them in 1799 and again in 1802. But by 1872, conflicts with white settlers and introduced diseases had taken a heavy toll with their numbers down to about 435 Aborigines. By 1880, there were only 230. The last Aborigines left the island in 1904 when the Anglican mission at Bogimbah was closed.

Although much of *Banyandah's* running gear had been renewed during her rebuild, a lot of it had simply come out of storage. Her outboard and tinny was one. Okay for the tinny, but the outboard was now an antique and barely ran. But we didn't want to part with the dollars to replace something we rarely used. While most of today's cruising folk have inflatable dinghies with new beaut outboards powerful enough to get them planing, Jude and I still prefer to row our dinghy. Why? Well for one, it keeps us fit, and being fit in your sixties is paramount, especially if sailing oceans. Secondly, an inflatable and outboard weigh a tonne. Well, maybe not quite that much, but they sure feel that heavy when pulling them up a beach or trying to get them back on board when ready to move on. Another reason we prefer our tinny are thieves. Expensive rubber duckies can be deflated and taken away in a car boot. It's just that bit harder to nick an alloy craft. But by far the most important reason for a hard rowing dinghy is safety. I was once coming back to *Banyandah* from an atoll situated 700 nm from the mainland, and it was blowing the usual 20-

knot trade winds when the outboard quit. Dunno why, and I didn't have time to work it out because I was being blown rather quickly towards the nasty stuff. So I did what I had to do to save my soul. I rowed. A rubber duck is a devil to row; it sideslips alarmingly fast in any sort of wind. So Jude and I rowed everywhere in those first weeks, and our tummies got flatter and once again our arm muscles starting standing up.

In 1974, when coming up this coast the very first time, the Great Sandy Strait had been a significant test. Imagine being a learner driver tackling a twisty mountain road, complicated here because the dangers cannot be seen, and there are invisible forces. We travelled in a convoy of six yachts, all newbies except our leader, a boat called *Crazy Jack*. After he got us safely across the Wide Bay Bar, like ducklings we followed him along the channel until he diverted towards an anchorage he remembered. Scared and nervous, not wanting to be lost I was first behind, and thought it odd when he came running out his wheelhouse madly waving his arms. That's when I noticed he'd suddenly stopped moving. Like a mouse surrounded by traps, I gulped then quickly dropped our anchor, and by the time we had launched our dinghy and rowed across, *Crazy Jack* had taken a distinct lean. Within the hour, dry sand started showing around his boat. And in another, *Crazy Jack* was on her side, and we could walk to the island.

Meanwhile, *Banyandah* had become entrapped in her own private pool. The fairies must have looked after us. Nevertheless, memories like that played silly buggers in my head every time Jude and I shifted anchorage. And once again we had to learn to control our fears, or we might as well park our lady in a marina and go home on a bus.

In our previous sailing life, communications had been limited to a two-way amateur radio that during good propagation could contact stations almost anywhere in the world. But it could not ring home nor could they call us. This time, in addition to a new amateur radio, we also had a mobile phone that could connect to the World Wide Web and under our particular plan gave us a free hour to any number in Australia. This proved heaven-sent. To converse with our children and grandchildren, to share our joys and mishaps took away much of the isolation, and that little device could also provide quick access to medical help if required – that is, when it could find a tower.

Over several weeks, every day we went to work, piloting our craft around dangers while familiarising ourselves with all our new gadgets, while the solitude created something like a second honeymoon. Quite different from our first time up this coast when the bonds of our marriage had been severely tested. Yachts can break unions. We've witnessed several examples.

In our case, back then, we had two young children to care for in a scary environment cut-off from help. The stress had been beyond anything we'd ever confronted before, and the bonds between Jude and I suffered through several hard years. Therefore, before leaving this time, we made a pact not to let stress put our marriage in jeopardy again. Candlelit dinners and quick rushes to study the aft cabin's new ceiling helped soothe the stress bumps, as did talking through our problems. Plus we found there is nothing like a quick cuddle before going into battle to turn something frightening into fun. In this way, we progressed up through the Great Sandy Strait to its remote north end. No cell-phone service up there. Not many visitors in boats or 4WD either. Just endless stretches of sugar-white sand, aquamarine sea, and land dotted with freshwater lakes.

Upon retiring from the sea and putting *Banyandah* on the land, Jude and I took up wilderness walking as a way to stay fit and in contact with Nature while practising the art of navigation. During those many years, we explored scores of forests and several deserts, spending hundreds of nights off track. Humping in supplies for a week at a time kept our bodies strong and our minds alert to survival. At first, we navigated solely by compass and observing the terrain, and we did fine until late one afternoon. We had set up the tent then went off to a rocky bluff for sundowners, but later, couldn't find the shelter in failing twilight. After spending that night huddled on the bare ground close to a fire, we invested nearly a week's wages on a new electronic gizmo, a handheld GPS. Once bitten, we became addicted to those magical devices that give a precise position whenever one's needed day or night.

While at its northern end near the narrowest part of Fraser Island, Jude and I went bush and that first safari was really hard yakka. Leaving our little red dinghy on the beach, we climbed the tall sand cliffs at Station Hill then pushed our way through the virgin forest over thick groundcover and understorey. This quite intrigued us as we didn't think trees, vines, and bushes could grow so big or thick in only sand. But they do.

Trudging on for a few more kilometres guided by our handheld GPS we came upon a large lake surrounded by a wide ring of reeds giving way to open sand flats. Braving the thick reeds that could hide any nasty, Jude swam *a la natural*, her pretty white bonnet seeming to glide over the murky water as if a saucer from outer space. That trek took about five hours.

The next day after moving the boat ten nautical miles down the island, we set off on a trail walk to the seaward side of the island to find Ocean Lake; the closest freshwater lake to the sea, only 600 m. Straightaway after gaining the track, some large dingo prints got our hearts thumping and our eyes searching the thick underbrush. A few hours walking through bedraggled eucalypts edging a swamp brought us to a gigantic sand blow that was ever so beautiful. Golden reddish sand stretched in waves for kilometres. Driven by the prevailing SE trade wind, it was invading the forest, consuming tall trees as it edged forward. That second walk of 15 km was much harder than the first.

We moved *Banyandah* further south after that, to a very calm spot off a small creek, calling the anchorage Ray Bay because of all the stingrays jumping out the water. A bit of seagrass on the bottom is home for small fish, and they attract the terns, eagles, and pelicans, so wildlife was on parade all day. A big old loggerhead turtle even popped up to say g'day while we were enjoying sundowners. Onshore next day we took advantage of a sandy 4WD track, packing a lunch for another trek into the interior. Our target, a 20 km round trip to yet another lake, taking heaps more video on our new camera and finding we are still very amateurish at filmmaking.

We had several sweet sails in the calm water behind this vast island. The southeast trades blew steadily across it at 20 knots giving us just the right conditions to test our new rig. The new mast, boom, and rigging took the load nicely, and our new second-hand sails kept their lovely aerofoil shape. Mom and pop were well tested too. And truthfully, we strained to keep up. When the wind blew extra-strong Jude and I practised reducing the mainsail by putting in *slab reefs*, which means lowering and tying off a portion of the sail, then re-tensioning it. Hard work requiring both balance and strength. Successful on a bright sunny day in protected waters, but what about a dark stormy night?

Our oldest son Jason, his wife Ally and two-year-old Jayden, came north for a weekend visit. They took the barge out from the mainland and joined us at Kingfisher Bay, which is presided over by an award-winning Eco-resort. Whist we did partake of the resorts facilities straight away, with drinks and a swim in their beachside pool, we soon went our own way. Picking up our anchor, we sailed a few miles around a headland to a freshwater creek Jude and I had discovered on the way up. Jason was in heaven. He raised the anchor, pulled out the headsail then took the helm. Little Jayden had a ball too. Boats are a natural playpen for little ones.

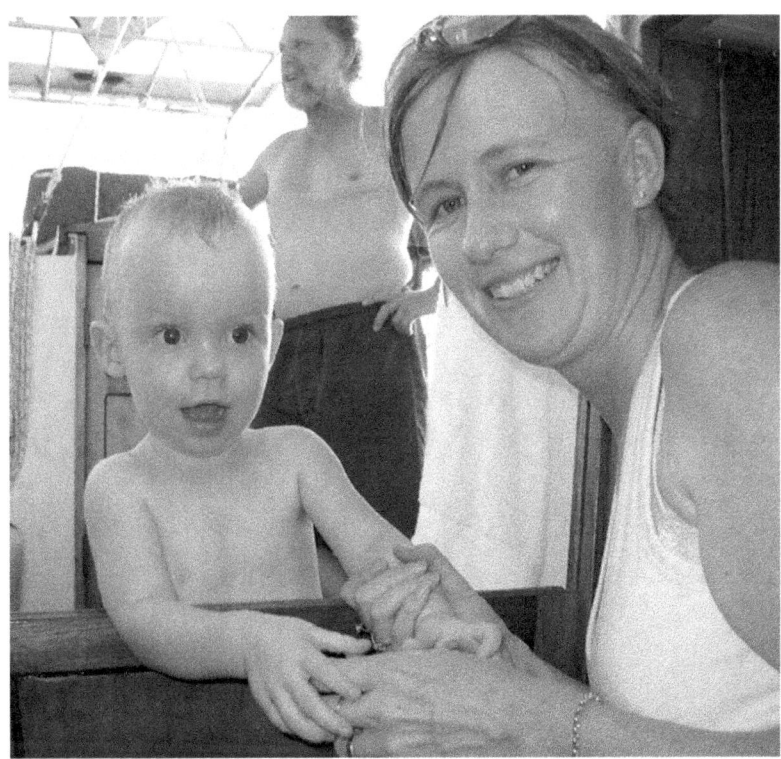

Banyandah has two living areas, one forward of the cockpit and one aft, each with a companionway ladder that provides a barrier to restrain a little man just able to walk. He loved driving the boat, and in no time changed from his usual "car-car-car" to "doat-doat" as the various watercraft went past.

Dear Ally loved every second of her first exposure to cruising too. Its laid back atmosphere has moments of excitement and discovery. There were little fishes, plenty of seabirds and several pods of porpoises, her favourite, splashing about. Plus a big old turtle popped his head up right next to her when she and Jas were messing about in the dinghy. It seemed so very lonely when they departed on the Sunday night ferry.

Fortunately for us, Carol and Lambert, old friends from our cruise through Micronesia nearly three decades earlier, came for a short stay a few days later. Lambert, bless him, was battling Myeloma, and little did we know, this would be the last time we would see him on his feet. In their younger days, these two had travelled extensively and had raced some of the fastest catamarans. The idyllic atmosphere aboard *Banyandah,* with a rather plush comfy eco-lodge close at hand, proved a perfect place for Lambert to recover from chemotherapy. Jude was her usual cheery self, but I sensed her sadness at seeing our once virile friend unsteady and so out of breath. Their visit reminded us how every moment of life is so very precious.

LUCKY, LUCKY, LUCKY

I should have known better. Tradition says beginning a voyage on a Friday is a bad omen. Fuelling this ominous portent – our last shakedown started on Friday the 13th.

We had just spent weeks provisioning our vessel for two months in the Never-Never to search for a shipwreck with our plan requiring *Banyandah* to sail to the furthest reaches of Australian territorial waters, to a mini sand islet twice visited in our younger years where we had found a bronze ringbolt from a little known French frigate.

Flexi-cabs Dave arrived early from Brisbane, and we used his transport to hit the town for last-minute items: Dave needed shorts; we all needed booze, and Jude needed fresh veggies and other delicacies to tantalise our taste buds while we worked out our last sailing kinks.

By noon, *Banyandah* was free of her marina berth and on course for the first of three obstacles needed to be passed to reach Moon Point on the inland side of Fraser Island.

Fraser, the largest sand island in the entire world, is surprisingly thickly forested. But not so surprising, it is surrounded by sandbanks continually being shifted by fast tidal streams. These banks are vast and easily seen, but difficult to navigate, as the channels between them are quite shallow. Harry, our 73-year-old neighbour aboard a 39 foot Cavalier, primed me with local knowledge then assured me we'd neatly clear the first sandbank at half tide. Nevertheless, as we approached the yellow cross, my bum hole began to tighten as Jude called decreasing water under our keel.

"Five feet," came from the wheel, quickly followed by, "four….three!"

Desperately not wanting a reoccurrence of our last attempt to cross, when I had driven *Banyandah* hard aground in front of a zillion townhouses, I scanned side to side hoping to perceive a darkening colour that would mark deeper water.

"Two feet," called Jude, her voice steady although now there was a constant pinging of alarm from our sounder.

And still that yellow cross lay several boat lengths ahead. At the front of our ship, I jerked my hand back as if physically moving the shift lever into neutral and we drifted forward under our own momentum. With skinny water all around, cool heads prevailed. Dave was stretched on the aft locker, calmly smoking a fag as if dockside aboard a luxury yacht. Jude, the professional she is, watched me intently for directions while the continuous pinging reminded her that we had less than a mini swell under our keel. Still re-learning my old trade after years on the land, I remembered to remain calm in tight situations as tension only clouds my thinking. So I let *Banyandah* drift forward, my toes tingling, waiting for that first jolt of hitting bottom, which never came before Jude sang out, "Three feet," as the yellow cross slipped past.

Later, when securely anchored close to an uninhabited shore backed by low forest, the day's mini-adventures were toasted time and again, all onboard darn pleased to have had an experience worth recounting. And so, with one of Jude's sumptuous curries warming our bellies and fine port warming our throats, we collectively called it a day, deeply satisfied our cruise had begun so auspiciously.

Upon first light, some thick heads and cottonmouths were soon cleared by a fresh breeze.

"Onwards to Rooney Point," I called. A twenty-five-mile voyage across an increasing wind.

With the first reef tied in, but still flying her full headsail, *Banyandah* was soon barrelling along at top speed under Fraser's lee. All was good. No! All was great! I was nearly in heaven when Jude offered round a yummy tray of tropical fruits. Strange – my first bite of banana tasted off. Saliva flooded my cavern and swallowing it mouthful after mouthful, I knew what was coming next. From deep within, breakfast flew over the side. Odd, I have never been seasick in my life, but felt much better for the experience – until, minutes later, more salvia, followed by frothy white stuff jettisoned into the sea. Better again, I reassured my crew that their captain was okay, to be immediately debunked by another explosion of white foam. Concerned faces now watched my every move. So I casually took up a confident stance that was quickly reduced to white knuckles gripping the rail during dry retching.

Passing Rooney Point put an end to what all had thought was a bout of Mal-de-Mar, except I was left with a tight stitch up under my right ribcage. Probably from the violent retching, we deduced. But why the elevated temperature that nurse Jude detected after removing her thermometer from under my armpit?

There was no party that night, only tired bodies and subdued supposition as to the captain's health. Oh well, I thought, we'd had a big day. Let's see what tomorrow brings.

Next day was Jude's birthday. I was still running a mild fever after sweating profusely overnight but took my part in the gift opening and photoshoot. Dave had a business to run, and as *Banyandah* was out of mobile phone range, I used that as an excuse to backtrack towards the mainland. This put our course hard on the wind. Sailing full and by, *Banyandah* performed like a racehorse, cutting swiftly through the calm sea, a mild headache my worst issue for most of that day. Until, close to the anchorage when we tacked through the wind. Jude turned the helm up, the headsail backed then I let it fly. Dave, being on his first stress-free holiday in living memory, lay flat like a lizard, soaking up his umpteenth cleansing ale. He wouldn't be taking any physical part in our sail training unless pressed into service, so I did my usual bit of winching in our large headsail. Job done, a bit out of breath, I took the helm to allow Jude to sort out her galley. When her foot just touched the threshold, a Nordic Viking drew his broad sword then ran it through my guts, pouring molten fire through my testicles and penis. Not caring if my ship was about to go over Niagara Falls, I fell to the deck incapacitated while my hands, with the strength of Titan's grip, crushed my poor Willy. And although praying for death had always been a ridiculous thought, I would have welcomed my God's hand at that moment.

Gasping, a rush of bodies closed around me, and although what followed is somewhat blurred, I recall trying to calm the pain away in a technique I have used to get through other horrible moments. And I somewhat succeeded. Chills replaced the fear I'd crushed my testicles, and next, I was in bed under a mountain of blankets with Jude's warm caresses containing my shakes. Sweat soon displaced the chills; pouring from me as if the sluice gates had been fully opened. What a party pooper! Jude's birthday and I was to have made her a chocolate cake.

Well, what to do now? Raise anchor and return to the mainland threading through sandbanks at night? Or flip open our phones to call for help? As quickly as the pain had come, it left. But what had caused it? A torn muscle? Bad prawns? Never one to call unnecessarily for help, against advice I decided it would endanger all to shift in darkness. And what would it achieve? The emergency ward would be on standby. So, I sweated and slept remarkably well.

Morning found me feeling a bit sluggish. But that wasn't as bad as the lump bulging out my right side. Uh oh, it was time for action, and off we went at full speed towards Hervey Bay. A passenger now, I lay on my bunk lamenting: Our search for the shipwreck would not go ahead.

How blessed I am to live in Australia. The noontime emergency room had ambulances arriving every ten minutes, but I was admitted and clinically checked within an hour. What I didn't like so well was the painful prodding and pushing by the registrar, who at first thought my kidney had stones. A CAT scan threw this out, so I was admitted to the surgical ward for observations. Next morning the head surgeon and his large multinational team prodded me some more then whispered amongst themselves with much nodding of heads. The head surgeon suggested he cut a hole in my abdomen to insert a camera then they'd all have a better look around. Seemed a good idea to me, and in short order, after signing several consent slips for a myriad of surgical procedures, they wheeled me off to theatre. The last I remember was the good doctor asking me if I wanted him to put right anything else not on the list. A sucker for a bargain, I agreed.

"Fix me up Doc. I got a lot of life ahead."

Not the thirty minutes suggested, but several hours later, I came to - somewhat. A nurse kept calling my name, and when I was coherent, she told me my ruptured appendix had been taken out. But that was not all. It was the biggest ever seen and full of pus. Yuk! Confusing everyone's diagnoses, my appendix had been found sitting atop my liver, which they all thought unusual. Oh well, It's g-o-o-one. And I'm better now though my chances of winning any modelling jobs have gone out the window unless it's to impersonate Frankenstein.

Our sincere thanks to the staff of the Hervey Bay General Hospital for their excellent care. And, our sincere appreciation to our mate Dave for his assistance and for just being there when needed. Can't imagine what would have been the outcome if my appendix had burst mid-ocean a week later.

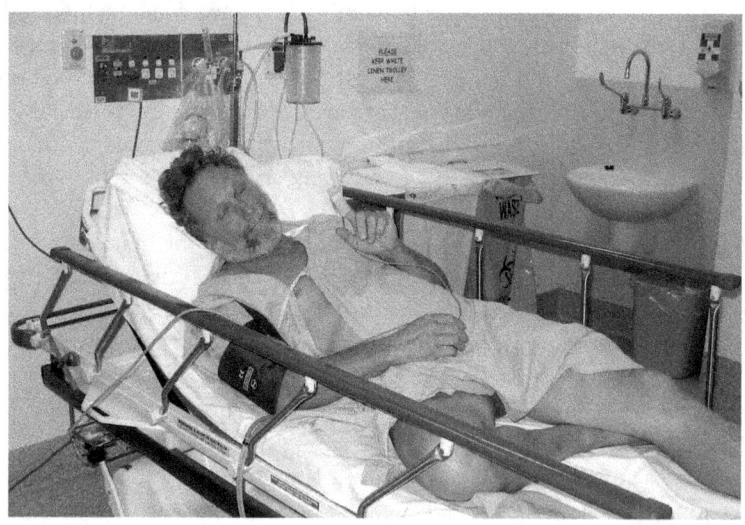

Le Top

Hello from the tippy-top of the world's oldest island. Once again *Banyandah* has successfully reached Torres Straits, those reef strewn, fast-flowing waters separating Australia from New Guinea that was discovered by Luis Vaez de Torres in 1605 when he was searching for *Terra Australis Incognita*. No longer does our compass point north. At last, we see it pointing west towards our first target, the Kimberley Coast. On board both oldies are in fine spirits and good health except for sore, tender feet caused by our new, overly aggressive, anti-skid cockpit flooring.

It is one day short of four weeks since we cast off our mooring lines at Hervey Bay. I'm sure if I could find the right button on one of these new electronic gadgets I'd be able to tell you just how many hours we've spent under sail these last 27 days, but I can't, and using my old sailor's instincts, I'll simply say heaps.

Before leaving home, our first plan had us searching for a shipwreck far out in the Coral Sea, but after my appendix burst, the six weeks recuperating ruled that out. Instead, we thought we would sail north, outside the Great Barrier Reef, where it'd be less encumbered with reefs, and we'd be clear of coastal shipping. We could have simply set the sails, engaged the windvane then sat back to ponder the empty horizon for the ten days it would have taken *Banyandah* to reach *Le Top*. But, at Lady Musgrave Lagoon, our first offshore anchorage, grey clouds scudding in from the direction we wanted to take forced a re-think. Maybe King Neptune was sending us a message on those howling winds, telling us that we had to be realistic.

That mini-gale forced us to look beyond our dream of sailing the open sea once again, and we saw two older, rather unfit bodies on board a veteran ship that had sat 16 years on a front lawn. It also forced us to ask, "what if?"

The answers we saw were not too friendly. So, as always, we took the responsible action and set a course north along the coast after that gale blew itself out. Of course, that meant much more work. You cannot sail in a straight line through literally thousands of reefs and islands. And each start and stop requires raising and lowering sails then furling them away. Navigation, while easy when crossing an ocean, is a full-time occupation along the shore, all the more so with the many wind shifts around headlands and mountainous islands. So, instead of blissfully watching a flat horizon slip past, we had to work our butts off, as well as our flabby arms, legs, and stomachs too. But through it all, we have been enthralled by the myriad islands strewn along Australia's East Coast.

In the last four weeks, we have sailed nearly 1300 nm, but we did not stop at any ports or towns. We didn't have any meals ashore nor take in any movies, nor did we visit other yachts although there were several in some anchorages. In fact, we hardly spoke to another soul. Anti-social you might think, but that's not the case. Every day we had wind. And every day we had a new destination, a new challenge, and simply put, that was all we wanted.

In addition to our forced layover at Lady Musgrave Lagoon, we had a stopover at the very lovely Hinchinbrook Island, the wettest spot in Australia, receiving more than two metres of rain every year. Ghosting through its lush channel under a limp genoa, carried more by the tide than the breeze, we saw waterfalls burst from mountaintops. Our only other break was at the isolated Flinders Group where last century's fleet of luggers brought their harvests of pearl shell and beche-de-mer to merchants. It's also where Australia's ancient inhabitants painted scenes of sailing ships and sea creatures on the rock walls of caves. I celebrated sixty-three years of life at those islands.

Anchored behind Flinders, the first of three special days was spent scouring the main island's hillsides for caves known only to a few tribal elders. Having no success, *Banyandah* was shifted across a narrow channel to Stanley Island, a long thin mountainous ridge with a bold rock massif at its seaward end. There Jude and I mounted another expedition, tramping through the bush with lunch, water, and a medical kit in our backpacks.

Straight away we found remnants of houses abandoned mid-last century; old bottles, rusting water tanks and foundations, all being reclaimed by Nature. We trekked the rock cliffs fronting the channel marvelling at the bird's eye view of mangrove forests meeting green reef that ran into deep blue sea, a beautiful collage of colours that only Nature can create. Following the ridge down to a cove facing seaward, we discovered the Yindayin rock art site; overhanging rock faces filled with paintings of olden-day sailing ships, whales, lobster, interspersed with hundreds of fertility symbols. Just beyond it, a vast cave opens with a soft sand floor that could have easily accommodated many dozens of the Aba Yalgayi family, who were part of the Yiithuwarra clan that inhabited these islands and the land around Cape Melville. A flat area where it opens to the sky is littered with thousands upon thousands of bleached white seashells; a midden, and visible remains from many years of feasting.

Standing upon the threshold to their sleeping cave, a lagoon thick with mangroves lay before us. There must have been every imaginable form of food within that area; mud crabs, shellfish, eels, birds, and of course, many fish. Looking to sea and seeing nearby reefs spread to the far horizon, it was easy to imagine the simple good-life these early people enjoyed.

A sailor's birthday is dictated by the needs of his ship and so instead of a party hat, on my birthday I put on my mechanic's hat to change a leaky engine water pump. While Jude conjured up a lovely cake from basic ingredients, and tasty bread from simple flour and water, I grunted and groaned, muttered expletives until late afternoon when I arose from the ship's engine with grease on my cheeks and a smile across my gob. No more pesky leak! Now that's what I call a first-class birthday gift.

Jude lavished me with kisses then pampered me by washing my hair, followed by a freshwater shower – an extravagant treat. After such special treatment, we went fishing for our birthday dinner. While I steered Little Red close along the reef, Jude worked the trolling line, but without success. So we tried a bit of bottom fishing off the point. It was fantastic drinking the last of our beers while watching the orange sun melt into the steel grey sea, but again no fish.

Venus showing brightly in the twilight meant we had to get back. But our outboard, like many things on board, is old and tetchy, giving us some distress before finally deciding to fire. Trolling again, in the lessening light, I couldn't make out the edge of the reef and bumped the prop against a coral rock, and that caused a gut-wrenching mini-explosion in my tummy. I would have hated to row all the way home on my birthday.

At that very same instant, the troll line snapped taut with a force that nearly ripped it from Jude's grip. Thinking she had snagged the reef, I spun the dinghy around while praying the line wouldn't snap. It was difficult in the low light to see those propeller-eating coral heads, but I circled back while Jude hauled in nylon filament at a high rate of knots.

I was so sure she'd hook the reef that I was shocked when she hauled aboard a huge, brown-spotted coral trout with our lure poking out a mouth so big he could have swallowed my fist. In answer to our wishes, my birthday dinner had arrived, and feeling ever so pleased, we went home to continue the party.

But it has not been all party and smooth sailing. The tight quarters and stormy trade winds have again tested the bonds of our union. We are a team for sure. And like other teams, we rely on the other to perform. In our case, if one fails, the other can be seriously hurt or lost overboard. These are powerful sails driving this ship – massive spreads of tightly woven cloth harnessing the forces of Nature, and controlling them without causing injury requires timing and teamwork. Making it harder, this work is conducted within an environment that never stops rocking. Our bodies and minds get tired. More than tired, we become exhausted and sleep is sometimes hard to find, especially for the captain who is a bit of a worrywart and carries the burden of safely navigating the ship through all dangers, seen and unseen.

We are only human, with needs and shortcomings. We have egos and tempers that flare. But above all, and what allows us to control these fears, desires, and emotions, we have love. A love for Mother Earth and her creatures, a love for the heavenly stars that accompany us on lonely nights, a love for one another. We know each other's strengths; we know our weaknesses, which we never stop trying to correct.

Sometimes this gets a bit too much, and words are said that are later regretted. But the bigger picture always prevails. We are a team and we are going forward together through life, so we forgive and try to forget, and that lets our bonds grow stronger.

One or two days are all we plan to stay at *Le Top*. Adventure and discovery beckon, and there is no time to waste as the tick-tock of time continues to beat for all of us. And so, while we still have good health, we intend to keep on experiencing life the way we know best, by travel and observing.

SAILING OFF THE EDGE

In the old days, when it was our norm to pick up a mailbag six months out of date, Jude and I thrived on isolation. We were pioneers exploring the world with our children and we were totally self-contained. This time it is somewhat different. Although still self-contained for food, accommodation, and entertainment, the big difference is we are missing our family. Going up the East Coast was grand, our mobile phone found towers to keep us in touch, but here in the Kimberley, it's the true Aussie wilderness; hundreds of kilometres without the smallest settlement and no contact with the outside world. To counter this, we have put a collage of photos on the hull opposite our loo that is within sight from most seating places. We like to think we're taking our family and friends along with us as we explore this land of contrast.

William Dampier, the buccaneer and long-time privateer, one of the first to explore the north-west coast in 1699, wrote of his journey that except for the honour of discovering the *barrenness spot on the face of the globe*, he might just as well have stayed away.

We understand his feeling because this land is harshly barren, filled with rock and monotonous vegetation, and we're finding the seas unnerving. Troubled by fast currents created by enormous tides, whirlpools and eddies churn up the bottom making the water turbid so that even the little depth needed to float *Banyandah* cannot be perceived. This makes navigating near land very stressful. Worst of all, we had to give up exploring the underwater world because of crocodiles that lurk in so many places, some twice the length of our dinghy.

Nevertheless, our travels thus far have been rather delightful. We are discovering new interests and passions. And although the land is harsh, it's a land of contrasts bringing exceptional beauty to the eye. Reds and black dominate, especially glorious at dawn and sunset. There are no vast tracts of verdant forests. Instead, there is rock; bold, chiselled, eroded, some precariously balanced.

Our saga begins in Darwin with our ship fully laden. We've taken on 400 litres of diesel to totally fill our 600-litre tanks, topped up our 720-litre water tanks, and crammed our lockers with an array of canned, dried, and fresh foods, and boat spares. Jude claims she only needs to top up the fresh supplies for us to survive until Perth.

In this land of contrast we have found the wind blows at night and usually finishes before lunch, so we departed Darwin at first light to weave through the hundred-plus yachts waiting to race to Timor. A heroic beginning considering the previous night's "parting of the ways" party we had with our new American friends. The wind being light, we first day-hopped along the vacant coast west of Darwin until Cape Ford, that took three days. Then we set sail across the Joseph Bonaparte Gulf in a fast, sleepless 24-hour sail.

When leaving home we'd had scant knowledge of the Kimberley Coast and took no charts whatsoever, so we were quite fortunate in Darwin to straightaway meet Rick and Nadine who had sailed the Perth/Darwin route three times in their catamaran *Hard Yakka*. They were heading to SE Asia and must have been short of cash because they sold us all their West Australian charts plus a bundle of mud maps covering the rivers and smaller places.

During a pleasant afternoon aboard *Hard Yakka*, we went through what they considered the don't-miss highlights of that thousand miles of coastline. And topping their list was a river we had never heard mentioned before. While the King George River is renowned for waterfalls and deep gorges, Rick said the Berkeley River leaves it for dead. Then he described a cul-de-sac anchorage where you tie stern to a waterfall, bow to an island, and are surrounded by towering red cliffs. Above these falls, he said there lays several freshwater pools safe for swimming and rock caves adorned with paintings dating back thousands of years.

"What's the catch?" I asked. "Why is this, the best-kept secret?" Rick then explained that getting past the off-lying sandbanks was the secret guarding these wondrous sights.

Our sail across the Bonaparte Gulf was both exciting and worrisome. The strong wind blowing over our stern set us on a cracking pace and with the sails wing n' wing, we rocked savagely. When the sun set and dusk settled, I couldn't stop imagining the swells that were chasing up our stern breaking with destructive force on the sandbanks guarding the Berkeley River. But we maintained course knowing we could divert along the coast if entering the Berkeley proved too dangerous. Unfortunately, knowing what's "too dangerous" before it is, sometimes proves quite tricky.

In one regard the strong wind was helpful because we arrived at our waypoint a mile off the sandbanks an hour before dawn and two hours before the top of the tide. And our luck had prevailed. While closing the coast, the wind had backed to blow parallel to it, and contrary to the norm, it had eased to a mild breeze allowing the land to moderate the swell.

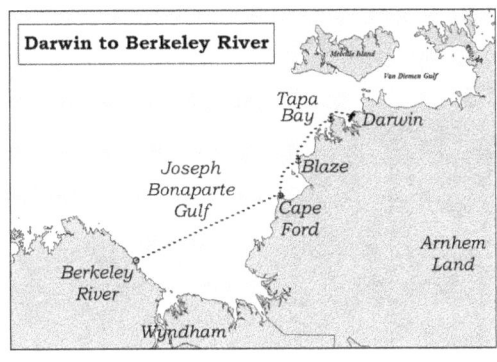

First light revealed an abrupt coastline with towering cliffs aglow in magnificent hues of red that alone were worth the sleepless journey. But, first light also showed metre high waves were rushing towards a shoreline so indented that finding the actual river mouth proved impossible.

Our CMaps digital charts depicted a doglegged entrance channel across sandbanks. But this data was several years old and knowing these northern lands suffer monsoonal rains that reshape not just the land but also the seabed, we were left scratching our heads. Had the sea been calm or had there been more hours of rising tide then we would have poked *Banyandah's* nose in to sound for the channel, but not with such a swell running and the tide soon to turn.

There was an anchorage two hours up the coast where we could wait for better conditions, and I was about to alter course when the thought struck of putting out a general call on our VHF. To our surprise, the *True North* answered. What luck! Without hesitation, its skipper read out the waypoints he'd made when entering that very night. Wondering what sort of captain would enter a dangerous river at night, I asked him and heard the *True North* was 50 m long and needed 2.2 m to float! Jude's cheers reverberated around the cabin as I began entering his 12 waypoints into our GPS. It charted a rather torturous route. Then we held our breaths and steered *Banyandah* for the land following the dots.

Straight away, we were in trouble. With Jude at the helm and myself below glued to the laptop calling out course changes, we first discovered a delay in the GPS tracking - from boat to satellite, back to boat, then computing to display while the current swept us sideways into "less than three feet!" A harried Judith called out, "Crikey!" We're nearly smacking the bottom in these swells."

But before we hit, the next blip showed us in a no go zone over-drying mudflats and my iron nerves shattered. "Turn hard left," I yelled. And for some minutes, a sweat-soaked T-shirt stuck to my armpits while *Banyandah* slowly edged back towards the supposed channel. On the edge of my seat, with a few hot words fired between us, during the next half-hour, we slowly

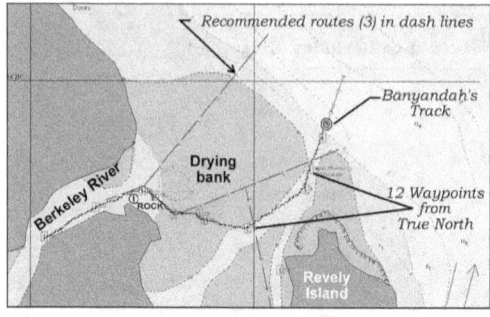

crept to each of *True North's* waypoints. Then came the least expected. The laptop ran out of power.

When my groans reached Jude, she called, "Hey! Back to basics. There's a current line running along the shoals showing us the way in."

Elated, and suddenly quite exhausted, we soon found ourselves in calm water with a strange flat-topped hill at the end of a somewhat murky broad river. We could have dropped the anchor and taken some much-needed rest, but instead, with the door now ajar, we wanted a peek, so continued midstream.

At first, we saw nothing more dramatic than on a journey up our home river the Richmond. Ordinary mangroves lined both shores and though we expected crocodiles under every branch, all we saw was turbid water. So we continued. Past the first tributary that snuck out the wall of green on our right, then past small outcrops of rock that had begun replacing the trees. After an hour of steady bottom and easy navigation, we felt like old river pros, avoiding the shoals and snags by taking the deeper water on the outside of each bend. Then while rounding a widening left-hander at mile five, a rock rampart shot up on our right, just where Casuarina Creek joined the river. This tributary held the magical anchorage Rick had described, but with the tide now falling, it looked little more than a drainage ditch. Tired and deflated we wondered if we dare take our vessel into it.

That junction seemed an ideal spot to take our rest, so down went the anchor. And before it had settled into soft gooey mud, Mr Resident Croc, four metres long if an inch, sauntered slowly past measuring us with his glassy reptilian stare. Jude said spying her first croc settled her nerves, claiming she now had a real-life image of her foe. But it did not settle mine.

Not long after finishing our celebratory big breakfast, the lovely sounds of birdsong were displaced by screaming outboards and bolting towards our cockpit we saw not one, but four large tinnies racing down river one behind the other. Filled with tourists, they swept past us and into Casuarina Creek, not slowing one little bit. *True North* stencilled on their transoms.

All was silent for half an hour until those same tinnies sped back out the creek and up to us. Over fifty tourists, performing synchronous waving, were suddenly upon our doorstep, and at a guess, fifty would have been their median age. While they drifted closer, we fielded questions like, "Just you two sail that boat?"

When we said we had been away six months and were circumnavigating Australia, several smiled in amazement, some just shook their heads. While chatting, we discovered that after entering the river the previous night, they had awoken in the gorge up ahead and that within the next hour they'd be on their way to the King George River.

Under my breath, I whispered to Judith, "Got to pack in a lot when you're shelling out $500 a day."

Just then a mini-liner turned the upper bend, looking so out of place, not only because of its size but also because it was sleek and all-white instead of pink and craggy. Its appearance had the four tinnies racing towards it like bumblebees towards sweet flowers. Then, while some sort of mechanical device plucked each tinnie from the water, I contacted their captain on VHF to thank him for his waypoints.

He was really quite pleased but quickly ended the chat with, "Got to keep moving. The river's all yours. There's no one else here." And I thought, "How fantastic! Probably no-one around for five hundred miles."

After the great white ship had eased around the downstream bend, we took a mini-sleep in blissful peace. When we rose again, the afternoon low tide had exposed vast mud banks skirting both banks. Little Red was quickly launched, the outboard mounted, and then we loaded drinking water, a sounding line marked every foot and the handheld GPS, before setting off to survey Casuarina Creek.

At first, we believed *Banyandah* could not navigate such a narrow waterway because the exposed mud banks left a channel barely wider than her length. Keeping a keen eye out for crocs, we moved up the tributary taking soundings and recording a track while taking visual bearings, which was pretty easy – no choice but to stay mid-channel, equidistant to the mangroves, except around the only bend. Quite surprised, we discovered there would be enough water to float *Banyandah* at half tide.

Past the bend, the falls appeared, breathtakingly cradled between sheer rock walls and pouring more water than expected for halfway through the dry season. The low tide had exposed a stripe of buff white shell low down on the red amphitheatre encircling the oval lagoon, and smack dab in the middle sat a little green island. Passing around it, we discovered a deeply scooped out basin.

Looking around, first in awe, then trepidation, Jude commented that it might be okay for a day visit, but you wouldn't anchor there overnight. But my sailor's eye had already found strong points to secure our ship fore and aft, and our soundings revealed deep water right up to the cliffs and island. After explaining how we would secure our vessel, Jude still remained unconvinced. Nonetheless, I had seen enough to know we'd give it a go on the morning's rising tide.

After a quick frolic under the falls, so refreshing after our many days cooped on the boat, we headed back, sounding some more to confirm the deepest track, and surprising a black Jabiru feeding almost knee-deep in mud. Once back, fishing took precedence. We had heard so much about the Barramundi fishing in the Kimberley, I expected to land a really big one within minutes – but all we landed was a catfish with slimy whiskers - a croaking, greenish thing that I chucked back and off he floated. But not for long. From out of nowhere, a shadow crossed the sun and a huge white-bellied sea eagle swooped down, its black fringed wings the width of our ship, talons extended from plump, downy legs and in flowing motion plucked that fish with the grace of a ballerina doing a pirouette.

Did you see that? Jude's expression asked. What's good enough for an eagle should be good enough for us was confirmed by *Grant's guide to fishes*. Blue Catfish – "very palatable white flesh when skinned." The next catfish we devoured.

Next morning the local croc was making his rounds, parading along the mangroves, their branches again underwater. My eye caught his while I dug out coils of mooring lines and laid them on deck. Tying the shorter ones together, I made up two piles, each about fifty metres in length. Then before setting off, Jude got out her croc basher, a hardwood axe handle purchased in Darwin.

Our well-prepared operation went reasonably smooth. Jude drove while I gauged our distance between the partly submerged trees, now looking close enough to stretch out and reach. Then after rounding the island, I simply plonked down our anchor. That held us central in the windless basin while Jude, bless her, rowed out the lines, securing the aft one to a huge boulder. Then with her croc basher always in reach, the bow line to a convenient tree on the island a few metres up the shore. Within half an hour, our baby was secure, floating next to a waterfall, the noise of which echoed off the surrounding cliffs.

A by-product of the northern heat is that our vessel becomes terribly salt-encrusted. Each wave hitting us sprays seawater that leaves salt when the water dries off. Layer upon layer, crystals hung like stalactites under the railing, the decks were sticky and cockpit timbers patterned in white. *Banyandah* needed a bath. Easy - Jude took off in a flash, rather sexy just in her knickers, and like a kid playing under a garden hose, she backed the dinghy under the falls then filled it with fresh water as full as she dared. Then hoping not to swamp, in teeter-totter fashion back to the boat to give our lady a bucket bath right from the dinghy. So refreshingly sweet, it was plain good fun. Jude also took the opportunity of doing a wee bit of laundry while I topped up our water tanks. Our work completed, after a well-earned lunch under a salt-free awning, we prepared for our first trek in the Kimberley.

Only a handful of times since reaching *Le Top* had we walked on the land; Cape Don for an hour, Darwin city and beaches before crossing the gulf. All those other weeks had been at sea level. When we arrived at the Berkeley, the abruptly rising coast had given us the impression of mountainous terrain. Even going ashore looked difficult for we had to scale a steep slope up loose boulders to gain the cliff top. But then to our surprise, we found the area relatively flat, not hilly at all. Just that strange flat-topped hill broke our view of stunted eucalypts, saltbush, and spinifex. A few paces into this unimpressive world exposed a cracked and fissured flat rock base, in which small, stiff, resilient plants had a toe hole. Following small cairns set by others that lead towards the falls, we found more rock, loose and tricky underfoot. Spinifex, sticky to our fingers, jabbed us through our trousers.

Around us, birdsong filtered through the still air while nearby a dead looking bush showed gorgeous, bright yellow flowers at the tips of leafless branches. Below it, a strange hard shrub was covered with what at first seemed ordinary pink flowers until we bent down and saw their centres were arrays of crimson spikes with tiny yellow streaks that made them look pink. Strange land this. Between the patches of rock, in sandy soil grew a mix of high grasses and what seemed like tall flannel flowers, reminding us of home except these were purple instead of cream. Then right beside us, a blue and green kingfisher landed on a leafless boab tree, its branches akimbo like an afro hairdo. Everywhere everything looked dead, but it is not.

Ten minutes later, we arrived at a broad tongue of rock painted black by water coursing over it in the wet season, and there we found several large pools with lush green vegetation in places along their perimeters. By this time, we were streaming sweat again, so the pools looked very enticing, but first, we couldn't resist a look over the edge. The scene was breathtaking. *Banyandah* looked suspended in space above a sapphire pool, like a jewel strung between island and rock face, a waterfall trickling beside her.

Rick had mentioned looking for rock art in this area, so we put off a swim and began searching the larger rock faces. This was even hotter work and far more dangerous pushing through thick grasses, watching for snakes and climbing over jagged rocks. And although we had no joy for over an hour, we persisted until rewarded by finding a faint sketch of an animal painted on an overhanging face.

"What's the big deal," I thought, wiping sweat off my face.

Just then Jude shouted from the next prominent outcrop that she'd found a wall of figures known as Bradshaws.

In crimson red on yellow stone were hunters holding boomerangs and spears. Intrigued, and beginning to know where to look, on flat faces not exposed to the elements and commanding positions overlooking the pools, we soon discovered several other sites that were a shutterbugs delight. Before setting up for photos, we studied the figures, some of which formed murals, to see details and try to figure out what the artists meant. For sure, after thousands of years, many had lost clarity, mostly by the natural oxidation of the stone we presumed, which changes the rock from pale to various depths of red that conceals the artwork. But clearly what we saw was a proud race of people depicted with armlets, fancy hairdos and ceremonial headdress, grass skirts, and a few of the animals they hunted; goannas, kangaroos, turtle.

We got so carried away searching for new treasures that we completely forgot the natural passage of the sun until a cool zephyr touched my cheek. Looking up, I saw the sun just about to dip behind the hills. Ignoring my first warning, Jude kept shooting photos until I more urgently spelt out the dangers of traversing an unknown, isolated rocky plain in darkness.

Setting our handheld GPS to lead us back to the dinghy, we set off racing the remaining light. And it wasn't until we were moving that the full danger become apparent, and this pushed me on even faster. But Jude lagged behind. And when I had to stop to let her catch up, I'd chide her to go more quickly. But Jude's an independent gal and knows to injure herself by too fast a pace would be more catastrophic than stumbling along after dark. So I would rush ahead a few hundred metres, locate the easiest route, and then wait for her to come to that point.

I don't know what Jude wrote in her diary about me verbally prodding her along, but the fact is we only got to the dangerous last slope with hardly enough light to see where to place our feet on that precarious jumble of loose rock. On the way down all I could think about was a croc waiting in the darkness at the bottom. But that turned out not to be our worse nightmare. The tide had dropped, hanging Little Red by its rope on rocks covered in sharp oysters that fronted what was now a vast plain of mud – soft gooey mud – the kind your boots sink into without stopping. And there could still be a nasty flesh-eating reptile waiting in the dark!

It wasn't nice, especially without a torch. Fortunately, Jude and I work best under adversity; bonds us into a team instead of two separate egos. So with care and a fair bit of determination, we managed to un-hang the poor dinghy by sliding its metal bottom over the oyster shells. When at last afloat and Jude rowing us home, she had me rub down her legs as the sandflies were having a feast. She'd rolled up her trousers so they'd not get muddy and the blighters had been savaging her from the start. A cold beer and wash on the deck put everything right – except for the dozens of bumps on her legs.

On that trek, we had seen that the terrain was level except for the flat-topped hill called Mount Casuarina that lay three or four kilometres away. And this gave us the idea that we would get a magnificent panorama from its top. So going there became the next day's destination. Only we'd start much earlier, and take a torch.

Just after daybreak, with a great sleep behind us even though the falls had kept a noisy vigil all night, we were off; this time carrying backpacks – Jude's filled with water, lunch, and the medical kit; mine containing cameras, tripod and some safety gear like our personal EPIRB that can send out a distress signal picked up by satellites. This time it was still fresh when we reached the flats and birds of many songs were welcoming the new day, their various tunes melding into a delightful chorus. Being sparsely vegetated with our destination always in sight, I just concentrated on finding the easiest route, which was away from the rocks forming Casuarina Creek.

After pushing through tall grasses within a kilometre of our destination and finding a dry creek bed lined with polished red stones, it became our path through the rougher countryside near Mount Casuarinas' base. Three hours after leaving the boat, we were slogging up its rocky slope, hampered by fallen trees and shoulder-high grass hiding our feet. We might be in our sixties, but we're still pretty good at climbing hills, so quite soon gained the top, finding it remarkably flat, as if this bit of land had been pushed up 220 metres. Same trees, same grasses, same scrub. The only difference, a beautiful view to a cerulean sea taking in thousands of hectares, slightly red, dotted with sparse, greenish vegetation and bisected by a twisted blue ribbon.

Further upstream from *Banyandah*, Casuarina Creek became a series of mini-gorges that tended round Mount Casuarina before disappearing in the west, while the Berkeley River narrowed to a multi-pronged gash in the earth that bobbed and weaved towards a large, flat pan maybe thirty kilometres inland. And, for the first time, in that direction we saw other mountains; they too were flat-topped. Majestic country – How I wish I knew more about it. Oh well, maybe one day - but on this day we were merely observers and looking back towards the sea we noticed a broad flood plain of bright white sand alongside the Berkeley near its mouth, and separated from it by a margin of viridian green mangroves. Upstream, where the Berkeley narrowed, its edges were rough and jagged as if the earth had been ripped apart. These were the sheer sides of the gorge we'd next take *Banyandah*.

A stroll around the flat top revealed eucalypt trees bearing clusters of bright orange flowers with yellow tips. A closer look showed each flower was made up of hundreds of tiny flame orange stalks emanating from a smoky grey cup. Interspersed amongst the eucalypts were acacia trees bursting in yellow blossoms that were a series of tassels radiating out along the last bit of every stem. All very pleasant, so we ate our lunch in dappled shade, cooled by a breeze while curious little wrens flitted over our heads. But such is life that we had to get home; back down into the heat, into the overgrowth, watching out for monsters; this time moving towards the upper reaches of Casuarina Creek to hunt for more rock art amongst the bold rock faces we'd seen from the mountaintop. From that point, the day became a bit of a slog. Even though we successfully reached the creek, it became thick, heavy going hampered by our packs, and search as we might, we didn't find any new art, eventually having to satisfy ourselves by re-examining what we'd found the day before. Still, the grand views had made the outing very worthwhile.

The next day, after a long shower under the falls on a convenient rock ledge, we un-did our shorelines and left Casuarina Creek, reaching the main river with ease. Turning upstream, within an hour, we entered a whole new world. Gone were green mangroves, gone too the crumbled slopes, replaced by sheer vertical walls of red-hued rock that marched closer and closer together like some sort of gigantic press. Around each bend, they seemed to draw nearer and taller until we had to crane our necks to see the sky above what sometimes appeared giant building blocks stacked atop another. The river's depth was not a problem. Nature had cut a slice out Earth, forming a flat bottom canal where the walls could be touched without fear our vessel would hit bottom. Such wondrous sights we'd never experienced, and to think we had *Banyandah* amongst this grandeur prompted us to stop often to prolong the experience. Right on an acute bend, we plonked down the anchor to enjoy lunch with views of the canyon in both directions. A gentle breeze countered the easy river flow, with the result our ship slowly revolved, providing a view upstream then downstream while we enjoyed salads and freshly baked bread. What a tough life!

Around three, just after the sun had dipped below the western wall throwing shadows down the gorge, new beauty came that added perspective. So we set off to further explore. Taking front row seats after setting the video camera on its tripod, we marvelled at the contrasting deep red colour as the shadows gave the numerous gashes in the cliffs a third dimension and let us better judge the enormous size of the building blocks.

With the engine silently ticking over, we sallied on until a breadknife of jagged rock marked the entry to a side channel. A quick glance revealed an impressive ruby-red vertical face slashed by a black tongue where water falls in the wet season. Opposite this, a small bank of mangroves looked perfect for hunting mud crabs, so we parked for the night. But before setting out our two crab pots, I needed bait. Down went the fishing lines and straightaway up came more catfish. Yum! We were getting rather partial to their chicken breast taste.

Next morning both baits had been savaged by something that didn't get its legs caught in the netting, and I returned with two twisted pots. But that didn't spoil the beautiful morning as we rowed into the crack to find a quiet pool in the cool shade at the base of an imposing, perfectly flat vertical face. A good spot for an hour's peaceful meditation. Returning home to hide from the rising heat, breaking the silence came the easy thump of machinery, and soon the sailing yacht *Wooshee* was slowing down beside us. We hailed them so heartily they quickly dropped their anchor and came over for a chat.

What a sweet couple. Matt and Gill were coming from Perth on their way to Darwin with ideas of going to Japan. With us going the opposite direction and having been to Japan years ago, we had plenty to chat about. Snacks became lunch, which then stretched to afternoon tea before finally they said they wanted to move on another half mile to the Red Amphitheatre and suggested we join them there for dinner. As they had been underway for more than a  month and were very low on supplies, we replied we'd be along just as soon as we caught the main course.

While we had been chatting, I'd been watching the shallows and had seen a few predators striking the tiddlers, so I thought pulling a lure would get results. And it did. Needing a workout, Nature Boy shunned the outboard, choosing instead to row his tinny while towing a white jig close along the mangroves. Rowing as fast as I could, in less than fifteen minutes, my throaty laugh echoed around the gorge when I landed a three kilo Silver Queenfish. Something to brag about later that evening.

The Red Amphitheatre is actually two waterfalls in separate round chasms side by side. Again, red is the keyword. With a slash of green between them and more vegetation spanning away each side, they made quite an impressive sight.

The morning after our dinner party, I was up before first light to film the sunrise on the cliff faces. And when Jude also popped out of bed, in a flash, we dressed in bush gear then madly rowed to a nearby slope to climb to the top. Racing first light, with galloping hearts we scrambled up loose scree then pushed through spinifex to be rewarded by a most spectacular view. Far below on a dark river floated two boats, overshadowed by the amphitheatre's wall of deep claret-red. Moments later, when the sun peeked over the eastern rim, dark shadows told the story of countless centuries of erosion and gave life to the scene. And as the day came alive, Jude and I walked along the edge, snapping photos and capturing video of the rapidly changing scene.

That sortie proved so enjoyable that as soon as we were back on board, we began thinking of other locations already passed where we might gain access to the high ground. But before turning back, we spent half the day doing maintenance then popped over to *Wooshee* to wish her crew good luck. Then with shadows lengthening, we turned our floating home around to meander downstream, looking for a perfect photo opportunity. A few miles below the Amphitheatre, the Berkeley zigs and zags in short runs of vertical cliffs called the "Z" and just past them we found a steep rocky slope we could climb. Parking *Banyandah* near it, straightaway we went fishing for dinner.

Just before dawn the next day, in cool darkness we were dressed in bush gear then putt-putted away in our dinghy, armed only with our camera gear. In the moonless light, with some difficulty, we found the slope straddled between steep walls and we landed to begin the climb; first on very loose scree, then pushing through bushes we found the ever-present spiky spinifex. The sun still had not risen above the opposite rim by the time we had gained the flat ground, but there was enough light to find our way to the edge carefully. And from there the view down was breathtaking. Before us lay an ancient world, gashed by eons of water gushing through it. While setting up our cameras, the first glint of sunlight cast an eerie glow across the craggy walls where they twisted and turned in the "Z." Far below lay *Banyandah*, a mere speck still in deep shadow, dominated by towering parapets so close they seemed to both guard and threatened her. While gaping at this breathtaking view, we saw an enormous croc slithering alongside the mangroves on the opposite shore; his prehistoric armour perfectly in keeping with the scene.

For the next few hours, we clicked dozens of photos from three commanding positions while the shadows receded. One was taken from a giant-truck-sized rock that plunged hundreds of metres straight into the river. I set up the tripod on an adjacent rock then asked Jude to sit right on the outer edge of that giant rock so I could get a photo of us with the entire Berkeley at our feet. She agreed, reluctantly, but took ages to edge forward on her bottom little by little. Lucky the Panasonic has a remote because I would never have made the run in a ten-second delay!

What matters here is we set ourselves a goal then achieved it. We got the photo, which puts the memories away for when we're not able to do these crazy things.

Back on board, to go with our pancakes, we celebrated by opening one of our few cans of grapefruit sections as a special treat. Later, we meandered back to the river mouth, intending to exit the river on the next morning's high tide. And to make sure we'd not have any dramas, after anchoring just inside, we took Little Red out at dead low water to plot on our GPS the then plainly visible dry sandbanks.

Next morning, as the sun's glow just lit the hills, we started the engine and went out on the same track we'd come in on and had not one drama. But I know when passing into deep water, it felt like a heavy burden had been lifted. A yacht needs water to float and plenty of open space, and that explains why it is always so much more comforting to be out mid-ocean.

With all sail up harnessing the light breeze, we engaged the windvane steering device then looked back to the Berkeley to reflect on our adventures. Ancient rock art, Earth's evolution on display, Nature in balance. And when the Berkeley's narrow opening was again lost to sight, we turned forward to think of what new discoveries lay ahead.

Shake down cruise behind Fraser Island

Flinders Island Group - Aboriginal Art on Stanley Island depict early sailing ships

Darwin sunset from Fanny Bay Yacht Club with 106 vessels ready for Timor Race

THE GIANT'S POOL

I don't know why, but as we sailed from Gallery Bay, old Mister Grumps was paying me a visit. I'm a strong-willed healthy lad who is sometimes under a bit of pressure, so periodically I get moody and you do not want to be near me until that tempest blows out. As a result, Jude was at one end of the boat making bread to go with the fish she'd caught that morning, while I was holed up at the other perusing my library of information. Meanwhile, the boat just sort of took care of herself. We weren't going very fast. In fact, I probably could have swum circles around her. But she was pointing in the right direction, with the current taking us forward at about a knot, and that was good enough for Mister Grumps while he waited for the afternoon sea breeze to pipe in. Bread making delayed lunch, fouling old Grumps even more. So instead of tending my business as captain, old Grumps just kept sifting through books and digital stuff looking for more info on Bradshaw paintings. As a result, the current changed direction without being noticed.

Only vaguely while eating my bread and fish did I wonder why the GPS showed increasing speed even though the sails still hung limply from the rigging. We were still pointed at Cape Rulhieres, a rocky headland five miles ahead, and that's all that mattered to Mister Grumps while he munched his lunch. But after the meal, when he looked closer and saw that we were actually being taken backwards by the current, well, that was enough for old Grumps to blow his stack. So I raged and stomped about while getting sail down and starting the engine. Not liking to fight, Jude stayed well out his way, so now old Grumps had nothing to battle. Instead, while the afternoon turned noisy and hot, with us slowly inching our way around the headland, he cursed the current, past more ungodly rocks, through the loneliest ocean - that should have been boiling with fish, but none wanted our lure. Seems even the fish knew to stay away.

Some time approaching beer o'clock I had *Banyandah* close off the cape, crabbing sideways across a current line, hoping to find a counter-current I was sure would be filling the bay fronting the King George River. And presto, at last, our GPS showed us getting a lift. Reason enough to crack open a cold one and immediately I began to feel better. Anchoring in Koolama Bay, we were surrounded by a rim of rosy red rock that looked from outer space with the lowering sun setting fire to one side, while the rising full moon highlighted the other. It was stunningly beautiful but looked even more wondrous when Jude slipped behind me and began nuzzling my ear.

Later, while we were examining the aft cabin headliner, I realised what had brought out old Mister Grumps. Back home when the moon waxed this big and I'd been holed up for a bit, Jude and I would bust out and go bush. We'd breathe the good air, gaze wide panoramas, stretch our legs and get stuck into challenging things like climbing mountains. So I turned to Jude and said, "Hey Babe, Why don't we go walkabout. I've read rock art has been reported somewhere up the east tributary. We could spend two or three days searching for it."

Jude's the original "yes girl", but she's also a thinker and suggested we first visit the famous twin falls and then head off if we found a suitable spot to leave *Banyandah*. Her more cautious approach certainly had merit, but I felt sure we'd find a safe haven to park our baby and pointed out, "It might be better to do the walk straight away or we'll miss the full moon."

"Tomorrow?" she queried in a voice hoping I'd say no. But I answered yes. "We'll get across the sandbank on tomorrow's early tide, and where the two arms meet, there's a wide basin that's just got to be secure. We could be anchored and on our way before noon. That'll give us plenty of time to trek upstream for a camp."

Once the pros and cons are thrashed out, Jude usually gets 100% enthusiastic and starts her planning. While Jude rattled off lists of foods, medical stuff, and the clothing she would take, I lay there thinking of what I had to do. And every few minutes she'd remind me not to forget the torch, and what about spare batteries…

The King George River enters Koolama Bay through sandbanks similar to those at the Berkeley, except these ones are deep within a protected bay that is calm and they have only one small dogleg. Making our crossing even easier, we had the waypoints *Wooshee* had used a month earlier. The morning's tide was a big one, and so *Banyandah* sallied across with a metre under her. We then found the lower reaches much like the Berkeley, mangroves giving way to abrupt rock. And although we got into a wee bit of trouble with shallow depth where the first side stream enters, it proved nothing more than an adrenalin rush that fully awakened us.

By seven o'clock, and nearly high tide, we came upon the basin where the east tributary joins the main river, and suddenly it became a half-a-mile wide pool looking especially huge as the mangroves were half underwater. We motored around taking soundings, and finding the bottom reasonably flat, placed our anchor pretty much in the middle. Then we pulled it in until even our strong engine didn't budge it. Probably sank it half a metre in good river mud. And that, with the surrounding hills assuring calm water, made *Banyandah* quite secure. Admittedly, a suburban marina this was not. There were no structures, no other vessels, no people; just us. So, would you leave your house unattended in the middle of nowhere to go bush, with no phone, or even informing a neighbour? That's what we must sometimes do, or we'd never take advantage of the moment. And we would not have experienced Easter Island, Kingman Reef, or the strange Malpelo, a mid-ocean rock 300 miles off Columbia.

Nothing in life is 100% sure. If you wait for it to be without risk, you will miss out. We just try to be smart and fresh the risks by confronting the dangers. Then, once precautions have been put in place, we put the worry out our heads and get on with our plan. And that's what we did that morning. Every locker was thrown open to dig out our tent, sleeping gear, rucksacks, and all the other gear needed to survive in a hostile land. Jude is an old pro and miraculously put together an excellent menu while I looked after the other essentials like wine, snacks, and sweets. We also packed our first aid and snake bite kit, EPRIB and GPS. I even remembered the torch and spare batteries.

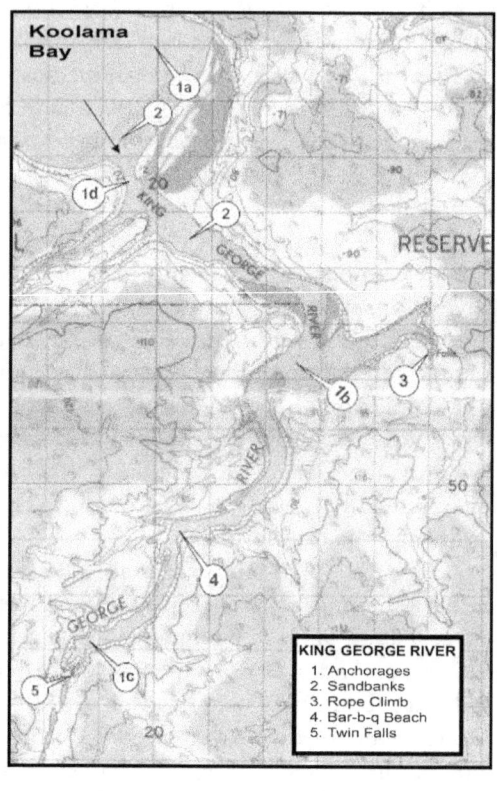

The east tributary is known to contain one of the Kimberley's most delightful freshwater pools. To reach them requires a two-kilometre dinghy ride across a shallow inlet then a climb up a waterfall using a rope slung down from the top by the Royal Navy. But, according to our Fremantle Sailing Club Guidebook, that rope had been removed and now access is via a rocky slope a few hundred metres downstream of the falls. I had seen a picture of a yachtie getting drenched going hand over hand up the falls and it not only looked dangerous, but impossible with fifteen kilos on my back. So the rocky slope sounded a good way up to me.

But, before setting off, we faced our hardest decision of the morning. Quite a quandary. Should we lock the boat and therefore advertise it's unattended, or leave it open as if the owners were about. In the end, we hedged our options by putting the valuables back aft and discreetly locking that cabin while leaving the forward area wide open.

Boarding Little Red, now amazingly loaded with two huge rucksacks, trolling gear, extra drink, sunscreen, insect repellent and Jude's hardwood croc basher, we shoved off at the impressive time of ten-thirty – only to return after a hundred metres to pick up the video gear I'd forgotten on the cockpit floor.

The ride up the inlet was lovely, surrounded by craggy rock abutments mirrored off flat water that our wake soon set wobbling. Having been hard at work since well before daybreak, we started to relax knowing we were prepared. After a half-hour ride, the inlet split into two vertical canyons. I steered into the right one and the towering walls narrowed to form a cul-de-sac of rusty red rock with a black tongue drooping down at its end. Impressed, we were also relieved to see a trickle of water falling off the edge indicating we'd have flowing water on our trek. But what didn't impress us as nicely was the four-metre saltwater croc barely afloat right ahead. The tops of its nostrils and the ridge above hooded eyes betraying its presence had us holding our breath while it glided past creating only a faint ripple.

The walls plunged straight into the murky water, so we were able to pull directly under the falls to take photos while the breeze kept the slight trickle of water away. Surprising us, off to one side dangled a very long, thick braided rope; a suicidal climb with gear on our backs. Maybe forty years ago, but on this day, I was keen to look for the rocky slope mentioned in the guidebook. But that wasn't so easy to find. The walls of rock ended in mangroves that we'd surely not enter for fear the crocs would have us for lunch. However, upon closer inspection, we found a tiny crack, a fissure in the wall that had rubble at the bottom. Crikey! Maybe the rope was the better way up. This crack had some ugly precipices to conquer; where a slip might land you with a broken back.

Suddenly my great plan began to unravel. Jude wasn't sure she could get up either route and returning to the boat was mentioned. Making it even more difficult, the mean hooded eyes of the croc were fastened onto us from just a few metres away. And then quite surprising me, when I suggested landing Jude at the crack so she could better decide, she agreed. Running the bow into the rubble, she scurried out and up the scree, somewhat safe from the reptile. Then she proceeded to climb over the bigger stuff while I sat in Little Red offering suggestions as to where to find handholds and put her feet. At one point she had to use a body press between the rock faces to shimmy around a ledge, but then she called out the rest was do-able.

"Can you do it with your pack?" I called up.

"No-way," echoed back. But then she offered, "Maybe we could hand them up over the ledge."

That seemed a positive enough response for me to park our tinnie and look for myself. And as the croc was momentarily off chasing an alternative meal, I drove in and scurried up the slope. Usually, Jude's the more cautious one, but I have to admit this crack had me worried. Guess I don't like body presses where there's nothing but empty air between you and sharp pointy rocks far below. But Jude was enthusiastic, and I surely didn't want to disappoint my lady, so we went down to sort out the dinghy while the croc was still out of sight. A bit scary that.

Storing our dinghy became a major headache, as we'd not be away a few hours, but days. Big tides can do horrendous things to small craft left unattended. In the end, we emptied all our trekking stuff, putting it on the first big rock. Then we removed the outboard and fuel tank, the oars, anchor and all the little gear, hauling that lot up the slope beyond the high tide mark. After that, we lifted the alloy craft out the water and onto a handy shelf cut into the wall, which was also above the high tide line. Only then did we secure its rope leash to a big rock. After that, buggered and hot, we turned to face the crack knowing there would be no turning back.

Taking great care now that we had extra weight on our backs, level by level we found footing, until the menacing overhanging ledge. Un-slinging our sacks, I handed them up to Jude after she had pressed her way up. Then I had to face my nemesis. Sort of reminded me of Malpelo off the Columbian coast where the boys and I had climbed this stupendous mid-ocean mountain peak. We got to the top okay, but on the way down I took the wrong fissure, which led us to a very narrow rock bridge that the nimble lads simply ran across and were gone. When I got to it, I stopped, looked far below to the sea and got rubbery legs. I did this time what I did then. Took a few calming breaths, went through what I expected, then berated myself until I felt a goose, and then just did it. Jude was right, the way up after that proved just plain hard work.

A few stone cairns at the top proved others had mastered the crack, and these took us through some terribly spiky bush to a vertical edge. Expecting to walk out onto the lip of the falls, I was startled. The edge dropped straight into a canyon. And way below was a gigantic aqua-blue pool. What a luscious sight - but unreachable. Surrounded by cliffs equal to those at the falls, it seems we had climbed double their height!

Others had come this way, so there had to be a way down. Maybe it lay back towards the falls. But carrying heavy packs through thick bush, we'd not be going back. Instead, we trekked ahead along the rim. Beyond the pool, the gorge narrowed and looked just as inaccessible, prompting me to wonder whether this trek had any chance of success. All this time the hot sun is beating down, my throat is like sandpaper, and my rumbling belly keeps reminding me lunch needs to be soon. But there's no shade in sight. So we continued pushing through the scrub, past the pool to a point where the cliff face is split by a slope that seemed slightly less than vertical. And while it didn't appear easy or direct, it led into the canyon. So I unloaded my sack to try it. Jude plopped down under an overhanging rock and waited. Down, down through dense spinifex, on sharp loose stones, I zigzagged until I was only my own height above the canyon floor, where a drop onto uneven rock stopped me. If I jumped, I might not get back up. Searching the canyon, I thought I saw a possible escape route, so I climbed back to present a new plan to the wife. Go back or take a chance. Nodding her acceptance, we slithered back down to the last drop, and that's where she baulked.

"I'm not dropping off that," she adamantly refused.

And I couldn't convince her we could do it, so I jumped. Not precisely a jump, more a slide on my belly until I hung then dropped the last few feet.

Safe and intact, I looked up, grinned, and then said, "Hand the bags down Sweetie." Then I gave her my shoulder to stand on.

The day took a much better turn after gaining the canyon floor. Right next to the wall, we found glorious shade with pools of freshwater at our feet. Jude immediately started digging into her bag looking for lunch. But instead of plopping down in the shade to wait, I wandered downstream and soon came to a series of giant steps dropping into that magnificent pool. Its magical bluish waters touched both sides of the red canyon and were so clear I could see its vertical walls descend more than ten metres. I reckon God must have designed this pool for giants, with the far end near the falls a baby giant's wading pool; its flat bottom was covered by only a metre of water. Like a ferret, I found a route down the series of giant steps and successfully reached the pool's edge, and then scampered back to find Jude busy laying out the meal.

"Leave that. Come have a look."

From the high vantage point, we looked in wonder. It was so massively beyond comprehension, our minds spun until we just had to accept it as another of Earth's magnificent creations. Scurrying down and stripping off, wasting not one second, we jumped into that deep body of pure water that stretched down red canyon walls like a blue football field. In a scene from some primeval past, our joyous shouts at first sounded rather puny before they doubled off those tall canyon walls. So clear, so pure, we drank while doing a few strokes then floated off to the far end. Lifting ourselves out and carefully creeping up to the edge, it dropped straight into the river. Way down below in the murky water we could see old croc guarding our gear. Or was he simply waiting? Who cared, the giant's pool had created giant appetites. So like a pair of noisy kids, our yelps echoed around the canyon as we dove back in.

Casuarina Creek, Berkeley River - anchored bow & stern to a waterfall with wonderful Bradshaw art upstream showing a proud race with armlets, fancy hairdos & ceremonial headdress

Berkeley River Gorge and zig-zags through the "Z"

Wooshee and *Banyandah* at the Red Amphitheatre with Mt. Casuarina in the distance

The Giants Pool   49

King George River
Top: "Giants Pool" saved us from heat stroke
Bottom: Who did this amazing Bradshaw Art? Jack worn out scampering in and out of caves.

Bottom: The most amazing billabong plants and a view from the top of the Twin Falls Banyandah alone amongst massive erosion.

VISITING ANCIENT FOLK

Returning to our shady spot next to the cliff, we ate lunch ravenously then the serious business started once again when we began studying the hot rock canyon for a way out. The day just kept moving on, and so must we, although we did consider swimming the afternoon away then sleep on a rock shelf that night. But the possibility of witnessing Bradshaw art around the next corner was the hook that got us up off our backsides.

Oh, how hard it was to get started after such an excellent stop. So full of water we gurgled, it soon started pouring out our skin as we faced our first hurdle; a lift up onto an eye height ledge using a lone sapling growing out a crack as a step. What looked easy proved hard. But with a few grunts and groans, our sacks and bodies got up on the ledge. Upon standing upright, several more similar obstacles rose ahead. Quickly in giant steps, the climb up led us into a much narrower gorge with a chaotic boulder floor that promised to break our legs each time we rock hopped. How much easier it would have been if unencumbered, but we had to carry the gear although it shifted our balance and momentum, making rock-hopping pure madness. Step by step, in the intense heat, another danger also had to be faced - fatigue. When pushing to the extreme, one must stay in touch with your body, otherwise thirst and fatigue cloud judgment. Just such a situation nearly jeopardised our expedition.

We had been on the move for several hours and were still climbing over or squeezing around the large boulders that filled the gorge as if thrown there by a giant's hand. According to the GPS, we'd travelled three kilometres from lunch, but with the afternoon sun heating the canyon walls like an oven, it felt more like we had walked eight. And we'd found nothing – no rock art, nor any flat ground for sleeping, and it was getting late. So, I pressed ahead – to sort of speed things up by searching for obstacles and art. Jude could then concentrate on keeping moving.

A change of scenery came; still within towering walls, a few saplings hid a pond with a sandy shore. And while I skirted it, I wondered whether here might be our first camp. But the water looked stale and the walls, which were magnificent colours and contained several ledges and caves, made the place feel claustrophobic. It'd be dark there once the sun set. So, I leapt across a shallow bit then paused to catch my breath, and gazing up, saw my first Bradshaw figures. That's when I heard the chilling shout, "Jack! Just gashed myself. Blood's spurting out."

When I raced back the hundred metres, Jude was down on the ground, her pack still on her back, one leg up on a rock, bright red blood all down it. She held a big wad of tissues firmly against her shin with more blood seeping through it. Immediately alarmed, I found some relief in seeing colour still in her face, so I tried reassuring her, but she was adamant that she'd punctured an artery because it was spurting. We got the pack off her back then she drank some water before digging for more tissues to replace the saturated ones. During the changeover, I saw a deep nasty gash forming an S in the meaty area alongside her shin. And while the skin did curl under, I did not see blood spurting, which was good. Speaking tersely, Jude explained how she had tripped on a root and fallen onto a sharp twig that had broken off in her leg. After tugging out the broken bit, she was now cleaning the wound to see if any bits had been left in it.

These medical emergencies are heart stoppers when they first happen. This one suddenly made us aware of how isolated we were, but that's when preparedness takes over. Our medical kit is very complete and our first aid training up to date. We even carry sutures and have the confidence to use them. But in this case, after applying pressure, the bleeding slowed to a point where good adhesive tape over a sterile pad drew the cut together, and the bleeding stopped. But how far could Judith move without aggravating the wound to bleed again?

It was reminiscent of the time she'd badly wrenched her knee many kilometres in the bush and couldn't put any weight on it. Faced with the dilemma of either leaving her and seeking help or standing by to assist, in that instance, as in this one, a shelter was needed, the nearer the better.

Leaving Jude to rest, I entered her as a waypoint in our GPS then forged ahead after deciding the immediate area could be a campsite, but a poor second choice. For a few hundred metres the way forward was just as tricky, then thankfully it opened up a bit, allowing me to climb up to the surrounding flats and seek water. In this, I was lucky. My search took me around some massive rocks then back to the dry riverbed just above where the gorge finished. Here grassy sand was dotted with a few trees between large flat rocks. And the dry, rocky river became a canal filled with clear water. Relief flooded through me. In a sweep, my eyes saw a perfect tent site, a place for our cooking fire and a sky open for moonlight. Racing back, the distance measured three-quarters of a kilometre, half on rock, including a rather difficult climb, the other half on flats. Explaining all this to Jude, she tested her leg and to our relief could put weight on it. But part of the problem was protecting the wound, so I dug out the wide crepe bandage that is part of our snakebite kit and firmly bandaged her ankle. Now could she carry her sack? I was prepared to make a second trip, but Jude's tough and was sure the load wouldn't bust open her leg, so we set off at a careful pace.

Camp at Billabong Two turned out to be nothing short of fantastic. A perfect site; flat, open, dotted with trees in blossom, and a pool that I immediately entered to cool off and bathe. The tent area also proved the best, soft with easy access. I erected our tent without the fly so we could see the moon and stars but not be troubled by snakes or pesky insects while we slept.

Jude recovered quickly and became cheerful, the wound causing her no pain after taking a few pills. So we celebrated. Out came the wine cask, the nuts and munchies; all very much enjoyed while watching gold tinge the fiery rays spreading across the rock-strewn landscape. Particularly beautiful were the flowers. Purple water lilies, which would have provided food for early Aborigines, lined one side of the canal, while on our side, purple bells popped out from what appeared to be succulents. Close to the tent, acacias, commonly known as wattles, perfumed the air with their furry yellow flowers. And scattered about, orange spiked Grevillea hummed with honeyeaters. What a day; afloat that morning, crossed a river bar, packed, climbed a crack, swam in a giant's pool, and then walked a canyon. No wonder we slept like two woodsmen sawing logs.

When adrift on *Banyandah* the day before, Old Grumps had found a handful of digital images showing some of this area's rock art although none gave their location other than the notation *Eastern Creek*. But from our two previous excursions, we knew these ancient artists preferred high sites exposed to water views, or so we thought. Therefore, we believed the art would be found back in the gorge near where Jude had injured herself. Having slept well, her leg felt good, but before trekking back into the heavy stuff, we thought we would take a more leisurely walk around the outcrops seen less than a kilometre further on. It looked mostly flat open country with plenty of shady places to rest, so we packed our camera gear, some water and left thinking we'd be back for a morning snack.

As often happens, Judith got interested in the flowering ephemerals growing just about everywhere. So I went ahead into the rocks that were not hugely tall or impressive; lacking large overhanging shelters, they overlooked pretty bland country. I remember videoing the first one and remarking on tape how the ancient artists would never have chosen sites like these. Famous last words. When I walked around the other side, I found a wall filled with Bradshaw art. What glorious stuff. Some of the best we'd seen, showing lovely minute hands, aprons, and cute little feet. One flowing figure had triple tassels mounted either side of its waist, while another appeared to wear a knee-length skirt.

First recorded in 1891 by Joseph Bradshaw who, after becoming lost while looking for new grazing lands in the northwest of Australia, sketched in his journal what has become known as Bradshaw Paintings. According to legend, they were made by birds. It's said these birds pecked the rocks until their beaks bled then created these exquisite paintings by using a tail feather and their own blood. I don't know about that, but what is known is this art is of such antiquity no pigments remain on the rock surface, making it impossible to use carbon-dating technology. Nor can the composition of the original paints be determined. Whatever pigments were used have been locked into the rock itself as shades of mulberry red and have become impervious to the elements. Their dating is based on a 1996 discovery by Mr Grahame Walsh of a Bradshaw Painting partly covered by a fossilised wasp nest, which scientists removed and analysed using a new technique of dating, determining it to be over 17,500 years old. To best gauge that timeframe, that's four to five times the age of classic Egyptian art. Some experts say the art is more than 50,000 years old. Hence the mystery surrounding who created it.

My discovery was conveyed to Jude in a series of yelps, yells and yahoos, and she came at a peg-leg trot. The wall displayed a collage of animals and human figures elegantly posed or running. One figure held what we thought to be a turtle. While another, a lady is strutting her stuff with her hair flowing back. It's mind-blowing to see such beautiful art on hard, barren rock and know some early beings not only had the technique but the subtle appreciation of style that's depicted. Witnessing this, not for the first time did we wonder whether the earliest Aborigines had that ability? Leaving that to the experts, Jude and I were there to witness and record, and that's what we did. The video camera hummed while both Jude's digitals beeped. Then we went in different directions to find more art.

Jude found the next collection in a mini cave hidden behind thick bushes. Here a figure wore armlets and other accoutrements of a ceremonial dress with a massive mop of hair gracefully held back by tasselled cords. Several other sites were found within ten minutes of camp, but the most intriguing came when I discovered a cave with a turtle painted on its ceiling in white. As usual, I called to Jude who was always keen to share the discovery, but I didn't describe my find, intending her to see the white figure and then gauge her reaction. Everything so far had been in red, so although the turtle was a bit more crudely painted, I thought it significant. Jude hardly reacted. At first, she just glared. Then rather affronted, "Looks like someone's graffiti. And what's this?" she said looking closely. "Acrylic? Looks like house paint." She didn't like its crudeness and I could understand her disgust because it overlaid other Bradshaw figures. I still thought being in white was significant, and silently, we set about looking at the art and recording it.

All this bush bashing, rock climbing, and looking under ledges took up most of the morning and feeling peckish, a break for drinks and the oranges Jude had in her day bag was suggested. But as there wasn't much shade under the white turtle, I investigated the backside of the rock and found some comfort under a large ledge that also contained more rock art, and something else. At first, I thought it was an animal bone from a big creature like a cow or maybe the thighbone of a kangaroo and wondered whether a dingo lived there. In fact, I got so nervous I backed into the open to scan the bushes and tall grasses. Doing that revealed more bones lying in the thin space between two rock faces, on top of what looked like wrinkled brown butcher paper. The bones were slightly red as if rouge had leached from the rock and permeated them. Jude came to my shout, and while quietly enjoying our snack, we pondered the find.

The juice from the orange was starting to act like electrolyte added to a battery when I spied a bleached bone in the grass near my feet. When it looked like a piece of someone's skull, a jolt shocked me and my arm shot out. Just a bit further from it, another bleached bone lay half-hidden under some leaf litter and picking it up another zap hit me when I identified someone's arm. Oh my, was this the scene of a gruesome murder? It was sure a lonely enough place to hide a body. But hey, who's going to come all the way out here. No way! And it began looking more like a ceremonial burial site. Either way, we recorded its exact GPS position to send the information to the authorities when we next made contact with the outside world. More recent research has revealed we did indeed find a ceremonial burial site; past chiefs and prominent tribal persons were laid to rest upon a bed of paperbark, their bones first treated with ochre.

Having found so much art did not dampen our desire for more. It's addictive like treasure hunting; no matter how many riches are discovered, more is wanted. So as the sun grew hotter, we continued to search like little mice for cheese, further and further from camp; finding another billabong, another waterfall without water, a flood plain where Nature's fury had moved masses of stones, shaping them into ocean waves. And of course, we found more artwork, but none as clear nor as lovely as the first ones. So, rather buggered and ravenously hungry, we reluctantly returned to camp.

A shady area was made using our tent fly strung between a tree and some rocks then we lay under it savouring the breeze that filtered around it. While eating lunch, a young goanna played peek-a-boo from behind our tree's loose bark, unwittingly posing for Jude's camera. And then afterwards, instead of going back to the gorge as intended, we alternated between swimming in the pool and lying under the shade until the sun sank nearer the horizon. That gave us some new vitality and not wanting to miss out on the opportunity of being where we were, we got up and crossed the dry bed to wander through the rock outcrops on the other side. But you know how it is when you've had a great time then try to repeat it. This time the bush was just that little more troublesome, the green ants a bit more ferocious, the fear of snakes in the tall spear grass a bit more real, and the rocks, well they were just rocks instead of potential living quarters for an ancient civilisation. And we found no further art.

But we did discover something of interest. The dry riverbed meandered as if a giant snakeskin, its floor both granite and sandstone, and amazingly we found patches where lava coated the granite-like thick bubbly fudge.

The Kimberley region extends from the red dunes of the Great Sandy Desert through the rugged sandstone escarpments of the Kimberley Plateau to the Timor Sea in the north. Covering some 423,500 square kilometres, it is near twice the size of Victoria and three times the size of England. The central part of the Kimberley, known as the Kimberley Plateau, is generally flat sedimentary rock; sandstone and quartzite deposited about 1800 million years ago by major river systems that flowed from north to south across the whole region. Then about 18,000 years ago, as sea levels rose from approximately 120 m below current levels, the Kimberley coastline became drowned with the sea filling what was once river valleys.

This area also contains considerable volumes of basalt lava flows, with intrusions of leucite lamproite enhancing the region. Of the Jurassic age, they are genetically related to kimberlite; wherein, lay their importance. Kimberlite is a type of potassic volcanic rock best known for sometimes containing diamonds.

Not far away is the Argyle diamond mine, the world's leading producer with an average annual production of 35 million carats (7000 kg), or about a third the global production of natural diamonds. No wonder as soon as we saw that bubbly volcanic stuff, Jude and I forgot about Bradshaw art and started looking for sparklers instead.

Our second night's sleep was even better than the first, and I arose in the predawn light to make tea for my lady, which we enjoyed in bed listening to birds sing love-songs to the waking day. We had achieved quite a lot in the previous two days, so were not so driven to get going. Instead, after rising, we lazily wandered our area, snooping into cracks and crannies, discovering strange animal tracks in the sand, and a small midden of seashells proving this billabong was a past tribal site. But hanging over us was the fact that we had to be heading back. Like it or not, we had a deadline.

What slowed our breaking camp was the night's heavy dew that had wetted the tent and took several hours to dry. Nevertheless, dry it did, and we finally left with both sadness and gladness filling our hearts. Jude's leg was still wrapped in crepe bandage but not causing pain. Unfortunately, that did not make the big rocks in the gorge any easier for either of us. In fact, it was me that slowed the pace. My dodgy knee kept complaining, and I didn't want it to collapse when jumping across a chasm. And carrying our packs on such a hot day only made them feel even heavier. So, several times we quite willingly dropped them when we saw a new overhang to investigate.

Around mid-morning break, we arrived back at billabong one, Jude's injury site. With the heat sucking the air out our lungs, with great relish, we dropped down under a monstrous rock tilted over a breezeway. And after taking a big drink, we ate the last of our crackers and cheese then I hobbled over towards the artwork I had first discovered. It certainly was impressive. On a vertical face looking over the pond, several people chatted in an arc, the outer ones being taller gave the illusion of perspective. The outer two seemed the leading figures, with their elaborate conical hairdos that trailed intricate "knotted" ponytails giving them a sophisticated and elegant look, while the other figures looked right and left up to them. All had accoutrements adorning their arms and waists.

Rediscovering this Bradshaw got us scanning the area, and we soon identified four other potential sites perched high above the watercourse. Balancing our need to get moving against our desire to make the most of this opportunity had me race off leaving Jude to search the local area. Skirting the stagnant pond, as quickly as I dare I climbed up a crack pushing through thick scrub then jumped boulder to boulder until I gained the first overhanging rock shelter. This quickly revealed a few stick figures painted on its ceiling. They were less elaborate than the others, more like simple cartoon characters. So I snapped a few photos, did a minute's video of the view then crabbed sideways to the next spot. More trouble than it was worth, the few simple animals painted in mulberry red held my interest for only a few minutes before I was hunting for a way down.

I hate being in a hurry. I lose patience, and then everything irritates me; like the green ants' nest, I failed to notice. Ouch! Suffering many bites, I wiped them off my neck along with my sweat, but while doing this, lost balance and crashed through a dead tree, whose breaking branches eased my tumble to the canyon floor. Getting up mumbling curses, I was looking up and across to the last cave, and wondering whether to bother. There was not even a crack to climb up, just a series of hollows washed out the wall by the wet season torrent.

Deciding to go over just for a look, I was straight away impressed with the worn, smooth, multi-coloured stone that made up the slight corner. Above, maybe twenty metres, I saw the cave and on its ceiling beheld a collection of small figures in several groups. Hmm, but how to get up?

Right before me, eons of rushing water had washed out a chamber that when entered, became a circular stairwell of sorts. Nimble youths might have used it to scamper up to the cave, but for me, the journey was a bit slower. Being careful not to fall and crack open my head, I took one level up at a time until I could slither over on my belly to view the rock art.

Pairs of figures arched back with bountiful flowing hair and were holding twin boomerangs in each hand. Elegant, but what did they mean? Another with petite feet held a large arrow that might have been a spear. Again, the artwork was well preserved and hardly looked to have been painted fifty millenniums ago. And although our time was running short, I could not pull myself away and kept wondering who had created these arched figures, so well proportioned that any art student would have been proud to claim them. Who, such a long time before the Pharaohs? It was truly mind-boggling.

The old tick-tock of time puts limits on us all, and so all too soon, we were on our way back to that magnificent giant's pool for a last swim before returning to reality. Our alloy dinghy was still perched high and dry. So were the oars, outboard, and the rest of our stuff. And in tedious, sweaty work, we assembled it again then off we went. Didn't even get a chance to say goodbye to Mr Croc, just put the trolling line out as the cliffs disappeared, and it felt like leaving Wonderland.

Ending this tale properly, we hooked a pan-sized trevally just before reaching *Banyandah*, and Jude's boot on its head kept it quiet till docking Little Red. Of course, *Banyandah* was still safe, with all our gear in its proper place. So, as the sun set, we drank a few lukewarm beers from the turned-off fridge, while reflecting on the sights we'd just been very privileged to witness. Around us, our decks were littered with the best camping gear. But where we had just visited, early man survived with nothing more than their strength and skills. A slip could have meant a broken limb, for which we have a remedy. But for early man, a broken arm or leg could have meant a slow, painful death.

Oh, but the next day, aches and pains appeared in our backs, legs, and my arm where I had fallen, and in Jude's hip, which never hurts until she stops. On a positive note, her wound began granulating nicely.

We kept low key all the next day; cleaned gear, moped about, talked very little. After a second sound sleep, we watched the video footage, reliving the adventure before writing up our journals. Once again, Earth and her creatures had provided wonder, adventure, and entertainment. They had revealed mysteries beyond wisdom, offered knowledge by simply observing life. And only when totally satiated and feeling fulfilled, did we start thinking about the twin waterfalls that still lay ahead.

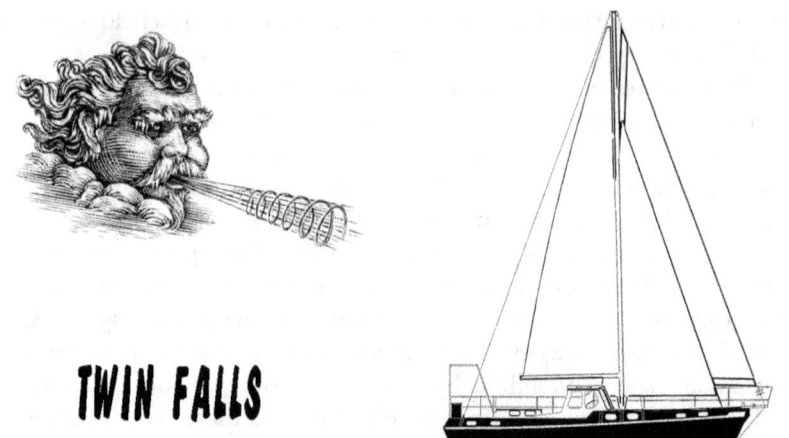

TWIN FALLS

The King George River is renowned for its twin falls that plummet off a plateau into a gorge of spectacular beauty. It's a destination on many world tours and one rarely missed by visitors to the *Top End*. In fact, when we first arrived in Koolama Bay, a mini-liner was anchored and taking its passengers through the gorge to the falls on giant-sized inflatable dinghies with powerful outboards. Well, we had our own ship. And you can bet we'd not be missing something of such great beauty. So, the other part of our King George Experience began late the second afternoon back from visiting the ancient folk. Immediately upstream after getting away, the river narrowed into a majestic gorge similar to the Berkeley, except the King George is bigger, wider, and we thought possibly older because there is more sloping ground at the base of the cliffs. According to our guidebooks, this river cuts through the high Kimberley Plateau whose rocks were deposited 1800 million years ago, making them some of the oldest on Earth.

We had also read that The Darwin Stress Busters, whoever they are, had named a spot on a bend partway up as *Bar-b-q Beach*, where behind a gap in the mangroves is a sandy beach with handy flat rocks that can be used for tables. Also noted is there's usually a three-metre croc patrolling this section of the river. In the Berkeley, we had seen that low light brings out the cragginess, so we were travelling upstream in the last hours of daylight and were rewarded by ever-changing colours. Just on dusk, we reached a tight corner where the outside wall plunged straight into unfathomable depths. Fortunately, it shoaled nicely across the channel opposite *Bar-b-q Beach*.

Next morning, before the sun had peeked into the canyon, we were away, eager to see the fabled Twin Falls. But straightaway we were running through another wonder. The outer bend, where the deepwater ran, was thick with mauve coloured blobs of jellyfish; the kind without tentacles, big as footballs making a chunky jellyfish soup. Nowhere else, just on that bend. We were so amazed we turned the boat around and drifted through them again, snapping more photos and wondering whether simple creature like these can communicate in ways unknown to man. And that this was a jellyfish jamboree.

About this time, the wind started blowing straight up the channel, hastening our travels. And quite soon we were running down the last stretch of the gorge. Ahead a vertical wall of russet red rock blocked our passage. When closer, it parted both left and right. And once inside what is nearly a landlocked bowl sunk down from the surrounding earth, it became windless. So we just drifted, taking in the majestic beauty of the two scoured out basins, each trickling a waterfall.

Alone, surrounded by Nature in its purest form, we began noticing more than just the outstanding beauty. Indeed the walls were impressive, as were the trickles of water cascading through rainbows across the dark background. But there were also extra special treats. Hanging gardens of maidenhair and herringbone ferns shone through their own rainbows. Following the rainbows down, our eyes fastened onto the pockmarked nature of the sandstone nearer the water's edge. Strangely lovely how the wet season's torrent has eaten out equally spaced divots reminiscent of Swiss cheese. The colours intrigued us. Rusty red rock stretched high above. And in most places around the basin, it was that colour too. But in patches, some quite massive, the stone had an odd whitish appearance that when viewed close up was streaked with lavender and yellow. This troubled and intrigued us when seen from afar. Why such big and scattered chunks of white. Following several trains of thought, we concluded that this was the stone's natural colour and that these were patches of recent erosion, where the oxidised rusty colour had been blasted away by torrents of debris and water. With that thought in mind, when taking a broad panorama of the area, it became perfectly clear just how powerful a force comes into play during the wet season.

We anchored *Banyandah* outside the extremely deep falls area and prepared for a trek up to the plateau via a track located near the boat. Although the trail is used by dozens of tourists and yachties each year, we dressed in full bush gear. This is a remote wilderness, and we needed to be responsible and prepared to look after ourselves. Taking something to eat and our emergency equipment, as well as the snakebite kit, being dressed for rough terrain , also allowed closer inspection.

The wind had now become very boisterous, its gusts bowling *Banyandah* over, sending her racing off on a tangent whenever they attacked. But our anchor must have been stuck in some real gooey mud for she always danced sharply back. My only problem, rowing against the blasts down the slopes. But after my back warmed to the task, we made headway. And thankfully before I tired, we found some protection and crunched into the rocky shore. Standing there catching my breath, finding a rough track up the slope was a welcome treat. Then after gaining high ground and finding another well-trodden path, not being pioneers took nothing away from the spectacular views. Far below between towering ramparts lay *Banyandah* as if a toy boat blown this way then that upon wind darkened waters freckled white.

The blast from the heavens also seemed to add an extra dimension to the raw natural scene and had us lingering at each vantage point to marvel at the changing colours. In fact, it took so long to traverse the short distance that when we finally came upon the black river flats, we took a snack break before scampering to the edge for a look over.

Oh my, looking down had our toes tingling, especially with the wind buffeting us even though we clung to a huge rock as a gecko clings to a ceiling. Thankfully the wind blew us away from the edge, bringing spray wetting our faces. The thought of losing grip never left me as I leant over the edge to gauge the amount of water that could flood over during the monsoon. A better appreciation was found by looking sideways to the flattened vegetation. It told the story of a torrent more than three times my height across a gap of several hundred metres, while at the moment it would have comfortably flowed along a street gutter.

After exploring the first waterfall, we climbed up and across the rock island splitting the two flows then down onto the other flats where our earlier snack was deemed insufficient, so lunch was declared. Discovering a cover of shade over a ledge providing seats from which we could dip our feet in a pool, sandwiches and fruit disappeared from between us. Once fuelled up, I was ready to explore the waterfall's edge further, but Jude was too comfortable to move, wanting instead to review the photos she had taken. So I went alone, video bag over my shoulder, to film a monumental documentary showing Nature in action for my grandchildren.

With those patches of exposed rock foremost in my thoughts, I wanted to demonstrate how mighty rivers shape Mother Earth. This required a sequence of the water tumbling over the edge and down the hundred metres of height. And so I started making my way across the flats towards the sharp edge exposed to the vast Kimberley red canyon. But every time I reached a drop-off, instead of finding the pool, I found another ledge hidden just below. And again, I would have to find a way to reach that one. This kept happening, three, four times until I was about to give up on getting the shot. By this time, I was down a bit from the top and off to one side with a good camera angle, but I could not see the bottom. It was still obscured by a minuscule projection jutting out just a small step below. My heart quickened. Did I dare? I'm a safety-first person. I just have to be. But there's a demon inside on a tight leash ninety-nine percent of the time.

Not knowing what I'd see, that demon lent out. Holding the camera at full stretch, pointing it down, I was trying to see what was on the screen. Shaky to say the least, but I thought there were white splashes amongst the black. And this had the demon put a foot out on the tiny ledge. Now my toes really started tingling, and my other senses began working overtime as little by little that demon edged out till we could actually see past the edge to splashes in the pool far below. Quickly before losing nerve, I hit the record button then concentrated on not losing balance. Especially tricky as I only had vision through the viewfinder. The moment I completed the shot, I jumped back and scolded myself for being just plain stupid. One errant blast and I would have been sent flying. But, after playing the scene on the screen, half of me was delighted. The other half was still furious. So, to bring peace, I promised once, then twice, to never take silly risks like that again.

Back up top, I kept mum on my doco. With the sun stretching shadows down the ridgeline, I called, "C'mon, let's get going." We needed to be retracing our steps down the slope and get safely home after yet another lovely day; the last in the King George River.

Well, not quite our last day. The next morning, while bucking that headwind, we had to shift *Banyandah* downriver, parking our lady just inside the sandbar to pack up for sea. And because the high tide would not arrive until quite late, we had an early dinner then went straight to bed with the alarm set to ring just before midnight. That's when the moon would rise and there'd be an hour of tide still to run.

Usually, crossing a river bar at night would be unwise. In all our years, we had never attempted it. But because the daytime high tide was too small for *Banyandah's* six-foot draught and we'd be stuck inside another week, and because the King George is calm with no swell and little current, I decided to use GPS navigation to follow the track we made coming in.

Getting up in the dark, we both were very nervous. Like flying blind the first time, me intently watching the GPS screen (actually we used both, our ship's and handheld - one as backup), and Jude steering to my directions. But, in a short hour's work, we were out, with the anchor down in Koolama Bay, going back to bed with the alarm reset for five. Why five? Well, Cape Londonderry lay just ahead; the most northerly point in the Kimberley. Real nasty currents there, best tackled at slack water.

Goodbye Timor Sea. We'll soon be bouncing over the Indian Ocean swells again for the first time in twenty years.

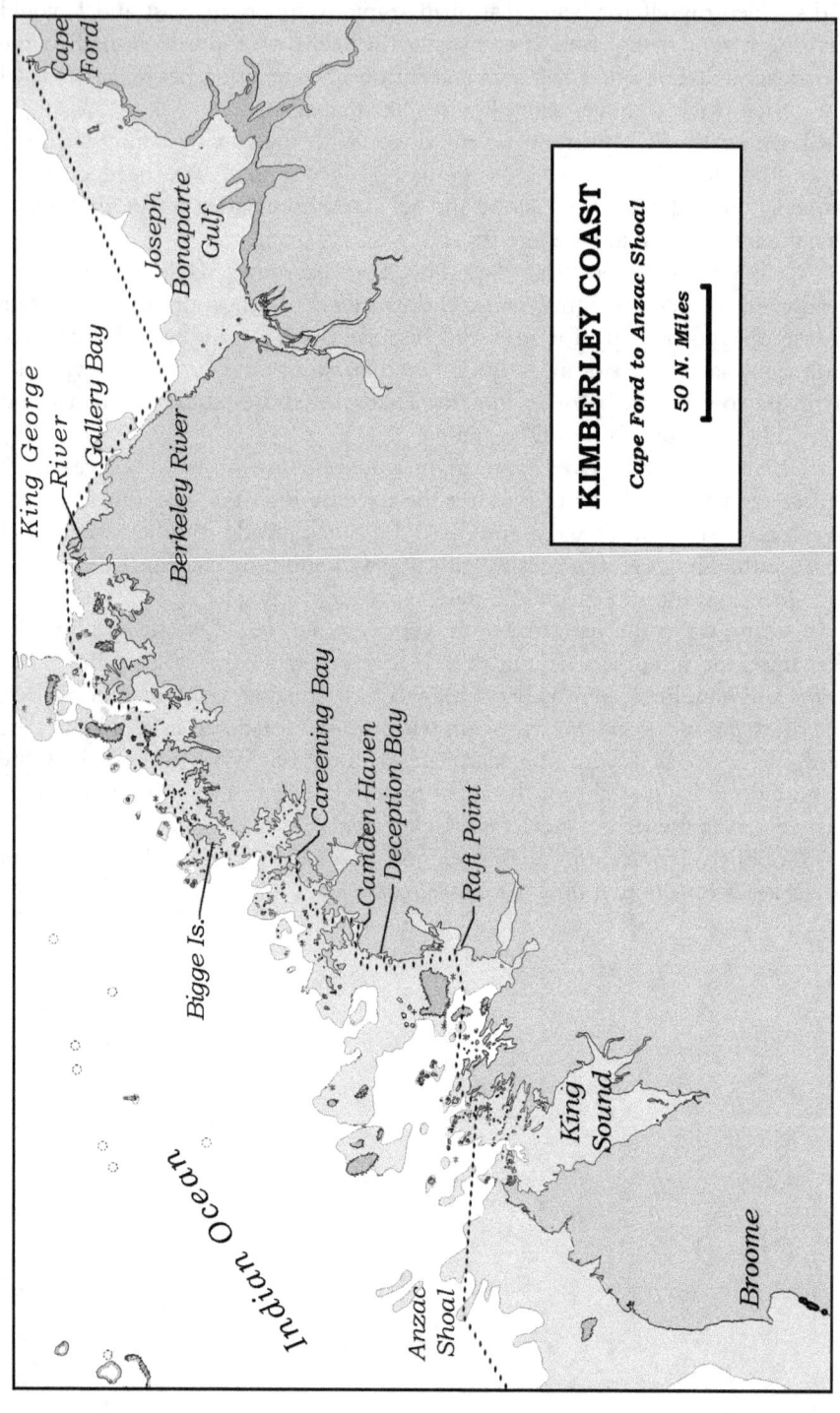

CAREENING BAY

Matt and Gill off *Wooshee* gave us a great gift when we first met them in the Berkeley. We were discussing early explorers when they asked if we'd read much about a Royal Navy Lieutenant named King. Admitting we knew nothing, they loaned us *KING of the Australian Coast*, a terrific book by Marsden Hordern, covering Lieutenant Phillip Parker King's many voyages when surveying the Kimberley Coast between 1817 and 1823.

Reading his story while travelling along King's Australian Coast, this is what we learnt. When Napoleon lost his last battle at Waterloo, the great rundown in the Royal Navy began. In 1815, over 700 ships were in commission. Three years later, only 130 remained. Disbanding them put thousands of sailors and four out of five officers on the beach. While officers received halfpay, the sailors got nothing.

Consequently, crime increased and the Brits suddenly needed more prisons. Back then, they sent their convicts to Australia; to settlements at Sydney Cove, Norfolk Island, and Tasmania. All became stretched to their limits. Little else of this vast continent had been explored.

After mucking up their navigation to Batavia, the Dutch had landed at a few places along Australia's west coast and thought it a hostile, barren place. Then in 1770, Captain Cook discovered the east coast. That opened the floodgate of discovery. France had their eyes on the southern continent and in 1800 dipped deeply into its pocket to send Nicolas Baudin aboard the *Geographe* to survey all he could. In convoy with another corvette, the *Naturaliste*, he carried astronomers, hydrographers, a zoologist, historian, and artists. But finding the north and west coasts horrible, dangerous places, they mostly stayed many miles offshore. Only Matthew Flinders aboard the 334-ton *Investigator* in 1801 was bold enough to have a closer look, but he didn't find any big rivers when making a detailed survey of the south and west coasts. And it was big rivers, the Admiralty wanted to find. Because, in the early 1800s, no one had yet crossed Australia's vast inland, and the British hoped to find rivers emptying melted snow off inland mountains that would herald large tracts of fertile land with easy access from the sea.

The Napoleonic wars had severely drained the British treasury, but with other nations in the hunt, and under constant hammering from distinguished scientists like Sir Joseph Banks, the Admiralty were put under enormous pressure to launch an expedition. They finally agreed in 1817 to commission a survey of the northwest coast. However, only a tiny amount of money was authorised for the task and they chose a little known officer whose talent lay mainly in chart-making and then did not even provide him with a ship. The job went to Australian born, Lieutenant Phillip Parker King, son of a former NSW governor, who, along with two midshipmen, had to find their own passage to Australia, and then once there, locate and buy a ship at the right price. Great opportunities allow some men to be great. So it came to be with King. Brave, persistent, clever, the Lucky Captain as he became known making not just one voyage but four through this dangerous and isolated part of our world; one each year, both winter and summer; once being absent from Sydney for 344 days. King knew he'd be on the beach and unemployed except for this opportunity, so to keep in the Admiralty's good books, he named almost every important discovery after influential military and government officials. Hence we have Port Nelson after the great Admiral, Vansittart Bay named for the Exchequer, King George and Prince Regent Rivers, and Admiralty Gulf. But he did not name the vast and dangerous King Sound. This came afterwards, as we'll explain later.

During his third voyage aboard the fifty-six-foot cutter *Mermaid*, which carried nineteen hands, she sprang a leak, such a bad one they feared she'd open up. So they looked for a place to careen her. Now in those days the natives weren't too friendly, nor was there a general store just down the road, and considering the terrain, currents and how little was known, fixing *Banyandah's* engine oil leak seems child's play. But men were super-sized back then, much more resourceful and cleverer in some ways, so they searched until they found a perfect bay; one that had a gently shelving beach, with no rocks or obstructions. This became their careening bay and they laid the *Mermaid* on this beach for repairs. After stripping the copper sheeting from her hull, they found the iron nails holding the planks corroding away. So, like a surgeon finding incurable cancer, they did what they could during the two-week cycle between big tides then closed her up, and prayed all the way back to Sydney.

Before they left Careening Bay, King had the ship's name carved in a massive boab tree; it is still clearly visible today. Reading this story while travelling through the same dangerous waters, we just had to visit this special site. So Careening Bay became our next destination.

After leaving the King George River, we day hopped past Cape Londonderry and Admiralty Gulf, and then rounded Cape Voltaire to anchor in Krait Bay; a tiny slit in red rock named after the well known Aussie craft that had set up a WWII training base there before running several raids on Singapore.

Late that afternoon, Bruce and Anna on *H2O* happened to sail in, and next morning we travelled in convoy across Montague Sound to Bigge Island, where Jude and I rowed in to visit a cave containing Wandjina rock art.

Crikey, it had been vandalised, robbing us of making that special connection. And even before we had much of a look, Bruce and Anna came racing into the beach waving frantically. Blood was pouring from Bruce's right hand while his other clutched something attached to it. It seems while fishing he had jagged himself with a treble hook.

"My best lure," he yelped as I snipped off its barb on board *Banyandah*. We found these two quite heroic. Not young kids anymore, after raising their children, these baby boomers were out doing something adventurous before they could not. They'd purchased their yacht in February, took a sailing course in March then spent heaps on new goodies before heading up the Queensland coast, never have sailed on their own before! The Great Barrier Reef is daunting enough, but the Kimberley Coast is a tester even for experienced sailors.

A rare strong wind struck that night at Bigge Island, allowing little sleep rolling about on the swells entering Wary Bay. The next morning, bleary-eyed and thick-headed, I renamed it "weary bay" in my last radio chat with *H2O*. For Bruce the goose and Frau Anna, this was as far as they'd go. They had decided to turn back and return across the top rather than face the Great Australian Bight.

With white breakers crashing just behind us, it was onwards under reefed main and headsail rolled to number two dot. Heeled over, seawater sluicing the decks, we had a powerful sail that day; Jude loving every moment, steering us through the string of Coronation Islands that obstruct Port Nelson Bay. Shortly after lunch, spent from so much excitement and too little sleep, we entered Careening Bay and set our anchor under sail, just as King would have done.

In the silence of barren hills, alone, a zillion miles from help, we suddenly became one with King and his men. His predicament energised us. Eager to walk the ground once used by the *Mermaid* crew, we dumped Little Red in the water, and then rowed towards the hostile shore just as King's men would have done nearly 200 years earlier when they towed in the *Mermaid*.

Protected by off-lying islands, the arms of this cove stilled the last trace of swell making its surface reflective as glass. Indeed, on such an inhospitable coast, Lieutenant King had been lucky to find such a perfect spot to dry out his ship.

The moment we landed on the hard, crisp sand free of stone, we imagined the *Mermaid* on her side dominating the beach. So deep in draught, King's men had to dig a large hole near the ship's rudder to replace its faulty iron keel bolts. Standing at the water's edge, with the beach sloping gently up to a grassy flat that is dotted with small trees dominated by a spectacularly large boab, a perfect campsite is formed, running level to the foot of timbered hills.

At the east end of the beach lay a wall of polished black stones, dumped there by a raging wet season creek, and closer to where we stood in the middle of the bay was another creek; its dry bed festooned with *mula-mula*, purple lamb's tails wagging in the breeze. To reach that one gigantic boab tree, we had to walk past the deep green leaves of healthy-looking strychnine trees intertwined with Crab's Eye vine. The seeds from both being equally poisonous; both native to Australia.

Entering a clearing, upon seeing the monstrous split double trunk, I recalled what King wrote in his journal: "The name of the vessel, etc. was marked on the large stem of a Capparis."

Before us, in giant lettering almost as clear today as when King's men had carved it: **HMC MERMAID 1820**.

When carved into the tree, its girth had measured 8.8 m, today it measures 12.3 m, stretching the letters slightly. I stood transfixed, hearing hearty voices of men unsure of their fate while my fingers traced every one of those letters. After our unhappy experience at Bigge finding the Wandjina art vandalised, we were happy not to see graffiti defacing this. And then, of course, we had to have our photoshoot; setting up our cameras on self-timers so we could be photographed together under this piece of living history.

Behind us, a trail led through tall grass, up the valley to the small pool King's men had used to replenish their water supply. To better connect with the past, Jude and I playacted their task and were darn pleased we only needed a small drink. Then we wandered back to where his company had camped on the flats and searched for a forgotten trinket, but only found other footprints.

Beginning with a weary night at Bigge Island, followed by a fast action sail, to end our rather full day we strolled hand in hand to the other end of the beach for a wander amongst the cool shade of the largest stand of coastal cycads in northern Australia. After reading King's own words then walking the exact spot of such high drama, finding a comfy place upon the dried fronds covering the ground caused visions of King and his men to begin passing through our thoughts. And while a bevy of birds warbled in concert with the sun's fiery golden rays filling Careening Bay, we watched King's men labouring on the careened *Mermaid*.

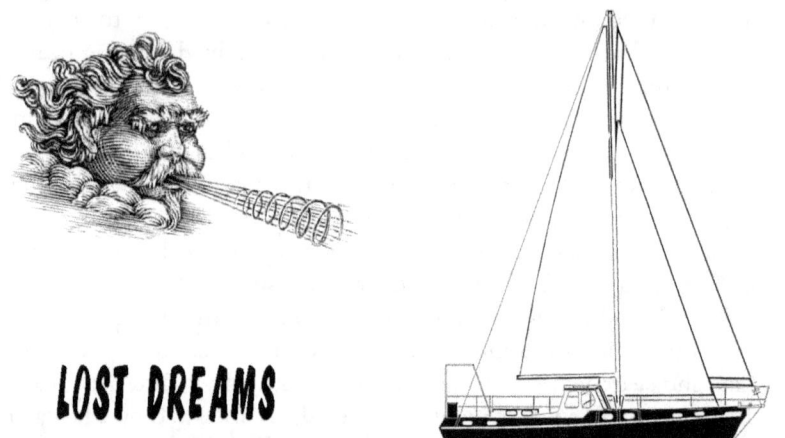

LOST DREAMS

Next morning straight from bed, I got up to take a whiz and nearly pissed on a croc nudging my ship! Okay, no early morning swim for me. Then, while rushing to grab my camera, I noticed black ash on the deck and looking towards the land saw billowing clouds of smoke rising up well behind Careening Bay. This surprised me. We'd had no lightening or storms; in fact, we'd not had one drop of rain since a stormy night sailing past Cairns a month earlier. So quite possibly this  fire had been deliberately lit. The smoke, drifting rapidly west, indicated a favourable wind outside our calm anchorage, and in quick time we were packed and sailing off with no idea where we'd end up. Nor did we care. There were plenty of parking spots further west. Or so we thought.

Once under sail in Port Nelson, a pleasant breeze sent us towards lofty red cliffs glowing like steel ingots straight out a furnace, which we identified as Cape Brewster and Bat Island, where King "having smelt an overpowering sulphureous smell" disturbed a colony of bats. We rounded these with the current assisting, and then stood horrified, watching thick smoke fan down the cliff face and engulf us. Suddenly from within dense smoke that caught our breath and made our eyes tear, the land disappeared. Before losing sight, we had been near the entrance to the Saint George Basin that leads to the Prince Regent River. Both are large bodies of water that rise and fall with the tides, and this creates enormous currents that change direction as the land changes shape. Compounding our dangerous situation, around us were several submerged rocks onto which our sightless ship could run. And adding to our woes, the wind chose that moment to abandon us. Left to drift in such a precarious position, using the engine became mandatory. But before starting it, I slid aft to fire up the CMaps chart on our laptop, and as expected, it showed we were in the middle of an intricate maze of reefs.

With the smoke seeming to originate from the Saint George Basin, I scratched any idea of visiting the Prince Regent River off our list, and as fast as I could, laid out a safe route weaving a route through the dangers to High Bluff, the next headland. Hardly able to see the front of our ship, I drove along that track while a nervous Jude kept a keen eye on the depth sounder, both of us on high alert. This might be the norm for space shuttle pilots, but it is nervous work for yachtsmen.

An intriguing tale of local history concerns Camden Harbour, the first white settlement in the Kimberley that lay a day's journey ahead. This is what we read in one of our guidebooks: *"The ruins at Camden Harbour are all that is left from a failed attempt at settlement in the 1860s. The Camden Harbour Pastoral Association conned many Victorian investors out of their life accumulated wealth, promising free passage, rations for a year, twenty head of cattle and a 12-year lease over 20,000 acres to every shareholder. The area was promoted as fertile country 270 miles from Perth. In reality, there was barely any soil for farming, unsuitable grazing, hostile Aborigines, cyclones, intense heat, crocodiles and it was located 2400 miles from Perth, not 270. The first of three ships, the Stag, arrived in December 1864 and was soon followed by the Calliance and the Helvetia. In total, 73 groups of investors and 4,500 purebred merino ewes were landed. The Calliance ran aground and was wrecked soon after unloading."*

And their story grew worse. They had arrived in the high heat of midsummer, and a high tide soon ruined the stores left on the shore. Finding little water or grass for the stock, without fences, the sheep wandered off or were taken by natives and dingoes. To remedy this, a small island across from the proposed settlement was used as a holding pen; today it's called Sheep Island. That island also became the settlement's cemetery and is the final resting place for the first white woman to die in the Kimberley. Twenty investors did an immediate about-turn and left on the ship they arrived on. They took word of the mismanaged affair to Perth, after which a Government official and three policemen were sent to take charge. In February 1865, Robert Sholl, the Government official, arrived on the *Tien Tsin*, and a further 53 settlers departed on this ship. So, instead of helping to establish a settlement, Mr Sholl closed one down, noting, *"All were masters – There were no servants."*

We had to really search our charts for this lost settlement, eventually finding it well off the beaten track, lying on the other side of Rogers Strait, a hazardous bit of water with fast currents. The *Calliance* must have found it so. The point where she sank faces the ruins and carries her name.

Rogers Strait, between Augustus Island and the mainland, is filled with islands and rocks, and since it also drains a large body of water, we expected strong tidal flows. I did a bit of homework on CMaps, laying down a safe route through Rogers Strait then I looked up the tides and calculated when it would be slack water and came up with a departure time. The night before, irritating smoke and an eerie glow of bushfires from just over the hills in the St George Basin kept us awake, so we quite happily got underway even though we had to motor.

Taking up our usual positions for dangerous transits, I called out steering instructions off my screen while Jude yelped and yahoo as we sped through the whirlpools.

Down below, I also couldn't keep the excitement out my voice as I shouted, "We're going nine knots!"

But Jude's answer of, "Rock close by" subdued my glee and I rushed up.

Looking astern was like watching a fast-flowing river, smooth down the middle, ruffling along the edges, and it simply amazed me until I looked sideways and saw a jagged black rock poking up about a boat length away. Jumping back down, my guts took a horrid turn. That rock was not on my screen. And then it became really frightening being locked to that laptop while topsides, unknown obstructions could be rushing at us like destructive torpedoes.

Thankfully, just then the current reversed. There was no slack water, it just stopped assisting and started setting against us. Surprised by its suddenness, fortunately, we only had to buck it for half a mile before losing the main flow by rounding Green Island. From there we headed into a tranquil bay that would have been absolutely lovely if smoke hadn't masked so much of it.

What a boon to have read Camden Harbour's history. As the land came into view, we could almost see the story unfold. The harbour could certainly accommodate quite a number of large ships, and the hills looked fairly verdant for a northern dry season. Most noticeable was the absence of the massive amounts of rock we had grown used to. So, why did the venture fail? Was it: *"Too many masters and no servants,"* as Robert Sholl had declared. For sure, the harsh land would demand hard work, but it can be productive as demonstrated by the immense cattle ranches occupying the land today.

Straight away, we found its first hurdle. Even when nearly high water there was no place to land amongst the shore rock, and the onshore breeze created inhospitable surf that swamped Little Red. Had we landed at low water, mud and mangroves would have blocked our way. As it was, we motored right over the mangrove treetops, dodging leafy branches to land on rocks, and that meant we'd have to leave before the falling tide blocked our exit. Climbing to higher ground, we found another major drawback, the soil. Promoted as a fertile country, it appeared granular, a residual soil with little or no compost or humus. And hidden within the tall grass that was so coarse I doubt any creature could digest it, were lots of much bigger rocks.

The ruins stand on a hill overlooking Camden Harbour, with pretty little Sheep Island and the barren Granite Isles in the offing. And as we took in its pleasant ambience, highlighted by numerous yellow flowering Kapoks and gouty boabs, we tried to imagine how those settlers might have felt on the day of their arrival. Jude and I like to playact our notions, and for a few minutes, we were young settlers looking over our promised land. Before us, we saw the elders place stones roughly drawing out the town and we could picture the few shops, civil buildings and the meeting hall where we'd sing and dance on Saturdays. Over the hill behind us, we imagined a dirt road leading to our holdings and imagined driving our dusty dray on it when coming to town. And across the waters dotted with islands, we saw nothing but adventure, a sea teeming with fish, and the fun we'd have learning new skills with our children.

In reality, when we looked around, we saw four collapsed dry rock walls overcome by tall weeds; totally deserted except for a pair of pigeons feeding on seed thrashed from the weeds by wind against a stone. A shard of Willow Pattern displaying two lovebirds had been placed on a waist-high wall, alongside a rusty forged nail and someone's buckle without a belt. It was all so very sad that upon the breeze I could almost hear an excited Victorian lady instructing her maid to pack the best china, so they could entertain in style in their new manor overlooking 20,000 acres.

Behind the largest remains, a stout boab tree stood with an inscribed brass plaque embedded in its thick grey bark. *In Memory of Robert Sholl, 1819-1886, who in 1865 as Registrar Magistrate came to the aid of the Camden Harbour Association.* It seems he departed a year after arriving and this place has been deserted ever since. That made Camden Harbour seem even more tragic as we silently kicked through the grass looking for forgotten relics. Then just as quickly we gave that up, fearing what we'd find would only add to our sorrow. Instead, we boarded Little Red and left the failed settlement to its peace.

A mile across the inlet, a pimple of land erupts, conspicuous by a large spit of buff sand against drab scrub. This is Sheep Island. How those settlers got four and a half thousand merino ewes on it is beyond my comprehension because to do that they must have stacked them one atop another like they do in a road train. As we approached, we soon discovered the beach is not sand but shell grit and rubble. Crunching into shore, we found it deceptively steep. And remembering the warnings of a resident croc liking to lie in a depression at the top, my protector took up an oar and approached cautiously. Meanwhile, I held the dinghy ready for an escape. With relief, instead of seeing Jude dash for safety with a croc snapping at her heels, I got the all clear.

On the top of the spit grows a single large boab tree with some barely legible inscriptions in its bark, and thinking something dramatic was about to unfold, I set my video whirling as I approached. Hidden behind the tree lay the gravestone of Mary Jane Pascoe, the first European woman known to be buried in the Kimberley. It is the most heart-wrenching sight. On this tiny speck, deep within a rarely visited inlet, amongst dozens of other bays on a coast that has no towns, nor even roads, lies this poor young woman who died giving birth to this settlement's first baby, who also died. No roses for Mary Jane on Sundays. She could be buried on the moon her every relative are so far away. Several other unmarked graves on the island are now unrecognisable, overgrown by scrub. It is reported that during the 1890s they were surrounded by wrought iron railings. But today all that remains alongside Mary Jane is a wide-mouth jar with a rusty lid. Inside, an information sheet lists the deceased. The first, Samuel Hart, died of overexertion on the day he arrived, departing this Earth on Christmas Day leaving a wife and six-year-old son. The next died three days later from sunstroke; both men in their early forties. The last of seven, on 17th August 1865, a young constable succumbed to a spear wound in the back. He left a pregnant wife and three children. A fellow not buried on the island was the blacksmith, Michael Quinlan, who drowned in Rogers Strait 5th September 1865, the body never found.

We went home to *Banyandah* after that and sat quietly on the stern locker gazing around the deserted landscape now shrouded in smoke haze and looking obscenely beautiful in the orange setting sun. Lost dreams every one of them. I could still imagine a road leading over the hill to estates, could even see a busy jetty with folk promenading and watching supply ships at anchor while on the breeze came the lowing of cattle fat for market. Not to be. Full marks for having dreams and risking all to achieve them for our time on Earth is limited. But because these ill-equipped people failed is no reason to give up trying. It is a reason to work harder. For dreams are the essence of life, and to not pursue them means our precious time here is squandered.

SPIRITUAL PLACE

The fast swirling waters of Rodgers Strait, with its uncharted rocks popping up next to our ship, had upset me. And while I tried not to spook Jude by showing my concern, it gnawed away inside and probably contributed to my navigational blunder the next morning. It happened when I was driving us away from Camden Harbour while Jude tidied up. The tide was down, so our surroundings looked different from when we arrived, and as a result, I mistook some rocks now high out the water for a small island we'd come around. My error came to light when the depth sounder started ringing its alarm, which is so high-pitched I can't hear it. Why do they do that? Must be heaps more industrially deaf people than just me. Anyways, Jude came running. And wondering what all the fuss was, that's when I noticed we had only a foot of water under us. Sharp left, wheel all the way over, hold on and pray; we'll either crunch or the sounder will stop beeping. Which it did as we regained safe depth. After that, I turned on the GPS and followed yesterday's track out. But that sort of put a curse on me for the next few days.

Fumbling through the smoke haze while trying to find rocks, reefs, and sightsee surely added more grey hairs to my beard that morning. But we got out of Rodgers Strait safely and seventeen nautical miles further along, in time for lunch, pulled into Sampson Inlet, a narrow waterway cleaving its way into the red interior. This inlet was scenic and had surprisingly clear water, but we could not see any point in staying the night once a chance to cover some miles by sail arrived with an afternoon sea breeze.

Unfortunately, sea breezes on this coast seem to act like a small yappy dog, in your face no matter which way you turn. So, after I had become quite frustrated, we ended up using the engine fairly hard against a lumpy head sea. Then my mood became even darker when we had to fight a current running between two islands. Clearing them and entering a bay filled with white caps, I had just battened down the hatches when right in front of us this black leviathan monster soared nearly out the water like a nuclear submarine being tested. And just like that sub, it landed in a gigantic white splash. Before either of us could grab a camera, a baby whale the size of a bus leapt out too. Now we had swirling currents, tumbling overfalls and giant mammals breaching all around and I couldn't be sure which was the greatest danger. But in that instant, my dark mood vanished. In a weird way, it was kind of fun. Never having seen a whale breach so close or flop a flipper up and down, we had never known they made such loud noises or such huge splashes.

A little further on we reached Deception Bay and anchored in time to drag a baited hook across the sandy bottom, pulling in a couple of silver trevally that fit nicely under the griller.

Next day a few chores kept me busy until midmorning, after which the drab scenery set boredom in. So I talked Jude into exploring a small creek shown on our mud-maps snaking out the corner of the bay like a Sidewinder crossing hot country. At first, she wasn't keen. And no wonder. Maybe I was trying to bolster my confidence after making a few poor decisions of late because the mud map showed high water was needed to get *Banyandah* in, just like at Casuarina Creek – except this entrance dries two feet at low water. And once inside, it showed the creek dramatically narrowing to a tiny gorge that I imagined to be very pretty.

As luck would have it, the tide was on the rise, so Jude agreed, and in a flash, we were motoring across Deception Bay. Half-hour later, we had skipped over the tricky entrance without any problem, and then quite enjoyed the twists around sandbanks, and past mangroves as we could see the bottom. Like any river, we mostly stuck to the outside of bends until the mangroves petered out and vertical rock walls began. Here the deeper water led us to within spitting distance of a very solid rock wall. It got rather scary after that, especially when the two walls started closing in like a funnel narrowing to hardly more than our boat's length. All this time we'd been continuously sounding, looking for deep holes, just in case we wanted or had to stay the night. But so far we hadn't found sufficient water to float at low tide. Three miles in, with a bit more than an hour of the tide still to rise, we rounded yet another tight corner and ahead it became even narrower. From the helm, Jude's pained look tripped the balance away from fun adventure, and that decided me.

"Okay. Let's get out of here," I called.

Showing relief, she asked, "Would you turn us around?"

So I took the helm. Full lock forward, followed by opposite lock astern; back and forth several times with lots of engine revs was needed to get our lady around without hitting the wall or smacking our rudder. Instead, I left a huge cloud of black smoke behind. And although I did get us facing the exit, my heart kept racing like a warhorse charging into battle. Jude got a bit flustered too, so to calm her, I suggested she grab the video camera and pour out her heart while recording the scenery. Bad timing for me.

Everything was going great. We had a wee bit deeper water, and I knew the way out because we'd just come in. But you know how it is when everything's going great. Somehow a rock Jude missed coming in, I hit with a sickening crunch, and we jolted to a stop, teetering this way then that while balancing on our keel. And no matter how hard I hit the engine astern, we didn't budge, except to rock more side to side. Jude had the floors up to monitor the bilge. But finding no water, no panic, just urgency. If we didn't get off, we'd fall over when the tide dropped; probably hit the rock wall and break off the mast.

Projecting a calmness not felt, I loaded the kedge anchor into the dinghy then rowed upstream, dropping it in deeper water then pulled. Actually, Jude did that. The extra bit of rising tide helped and to our relief, we rocked off. Picking up our gear, it was throttle down, and we skedaddled. Never been so relieved to get back into anchoring depth. But it sure cured my boredom.

A sail away start on the next morning's cool breeze took us out through the headlands into a sea so calm we made a close inspection of the wild rocky coastline. Ahead, a squat thimble rose from the tip of a low, narrow isthmus; where sailing in close under lightly taut sail, we hoped to entice a suicidal fish to strike our silver foil lure. Gosh, so beautiful watching the blue sea strike the deep red rock tiers and then foam white.

Aided by a favourable tide that breeze took us nearly 20 nm to Langii, a "spiritual cove" mentioned in one of our guides. Just a tiny thing, too shallow to enter; but right on cue, the breeze eased, allowing us to leave *Banyandah* exposed while we rowed in to explore.

Inside the small lagoon, pretty aqua blue sparkled over dazzlingly white sand. But that dramatically changed where the falling tide uncovered awesome strange shapes created by Nature. Rising out the water were creatures and other things only limited by one's imagination.

After a couple hours snapping photos and pondering the sandstone shapes, the afternoon sea breeze arrived on ruffled darkened water. Unleashing our sails, Langii was left to the wild. Continuing with good fortune, although tight on the wind, we could lay a direct course to our next destination. But to get the best from our ship required careful steering. Jude loves this. So, while she followed the wind's tiniest changes, we stood side by side, watching our next destination approach.

From ten miles out, the red bastions at Raft Point towered high above all else and glowed like hot pokers in the afternoon sun. Named by Phillip Parker King for the mangrove rafts found on the headland, the point also has a cave decorated with Wandjina art. Hundreds of towering rock fortresses adorn this coast but these guarding Raft Point are truly majestic. Maybe the thin layer of deep cherry red Carson volcanic at their base gives them extra heat adding to their grandeur. Whatever it is, towering majesty doesn't make anchoring easy as we found when we ghosted up to a sailboat and found him lying in more than eighty feet! Tacking about, we silently slipped across the bay to another yacht and found him still trying to find the bottom. Being in no great hurry, we came about once again then sat on the wheelhouse enjoying sundowners while soaking up the sights; letting *Banyandah* slip along in the breeze. Jude was loving every moment guiding her ship while I enjoyed the light sail work. Eventually, just as the sun slipped behind the red curtain, we tucked really close in near mangroves, where handing our sails, we let go our plough anchor.

Time to socialise? Hardly. We first had to fish up dinner then directly after a lovely repast, our bed started humming lullabies that kept us horizontally polarised till the following early hours. On our mud-map for this spot, others had written, "best in morning." Words that played around in my head until they woke me an hour before dawn. Whispering to Jude that I'd just move the boat out to photograph the cliffs at first light and that it was OK to stay in bed, she didn't. Up on deck, it was black, and wet from dew, and so eerily silent that when started, our engine rent the night like a big Mack truck at an all-nighter. But that was nothing. The anchor chain squealed over the bow roller sending shivers through the dead, as well as our neighbours. But, not to worry, we were soon underway and swallowed by night.

There's more than one headland at Raft Point. There are three. One of them shelters the bay we had anchored in, and off it a mile or so, a gigantic lump rises called Steep Island. The name says a lot, but it does not convey the magnificence of a rock mass erupting straight out a blue ocean. While waiting for its beauty to be spotlighted, the solitude and approaching sunrise on the quiet sea unleashed thoughts of being mortal. Maybe it's because every sunrise eventually sets. But when the first glow defined the far horizon then gained brightness to paint the east sea golden yellow, it not only brought life to Steep Island's dark hunk, it also opened the floodgates to warm thoughts of our family. Dearly wishing we could all be together sharing this loveliness, in spirit they were as we watched Steep Island magically change. The rising orb parading so many colours across Steep Island, it seemed to grow even larger.

Next on our agenda was a look at the rock art, access to which lay in another bay, so off we motored. The small swell gently rolling under the cliffs did not stop us from finding a safe spot off the beach where we parked and got dressed in our bush gear. Being still quite early, we were surprised to catch sight of a big black zodiac screaming through the water around the far distant point. After rowing in and landing on the pebbles fronting the sand beach, that inflatable crunched ashore right alongside us - *Orion* boldly stencilled in white on its side. Quite urgently, three strapping big fellas jumped out carrying garbage bins filled with protective gear and walking sticks, a giant size drinks chest, even a marquee and collapsible tables.

"What's up?" I called.

To which one replied, "Tourists coming."

Oh no, I thought, "How many?"

Another turned, dropped his load as if bored, and his eyes showed pity, but his lips toyed with mischief, "Ninety-seven in five minutes." Then grinning, "Better hurry."

Unbeknownst to us, the cave at Raft Point is the singularly most visited rock art site on the entire North West Coast.

The art resides up a steep hill where a saddle meets a rock face. Access is via a worn track that Jude and I raced up. Then catching our breaths under a shady gumtree at the top, the view was nothing short of spectacular. The red monolithic Steep Island dominated a smooth expanse of blue stretching to the far horizon. So peaceful, for a few moments. Racing around the same point the zodiac had come, in a swath of white foam came a flotilla of black craft carrying a small army of people. With limited time, we turned for the cave. These examples of Wandjina art are lovely. They tell the story of their Kaiara God trapping cod at Langgi, that spiritual place we'd visited the day before.

No matter our preference, each site has its own presence that can permeate your soul, reflecting as they do the spiritual beliefs of a people who mastered this harsh land. And for a while, we soaked up the aura inside the cave as we once had inside the Pharaoh's tombs. And like that time, a bond with the past was created before being broken by a gaggle of babbling, panting tourists. There's just never enough time. To their credit, they apologised for intruding. And we answered that we'd had our moment, and then stood back to let them have theirs. They were like us, old. But rather unhealthy.

Although, as Jude remarked to the ladies, "How heavenly you smell of flowers and soap."

We turned to leave after answering a few questions on our vessel and journey and met a stocky young man labouring up the track with a massive pack on his back.

"Lunch," I quipped. And he laughed then replied, "Defibrillator, oxygen and respirators," knocking the severity of the situation into my head like a hammer blow.

Ninety-seven unfit oldies trudging up an isolated steep hill in increasing tropical heat, I didn't like the odds. While mulling this over, a lean beanpole strode up ahead of another group of tourists. And I don't know how he could have thought we were part of his group, but he gathered them around us then began an impromptu lecture on the art. It was much the same as in our guidebook.

After his charges went to see the rock art, we mentioned seeing Bradshaw art in other locations, and as if we had touched a nerve, he became animated, imparting a whole lot of information on their meaning and origin. We now know most of what he said was pure conjecture. Science has yet to figure out who created the Bradshaw paintings that are so different from Wandjina art. Some say, space travellers.

Steep Island near Raft Point, Kimberley
The rising sun paraded so many colours across Steep Island, it seemed to grow even larger.

Wandjina Art at Raft Point - Kiaria God trapping cod

High & Low tide from the same spot
12 metre tides at King Sound

Mother and child - 'Please mommy.....'

Langgi - spiritual spot for anicient Aborigines - filled with "creatures"

MAKING OUR ESCAPE

Raft Point marked five weeks without contact with family or friends. In that time, we had explored six of the eight large bays making up the Kimberley. And while it had been a fantastic experience, several niggly irritations were getting on top of us. Midges that fly great distances to nip, dangerously high temperatures when exposed to the sun, crocodiles that nuzzled our ship, not being able to swim in the sea, and our nemesis, the long hours of having to use our sick engine, they all began spoiling the wondrous sights. We were a week from September and weighing increasingly on our thoughts was the lateness in the season and the many miles still to go. As a result, we became extremely selective in our route. The Horizontal Falls were bypassed for being too far off our track; Montgomery Reef was skirted due to insufficient tide to create the famous cascade, and several other side trips were put on a list for our next visit. These proved wise decisions as we found little sailable wind after Raft Point.

Leaving Raft Point's bold majesty in our wake, we motored passed the sleek cruise ship *Orion* anchored in deep water and then onwards twenty miles to the Kingfisher Group, a collection of islands connected by submerged reefs. On the way, more humpback whales kept us company. They are the world's fifth-biggest creature, growing to a length of nineteen metres and weighing forty tonnes, three times heavier than *Banyandah*. Humpbacks are baleen whales, they have plates, not teeth; sieves fashioned from a material similar to our fingernails through which they filter small marine creatures from great mouthfuls of seawater. Travelling north from Antarctica during early winter, they give birth in these warmer climes before heading back south in September. They are particularly active in the western Kimberley about the time we were there and can be aggressive if suckling young, often shown by lob tailing; where they stick their tail out the water and smack it back and forth like waving goodbye. They're also known for pec slapping; rolling on their side, slapping the water with their immensely long pectoral fins. They are also the world's best at getting airborne by breaching; shooting out the water then crashing down in a smack heard miles. And that is what three of them were doing as we motored out to the Kingfisher Islands. One old bull swam straight at us giving us the willies. My shaking hands clutched the video while the beast charged to within metres. Then he dove, showering us with his wet breath.

For all its reefs, the fishing at Kingfisher was pretty ordinary, and that was the clincher for us to quit the coast and make a beeline for the open ocean where we hoped to find clear water, a feed of fish, and some wind. But between us and the open sea lay the much-feared King Sound with the second largest tidal range in the world. Only the Bay of Fundy in Nova Scotia is greater. Making it even more frightening for us, the waxing moon had begun to align with the sun to create what are called spring tides, the highest and lowest of the cycle.

King Sound is a massive body of water indenting the land sixty nautical miles in a southerly direction to the township of Derby, which has a maze of mudflats on its doorstep. Historically it's important as the first town settled in the Kimberley. Today it's a petrol stop on the Great Northern Highway and is best known for having Australia's largest tides.

King Sound was not named by Lieutenant King. He was so spent after having survived two narrow escapes in as many hours that he plum forgot to name the place of their near disaster. Sixteen years later, that task fell to Commander Wickham, who completed King's survey in the *Beagle*. Reading of King being helplessly sucked in over reefs then spewed out through microscopic channels became more understandable once we saw the clutter of islands and narrow channels. It's quite frightening to see all that water, a far higher volume than Sydney Harbour, pouring both in and out twice each day in a height change that exceeds a three-story building. Reading the placenames gives an even better idea of the danger: The Graveyard, Whirlpool Pass, Hells Gate, and Disaster Bay. Daunting, terrifying, there are swirls, eddies and legendary whirlpools. An account in *The West Magazine* dated August 1991 told the story of what happened to Roland Long, master of a tug servicing iron ore ships caught in one of these whirlpools. His height of eye above sea level was usually sixteen feet, but his vessel was sucked down into a vortex so deep he barely could see out of it. Only the weakening tide enabled him to climb out using the tug's full power. In addition to whirlpools, there are roaring tides that sluice over reefs at speeds up to twelve knots creating metre high standing waves. King Sound is not a place for the faint-hearted.

Our last stop on the Kimberley Coast was a bay at the entrance to Coppermine Creek, just a lonely obscure place where whole islands rose from the sea and then disappeared, up and down each tide cycle. I never went ashore, but Jude did, for a few minutes. The tide line was receding so fast she would have been stranded if she hadn't started dragging the dinghy back straightaway. During slack water, we tried fishing but didn't catch anything. Poor fish must have been too tired from battling the large currents.

What made Coppermine Creek extra special was our connecting to the phone system and hearing the kids say everything was OK. For nearly a whole day I surfed the internet, and although it was patchy, working best at the top of the tide with the mobile phone held aloft in a string bag, I was lucky to pick up our mail and publish a few newsletters.

How's this for bravado, or was it plain stupidity. On the day of the most significant tidal flow for the month, a Friday, which is a bad omen for sailors, we departed Coppermine Creek. To escape, we needed to negotiate a narrow passage ten miles further on that had claimed a yacht just a few years earlier. All things working out just right, we'd be taking the last of the rising tide to that gap then have the flow go slack as we passed through its dangers, then have the falling tide take us as far away as possible, so we'd not get sucked back.

We were underway when the tide still had two hours to run, but to our horror when we reached the mouth of King Sound, we discovered the flow actually never stops but rotates around the compass like a runaway fire hose on a merry-go-round. As we approached the tiny gap between the two reefs off Silica Beach, it became frighteningly clear I had mucked up. The waters before us were a millrace with mountainous overfalls cascading off the reefs. Once near them, we got sucked in so fast, there was no turning back. After that, things got so crazy there was no time to capture a CMaps display of our track. But at one point we were being sucked in so fast, Jude had us powering full speed directly towards one reef, with the result, we slid sideways between them both.

Unlike Lieutenant King, our timing turned out perfect. Just after squirting through that nozzle, we started being spewed out towards the open sea as the tide began falling. To assist putting as much distance between King Sound and us before the tide turned, we motored hard through a seascape of humpback whales and whirlpools.

The tide eventually nabbed us. Around ten that evening when forty-mile offshore, I shut down the engine after a marathon eleven hours running that had required two oil fill-ups. Our oil leak was getting worse. Notwithstanding our efforts to continue under sail, in the breezeless night, we were being taken back at nearly three knots. Not to worry, by that time, all dangers had been passed. So, for the rest of the night, we drifted in then out with the tide, ending up pretty much in the same spot at first light.

On watch that night, I was reading *King of the Australian Coast* when vague, strange sounds slowly crept into my consciousness. On a yacht, especially at sea, there are plenty of noises. A good sailor puts each in a category, some to background and others in focus. Otherwise, you'd never relax. In our first years sailing, even the slosh of bilge water kept me awake, and a tin that clunked as it rolled back and forth would drive me to tear lockers apart. Thankfully, I can now pretty much put each sound aside. Therefore, when those weird sounds that seemed to come from everywhere entered my weary head, they were so foreign my mind ignored them as hallucinations I guess.

When a kid, we had a "party line," several phones were sharing a common line. You could listen to what your neighbours were saying by lifting the handset. Although I hardly understood much of what I heard, it was still a thrill to listen to different voices saying different things, and my young mind imagined stories to go with them. It's the same when hearing whale song.

Mewing like a cat, moans, grunts, wails, and whistles kept both Jude and me company through that night and although we often went on deck to look for their source, we only saw a big silver moon surrounded by stars and an occasional white splash. Sound travels much further and faster in water than in air, and humpback whales have excellent hearing, picking up sounds from hundreds of miles away. And so I could hear individual creatures say something that another animal would answer and by their tone and inflection, imagined a story to match the melody. "Oooh, you're so pretty – Betsy," mewed sweetly. "Lovely krill-ll this arvo," followed by a grunt. "Where's the little one-e-e," ending on a shrill wail and whistle.

Some humans believe we were put here to master all other creatures. That seems abhorrently arrogant to us, and out of touch with the real Earth, where other animals communicate very nicely with each other, where they seem to get along pretty well making their own decisions with what we leave them. The oceans, deserts, mountains, in fact, almost everywhere man is not, are clean and well managed. Sorry if this offends, but we think the ancient concept of mankind tending the flock should be chucked out the window. And it's time those clinging to last century's hopes that science will solve all our ills should realise the apple cart has already toppled. A chain reaction is underway. The world's poor, after watching the wealthy burn energy and resources for so long, are now reaching for their share. The business world and politicians love it. They sell it to the masses as more jobs, more products needing more buyers, which unfortunately results in more pollution and taking more of the planet.

Of course, it's past time for a completely new approach. One based on putting Earth First. This will sound like I have drifted across one too many oceans, but maybe what we need is an entirely new system. So there is the challenge. Not a faster Ipod or wristwatch notebook, but a system that puts Earth First and still manages man's aspirations.

When setting out from Coppermine Creek, we had no destination in mind. Even on the day of our great escape when the red and white Aussie Coastwatch plane had silently snuck up on us then blared out on our VHF, "Last Port – Next Port?" All I could honestly answer was, "Dunno." I could tell by his voice that the operator was a young fellah and probably not used to anything but direct answers. So when I asked him which he thought best, Broome or Dampier, he gushed into the mike, "Broome's got lots of action."

Amused, I answered wistfully, "Well, maybe we'll go there. Or, maybe Dampier. Depends on the wind."

Still adrift that next morning, we badly needed wind and less current. So when the wind hadn't come by eleven, we started motoring to flee the flood tide's clutches even though oil poured out our engine. Desperate to make our escape, during my night watch, I had studied the chart covering King Sound south to Broome and many miles to seaward, looking for where we might find wind and less current. Being near the land was the problem. Its excessive heat was creating fat lazy air that didn't want to move and the shallower seabed exacerbated tidal flows because the same amount of water had to flow in less depth and that makes stronger currents. On the chart, I followed the shallow water extending forty miles out to where the continental shelf drops into several hundreds of metres, and that is where I thought both our needs would be found. Following the wavy line representing that undersea drop-off, I spied a small dotted circle surrounding the number twelve. I knew that meant a pinnacle of rock rising to within twelve metres of the sea's surface. In italics alongside was *Anzac Shoal*. A tower rising to within forty feet was plenty safe and probably busting with fish, so that became our destination. Easy after that, I only had to put its position into our GPS and follow the track.

All that second day, our leaking engine carried us across a flat sea except when we stopped to top up its oil. Then again we'd droned on towards the flat horizon while the blinking icon on the GPS tracked along the dotted line leading to *Anzac Shoal*. Behind us, desperate for fresh fish, two lures trolled our wake inviting anything to bite. But nothing did. Not until hours of noise else had pretty well numbed us. Then suddenly we had plenty of action.

It started with a bang when a trolling line snapped taut knocking its plastic spool against the tower. Way aft, a big splash whitened the calm sea, and as Jude rushed to heave on the line, I cautioned her, "Better wait, it looks big. Best let it tire."

We don't use rods and reels on *Banyandah*. Maybe we should, but it has always been simple hand lines of braided cord and monofilament, which works well for hauling in little monsters, but quite challenging for anything of size putting up a fight. In my youth, I may have pitted myself against the big ones, once landing a 60 kg yellowfin tuna with bare hands. But in my mature years, I would instead drag the big ones for a while, takes the fight out of them. Only worry, sharks – a real concern out where we were.

While the big fella was being towed astern, I saw mini-breakers ahead, and although the sounder is still showing a steady bottom at 120', I know our undersea tower is just ahead. Damn, better get that fish in or the sharks will get him for sure. So Jude jumped to the line hauling hand over hand while I caught the action on video after cautioning her to watch getting a wrap around any of her precious fingers. But when that big fish jumped, showing his strength by tail walking, she handed the task to me. And while Jude fumbled with the video camera, I hauled a yummy looking, narrow-banded Spanish mackerel alongside. Dazed by his useless fight, before the monster woke up, Jude and I pulled that fish over the rail, giving us enough food for that night and the next.

But there's no time for photos or chatter, there's swirling water right ahead, and suddenly our sounder's flashing small numbers. A couple of reef knots tied around the brute's tail and slitting its throat took care of Mr Fish. Then I rushed forward where we're surrounded by light green water. With no land in sight, there's sea gushing up, turbulent in swirls and eddies, and *Banyandah* is bucking and throwing her head like she's a star rodeo performer while I'm clinging to the rail watching a rocky bottom rush past.

Managing to capture some of that on camera, *Banyandah* slammed into a wall of white-water marking the far edge. Once past that, we were floating over the smooth abyss of the deep Indian Ocean, and everything went as quiet as if it had never happened.

It was then an hour before dark and having no need to go further, Jude shut down the engine and we drifted to a silent standstill while I grabbed two cold beers to congratulate ourselves on mission accomplished. That was short-lived. There'd be no moon for the first hour after sunset and since Jude would soon be off to bed, after a few gulps, I set to chopping up our trophy. And before I'd finished, Jude had the first steaks sizzling in the galley.

Lovely, delicious, juicy, firm white flesh served with one of our last Darwin potatoes along with a can of sugar peas; a royal feast that immensely raised our spirits. And for dessert, we were given a reward.

Getting away from the land seemed to usher forth a slight breeze that arrived with the loom of the rising moon. Before slipping off to bed, Jude helped unfurl the sails, and then as she descended the cabin, I engaged the windvane to have *Banyandah* whispering off in a new direction

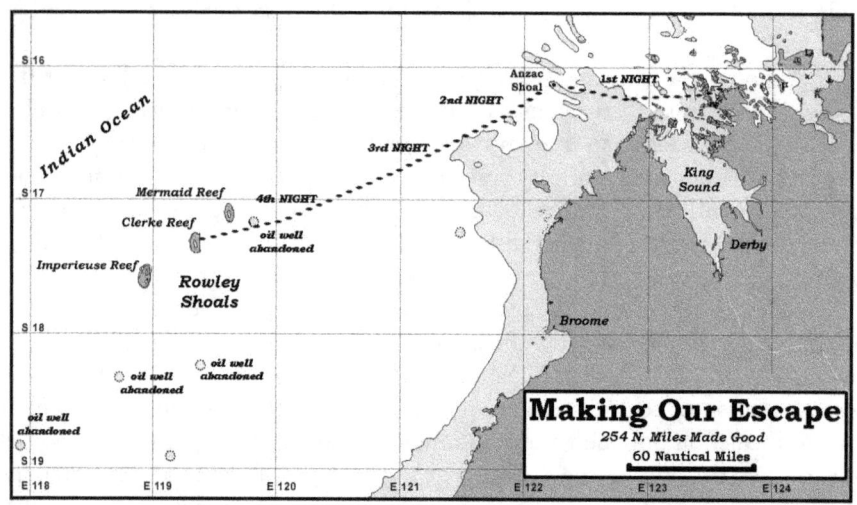

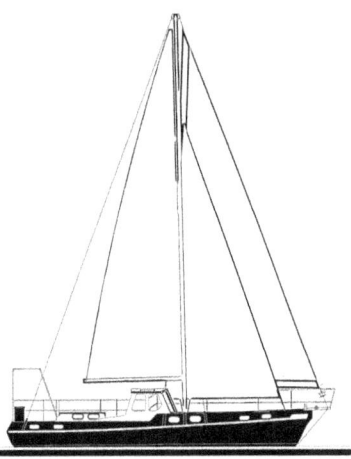

PRISTINE OASIS
THE JOURNEY

It's weary work standing watch at sea. Especially if just two crew split the long night when after a while, a tired mind tends to play tricks. About the time the moon was half up, a red light ahead on our left had me wondering who shared our bit of ocean. My tired brain is thinking the slow-moving light was a vessel travelling in a similar direction. With nothing else happening, I went below to make a hot drink, hoping it would wake me. Returning with a mug of Milo and finding the red light in much the same spot reinforced my thought of two vessels on similar courses. The ocean's a big place and boats are so tiny it's easy to think two would never get close. But to think that would be a mistake, just like the one I was making. Green to green, red to red is safe, but a light on an unchanging bearing means collision; something my tired mind seemed to forget. Until I heard the roar of its engines. In a sudden fright, I raced to turn on the deck lights to show we were under sail, but the only reaction was the roaring got louder. I hoped I'd not have to start the engine. That would wake Jude with a fright. Not again. Not like that horrible night in Japan when a ship nearly ran over us.

This one's un-winking red light kept moving forward and would pass in front of us. Bugger, my course changes had been putting us more into its path. It's a bit spooky when vision is limited and distances hard to fathom, and for minutes my heart raced. But, we didn't hit. Didn't really get close. Nothing like when I surfed down a ship's bow wave. Just a noisy craft pushing lots of water whose wake slammed into us long after it went past. But being tired, the whole incident put me on edge.

Finishing my Milo, I looked again to make sure that noisy boat's stern light had well and truly vanished. But instead of an empty horizon, I noticed his white light had changed to green. Hey, what's going on? Was he coming back? Strange thoughts started invading my poor brain. Maybe he's a pirate. We were close to Indonesia. Nah, has to be a Navy Patrol coming back to check who we are. Eventually, the green light caught up and paralleled our course, but never approached. He was still stalking us when Jude got up for her watch and wanted an answer. So I gave a general call on the VHF.

"To the vessel paralleling a yacht," I called, thinking I would hear an Aussie naval officer ask, "Last Port – Next Port."

Instead, the vessel turned out to be an oilrig tender, not the same ship that had passed us earlier, but a similar one. The vessel it was replacing, on its way home to Broome. I ended up chatting with a friendly sort about getting supplies in Broome versus Dampier. And he waxed lyrical about Broome's Cable Beach and its other tourist facilities, but he didn't know much about Dampier. So, once my exhausted body finally hit the bunk, I dreamt of bikini-clad tourists swarming through a bazaar while red and green-eyed monsters ran amuck down the lanes.

We sailed unhampered, west then southwest on a smooth sea the remainder of the night and I arose the same time as the sun, to an empty world except for two black and white terns hitching a free ride on the bow rail. Jude looked like death warmed up, so after three kisses, she headed straight to bed, leaving me to my own devices. Relishing this time alone, I had just settled into some writing when I heard a great splash and knew we had company. Spouting not too far off, sighting a family of whales reawakened my awareness that they enjoyed travelling oceans as well as the coast.

Our night's travel had taken us further from the coast, which dips back forming a crescent-shaped beach that's mostly uninhabited in its long-run south to the Dampier Archipelago. Tucked in near the top of that beach is the port of Broome and 180 nm offshore are the Rowley Shoals. First discovered by the French explorer Baudin, they were renamed by Lieutenant King on his second voyage. Rowley Shoals were no further off the rhumb line to Dampier than was Broome and appeared to be a Nature lover's paradise, untouched except by global warming.

Social contact and new supplies awaited us in Broome, accompanied by an exposed anchorage with enormous tides that uncovered extensive sand flats. Rowley Shoals, the alternative, offered Nature pure and simple. And that, even after seven weeks of mostly our own company, was our preference.

Around midday, the wind disappeared, leaving us drifting so peacefully it was perfect for a picnic on the foredeck. A shimmering sea under a pale cloudless sky stopped time while Jude laid out lunch in the shade of the mainsail. Remaining windless after lunch, we continued to drift into our third night, until just before my watch finished when the rising moon brought a baby wind with it. From the wind gods to us, that newborn breeze flowed down the moon's path, and it would not let us point anywhere near Broome. Providence had stepped in. And all sails were set to harness its faint strength, barely giving *Banyandah* steerage towards the atolls of Rowley Shoals.

On Jude's watch, she must have sweet-talked that baby wind because *Banyandah* ticked over twenty miles towards her new destination by the time the sun peeked over the rim like a careful eye. Exchanging short monosyllables about the night, after a few quick kisses and a hug, Jude slipped off to bed while I gulped down an instant coffee and sucked in some deep breaths to help prise open my eyes. Then pulling a few ropes, I reset the sails to squeeze another mile an hour out of that child. With a blue world stretching to a crisp, sharp horizon, there was nothing to stop my desires. No rules, no one to say no, nothing complicated, just plenty of time to ponder my thoughts while the cool breeze caressed my cheeks and raised my nipples.

Unfortunately, the rising sun's heat eased that child to sleep. So by the time the yellow orb passed its highest point, *Banyandah* moved only in puffs that came and went as if the Earth was breathing. But we never came to a complete standstill, logging a grand total of eleven miles in the eight hours from noon.

Afloat upon an aquatic slab, we had another comfortable night, our fourth since Coppermine Creek, with Jude again getting the best from the ship. I only managed nine miles in my six-hour watch, at one point threatening to launch Little Red to tow our ship after recording a measly point nine of a mile one hour, while Jude bested me by logging twenty-one miles in her six-hour shift.

With the moon not rising until after midnight, my watch was pitch-black except for the stars that sparkled off the sea but did not show the hand railing. That made it sort of spooky-looking out into the never-never where I could hear splashing, tail lobbing and breaching. The whales were some way off and never got closer, nor did they go away. It was as if they were holding a jamboree somewhere near the horizon.

It wasn't till much later, when I was quite tired and a bit jumpy, that without any warning a whoosh erupted close beside me. For the next couple of hours, while the noisier splashing nearer the horizon slowly went past, this beast continued breaching right next to our ship as we slipped all too silently through the water. It was more than just a bit eerie having a giant leviathan escort us. For although he mostly kept a safe distance with his whooshes a few boat lengths away, occasionally he'd come in real close, and then I'd see his splashes sparkle right next to our ship. And once, when his giant body nearly touched us, his exhaled breath wet my face - a moment to treasure had I not been quite so frightened.

After my watch, Jude charmed the soft breeze into a spunky one that started her recording more than three knots every hour. In fact, she got *Banyandah* going so fast I had to get out my warm bed to set safe points on the GPS. Otherwise, she might have crunched into one of the coral reefs.

Rowley Shoals consist of three coral atolls twenty miles apart, unique because their tidal range is greater than any other oceanic atoll in the world. Two have channels leading inside their lagoons, and two have islands. The northernmost, Mermaid Reef, given the name of Lieutenant King's first ship, is the youngest with the widest entry, but no island. The middle one, called Clerke Reef, after King's first midshipman, has an island, but an extremely narrow entrance. And the most southern and oldest, named Imperieuse Reef by Nicolas Baudin, has a huge island, but the fringing reef has completely closed, locking that island inside its lagoon.

Our pilot states the middle one has a permanent sand cay comprising coarse sand at its northern end with an entrance channel only ten metres wide and three metres deep that is best traversed at high water. At other times, the channel can have a fierce tidal race between jagged coral edges. My first thought was to go for the northern atoll with a more accessible entry than Clerke Reef's ten-metre wide channel. That is narrower than my boat's length, making it impossible to turn around if we had to. But then I had a second thought. Others must get in. And we are experienced with reefs, plus it has an island, while Mermaid Reef does not. Therefore the course I set Jude late that night passed south under Mermaid Reef then up to Clerke Reef's entrance.

Shortly after dawn on day five, I recorded a twelve-knot breeze from the southeast with *Banyandah* travelling at a little better than five knots - my remarks: Fridge On - Lure Out - Yacht in anchorage? I can still recall my first vision of something other than blue ocean being the mast of a yacht standing vertically out an empty sea five miles off. While Jude slept like a kitten back aft, I watched a yellow bump form under that mast, and then a large catamaran hull came up.

It then took the longest time for the blinking icon on our GPS to creep closer to the dotted danger line before I actually saw white breakers. Breakers on reefs usually do not show until you're a mile or two off, while the hull of a ship can be seen for four or five. In times gone by, when a ship's position was determined by taking sextant observations of heavenly bodies, an excellent navigator might have achieved an accuracy of a mile or two. And that made finding oceanic reefs like this one, and the tiny ones we used to find for our amateur radio expeditions, somewhat daunting, requiring a bit of luck as well as watching for other signs like flights of seabirds or changes in sea motion.

This became the windiest day of the passage but isn't that life. When you want something, you don't get it, and when you don't want it, well, you get a bag full. I'm not complaining. *Banyandah* was doing everything in such comfort I became just a passenger, sitting back enjoying the sights, mesmerised while the catamaran and sand cay grew larger. So comfy and serene, I let Jude sleep till the entrance was just a half-mile off and the yacht appeared quite big. Anchored just inside the lagoon, she was floating over a breath-taking patch of aqua blue, in contrast to *Banyandah* just a short distance away, still in the darkest mile deep ocean. The difference was so startling, Jude gasped as she rose from the cabin, then she shrieked when she saw white water raging dead ahead.

Our GPS had led us directly to the entrance channel, which even blind Freddy would have identified because the water there was an audible torrent. When the sea level drops below the coral surface, Clerke Reef becomes a closed lagoon except for this one channel, which then becomes something like the biggest fire hose imaginable. Such turbulence reminded me of King Sound because where the lagoon's stream hit the open ocean, it boiled and fanned out for miles. From my first look, I knew it would be impossible to attempt an entry until after the tide rose above the fringing reef when the lagoon could fill from all sides. A wait of five or six hours.

Before heaving to and having brekkie, the big cat's captain must have become worried when he saw us nosing into the torrent to test its strength because he gave us a shout on the VHF and asked our intentions.

"What's your advice," I answered back, to which he advised not even to consider coming in until slack water low.

That is when the outflow ceases before turning about to refill the lagoon. I told him we'd not be trying till slack water high because at dead low that channel would be a narrow causeway lined with jagged teeth that would suck in a vessel the moment the slack period ended. If it did that, you had better know the way in and be ready for fast action.

A few hours later, when the torrent had temporarily ceased at the bottom of the tide, Captain Trevor came out in his big tender to have a chat. Nice of him to do that. And while he floated close by, he gave us directions on how to get in then agreed it would be better to wait for high water. Seemed wise, we weren't in a hurry, we'd just taken nearly a week to get there.

So, we continued drifting until after lunch, and it was all quite lovely watching the reef slowly cover over and the fire hose, whose torrent had turned about with the tide, gradually decrease. In fact, Jude and I became so involved with other things that we didn't notice the big catamaran come out. Not until we heard the blare of his horn, and there he was powering into the slight head sea, his passengers sprawled in deck chairs on the broad upper deck. Waving enthusiastically as you do when meeting someone miles out to sea, we watched deep in thought as she headed towards Broome.

With *Karma IV* gone, Clerke Reef was totally deserted. Except for a tiny sand island without any vegetation, there was nothing but empty ocean for as far as the eye could see. Suddenly feeling quite alone, now that there was no one to help if we ran into trouble, the extra brewed coffee at brekkie started eating my stomach lining. Funny, that's just what we had expected before sighting *Karma IV*.

Jude had butterflies too. I could tell because she kept asking questions about things she already knew. Should we do this, what about that; as if we had never faced dangerous situations before. We all handle stress in our own way. Jude jabbers on, but I go quiet while I try to conjure up the dangers and work out contingency plans. Therefore her habit smokes my wick because it halts my mental process. I stopped her prattle this time by rushing out a series of orders in a no-nonsense voice that got her busy checking valves, connecting batteries, starting the engine, and turning *Banyandah* towards that narrow channel. Happy to be in action again, she drove while I laid out what we'd do if specific emergencies occurred. She either agrees or offers suggestions; then we both know what to expect. If time permits, it's a routine we go through every time something tricky comes up.

Each situation differs. Mighty breaking seas directly threaten life. Therefore each step, every grip, every life-saving device must be examined.

Navigating through coral does not directly threaten life unless our precious ship is lost. Balance is not the issue, vision is. Reefs sit below the sea's surface at most tides and can be challenging to detect in low reflective light. Also, in channels, crosscurrents can be an invisible force setting vessels sideways. And like here, where the ship cannot be turned about, once committed, you must carry through, and that demands no mechanical failures or panic. I brokered that by keeping the mainsail up, ready to use as alternative power in the worst-case scenario should our engine suddenly pack up, which it did once during a gale entry into a Greek isle when the fuel pump coupling sheared apart.

Having gone through our contingency plans, I think we both relaxed and started looking forward to the challenge. We even giggled like kids and shared a couple of good luck kisses. Aglow for a few minutes, the first inkling of trouble hit when I couldn't find the opening. Well, not straight away. Everything looked different with the water up, flatter, more uniform. When at last I spied the divide between deep blue and yellow-green coral, the channel I found was even narrower than imagined and that last cuppa burned deeper into my guts while my heartbeat throbbed behind my eye sockets.

Then things got worse. Standing at the front, I could see some nasty looking detached coral heads that I didn't think we could get over, and that stoked my belly fire into a four-alarm fire that had my eyes thumping while doubts filled my head. But, going on the premise that others could do it, I swallowed hard to wet my dry throat then signalled Jude.

"Okay, let's go ahead."

And with that, she engaged the gears, and we started in.

How's that saying go; the first moments on a new job are the hardest. Well, those nasty bits at the start only looked like they'd rip out our bottom; they were actually fairly deep, the water was just so transparent. In clearing them, we entered a long conduit akin to what the white rabbit went in and putting my simple plan into action, we kept to the centre and prayed the engine would keep going while Wonderland went past. Quite quickly, coral flats began hemming us in until we could have literally jumped onto them, while from deck level we watched fish scatter. A ray shot ahead like a jet fighter, and on the sides, there were movements of shimmering bluefish amongst the purple, green and red of living coral.

"Right a bit.... Steady."

Hearing Jude routinely repeats my instructions temporarily eased my apprehension, until I next looked along the aqua blue tongue and saw brown reef spreading either side to the horizons. Marvelling at the beauty one moment, I feared for our safety the next.

At the very start of these travels, we made a pledge to take others along by way of a video, so while I am directing ship from the bows, I'm also trying to record the exquisite natural beauty. But something in the viewfinder seemed out of kilter. Looking up, our hull is getting dangerously close to the wall, so I turned to shout a steering correction but saw that Jude had left the helm to capture a few still shots. Racing amidships still holding the video, I lent over to turn the helm just as Jude brushed past.

"Lovely isn't it," she said, beaming like a schoolkid before giving me a pert peck on my cheek, and then turned sideways to nudge the helm.

"Don't move," she commanded, flashing another cute grin.

And stepping aft, she took my photo. Behind her, I saw that same aqua blue tongue with coral shelves either side, but this time I was struck by how far we had come. Turning ahead, the white mound of sand stood alone like a diamond in a field of sparkling sapphires, and in that instant, our amazingly beautiful interaction with Mother Earth brought an inner peace that extinguished the blaze and slowed my pulse to a bradycardia beat. For this was Nature in all her glory – Nirvana - or maybe heaven.

And then we were in. Safely in calm water, we yahooed to the heavens so loud it may have been heard on the mainland. But there was no time to go dreamy-eyed round a coral studded lagoon. We still had to anchor our baby.

While Jude drove, I climbed the mast a few steps for a better lookout and saw a red mooring buoy with a couple of dinghies attached some ways off. Near them, we could anchor in clear water, but that was a fair way from the island. Much closer to it, I could see a dark blue area in which *Banyandah* might swing, so we went to investigate. Like driving an amusement ride, Jude dodged several coral heads then we entered an area bounded by shore reef and three separate coral heads, between which, with careful placement, we would have room to swing to all winds. If it was good holding, we'd be safe. Choosing a clean patch of sand, we put our hook down then gave it a good tug with the engine. After that, we waited to see how our darling would sit.

Engine off, peace descended, but only for the moment, it took our ears to retune to the noisy cawing of seabirds wheeling above the cay. Bedwell Island, named after another of Lieutenant King's midshipmen, is absolutely bare of vegetation; a yellowish-white oval with a length of dark half-tide rock along its longest edge. Reaching out from the island to us lay shallow flats of aquamarine dotted with dark patches that abruptly dropped into deep blue a few boat lengths from us. Following that blue to our ship, we could easily see the bottom, and plenty of fish; schools of 'em; big ones, little ones, and a family of tiny squid, already fluttering like fan dancers next to our anchor chain.

The transformation from days of sailing the vast ocean to being anchored in its midst was so great and sudden, it took a while just looking about for Jude and me to adjust. Just above the horizon, distant white rolls looking like clouds mysteriously disappeared then reappeared. Slightly weird, they were ocean waves breaking on the protecting outer reef. Between them and us lay an almost perfectly flat surface like a polished floor on which to dance. So peaceful, it was hard to remember that we still needed to look after our ship. Recording the stats of our voyage was a reminder that this is still a business with routines and procedures that look after our well-being.

When taking down the stats, we noted that *Banyandah* had logged 209 nm to make good 254 nm, meaning we had quite a good lift from the current. We only averaged 2.7 nm an hour, that's about 5.4 kph, which isn't so bad when the amount of time drifting is considered. And we calculated that we still had 253 nm yet to go to Dampier, which meant we were halfway. Another interesting fact: the lagoon temperature was 28.3° C, that's 83° F. Perfect!

Our escape was complete. We had left behind the crocs, bities, and murky water. We had even caught a good fish, which had been eaten. So the next task after tidying up was to catch our dinner. According to the sounder, the bottom lay nine metres under our keel, add another 1.8 for our draft, and yet, sand waves and coral lumps could be clearly seen on the bottom. Further out towards the coral heads, it was deeper and darker. Between them and us swam schools of fish.

In my younger years, I pulled up so many reef fish, I have a permanent crease from the line cutting my finger. And since Jude was the most excited, and I love to share that, I helped her replace the tiny wee hook we'd use in the murky Kimberley waters with a big number four. Reef fish are opportunistic feeders with big mouths. They don't nibble their prey. They strike it and run. Then you'd better pull hard and fast, or the Noahs might get your catch. Looking over the side, these ones would weigh in at a kilo or two, so they'd pack plenty of fight and I looked forward to watching Jude take them on.

Without fish bait, our standard starter is cheese because it usually stays on the hook. Down it went, and before reaching the bottom, she had a strike that pulled her arm down to the rail and made her grimace. Fighting back, the line twanged. After urging her to use her shoulders to turn the brute, I then shouted to pull quickly hand over hand. God, it was exciting. At that moment, years of making furniture were shredded and I was back on charter boats running fishing parties out of Cairns. She grunted, her eyes popped, and I laughed and hopped about yelling, "You're winning - Keep pulling." And then with a big splash that wet us both, a monster came flying out that transparent water, and it didn't just wiggle, it threw itself about while Judith muscled it aboard.

"You beauty, a mangrove jack," I called over my shoulder while grabbing a glove. "What a great fighter."

But my mind was remembering the similarity between the fine tasting jack and red bass, which can carry ciguatera poisoning. While Jude gloved up, I readied the still camera and reminded her of the fish poisoning we'd had in the Tuamotu Archipelago when Benjii was on board. Benjii is the son of Orlando, an Easter Islander who had escaped Rapa Nui in an open boat way back when Chile wouldn't let any of the locals leave the island. Jude would have remembered that, and at the first mention of ciguatera, her gleeful smile vanished.

"Is this the same fish?" She asked, curling up her nose.

The poisoning, sometimes called "old mans disease" causes joints to ache and muscles to go weak, had laid the three adults flat on our backs for several days. But it hadn't come from this particular fish.

So I said, "Nah, we got it from eating too many flower cods, remember?"

Then I shrugged my shoulders. "I still say it was nuclear pollution. We were only twenty-miles from Mururoa where the atom bombs were set off."

Jude's face showed she had heard all this before, so I made my point. "If this is a red bass, they can carry the disease too."

"I'm not eating it then," came back with venom.

And having dislodged the hook, she was about to chuck it back when I called, "Hey wait, let me look him up in the fish book."

And I rushed forward to the bookcase, quickly finding the thickest book, which I knew was *Grant's guide to fishes*, the bible, filled with photos. Then, in a matter of seconds, I found the page and ran back with it.

"Yep, see that dent by his nostril, he's a red bass."

And hearing me say this, Jude gently released him. It's incredible how long a fish can live out of water, this one shot straight out of sight.

Down went a newly baited hook, and again, before hitting bottom, Jude was hauling it up with not so much grunting required this time. Still, a reasonably large creature came hurtling over the railing and we both bent down to see what she'd caught. Multiple colours with bizarre Maori designs covered the gill flaps of this purplish-white fish with rather large lips.

"Ah-ha! A wrasse," I said.

"But okay to eat?" Jude asked.

And when I nodded, she started to put on the glove.

"But they can be a bit mushy and soft."

And I had to smile at her look of dismay.

"You remember those fish Rolly and Anna ate the night they bayed at the moon till they dropped asleep at daylight?"

She frowned in concentration.

"Geez, that was a long time ago. We used to run them down in the shallows and step on them."

"Yep. Same fish. Or the same family I should say."

This one was so pretty we took its picture before it too went back into the briny. Down a third time with more cheese and again before hitting bottom, she was hauling it back up and looking a little tired. This time a big brown and white thing with a monstrous mouth came over the railing and while it flopped about our aft deck, I didn't say a word because we both knew it to be a cod by its rounded tail. Quite yummy when fried whole. Jude didn't ask either. She just slipped on the glove, dislodged the hook then slit this fellow's throat. And with that, the fishing was over.

The day had been long, eventful, and exhausting, just one of many on the trot. The breeze, which had been easing all afternoon, ceased as the sun shone low across Bedwell Island. And its shining on the lagoon nearly blinded us like reflections off the glass of a high-rise building. But there were no buildings in sight. In fact, looking everywhere except the sand isle, we could have been adrift in the middle of the calmest sea.

There's a particular peace when afloat in the never-never and surrounded by air, so still, you can hear your own breathing. There's a softness. A nearly imperceptible caress by Mother Earth that slows movement to a standstill - until She becomes an Immovable Spot. A place where enlightenment flows from the creator, relieving us of our wanton desires, replacing them with love for Earth and her creatures. Maybe we had been at sea too long, perhaps the brilliant rays of the sun were befuddling our brains, but floating somewhere between heaven and Earth as we were, we knew that neither the world nor her creatures can survive under the present model of life.

Humans have developed many management systems. Each has strengths and weaknesses. Capitalism has us digging up every resource the minute we find it, has us cutting down trees never mind how many creatures are made homeless, has us using too much water and fuel in the pursuit of a happier, more comfortable life. But how many are happier? And what will our great-grandchildren know of the other creatures - or of Earth, the mother of all life?

We are not saying do this or do that. We are merely observers on our own path through Earth life. But what we have concluded from this journey that has taken us to so many lands is that the purpose of life is to experience Earth and share the burden of our fellow companions. This requires a respect for Earth that many have never learnt, blinded as they are by their quest for material things, or living in a human-only world isolated from all wild things.

When is enough, enough? When attaining material is the only satisfaction obtained in life? The Buddhist believe having less brings more, and I wonder if they're not right after seeing so many folk rush about attaining that which is transient, and by doing so, miss out on the real purpose of life.

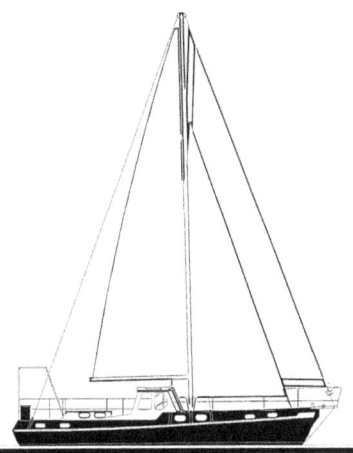

PRISTINE OASIS
THE ISLAND

Ten out of ten. That's how the night was. So still and peaceful, no anchor chain grumbling, no movement, just a softness that drained away fatigue and restored energies, so we awoke as if newborn turtles hatching out warm sand. On deck, the lagoon's water shone a darker blue than the sky and this had the effect of levitating the bone-white island, creating a dark emptiness under it that shimmered in the soft morning light. Wiping sleep from my eyes, that emptiness turned to unblemished sand washed smooth by the night's tide as if it too had been restored by a wonderful rest.

After breaking our fast, we assembled gear for a sortie ashore, trading our boots for sandshoes, shorts instead of long pants, but still taking wide-brim hats, water bottles and all our cameras, plus for the first time, our flippers and dive masks. Also, for the first time, I packed my small backpack with a remote video camera in its waterproof housing. The actual video head is a handheld sealed unit that supposedly can withstand several metres of water pressure while the recorder is a Sony Handycam housed in a Pelican Case. The case is brand new and came with a sticker on its lid stating *waterproof.*

Launching Little Red and muscling the 5 hp outboard down to it was followed by coaxing that decrepit lump of machinery into life. When it finally fired, its scream of protest destroyed the serene ambience. But that was soon forgotten after shoving off and finding a barricade of coral suddenly jumping out the blue between the island and us, where a hit could rip off the prop. We taxied up and down looking for a break wide enough for our dinghy, and finally finding one, snuck in only to discover too little water and our prop hitting rippled sand.

In a broad fan radiating from the island, the shallows spread in a sparkling aquamarine dotted with patches of purple we identified as tips of staghorn coral poking out the flat sea as if asparagus shoots. Silencing the machinery, Jude took to the oars and I stood in the stern to guide us through the maze of obstructions.

In our younger years, Jude and I used to take amateur radio operators to extremely remote coral reefs to set up radio stations making contact with tens of thousands around the world. On one expedition we landed on a sand island a few weeks after a cyclone had passed over it and like here, the part visible from a low dinghy was silky smooth and flawless, allowing us to feel like its first discoverers. Wondering what we would find, maybe treasure or skeletons, having seen both in the past had our curiosity peaking like week old kittens when our dinghy finally crunched into shore.

Jude had the honour of placing the first footprint on Bedwell Island while I sat on the aft seat, filming the event like a big-time producer. But I wasn't denied my moment of glory. While Jude set the dinghy's anchor, I marched up the slope to create my own marks in the crisp sand.

Our first view of Bedwell brought back memories of other sand islands similarly remote and untouched by man. Here life is basic. It's pure survival. Find food, find shelter, and find protection from predators. Sounds grim, but in an environment of unbridled vistas reaching to infinity, views filled with the music of distant sea accompanied by the chorus of Nature's creatures, a freedom comes that encourages thought without haste. But I won't understate. It's harsh. There is no shade. There are no structures to block out the wind should it become stormy. And there is no fresh water at all. But, there is plenty to nourish one's grey matter.

After trying to absorb all the sights in one turn, we strolled round to the side facing *Banyandah*, and while documenting our landing, we made our first find, a black float. Exactly like those used on the Kimberley pearling leases, this one heavily encrusted with barnacles had obviously travelled that distance. A few metres further up the easy slope, Jude nearly trod on an egg, spying it just as she was putting her foot down; its pink shell, darkened with freckles, matched the scattered sandy rubble perfectly. Further along, white birds wheeled in the air and we surmised this egg was theirs. These seabirds, not having the luxury of twigs or leaves, simply plop their unborn down on the sand and hope there are no predators or savage weather.

It just felt so grand stretching our sea legs along the high tide mark while searching for the unknown. And as we strolled, our inner beings expanded, losing civilised restrictions until we too were wild.

Upon gaining the island's flat top, we could see its far end perhaps a kilometre away. Although quite level, it wasn't smooth, but coral rubble and slabs of sand glued together by Nature, and in such a jumble. As if God had tossed them from heaven and they'd tumbled on their way to Earth.

Near to us were several small structures created from these slabs, so we set off for a closer look. Never before had we seen such things on any of the sand islands we had been to. Like card houses, made from sand slabs stacked or put on edge leaning against another with a slab roof on top. When I went for a closer look, I heard a squawk that had me ducking just as a shiny white missile whizzed past. Looking up, I caught a glimpse of two long red streamers. And then that missile turned and exposed itself as a red-billed tropicbird coming round for another attack.

The reason for its reckless attack lay at my feet, a minute puffball twittering in the shade of the card house. It was ever so cute. Hardly larger than a golf ball made up of baby feathers, all white with a tiny black beak wide open and panting in the morning's heat.

A few metres across the sand stood another house and walking round to its front, I jumped back after startling a full-size mama bird into flight. She left behind a mottled egg with the same freckles as the one exposed on the beach. Not waiting for my heartbeat to settle, I walked away hoping mama would come back and roost on her egg. But, she did not. Not straight away. She joined the few others wheeling round our heads, cawing and occasionally taking a swoop at us.

A full-size tropicbird, a true beauty of Nature with silky white feathers and twin bright red streamers for tails are not to be messed with. They gather their food by dive-bombing fish with their sharp-pointed beak; so they are agile, fearless, and know how to hunt. Plus, these were parents protecting their young, making them even more dangerous.

Not wanting to give them a reason for alarm, Jude and I moved away from the sand houses, counting fifteen structures at this end of the beach. There was another suburb built nearer the far end. As we passed the last we noticed a small sign at ground level. Two badly rusted metal stakes like cheap tent pegs held it just off the sand. And much of what it said was obscured by the deterioration of its plastic covering. But it was a government agency sign informing us of the manmade roosting colony, perhaps boasting which government funding had accomplished it, and probably telling us to keep clear.

Crikey, are red-billed tropicbirds so endangered we have to build them shelters? Haven't they been recreating their species for countless centuries without our interference? Or have we taken their food source and their numbers are dwindling? Or taken their space and this is someone's brainchild to help save the species. Many may think, isn't that nice, we're giving the poor little creatures a helping hand. But they were doing fine long before we spread across the planet. Why interfere?

It's something like feeding wild creatures. Sounds fine to give a helping hand, but it lessens their ability to survive without our interference and leads us to interfere more. Jude and I believe that if we want to save wild creatures then give them back their space. They'll not live around man, and man doesn't want them as competition around him.

There's the puzzle. We have taken their space and their food and replaced it with manmade housing. Probably sounded marvellous in someone's report, until a future cyclone washes their huts off the island and the whole colony can't figure out where to reproduce. Does that sound over the top? Well, maybe you have not witnessed the decimation of the wild kingdom that we have.

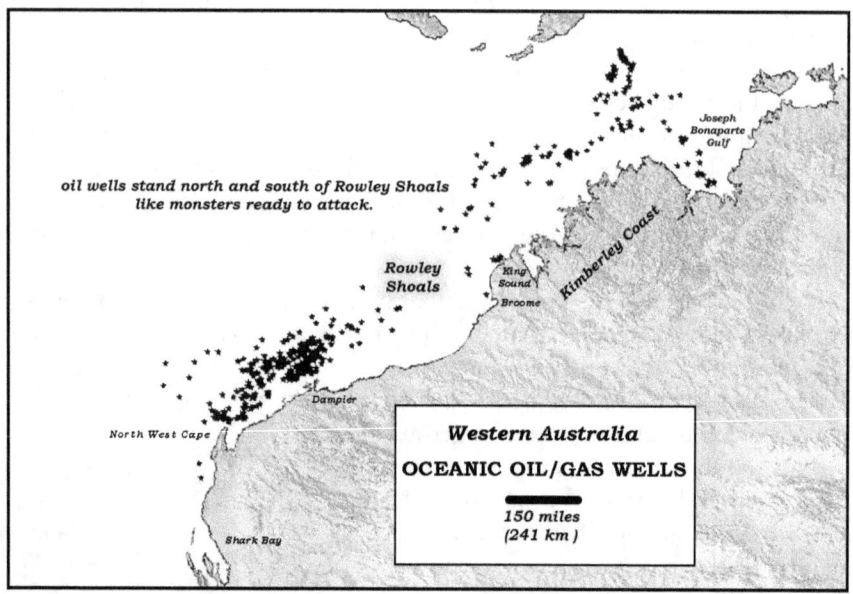

We have been to islands where every square inch was covered by roosting seabirds and come back a decade later to find buildings and far fewer birds in disarray. When Jude and I first got together, we explored a lot of East Africa and saw the ground black with wild creatures, only to go back twenty years later and see hotels catering for humans in their thousands, all wanting to view the last animals eke out their survival. Time will not halt their demise. It's their enemy. As humans spread, as we must under our present regime, our growing population needs more resources thereby displacing the wild ones, taking their territory and their chance for continued survival. To the south and to the north are oil wells standing over the Rowley Shoals like monsters ready to attack.

Resuming our exploration of Bedwell Island, we strolled to the far end where Nature plays havoc. Here the ocean forms the landscape by storm and tidal flow. We found steep sand cliffs ready to slide back into the sea. And rippled flats where the ebbing water created a most beautiful pattern of sparkles; multitudes of them dancing within a mosaic of minute rippled shadows. In this small pocket of Earth, our cameras whirled for nearly an hour.

Coming back along the eastern shore, the one closest to the barrier reef, we investigated a long run of half-tide rock. Formed by seawater draining out the island and carrying cementing calcium carbonate that binds coral sands and broken shell into a solid shelf about the half-tide line. This process builds the backbone of every coral reef in the world. It creates solid structures from particles that were first broken up by the action of the sea. Over eons of time, this natural action has created platforms stronger than the Empire State Building, able to withstand the full fury of a wild sea and support massive biodiversity of life.

It saddened me to wander over something made up of the dead. Not because the process isn't a magical one. It is, but it's in decline. Warming seas are robbing the world of coral polyps. That's a fact. By the waters getting hotter, billions of tiny polyps are being boiled in their limestone homes. Maybe their sheer numbers numb the human brain into taking so little action.

This sortie on a wild sea island after so many years in civilisation awoke in me the imminent loss of the world's coral reefs. And troubled by these thoughts, I left Jude to wander on her own and went back to the dinghy supposedly to quench my thirst. After drinking down half a litre, to brighten my spirits, I donned the backpack containing the video recorder then waded into the shallows that now had heaps more coral poking up from a beautiful floral garden.

So clear and still, like a mirror, only by looking vertically down could I see the life just around my feet. Within one step lived heaps of critters. A cleaner fish nipped my old Dunlops, an anemone shrank for safety, and a small crab ran at my intrusion. And this reminded me of the first time my father donned a facemask and put his head underwater. We were celebrating New Years at the Duke of York Islands near Rabaul in Papua New Guinea. Dear dad could not swim a stroke and had a terrible fear of the sea, yet he had conquered this fear to join his son's ship to experience a little of the wild side of life. At the Duke of York Islands, the sandy shore falls away so steeply we could anchor really close, with *Banyandah's* stern tied to coconut trees. It was under their shade in waist-deep shallows where I wet a mask and put it on my pop's balding head then said, "Hold your breath and dip your head underwater."

As soon as his head went under, it popped back up.

"There's fish all around me!" He'd exclaimed, and of course, I wore a tremendous loving smile.

I suggested he wander around ducking his head under until he got used to it, and then I'd show him how to use a snorkel. Pop waded about taking bigger and bigger gulps of air, staying under longer and longer until he came charging back asking about the snorkel. Real snorkels don't have those silly ping-pong balls supposedly to stop water filling the tube. You either don't put your head under so it doesn't fill, or note the sound of water entering the tube and learn how to blow it out. Takes practice to master. Pop was a determined man and after choking once or twice, soon got the hang of it. Then he was off. We put a shirt on him so he'd not burn as he scouted further and further afield with his head underwater watching all the life. Every so often he'd surface and yell that he'd just seen a starfish, an octopus, or a pretty blue fish that kept pecking his leg hairs. Well, with his head and facemask in the water, a man's body just floats, and after a couple hours, I noticed he was paddling in water over his head with his two grandsons bobbing next to him like seal pups. He became so engrossed with the undersea world that he lost his fear of water, and for the first time in his life, he was swimming.

As a hardworking businessman from L.A., he had never interacted with Nature before. But this one experience changed him. And many years later, just before he passed away, he was still telling anyone who would listen about his moment living on the wild side in Nature's world.

Rowley Shoals - Australia's Most Pristine Coral Reef 180 nm offshore of Broome

Time has passed, and it is now my moment to be a grandfather. And wanting so much to pass this gift to my own little ones, I entered the water with the untested remote camera in hand. Reaching the first clump of beautiful staghorn coral, I took a calming breath, uttered a prayer then thrust the camera underwater. It's not funny how seawater can invade just about anything; just ask any boatie about that. And it put the fear right through me that this small tube contained heaps of electronic bits, which the slightest whiff of salt would snuff out in a wink. But, to its credit, when I pulled it out the briny, the lens looked clear and normal. And when I went back to shore and opened the case then rewound the tape to review it, I was astounded.

There, in living colour, little damselfish swam in front of purple coral. Wow! Reassembling the gadget, I rushed back into the shallows, and suddenly I was a moviemaker looking for the beautiful and exciting. Almost everywhere, there was something to record. First, I found a live cowry shell with its mantle half out. It was tucked under some coral branches and it took a bit of acrobatics to get the camera lens down. But I did. Then I recorded an assortment of painted lip clams; at one point thinking I'd categorise just how many colour variations these animals have. Then I turned to the fishes. Schools of iridescent blue damselfish like the one that nipped dad were in abundance. As were families of yellow butterfly-fish swimming in such a straight line their thin black stripes seemed to align. They would scatter whenever I turned the lens towards them until I learnt to keep my body turned away. Then they'd get curious and come close. There were also black surgeonfish that have a nasty spike laid flat in a socket in their tail. And plenty of the always present multicoloured parrotfish, who get their name not from their gaudy colours but from their parrot-like beak that enables them to graze on living coral. Crunching bits off, a toothed crusher located behind their gills grinds it fine.

The oceans are amazingly clean, much cleaner than land. One never sees the slightest bit of waste; no roadkill, no rotting flesh, no bones, nor insect carcasses; only human waste like plastic bags, plastic string, bottles, and cans. That is because there's a well-organized hierarchy of animals eating every trace of edible matter. From the most massive shark that gobbles great chunks of flesh, right down to the tiniest cleaner-fish that nips parasites from the gills of larger aquatic creatures. There are several species that eat sand to filter out nourishment. Goatfish are one; named for their fleshy barbels or "whiskers" attached to their chins that assist them as they suck up sand. But one of the strangest seen around my feet was a blenny, a tiny eel-like creature with the agility of movement that defies capture. They live in a burrow and when the tide is up, they sit at its doorstep plucking nourishment from the stream as it passes. But when the tide is down, they can fling themselves out and skip across the dry flats to another pool.

When Jude approached carrying our diving masks, I came out and set aside the movie-making gear. We put sandshoes on in preference to flippers so we could push ourselves about.

The moment my head went under my heart leapt just like my dad's. Such a diverse abundance of life flung open a closet and out flashed memories of when Jude and I hunted for our dinner in coral gardens. We would explore the undersea world for hours, noting where a particular delicacy lived. In this way we learnt the habits of many creatures - like coral trout, they run to a hole at first sight of strangers. But once safe in a hole, they'll turn to see what they were fleeing. That's the moment to drift in with eyes averted not to alert them that a spearhead is directed at them. But here at Bedwell, we were not in these shallows to hunt. Animals soon learn what to fear.

One of Jude's cameras, the Pentax W20, is waterproof to nearly two metres, so she, like me, took a calming breath then plunged it underwater. And like me, was pleased to see it still functioning after its first dunking. Hesitantly, then soon with vigour, she took off photographing everything that didn't move. Then changing to movie mode, she captured heaps of little critters as they zoomed about. Unlike my video, her camera has a large screen, so results could be viewed immediately, which added to our enjoyment.

Eventually, time beat us. Hunger rumbled so loud in my belly, we both heard it underwater. And although the water was warm, it wasn't blood temperature so I became chilled and was thankful when Jude's camera battery finally went flat.

Pushing through the shallows towards our dinghy, *Banyandah* seemed to hover in a blue world of sky and water merged into one, and I uttered my thanks to the heavens for allowing us to witness it. I find it humbling. We are but a cog in a much bigger creation, a marvellously complex and intricate creation that I do not pretend to understand. Nor should I tamper, for I am merely an observer who will be gone after my moment on Earth.

Back on board and cooling down with an orange juice diluted to half-strength, we had just sat down to a cold lunch when our quiet existence was shattered by the faint sound of machinery. Not surprising it sounded so loud, our world was as peaceful as the far side of the moon. Jumping to the cockpit, we scanned the horizon and spotted a vessel heading towards the pass. Could it be a government vessel coming to renew the tropicbird signage? Or an Indonesian fishing vessel coming to harvest the abundant marine life? Or was it just another visitor like us?

The tide wasn't slack nor was it very high, but that was not going to stop this cruiser. He didn't even slow down before turning into the pass, and in a matter of minutes, we had the *M.V. Reel Teaser* steaming by us heading straight for the mooring and what were obviously his tinnies. In a whisker of time, he had sorted himself out, and in another, we witnessed a few hardy souls jumping over the side with gusto, splashing about with a fair bit of hop-de-la. And that ended our being far distant explorers.

While finishing lunch, there was more action with the neighbours when about ten of them boarded one of the tinnies, which then powered over to the island. Jude and I had had our exercise, so while lazing about under the shade of our awning, we watched those hardy souls traipse around Bedwell's hot glaring sand, doing pretty much what we had that morning. And once again, in a flurry, the red tropicbirds took flight then wheeled round over their heads, a few swooping down as a warning. And, the visitors took heed, snapped their photos then left them in peace to continue their wander around the island.

About an hour after they had gone ashore, the second dinghy left the cruiser and headed our way. In it was a slender fellow wearing sensible long sleeves, straw hat, and quality sunnies. As he pulled alongside, when I asked him aboard, he said he hadn't time, but wanted to know if we had the CALM brochure on the Rowley's.

Jude straight away burst out, "Who's CALM?"

Then I put my hand out. "By the way, we're Jack and Jude from the East Coast. Pleased to meet you."

The tall, lanky guy with sun bleach hair smiled then reached across the two boats and we shook hands while he introduced himself, "I'm Ross from Broome."

"You run charters, Ross?" I asked, inviting him to give us a run down on his operations, which naturally lead to discussing his boat.

With evident pride, Ross described *Reel Teaser* as a sixteen-metre fibreglass flybridge cruiser that had been custom-built for extended trips.

"She's got two 430 hp Cummings diesel engines and is loaded with gear," he continued, looking from his boat back to me. "We've been coming out to the Rowley's since the mid-'90s," he said with a slight nod of his head. "Mostly we catch and release sailfish and marlin and heaps of wahoo. But we also take charters to the Kimberley and fishing trips to Scott Reef north of King Sound. That's from Broome. From Exmouth, we go as far south as Ningaloo Reef and fish off the continental shelf which comes in close at North-West Cape."

"Sounds good, mate," I said with real admiration. "Jude and I used to work charter boats out of Cairns. One, a twenty-metre mother ship during the Black Marlin season. Pretty hard work, hey?"

"Yeah, can be. But we've been lucky to get good groups mostly. No one's really been sick because no one really boozes it up. They're pretty serious fishers."

Shifting his stance, he changed the subject.

"Now do you know that Clerke Reef and Imperieuse Reef form the Rowley Shoals Marine Park? It's managed by the Department of Conservation and Land Management. I've some brochures onboard. If you like, I'll give you one before we go."

I wasn't sure just what would be in the brochure, but hoped it would have information for my newsletters, so I was eager to get my hands on one and said. "Yeah, love to see it. When you off?"

"We'll be going in another hour. This has been a five-day charter and we've mostly fished off Imperieuse catching sailfish." When he smiled, the fatigue faded from his eyes and some excitement entered his voice. "Tagged and released seventeen this season, five this trip. We'll be back in Broome sometime tomorrow."

His gaze went to the distant horizon. "Then we have a late charter up to the Kimberley, and one more here before the season ends."

With a giant smile, Jude piped in, "Well, if you've any extra veggies or an extra case of beer that I can buy, that'd be great. We've been eight weeks since Darwin and we're nearly out of everything but basics. And we're keen to stay here as long as we can. Who wouldn't?"

Ross gave her a boyish grin. "Not sure about the beer. That's precious stuff and the passengers look after it, but when I get back I'll talk to the cook about what's left onboard."

And with that, he pushed off, started his outboard, and left us wondering if we'd be lucky enough to score some fresh veggies or a six-pack. Our last tot would be finished that night. After that, there'd be only the dregs of some port and a tot of rum left by FlexiCABS Dave.

Although we continued with afternoon chores, both Jude and I kept a watchful eye on the flybridge cruiser hoping to see some goodies loaded into their dinghy and head our way. But it was a futile wait. In the end, we heard the big boat's engines start. Then after dropping the mooring rope, they cruised right past us heading for the channel. Within minutes, they were fast becoming just a blip edging down the reef towards the mainland. Through the binoculars, I could only make out the glint of their two tinnies trailing astern on long lines. And I thought they had better not run into any nasty weather. Goodbye brochure, goodbye veggies, goodbye cold beer.

But little did we know we had not seen the last of *Reel Teaser*.

Manmade breeding sites on Bedwell Island

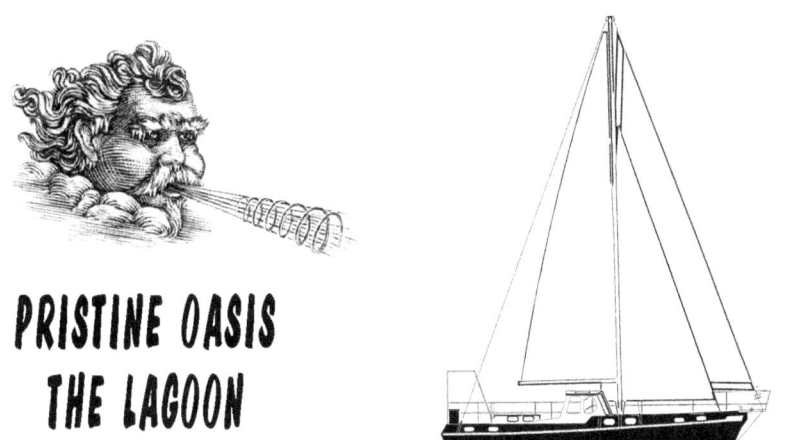

PRISTINE OASIS
THE LAGOON

Once *Reel Teaser* had slipped below the horizon, Clerke Reef once again became our private domain, and we set about procuring our dinner in an exercise that pretty much mimicked our first night, line down, fish up. After what had been a marvellously enjoyable day, upon finishing our tucker and feeling somewhat exhausted, we were quickly in bed.

Following a second blissful night's sleep, day three began just like the day before, a windless, ethereal world where time seemed to have stopped, and the far horizon marked the limits of our world. So distinctive was the mood, we didn't feel like squandering it by being busy so I sat gazing into the never-never letting various thoughts and memories percolate through my head. Jude made believe she was writing up her journal, but she too was gazing at the combination of calm blue expanse and buff island more than she had pen to paper. We didn't tire of this but eventually, hunger took control, motivating us toward an easily made breakfast of cereal. Jude had wanted toast, but we had no bread. That prompted her to make some right after we'd finished eating.

With activity stirring the boat, I mentioned I'd get the underwater video gear ready for its first total dunking and suggested we row to the nearby coral bombie for a dive before lunch. Jude's eagerness triggered thoughts of us meeting a big nasty shark like the dusky brown one that had come out of nowhere to snaffle the fish frame chucked overboard last night. This was not some inshore coral patch close to a busy resort, but a mid-ocean coral atoll. And while we had encountered plenty of sharks in our younger years, even having to fend off a few when shooting fish, I was not quite that same man and became a bit apprehensive.

The remote video equipment we have is not a cheap toy, but a professional kit used by motorcycle racers, mountain climbers, kayakers, and extreme action sportspeople of many disciplines. Its main bit is a Sony 540 line video head housed in a robust alloy tube that is totally sealed. For the actual recording of images, a miniDV Handycam is used. This needs to be housed inside a waterproof box along with an amazing amount of cabling that connects the various components, including a set of batteries for the remote video head. To turn the Handycam on or off, a separate controller is used, a small handheld gizmo with a single red button dead centre and a LED light that either glows or blinks red and/or green to indicate one of several things: On, record, low power, out of tape, and when rapidly blinking, switching off. While it looked a simple device, inside were loads of transistors. Therefore, when I waterproofed it as instructed by the supplier, I used heaps of silicon over the red button and around where the LED pokes out. But maybe not heaps enough.

Originally the equipment had been purchased for recording us working *Banyandah* under sail. That's one thing we often discussed when crossing oceans all those years ago. The four of us would fantasize about having movie cameras on scissor arms that would extend away from the ship to capture some of our crazier shenanigans while gliding through the seas.

Older, wiser, with a few more assets, we were not going to let this opportunity slip past without snapping images everywhere we went. And so we put together a remote digital recorder that would capture us flying across oceans. Unfortunately, after fixing it to our aft tower, great disappointment came with the results. Not just the poor video quality, it's more that the boat never moves. The ocean and horizon did the moving, which somehow took away the drama and excitement. We thought it beautiful in small doses, no one would get seasick watching the footage, but, ho-hum, no matter how nasty the real action was, the video soon put us to sleep.

Therefore this expensive bit of gear sat in the camera locker for most of the trip. That is, until arriving at Clerke Reef when I poked the recording head underwater but kept the recorder dry on my back. Now, on this third day at Clerke, it was about to get its first real underwater test.

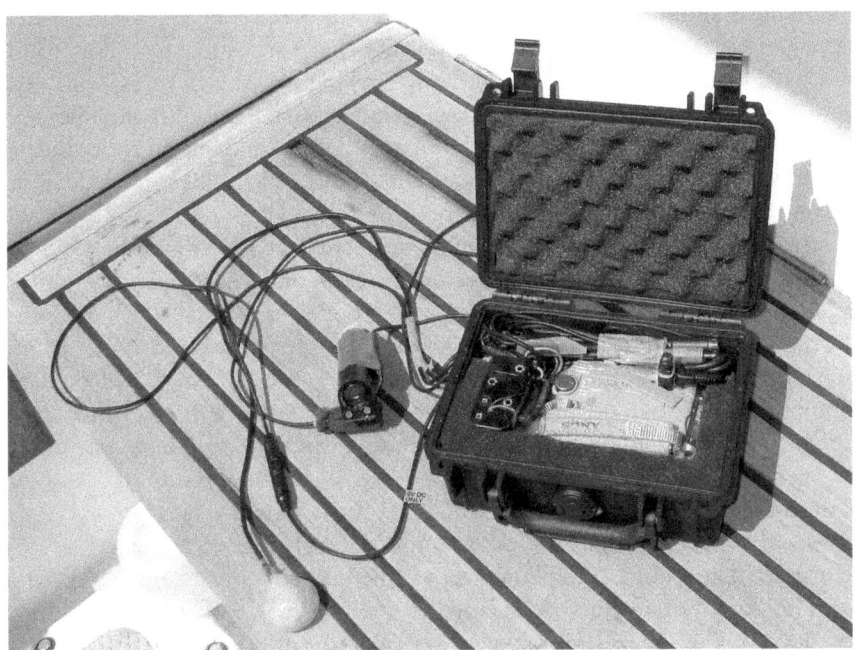

About eleven, under a cloudless sky straight from a Dulux commercial, we rowed a hundred metres to the largest of the three nearby coral outcrops, finding it with a half metre of water over it. I don't know about Jude, but as the group's designated protector, I was still a wee bit nervous thinking of last night's dusky brown shark. So I sort of dragged my feet when it came to jumping in. I fussed over my diving mask then found something not exactly right with the backpack that held the video device. Jude mustn't have been in a hurry either. So, in the end, I jumped in first.

With bubbles blocking my view, I lifted my legs up around my chest just in case Noah had been waiting for lunch. Then I spun around as I used to do, searching for anything that might be rushing towards me. But spying nothing more threatening than a few thousand tiny fish and a whole bunch of colourful coral, I signalled Jude to come on in.

At its edge, this plateau of coral dropped straight into twelve metres of water with vertical walls festooned in red fans and other beautiful corals bustling with tiny school fish on parade and a few bigger ones zooming every which way. Going deep was not on our agenda. We wanted to record the pretty colours, and that requires good light, so we swam over to the top, which was adorned with an endless profusion of every imaginable type of coral. You see, corals do not come in just one variety. I'm not even sure why they have so many shapes; they're all the same creature, in the class Anthozoa from the phylum Coelenterata, which means hollow bodied. Being the same creature, they sure can form into a multitude of fascinating structures; domes with furrows like our brain, branches like winter trees, some are fan-shaped, others have smooth thick coatings or look like pretty lace or like red organ pipes. There are hard corals that can be very sharp and soft ones slimy to the touch. All together, they form the reef, growing out the dead skeletal mass from countless eons of their ancestors. And scattered amongst the living are the dead, or partially dead, for coral is made of thousands upon thousands of individual creatures in a colony not unlike our major cities. The dead are usually white; the magical colours come from the living ones.

Around this reef, there wasn't much dead coral. It was vibrant; not like the reefs dying on the East Coast, killed by trawlers mucking up the bottom for decades and from farmer's fertiliser washing out rivers for far too long. Being 180 nm from a nearly uninhabited shore has kept this coral reef pristine. Tragically, global warming will probably kill every one of these reef builders, robbing our great-grandchildren of the wonder and beauty, the miracle of biodiversity. If not global warming, then an oil spill. It would take only one to kill everything here. So, without further ado, I pushed the red button and was pleased to see the LED turn red. Suddenly I was a filmmaker.

What a sweet world. So clear was the water, Jude and I seemed to float effortlessly like giant eagles gliding across the heavens. I, with my hand out in front holding the camera tube, seemed to attract a crowd of fish scrambling to audition for the next *Nemo* movie. I was joyous and just knuckling down to perfecting my technique when I pulled the controller from inside my wetsuit and noticed with alarm that the LED had gone out.

Pressing the red button repeatedly failed to change its state, and in despair, I raced back to the dinghy and threw the whole waterlogged backpack over the gunwale. Jude surfaced next to me and asked, "What's up?" To which, I groaned that it had just suddenly quit. Since it was impossible to open the recorder case with so much seawater about, we abandoned the device and continued our dive. Jude still had her Pentax W20 with nearly a full battery.

Later, onboard, the news was not good. A small amount of seawater had entered the recorder housing. Bugger! So much for those stickers proclaiming, "Waterproof." But that was not what put me out of action. Fortunately, that little bit of saltwater had not gotten inside the Handycam. What shut me down had been the LANC controller springing a leak. This I discovered when pushing the red button and saw water bubbling from under the sealant. After I sliced its cover in half, a cute little circuit board loaded with transistors was exposed; some had white froth growing out them.

On a voyage years ago, when hundreds of miles from land, our radio transmitter took a direct hit from a king wave, after that it sputtered and went dead. With it absolutely useless, I felt no remorse dunking the whole thing into a bucket of fresh water then letting it dry out for a few days before turning it on. Miraculously that radio came back to life and I let that guide me in what to do with this device. First I dipped it several times in a glass of fresh water then cleaned away the froth before another wash, and then put it on deck to dry. And would you believe - another miracle. By nightfall, we were back in action!

But the slight ingress of seawater into the recorder case was another matter. I inspected where the cables passed through the housing and decided to add more sealant around them on both sides. Then the case was set aside to cure for a few days before we made a second dive.

By Tuesday's dawn, we had been living at Clerke Reef for a week and a day and had neither budged nor charged the ship's batteries except by whatever the solar panels put in. In that time, we had used our laptop considerably, writing notes and completing a newsletter. Plus we had other drains on the system like recharging four different camera batteries. There are two battery banks on board *Banyandah* and when anchored, we isolate them to ensure we always have enough in reserve to start our rather large diesel engine. Imagine how disastrous it would be to be engineless inside Clerke Lagoon! Therefore, when the system dropped to minimum voltage, as indicated on the electrical panel above our dresser, we knew the engine needed a run.

Battery issues aside, having been in one location for over a week, it was time for a change of scenery. And since we had not seen the bottom of our boat since her out of water refit some seven months back, we decided to shift to a shallow sand flat to inspect under the ship, charging the batteries enroute.

Near the entrance channel was an acre or two of white sand with a couple metres of shimmering aqua blue water over it. This was where *Karma IV* was anchored when first sighted. After picking up the anchor, we first weaved our way into the deeper part of the lagoon then I directed Jude to test the depths over this sandy area, where we found a few lumps and bumps, but sufficient water for the middle part of these larger tides. After that, *Banyandah* might sit on the bottom. The Rowley Shoals have the highest tidal range of any coral atoll in the world.

We continued charging batteries, investigating the next shallow sand flat further along the reef. The brilliant aquamarine patch after that looked inviting, so we advanced farther into the lagoon. Like a Sunday drive through the countryside, me perched on the wheelhouse next to my lady weaving around whatever coral heads blocked her way. Both absolutely spellbound by the beauty. Fringing the inside of the barrier reef were countless numbers of pure white sandy areas with about *Banyandah's* depth over them, all in a mesmerising Caribbean Blue that sparkled with the slight surface movement. Even after an hour, it was still exciting, but finding no more a suitable spot than the patch by the channel; we rounded ship and headed back to do our underwater reconnaissance.

It took several minutes to position her so she'd not stand on the bottom if conditions changed; an unfortunate event, especially if underwater. This happened once in a situation similar to this. The whole family was underwater using the hookah; the boys were playing on the sand floor while Jude and I searched for seashells. Unbeknownst to us a sudden squall passed overhead dislodging our anchor and dragging our ship merrily along with us attached by our air lines. We could see the water getting shallower, but could do nothing until *Banyandah* was driven up on a sand spit.

But there was nothing sinister lurking in this day's clear sky as we donned our masks and flippers. Feeling assured *Banyandah* would behave this time, we both slipped into the warm lagoon. Straight away, I was pleased to see little growth on the hull. The many coats of black antifouling we would put on her in Hervey Bay were almost perfect. Just a bit of green algae grew on our white boot topping and some harder shell on the blades of our propeller. While I dove down to check the bottom rudder bearing and two anodes, Jude did a swim around the boat. When she came back, she tapped me on the shoulder and wiggled her finger. Intrigued, I followed. When amidships she pointed to where the keel turns up towards the front and I could see a hand-sized chip of bare concrete and knew immediately that it had happened when running up on that rock in Deception Bay. Fortunately, *Banyandah's* keel is solid reinforced concrete for the first foot up, and only my pride was severely damaged.

It took about two breaths of air to clean one side of our three-bladed prop. Not that they were heavy with growth, more that my body was not quite what it once was. My panting on the surface was also considerably longer. So the whole process took a quarter-hour and left me with little puff. Nevertheless, the results were worth it - a clean, efficient prop. I then went round to each through-hull fitting with the long slender filleting knife and scraped out any barnacles that had made their home inside them. Those quiet areas are the first place shells attach. If left alone, they will block the toilet and sink drains.

After cleaning her bottom, I climbed back on deck to pick up the remote video camera then together Jude and I swam to have a look at our anchor. As per usual in light weather, the anchor was lying atop the sand like a sleepy puppy. Pushing the red button, I was reassured to see the LED glow red indicating we were recording. So I started a sequence beginning with the anchor, following the chain back to feature the underwater shape of *Banyandah*. Everything was sweet. I even documented the chip of bare concrete.

Returning topsides intending to do another dive after a quick bite to eat, I was dismayed not to hear the telltale whirring from the camera even though the controller still glowed red. Dreading what I might find, I removed the waterproof case from the backpack, dipped it in a bucket of freshwater, shook it dry then popped open its catches. My heart nearly stopped when a runnel of seawater poured out. Prizing the Sony camera from its foam surrounds found more seawater under it. My worst fears were justified when I tried powering up the Handycam, and it insisted on staying dead.

I was reluctant to chuck the camera into a bucket of fresh as I had recorded tape that I did not want to lose. Instead, after popping off the battery, I began disassembling it using jeweller's tools to loosen the minute screws. After removing the three leaves making up the outer case, a circuit board was exposed that had a little saltwater on it and looking closely, I saw the dreaded white froth on several of its semiconductors. Taking courage in hand, I sponged this area with fresh water then laid the bits out in a sci-fi array that looked somewhat out of place on my foredeck.

Earlier that morning, while touring, another yacht had approached the channel at high tide. From our distant position, it appeared a charter vessel with two masts whose ratlines were festooned with several male bodies as it came in through the entrance. Crossing the lagoon, they took the vacant red mooring then turned up their sound system and began yahooing from the rigging and jumping into the water.

Not wanting our close encounter with Nature to be spoiled by a bunch of cowboys on holiday just added to our desire to live in another part of the lagoon; a bit further away from the island perhaps. After lunch, with the tide dropping and *Banyandah* nearly touching the bottom, we upped anchor then headed to a nest of coral heads we'd found earlier that morning. Anchoring there gave the whole place a new perspective. We were now closer to the outer edge of the atoll and with the tide nearly at its lowest, had a perfect vantage point to witness what we'd read about; the entrapment of lagoon waters making them, and us, higher than the surrounding sea.

Not long after getting settled, we heard more machinery and stood amazed as a familiar shape approached the channel. The motor vessel *Reel Teaser* was back, and she didn't wait for anything like slack water to attempt her entry. Instead, without her engines missing a beat, she turned into the full force of the fire hose shooting out the channel. We watched, holding our breath, hoping a disaster wouldn't occur. But Captain Ross knew his boat and this channel. Within minutes, he was inside the reef. Instead of going over to the red buoy that was now taken; he turned for the shallow patch we had just vacated. Once there, his offsider jumped into one of their two dinghies, and with the other in tow, a few moments later had both of them anchored in the sandy patch. Then Ross picked him up with the big boat.

While Jude and I wondered whether he'd anchor next to the other vessel, or maybe park where *Banyandah* had first stopped, he did neither. That flybridge cruiser screwed back around for the pass. Now it is one thing to come in against an outgoing tide, and quite another to rush out with it. Most will know aircraft always land into the wind to get maximum airflow over the aircraft's control surfaces, giving the pilot better command of the plane. Same with watercraft. But Ross was doing the exact opposite, with a horrendous amount of jagged coral on either side to crash into if he lost control. And plenty of whirls in the channel to help him do that. Thinking he was somewhat mad, we watched him line up *Reel Teaser*. Then with a noisy burst of engines, they headed out. Don't think I've ever seen anything quite like it. With something as substantial as that sixteen-metre vessel for a gauge, it was quite apparent that the lagoon was maybe a couple of metres higher than the surrounding sea, which meant *Reel Teaser* was powering downhill! Assisted by the outgoing torrent, she just zipped along over what appeared high and dry coral reef. It defied logic.

I had been winded by holding my breath when he'd come in, and damn near passed out after my heart forgot to beat during the unfolding drama. As we watched, *Reel Teaser* seemed to fly like a kayak down furious rapids - that is until she hit the solid wall of turbulence where that fire hose hits the sea. An arrow smacking into solid oak could not have stopped more suddenly. Seawater flew over his flybridge, the wave shattering into a million pretty rainbows as soon as the low sun passed through it. Obviously, they made it or I'd be writing about the deaths of several souls and the sinking of a magnificent ship, and lamenting that hundreds of litres of fuel and oil had killed a portion of that exceptional reef. In hindsight, it seems extraordinarily high risk, especially considering it would have taken the shearing of one fibre coupling to have put them in deep trouble. Now that is something I know about.

I have been taking mechanical things apart since a little kid. Maybe it's the mystery of what makes things work, or the admiration of well-made bits fitting perfectly together to achieve a task or the challenge of tackling something new. But over the years I have built up a reasonably good knowledge of gears and cams, shafts and bushes, pulleys and sprockets; and with the coming of electronic gadgets, this has expanded to know a bit about circuitry and those little black chips that do mysterious things to electrons. Therefore, taking apart the Sony Handycam had not been frightening, but a challenge to overcome, with the primary task figuring out how their engineers got all the bits crammed into such a small package. When younger, I always had bits left over after reassembling whatever I'd taken apart. Spare parts I called them.

Consequently, I was more apprehensive about reassembling the Sony than I had been when taking the first screw out. It was so delicate. Fine ribbon wiring pushed into plastic connectors, the tiniest of screws holding odd-shaped thin metal components in precise arrangements. But the recorder was useless as it was and I had nothing to lose, everything to gain. Therefore, I got out my magnifying glass, turned on the brightest light then sat at the chart table to try to figure it all out. And if I could, have no spare parts left over.

Getting the bits back into their proper place was the first hurdle, and that went reasonably well as they had notched places to rest in. But I came unstuck when trying to close up the whole shemozzle. Try as I might, there was a trick I wasn't seeing, and losing patience I threatened just to tape the damn thing together to see if it even lit up. But then I noticed the tiniest little tabs on one of the pieces that lead me to push them under another, and with a click, the Sony snapped together. Now would it work? That would be the biggest miracle. So I uttered a prayer and rotated the switch. What a beautiful warm glow rushed through me when the ready light lit up accompanied by its familiar ping. *Banyandah's* underwater production was back in business.

Early the next day, the big gaff-rigged ketch motored out on the high tide. I spoke briefly with them on VHF and learnt they were on a dive charter and going out for an underwater look at the outer edge. They planned to do a night dive then sail before dawn for Mermaid Reef. With them gone, we had the place to ourselves again and decided to do the dive we'd put off. I was particularly keen to try out my newly resealed Pelican case whose lid I had discovered was warped and not compressing the sealing gasket along both ends. This I tried to fix by seizing it round and round with cord that I twisted tight as if a tourniquet.

In choosing where to dive, we remembered the area around that large sand area as being exceptionally colourful and decided to check it out underwater. After loading Little Red, in just a few minutes, we were back in the sandy patch up against a coral wall in chest-deep water.

Slipping into the water was like entering an aquarium. Straight away, our bodies were weightlessly aloft in a transparent medium only noticeable by the slight chill that heightened our senses. Instantly we were aware of life. There was so much of it, depicted by movement by both, the creatures and the sand that mirrored the twinkle of the sea surface. It reminded me of my first visit to Disneyland. Holding tightly to my father's hand, I'd been gobsmacked by amazing sights no matter where we looked and had wanted to rush off to one, but before I could, was drawn to another, with the result I hovered in one spot turning round and round. I did the same here. But unlike then, as the realisation that this was real sank in, a warm blush of reverence coursed through me.

The wall trend away in a wrinkled vertical face splashed with almost every colour and was adorned with lovely red fans and hard, straw yellow corals shaped like enormously large mushrooms. Randomly scattered were brain corals in a variety of sizes, as well as soft blue-grey sponges that had fleshy succulent leaves, and other sponges shaped like rose flowers. Amongst all this wonder, shadowy caverns fired up our curiosity when we saw dark shapes lurking with mouths of sharp teeth. Everywhere else, filling the open spaces, a myriad of fish darted about, some stopping to watch us before zipping away whenever we moved. Then, as children sometimes do after seeing a stranger, when a safe distance away, their curiosity compelled them to turn about.

Jude got busy straight away. Pulling the slim silver Pentax out from her blue Lycra skinsuit, she glided in on four yellow-banded angelfish sheltering within the gaps. After she passed, they came out to follow a safe distance behind her. Swimming around a corner into a sandy cul-de-sac, she pointed her camera at a dozen rainbow parrotfish grazing upon lumps of hard coral while jettisoning white plumes just like shags do when lifting aloft.

Right in close amongst the coral garden were hundreds of tiny wild blue damsels along with straw-coloured ones too. I was there delving through the individual corals playing with a field of feather duster worms, their tails out their holes and fanned like their namesake filtering the stream. In a game played since our earliest dives, I touched a tail and laughed noiselessly when it instantly snapped shut. Jude then nudged me aside to frame up a shot of the multicoloured forest of tails, and while waiting I caught sight of a sea slug, a nudibranch, travelling over a lump of dead coral. Sea slug is an unfortunate name for nudibranch, implying something loathsome and objectionable when in fact they are one of Nature's most beautiful creatures. This one was a *Glossodorus*, a shell-less mollusc about an inch long, brilliant azure blue with shocking red markings, its mantle edged by an orange stripe and a fascinating red plume that its gills towards its rear end. It has been written by Professor Daiken, in his book *Australian Seashores*, "They cannot be beaten for decorativeness – even allowing for butterflies."

Strange creature, but aren't most sea creatures foreign to us. Nevertheless, here they are living their lives, finding food, replicating their species, doing their bit to keep the underwater world clean and in good running order. Maybe they don't sit on their tails chatting to one another, or perhaps they do and we do not see it that way. For sure, they do not record their history or their knowledge as we Homo sapiens do. But they do live, they replicate, and by doing so add immensely to Earth's kingdom.

All this I recorded with moist tears fogging my facemask while feeling very privileged. Here was proof that the seemingly vacant sea that encompasses two-thirds of the world was not lifeless, but was in fact filled with more creatures than all humanity. Are these undersea creatures any less deserving of life? Do they do harmful deeds? Do they destroy their environment or squander the world's assets? Do they lie and plot for their own gain? Maybe I'm off the deep end, for are they not only dumb animals and we the King of all beasts, and don't we set the rules because might is right and whose mightier than Man, but does that make us wise?

We claim great wisdom. Give accolades and awards to our brightest. And that leaves me confused. If we are so darn smart, why have we gotten Earth into such a mess? Could there be forces beyond our knowledge, beyond our control? Mark Twain, that humble philosopher once quipped, "What gets us into trouble is not what we don't know. It's what we know for sure - that just ain't so."

Maybe we ought to take things a bit slower – dig fewer mines, drill fewer wells, have fewer babies – until our knowledge of Earth and her creatures catch up to *what we know for sure - that just ain't so.*

With those thoughts running rampant around my poor head, a gang of hump-head snapper marched around a coral bluff and proceeded in formation across the sand flats as if on a mission. These large predatory fish were out searching for prey, their eyes twitching this way then that, searching for a school of tasty tiddlers to attack. Might is right for them too and so it's a good thing Nature keeps them in balance or the world would have only marauding bands of hump-heads gobbling up everything in their path.

Humans once had predators keeping us in balance. But clever man has found clever defences and now our population soars, forecast to reach over

9 billion by mid-century. Crikey! If I live to a hundred, the world population will have quadrupled in my lifetime!

Swinging my lens towards the hump-heads to capture their purposeful march, I was alarmed to notice two grey sharks bringing up the rear. A bit less than my height in length, they displayed effortless fluidity of movement to keep pace with the squadron. My first thoughts were they were waiting to attack a straggler, or just tagging along knowing there'd be leftovers from anything the snappers attacked.

Mesmerised and motionless, I watched the group swim past Jude without her even being aware, and then I nearly sucked in a lungful of water when the two sharks spotted me and abruptly turned my way. One lost interest as soon as I started back-pedalling, but the other came head-on, its two small eyes never leaving mine showed nerveless determination. At first, remembering I'd had previous run-ins with these animals, I felt totally in charge. They act much like bullies; when mounting an offence has them dashing away. My resolve started to weaken when his smiling slit opened to expose rows of dagger-like teeth. Remembering to take the offensive when he was just a metre away, I blew out a burst of bubbles that unfortunately blocked my vision. Expecting to see his tail flapping away when my vision cleared, real fear gripped me when I saw his toothy grin nearly upon my feet. Instinctively I lashed out, kicking furiously with my flippers, to not only move back but to hit that wild beast who might at that instant be lunging for a bite. Sand clouded the water but I felt my flipper hit something substantial and kicked harder and faster to reach the safety of the coral. Whether that grey shark was just plain dumb and did not understand that I was King of all beasts, or whether he would have taken a chunk out my foot, I will never know because in that defining moment we were both going high speed in opposite directions.

I rushed back to Jude, who was happily snapping photos, oblivious to my drama. And I tried to seem relaxed while wanting to blurt out that I had just fended off a shark attack. With our heads just above the water, I gave her a quick, somewhat subdued, rundown. Her one probing question drew a little white fib, "Nah, wasn't scared a bit."

Guess I shouldn't fib to my lady, for when I picked up the controller to turn off the remote camera, its light was already dead. A new groan escaped me when I showed Jude the failed device, and that ended our dive.

My day went from bad to worse. After opening the Pelican case, seawater streamed out, and this time the Sony looked kaput. There was much more than droplets coming out the camera, so much that I feared the tape might be ruined.

I worked the rest of that day disassembling the video camera, once again washing the tiny circuit boards before setting them in the sun to dry. But to no avail. Nothing I did would get its little ready light to glow again. So I had to come up with a way of getting the recorded cassette out. But without power to the circuit boards, there was no mechanical way of doing this. I soon found prising the cassette-loading device with a screwdriver, and other levers only succeeded in bending the tin work, and so I began to despair. My only recording of life under the waves was on that tape and short of taking a pair of tin snips to it, something I was heading towards doing, I could not retrieve my treasure.

Of course, now I wish I'd taken a photo of the mess lying on my chart table. I tried to be gentle as I actually had high hopes of getting the whole thing working again. But that was not to be. After several frustrating hours, I lost patience and wrenched open the holder to retrieve my treasured cassette, its delicate tape still caught between the pinch wheel and recording head. Thankfully, the tape did not look wet. After rewinding it by hand, I took courage and placed the DV cassette into our much bigger Panasonic video machine to replay it. Then, eager like two kids eyeing a toyshop window, I pushed play and immediately underwater images came alive, and while the quality was only average for such clear conditions, at least there were usable images of little critters swimming nonchalantly about a magnificent coral garden. But I did not get anything of the hump-head snappers nor the sharks. It just jumped around a few frames before their arrival, and then went blank. Oh well, one's got to be grateful for what one gets.

Nevertheless, that was the last underwater recording at Rowley Shoals. I had already decided not to risk the backup Sony in that supposedly waterproof case. Next time, I'll make my own.

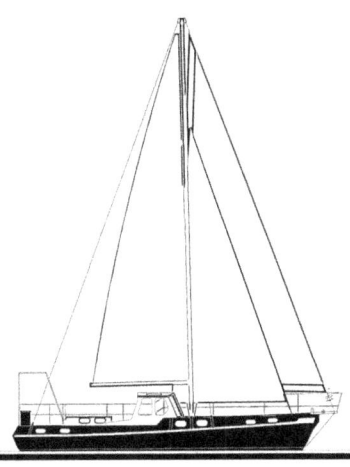

PRISTINE OASIS
THE REALITY

We were getting quite used to the lovely calm nights blissfully floating between heaven and Earth in deep untroubled sleep. We were also getting used to rising each morning to a mirror-like lagoon of molten gold that energised our souls in a slow, relaxed way. With such beauty around, why hurry? Jude and I often enjoyed a brewed coffee while the sun rises, followed by brekkie with the radio spouting the latest ABC news. It usually just waffles on in the background with who killed who, or what this or that politician claimed overnight. But this morning's headline grabbed our attention when it reported an 8.4 magnitude earthquake just north in Indonesia sending a chill through both of us.

The same size quake two Christmas's past had created a catastrophic tsunami devastating a considerable area along the Indian Ocean coast with significant loss of life. Not wanting to show alarm, but the instant we heard the news, both of us rushed into the cockpit to scan the horizon praying we'd not see a killer wave heading towards us. We felt a bit shaken that neither of us really knew what we should do. From a warm, cosy feeling to fearing for our lives happened in the few seconds, it took to look around our small world. At deck level, our blue world stretched about seven miles in every direction. A tsunami would travel that in maybe two or three minutes. Hardly time to raise the anchor, and images formed of the ultimate wave sweeping over *Banyandah*, her chain snapping, the sea rolling us faster and faster once the mast broke off.

Breakfast was tense after that. I was torn between skedaddling out that lagoon as fast as *Banyandah* could travel, or staying put and praying nothing would happen. An agonising hour passed, oscillating between despair and hope, depending on whether we heard there was considerable scale damage throughout the islands or that no tsunamis had been reported. Then a report came from a teacher based on Cocos Keeling Atoll, not that distant from us and closer to the epicentre. Relief poured through us when he reported a super fine day with only a slight ripple observed. Our spirits soared higher still when an expert then explained why a tsunami should not affect mid-ocean atolls; something to do with the abruptness they pop out the seabed. Seems for giant waves to form, a gentle shoaling has to occur. Phew, we were relieved to hear that. But wondering whether the experts are always 100% correct, we noted our small body of water was contained by sharp coral and that any sort of wave would cause havoc.

An hour after reports of after-shocks, an Australian Coastwatch plane flew over. Sometimes I am keen to answer their call, sometimes not, but this day I didn't wait for their call; I grabbed the VHF as soon as we heard the whoosh of her engines. To our great relief they had not heard of a tsunami, and to reassure us, they called back to base to confirm this. There were smiles all round when we got the all-clear.

To celebrate now that we were back in go-slow mode, we went for another dive in the aquarium, this time Jude making sure she had not only a full battery but also an empty memory card. With my remote video out of action, I again took the role of a chaperone, either keeping a lookout for those pesky sharks or searching for interesting things to photograph. Our teamwork not only got some great underwater photos, but Jude also recorded nearly a dozen video clips. Watching how easily she worked the Pentax W20 got me thinking it would be far simpler to ditch the troublesome remote and buy another camera like hers.

By the next morning, our second Friday at Clerke, we had just about dove ourselves to saturation. With another run of newsletters completed, I suppose our feet started to itch and we began wondering what lay beyond our horizon. Plus I was nagged by the worry we were dragging our feet, fearing we'd get in all sorts of bother if the southerlies started blowing against us. Little did we suspect they would arrive early.

From our coral nest, we motored over to the red mooring buoy to experience the views from that vantage point while we packed away some of our clutter left adrift in the calm conditions. But before starting that, we rowed ashore for one last look; to say goodbye and good luck to the red-tailed tropicbirds, and feast on the island's beauty at the lowest tide of that cycle.

Upon landing, we were once again her first explorers; the broad fringe of sand was perfect, stretching for what seemed miles into the lagoon. Setting off following the tide line, about every twenty paces we found giant spider shells chasing the receding tide, digging their spiky operculum into the sand then lunging forward, or was that sideways. It's so hard to tell with something shaped like a spider with legs only on one side. When picked up, they'd suck in their foot, pulling close their protective operculum that would then expose a rim of glossy crimson and golden shell.

Far ahead, amongst the acres of smooth sand lay a lump that was hard to tell what it might be. Neither Jude nor I wanted to let on that we had seen it because it looked like a rather large shell. Making our separate ways down the beach, we both migrated towards it, hoping to claim the prize if it proved something special.

When within dashing distance, both of us made a run, for we could see it was a giant nautilus shell. The nautilus is a strange creature, a cross between two types of molluscs. They have a hard shell on their outside, but like squids, have tentacles and propel themselves by expelling a jet of water. As a creature of the open sea, any found on a beach are dead, so when Jude lifted this one off the sand, the critter hung limply from its shell and smelt horribly. But what a fantastic sight! Something like an octopus stuck out an attractive cream-coloured shell that was near as round as a dinner plate and decorated with radial terra-cotta stripes. Nautilus shells are symmetrical and inside are several chambers. The creature lives in the outermost and largest chamber with all the others connected by a tube called a *siphuncle* through which the animal changes its buoyancy, and thus its depth undersea.

Arising the next morning, Saturday, wind ripples kept our dinghy tugging against a tight painter, and this reinforced our thought to depart on the noontide. After brekkie, we went off for a quick last dive, this time to the shore wall close to the mooring. Like a bitter last taste, poor visibility made it feel like swimming in a snowstorm. Needing something better than that had me turning the outboard towards the breakers on the outer barrier. As we ran on, *Banyandah* got smaller, the island shrank, until a gnawing fear we'd be stranded by our cantankerous outboard forced me to alter course for the seaward end of the island.

Skimming over the transparent lagoon, I shouted to Jude. "Hey! How about circumnavigating Bedwell Island instead?"

Jude, so beautiful in the bows, her sweet Geordie smile acting like a beacon, simply nodded.

Approaching the end of the island taking the full impact of the Indian Ocean, it became riskier; curling breakers rose out the shallows and for some moments it didn't look like we could get safely through. With our small dinghy up on the plane, we searched for a pattern to the forming waves. Waves come in sets. Ask any surfer, they'll tell you that bigger ones often come three at a time followed by a calmer period, with every seventh set larger. That's the theory, Nature has her own I suppose, but we mortals need some sort of guide and this one told me if I timed my passage just right, I could dash through the shallows at an angle between the bigger breaking sets and reach deeper water, and then be able to continue around the island. The thought of shooting the waves added even more spice to the morning, and under such a brilliant blue sky, our cares seemed to evaporate. So, after waiting for a piece, I gave her hell. And off we shot on the backside of the last wave, Jude rapturously giggling with an outstretched neck as she watched the smooth sand pass close underneath. The next wave soon formed behind us and as it started lifting our transom, Little Red blasted down its face as if we were board riders taking a left-hander at Lennox. Assisted by that following sea the pitch of the outboard started to scream and now my main task was to keep her straight along its face. In a perfect moment that matched the ideal morning, we slid off that wave into deeper water, watching it crash in a mass of foam that washed high up the beach then swirl around the overhanging cliff before slipping sideways as the next wave came in. Watching that told us a lot about how the island was formed. Countless waves over eons have been washing broken bits of coral and dead seashells up onto that beach where they are pulverised; the resultant sand is washed off the far side and added to the extending sand spit.

Racing down the side closest to the sea was out the breeze, calm, and instead dreamily decked out in multiple shades of blue, backed by the island's bright white, cut horizontally by that run of greyish-black half-tide rock.

"Shall we take a look at the channel," I called above the engine whine, and again Jude merely nodded, so wrapped was she in the scenery.

Flying past a few isolated coral lumps, we entered the main lagoon where I glanced toward *Banyandah* when she hove back into view. Satisfied all was as it should be, we turned towards the outer reef to search for the way out. From dinghy or deck level, coral reefs present intricate patterns, so it would be reassuring to refresh our memories on the route out the lagoon.

Weaving in and out dodging coral heads along the inner edge while looking back over my shoulder to get my bearings off the island, I remembered seeing the three yellow buoys stationed near the channel, and then it all started to come back. Using the buoys as a guide, I located the long finger of the reef we had passed coming in, then directed the tinny down that lane to reach the channel. Here the water was flat, and slowing down we moseyed along towards the open sea, taking note of the few dangerous bumps sticking out. For the moment, the fun was gone and, back to business, we noted the few landmarks and where we'd do what when going out.

The day was just so superb I took the dinghy right out into the deep Indian Ocean. Where, from aqua blue to blue-black in just a few dinghy lengths had me quickly turn back to the relative protection of the shallow channel, the consequences of an engine failure too high.

The tide had turned by the time we'd finished our circumnavigation, and not feeling confident enough to take *Banyandah* out on a falling tide, we rescheduled our departure for the next day, opting instead for a leisurely lunch featuring Jude's freshly baked flaxseed bread.

Over the last months, Jude had grown increasingly alarmed at the large amount of gas her new oven used, and in an effort to conserve our limited supply she had started cooking bread in a cast-iron skillet. Making sufficient dough to fill the skillet then letting it rise to about three centimetres thick, she cooked it over a low flame for around ten minutes then stuck it under the griller for another ten. That produced a chewy loaf that had a crunchy crust. Ever so delicious when split to make open-face sandwiches.

The following morning, our new departure day, some form of excitement or nervousness must have disturbed my slumber for I was out of bed writing notes several hours before the eastern horizon saw any light. Jude, bless her, sleeps well no matter what, so my clunking about fixing coffee didn't budge her. She slept curled up like a kitten until I turned on the news at a quarter to eight. Smooching soft kisses and a warm caress, I went to make her a cuppa and noticed *Reel Teaser* cruising around the seaward edge. By the time I returned, he was starting into the channel. And before the news had finished, with Jude still in bed sipping her drink, *Reel Teaser* had her anchor going down, close enough to hear the throb of her engines. Roused into action, Jude held a sarong in front of her breasts then rose to the cockpit to welcome them with a wave, which Ross returned from his flybridge.

That same light southwesterly breeze that we'd had the previous morning cooled Jude's sleep warmed body so her bare buttocks became taut, making her appear like a tanned sea goddess, and when she leaned back against me for a warming cuddle, my limp heartbeat rose dramatically.

Having new neighbours didn't disrupt our usual Sunday morning ritual of a cooked breakfast of eggs, hash browns made with our last potato, our last tomatoes fried, along with several slices of yesterday's bread, toasted. Every few minutes, one of us would pop up to stickybeak the action. They must have eaten earlier for they loaded one of their tinnies with diving gear then eight guests and their driver sped off towards the aquarium, a popular spot.

Keen to meet Ross again, we kept a sharp lookout. Almost two weeks had slipped by since our first encounter when we'd mentioned we were running short of the basics. With a voyage ahead that could stretch another week, now that the last potato was gone the only veg left was a limp half cabbage and a lump of mouldy pumpkin. And worse, there was nothing left for sundowners.

For the best part of a week we'd had nothing to toast the gods, having spun out the last tot of rum over two nights by making weak punch.

About a half-hour, after their tinny had taken the clients off to the island, we heard an outboard come alongside. Having been waiting to listen to this very sound, we both came up to greet Ross who was alone and looking even more tanned, this shown by white crows feet accenting his eyes from too many hours in an open boat. To our delight, upon our invite, he started to board but then stopped. Signalling something forgotten, he reached back under his centre console and withdrew a bottle of white wine, which he ceremoniously handed across as if we had invited him for dinner.

"Surprised to see you still here," he said taking off his straw hat to get under our awning. Then indicating the wine, he sort of mumbled, "Thought you might want a treat."

To wit Jude replied, her eyes smiling, "Thanks heaps. Love it. I'll put this straight in the fridge. Thanks, Ross."

Shifting into our cockpit, his gaze took in our Spartan helm station that contains only a compass and four essential gauges and instruments. A slight shake of his head preceded a quick glance aft, followed by, "Nice cabin, spacious, yet compact."

To help round out his appraisal, I invited his inspection up forward.

"I really like the timber," he said, indicating our polished rosewood and cedar interior abundant with character.

"*Banyandah* has had two lives," I began, settling back onto the teak cockpit seat. "We built her in Sydney in the early seventies then during the following sixteen years we sailed around the world."

I have begun this story the same way hundreds of times and am still amazed to hear these words come out my mouth. Little Jackie Binder from the wrong side of L.A., a timid boy who always felt a little out of place, was a sailor, a traveller of the world, a comprehensive observer of this planet's life. I always feel so fortunate when I tell others how it began that sometimes my eyes give my emotions away. This time I had to look across the lagoon to Ross's clients now wandering the island before my vision cleared. Watching his clients follow our footsteps, I wondered how much they were paying for their short visit. These musings took but a second.

Turning back, I went on, "When our boys needed to finish high school, we craned *Banyandah* onto our front lawn, where she sat for… for about the same number of years we sailed her. We'd always planned to go sailing again; it just took a bit longer than expected to get the kids, and our affairs settled. During her shore time, we gutted her, removed the machinery then rebuilt her totally from an empty hull."

During my recital, Ross had looked about more intently, and when he turned back, his eyes held new respect.

"Been around the world?" he inquired softly.

Jude answered that. "Oh yeah, *Banyandah's* been more than twice round if you count her voyages to Japan and around the Pacific. But this voyage began just this year in February."

That's when I quickly added, "So, we're sort of sailing on our "P" plates, re-learning our trade, having older bodies makes a difference."

Feeling we had monopolised enough of the conversation and wanting to get round to other matters I asked, "But what about you? How's the charter going?"

Ross shifted his position, cast a wistful eye to his craft then told us he'd had a good trip, but was looking forward to getting home and having a break. "They're really good people, but looking after them 24/7 takes a bit of doing."

"You've been lucky with the weather." I piped in and then grinned. "It's been terrible for wind sailors."

"Yeah, there's not been much wind, but some is coming which will probably make our trip home to Broome a bit rough."

His mentioning going home gave Jude her opening. "Um, if you've got any leftover veggies, anything would be greatly appreciated. We're off for Dampier tomorrow, and we're totally out of fresh food."

Ross gave her his best boyish grin, saying he'd have his cook put together a *care package* of anything not needed.

"We're going back out the lagoon just as soon as our guests return from the island. They want another crack at the snapper along the outer edge. But I'll be back to pick up my dinghies early tomorrow morning. If I don't get over, just see Jenny, the cook."

As if her best Christmas had just visited Rowley Shoals, Jude gushed, "Oh, that'll be fantastic Ross. Thanks. What a super change it'll be from canned food."

"Short rations in paradise are not good," he said cutely nodding his head.

Then reaching into his hip pocket, he pulled out a folded pamphlet which he handed across. "This is the CALM guide mentioned last time. Sorry, I clean forgot in a rush to be underway."

On its front, besides the name, Rowley Shoals in bold yellow was a photo of an undersea coral cliff face with smaller pictures showing various types of corals and agency stamps along the bottom. Opening it out, I saw two graphic maps on facing pages. The left showed Imperieuse Reef, and the right displayed Clerke, both coloured in the light blue indicating ocean with other areas in yellow and green. Without needing to read the legend, I knew the colours marked zones of restricted activities.

Leaning over my shoulder, Ross pointed out, "You can only fish in the blue and yellow areas. The green is sanctuaries."

"Do you mean no spearfishing or trolling in the green?" I asked.

"No," Ross said, "It means no fishing at all. No line fishing either."

Hearing this and seeing that the green zone covered the entire accessible lagoon, my stomach suddenly seemed cast in lead.

"That seems excessive. This lagoon's nearly ten miles long, and they won't allow visitors to line fish! They're forcing us to go outside to get a feed." I angrily shook my head in disbelief. "That's okay for big charter boats like yours, but we'd be risking our lives if we went out in our small dinghy."

"No. That's not quite true. You can fish inside, in the other lagoon beyond those coral flats. See, it's marked in yellow," Ross said this pointing far away behind *Banyandah*.

We had been to the other lagoon, which is inaccessible for big boats, the day we tried reaching the ocean breakers, and it's quite a long journey from the anchorage.

I mentioned this to Ross saying, "You've got to have a good outboard and big rig to make that trip safely, and you know as well as I that reef fish bite early and late. They're asleep when the sun's brightest. So to catch a fish for dinner, I'd be forced to come home through the reef when nearly dark."

I stopped long enough to stab a finger at the pamphlet then started up again really disgruntled.

"Sorry, but that just doesn't make sense and seems totally unwarranted. I mean, it's not as if thousands of amateur fishermen use this atoll. It's a hundred and eighty miles from land, and they should have considered the safety aspect of their restrictions."

Every vestige of a smile had left Ross's face when he replied, "Well, the Rowlies are unique, special; we've got to protect them."

"That's okay for you. You are getting top dollar and have the right gear for fishing outside. But what about us? A bag limit would be just as effective and a ban on spearfishing because it spooks the fish."

My eyes had been scanning down the neatly organised list of what was allowed and what was not when suddenly they widened in astonishment.

"I agree to protect the future of these special places is a priority, but if you think the Rowlies are protected by this document, then you're mistaken."

I meant no disrespect and told Ross that I spoke my mind because so many citizens are repeatedly duped by agencies that quote facts and figures, issue reassurances, but are still beholden to a fickle population whose primary concern is "me and mine," not with Earth. Case in point: In the news, while at Clerke Reef was a proposal to build a liquefied natural gas plant on Barrow Island, a Class A Nature reserve just down the coast. It is so unique, the likes of you and I are forbidden to even land on its shores. But Australia's largest petroleum company was saying this new plant is essential to meet world demand and will employ thousands, and generate substantial export dollars. And of course, the government of the day who have the final say are hedging their bets by declaring world's best practice must be employed, that some fifty environmental conditions would have to be met, and that no wildlife will be disturbed. It beggars belief that 5000 workmen, cutting and grinding steel, running cranes, driving trucks, shifting earth and changing the terrain, over the number of years the construction will take, and then onwards while running the plant, won't scatter the wildlife to hell and gone. But a blinkered population sees jobs and money and quotes "need" to relieve themselves of ill-doing. Well! Know what? In that morning's news, the Minister just gave the go-ahead for that LNG plant on Barrow Island.

In looking down the list of allowable activities at Rowley Shoals, fishing for dinner was not on it. But mining and oil exploration were. That made me see red.

"Do you know they could put the world's biggest oil drilling platform within cooee of Bedwell Island and that'd drive those birds to the far horizons, destroy their breeding colony, and yet it would still be legal according to this document."

Ross's brows arched towards the top of his head.

"Won't happen, you're thinking, but you watch. This whole west coast is one vast gas and oil field, the North West Shelf, and it runs straight through Rowley Shoals. When mankind gets desperately short of energy in a few years if they find oil or gas under Bedwell, will our brethren reduce their energy needs, or will the government of the day present us with a nice neat package with plenty of conditions supposedly protecting the birds and underwater world? You'll still be able to fish, maybe, but the beauty and pristine Nature will be gone - forever - never ever to return. That is what humans do. Our greed, our need, is destroying Earth life."

Ross listened to me spout off with a cautious face, and why shouldn't he? This policy suited him so perfectly it was as if he'd written it himself. Thinking that, I asked, "You've been coming here a long time?"

Squirming around on the hard seat, he replied, "Since the early '90s. We pioneered charter work out here and discovered just where the sailfish roam."

"So CALM would have gotten your input before enacting these restrictions?" I asked inclining my head towards the pamphlet between us on the seat.

Again his smile became fixed, and his eyes narrowed when he said, "Yeah, we were asked for our recommendations."

You will never get everybody agreeing. And I think it is true that some interest groups get special treatment while the minority voice is not always represented. What is right? Who's correct? Do we know? Are scientists always precisely right and even if they are, do politicians follow their advice?

But none of this is really the crust of the situation because we live on such a marvellous creation, the closest proof of God if you believe in one. Earth can sustain a multitude of life - but only when Earth life is in balance. If man reduced his footprint, then all the world's dilemmas would be solved. It would limit pollution, reverse climate change, provide all the hunting and fishing a smaller population could want while still maintaining a diversity of life. Imagine how enriching a journey through Earth Life would be without so many of us clamouring for space and resources.

Some may think Jude and I are save-every-critter nutters, while others may believe we are just antisocial, but we're neither. We love the uniqueness of our species, but we are a realist. We just have to be to survive sailing the seas. And we have lived long enough to recognise that our brilliance is not infallible, just the opposite in fact. Sometimes mankind achieves such great feats, pride wants to burst out our chests; other times we paint ourselves into a corner expecting a door to be there, and when it's not…well, the consequences are dire.

I once made a voyage on a big cargo ship with a captain who drank so much scotch his eyes were brown instead of white, and when he was in his cups, he used to lord it over me that he knew the sea so much better because he was a Grade I Master and I was just a lowly yachtsmen. But, looking about his air-conditioned stateroom six stories above the ocean and noticing only the one porthole to the real world had me wondering what he really knew compared to a sailor who can lean out and touch the sea's wetness. There is a difference in what you experience driving fast with the windows up to strolling a country lane.

Some think Jude and I are barmy living our dreams and thinking up new ones all the time. Well, now we're thinking if all the young ones set aside their electronic devices and go outside to experience this amazingly beautiful planet they will learn about the other creatures, and then maybe they would see that the other animals have a right to their time on Earth too.

The rest of this tale pales in comparison to what went before. I could write pages about our visit to the *Reel Teaser* and dear Jenny who loaded us up with enough of her extra veggies that we dined sublimely on our trip south. And I could describe the apprehension and excitement we felt when finding our way out through the channel, but that would be anticlimactic because it would not come anywhere near the fright of our passage in. So I'll just mention the unusual event of once again meeting the big catamaran *Karma IV*, this time as we cleared Clerke Reef. And when giving Captain Trevor a big wave before setting our sails against a fair southerly wind, we wondered whether it had been our karma to visit Rowley Shoals. The *Karma IV* had helped us in and was there waiting to see us safely out, and the visit helped solidify many vague notions we'd had floating around our heads since our first encounters with pristine Nature. Long live Mother Earth.

PAYING THE PIPER

We started paying the piper for our good times at Rowley Shoals just after blowing kisses to *Karma IV* and waving goodbye to Ross and his fishing gang. What had been a lovely day changed the moment we motor-sailed around the seaward edge of Clerke Reef and got laid over 20° by the strength of the southwest wind. The first of this stronger airflow had found us the previous evening when it had made Ross's night fishing pure hell. *Reel Teaser* had dragged her anchor several times and Ross had come back into the lagoon looking like a father up all night with a sick child.

After losing Clerke Reef's protection, we found ourselves driving our veteran craft too hard into the perpendicular lines of soldiers charging at us. One after another, *Banyandah* smashed them into sheets of spray, which then washed her wheelhouse, and whosoever foolishly did not duck out their way. With some power restored to our batteries, the engine was reduced to a fast tick-over that kept the charge flowing while helping *Banyandah's* blunt bows part the oncoming seas. Free again, with a new adventure beckoning, apart from the mechanical noise, pounding sea, and angle of heel, the afternoon became rather pleasant. Bedwell Island growing smaller acted as a catalyst to flood memories of our visit through our heads while we gazed upon the sea ahead.

Losing view of Bedwell as the sun slipped below the horizon left us all alone upon the planet's surface, and as strange as it sounds that brought further relief from worry, like sitting a child in a corner brings calmness. Having no alcohol on board, we had nothing to toast the Gods as the fire along the western horizon became quenched by steel-blue sea. Instead, I wrapped my arms around my darling, and her warmth leaning back against me bonded us into one as I held us snugly against the trim on the wheelhouse.

"Back to work," I said, nibbling her ear then felt her buttocks jiggle in laughter.

"I mean it," I said as seriously as I could with my lover's warmth now penetrating my torso while golden rays burst skyward. "You're going to bed."

Jude turned within my arms, and together we moved with *Banyandah*, rocking fore and aft as she cut through the sea.

"What'll you do for dinner?" she asked.

I gave her a squeeze. "Maybe I'll eat you."

And we laughed, her glowing face mirroring the golden radiance as our first day at sea came to an end.

After Jude slipped off to bed, it became quiet and lonely, and wondering if I would see the blinking light emanating from Imperieuse Reef, I stayed topsides watching the stars emerge above the darkening horizon. I wasn't concerned. The GPS showed us well clear and being strapped in as close to the wind as our good ship could go, there was nothing to do but wait and enjoy the journey.

I didn't have to wait long. Just after full darkness, the quarter moon was joined by a loom sweeping around the southern horizon nearly straight upwind. Watching its repetitious arc, I hoped we'd pass close enough to catch a glimpse of its full light, which the chart indicated reached out fifteen nautical miles. That took another hour and didn't last long. By the time I was rousing my shipmate for her watch, the beacon light had retreated again to be only a quick flashing loom across the moonlit sky.

Dawn brought more wind so my first task upon waking was to shorten sail. Jude eased our headsail until it fluttered and I hauled in its reefing line to roll the sail in to number one dot. To reset its shape, Jude pulled on the sheet, keeping it tight around the winch drum while I cranked. Our new roller furler is so much easier to reduce sail area than the old days when it was necessary to lower one sail and raise another. Removing one sail then hanking on another not only took time, it often led to a wetting and was dangerous in heavy weather. Now, not only do I not have to go forward at all, I do not have the difficult task of cramming a sail into its bag, nor do I have to brace myself to the ship's wild movements while doing the work.

Reducing the mainsail also had to be done, and it is shortened in much the same method as in the past. Our mainsail has *slab reefing*, called this because horizontal slabs of sailcloth are shortened out by partially lowering the sail down to reefing eyelets at the front and back edges. Three sets on our main allow us to take out one, two, or three slabs of sail area. Unfortunately, on *Banyandah*, it is still necessary to go forward to the mast to do this. So, while Jude let the mainsail run out until it fluttered, I released the tension on the line holding the sail aloft then pulled handfuls of cloth down till the first reefing cringle could be engaged on its hook then I re-tensioned the halyard using the hand winch on the mast. That stretches the leading edge. Tensioning the back edge, the *leech*, is achieved by winching in a special reefing line that passes through a cringle on the back edge.

Since leaving Clerke, the wind had blown straight from where we wanted to go, and this had forced us to sail further out into the Indian Ocean. Our guidebooks had warned that summer heat troughs produce strong southerly winds, and so we wondered, could this be the dreaded summer wind. We hoped not. We still had another twelve hundred miles to go before reaching Perth. It was only September and our guides indicated mid-October as a typical start for them.

After reducing sail, we tacked ship, passing through the eye of the wind, taking it on the other side, thus changing our direction of travel. *Banyandah* can make headway when pointing about 45° off the breeze, but she'll sail much faster if we let her fall off another 5°, therefore we usually tack through 100°. Furthermore, when the wind is strong and we are pressed over more than 20° of heel, she doesn't perform as well either, punishing her crew for the punishment she receives from having too much sail for wind and sea. Reducing sail keeps her upright, and we find she may even go faster.

Late our second afternoon, when the wind eased and the white caps diminished, we reversed the reefing process, resetting full sail. And that's how we stayed during sunset, through the night and the following early hours. Our only special event, Jude noted whales breaching close to our ship. When we started sighting an increasing number of vessels on the third day, it was becoming decidedly more crowded, leading us to suspect that we were approaching civilisation.

On the fourth night, we knew Mankind was very near when our mobile phone found a tower and Jude said hello to our sons and grandchildren, spinning tales of adventures at Rowley Shoals. Sunset occurs during our free phone hour, and while chatting with Jerome, a strange and wondrous phenomenon occurred; a phosphorus red fireball scorched the sky horizontally, leaving a pink vapour trail as a mark of its passage from horizon to horizon. Many years ago, when approaching the island of Sri Lanka, a similar fireball was sighted, that time in a hue of lime green. Four backpacking passengers were on board for that trip and all of us had wondered what it meant. Thinking it might have been an emergency flare, we had notified radio friends then spent the night searching for shipwreck survivors. But it hadn't been a flare. Later research indicated we'd witnessed an enormous meteorite entering Earth's atmosphere.

When changing watch our fourth night out, we were only five miles off an inshore island, so again we tacked ship, and before retiring, I instructed Jude to watch for the light on Legendre Island, the entry point for Dampier. Jude searched the night but saw no light even though our GPS declared it within sight. Perturbed by this anomaly, she twice thought of waking me, but twice became sidetracked by the strange melodious sounds of whales through our hull. As *Banyandah* eased offshore, with the sounder showing increasing depths, she figured we were safe and settled back to enjoy the concert.

Rubbing the sleep from my eyes in the half-light of early dawn, a litter of ships surrounded us like water beetles skating on a pond. Ships were passing to starboard, others approached astern, while to seaward, a strange glow akin to a giant city lit the sky. And dead in front was a massive oilrig on its side being towed northward. Knowing we were close to Export Central, I rushed to make breakfast but wasn't half done before an even stranger sight passed close by. Four massive white domes adorned this vessel that had *LNG* in two-story-high letters on its side, indicating she carried Liquefied Natural Gas. Starting her twenty-one-day round trip to Japan was the *Northwest Sandpiper*, one of nine ships, each with a carrying capacity of 125,000 cubic metres of LNG that was held at temperatures of minus 161° C. From what we learnt later, she was undertaking the 2500th voyage since the export of this resource began in 1989. Little did we realise we would soon be learning a great deal more about the procurement, processing, and shipping of North West Shelf gas.

Feeling sure we'd sailed far enough to lay a course for the port entrance, I tacked *Banyandah* on my own. Jude was sleeping so peacefully, I hadn't the heart to wake her. *Banyandah* doesn't have self-tailing winches, so I had to pull the rope controlling the big headsail while cranking the winch, and regrettably, the extra strain was more than my back would take. I usually don't suffer back spasms. My winch cranking shoulder is the joint of choice causing pain. But not this time. A surge of pain doubled me over and unable to straighten up, I had little choice but to slump to the cockpit floor where I tried to stretch out my crippled body. Unable to do so, with horrid thoughts of getting too old for jaunting around in a yacht, I then decided to pull myself up. But in vain.

Life at sea is non-stop. It cares not about age, relentlessly attacking both young and old. Lying helpless, knowing I risked being run down, I knew if I wanted to keep managing this vessel, it would be on the sea's terms. And that meant getting more fit.

By the time I could pull myself up onto my feet, the breakers on Legendre Island were in sight. Also visible was the single column of its light structure; strange the light had not been sighted during the night. When close to the breakers I could have tacked and begun a series of zigzags upwind for the channel but chose instead to start motoring into the light morning breeze. By half ten, we were entering the outer harbour.

Jude joined me when she heard the engine fire up, and for quite some time, the binoculars swung like a pendulum between the two of us while we pointed them at strange sights. Before us lay an archipelago of forty-two islands, beautiful in their dry scrubby montage, while to our left ran the Burrup Peninsula; gloriously unusual, desiccated, and decorated by runs of deep red rock. Also adorning it, a confusion of shiny steel towers shooting columns of flame. After nearly two and a half months of only unaltered Earth, we almost needed treatment for shock upon seeing man's footprint so boldly stamped upon Earth's hostile landscape.

Ahead, across a broad waterway reflecting the cornflower blue sky, numerous green and red towers marked a confusing array of navigational channels. But *Banyandah* did not need all that clutter to guide her in; she was not a deep draught cargo carrier needing to follow a predetermined path. So, with a lazy wind now in a more favourable quarter, we shut down our diesel, and by sail enjoyed in silence the passing parade of new sights. One of which came into view after two giant-sized tugs chugged seaward past us, their departure exposing the most gigantic leviathan we'd ever seen. At first, it appeared as two ships lying one after the other alongside a loading jetty. But seeing only one superstructure through the binoculars, we soon realised it was a single vessel running on for what looked a mile.

Using our GPS, we found safe passage through that maze of islands and channel markers only to be then confronted by a collage of ships, tugs, personnel carriers, barges, and service craft. Complicating our approach, that lazy breeze suddenly gained sufficient strength to put *Banyandah's* gunwale underwater. Gusty winds, close quarters, and flying across the water forced Jude to take the helm for final manoeuvres into Hampton Harbour.

Heartbeats increased with the wind. Coming fast on our right, more ships were berthed alongside the long slender East Intercourse Island. One was loading a cargo of fine red earth that spewed off a conveyor system; while beyond it further south, a contrasting snow-white mountain of sea-salt glistened in the midday sun while it was being dumped into the bowels of another ship. Then I saw Jude reach for her camera and restrained her because rushing at us were hungry red rocks right in our path, requiring careful navigation if we were not to make fools of ourselves. Adding to the confusion, small craft churned the waters around us. A quick rush below brought up our Fremantle Sailing Club Guidebook. Opened next to our compass, we first picked out number three marker. A heartbeat later, at number two, we turned sharp left to pass close to a grotesquely craggy lump called East Rock, dumping all sail as it passed. While still tidying up, a minefield of mooring buoys opened out.

Some find trouble in shopping centres when the simple task of choosing a parking spot can make horns blare and tempers flare. So imagine no lines, no signs, only obstructions and confusion of others bearing down while unseen forces shifted you sideways. Bamboozled and unable to decide whether to take up a mooring or put down the anchor, a building onshore suddenly matched the photo of the yacht club in our guidebook.

Weaving this way then that past moving and moored craft unveiled a dozen yachts aligned to the stiff breeze. Ahead by a hundred metres, a low causeway connected East Intercourse Island to the mainland, sheltering the anchorage from seaward. With the shore to our east, the small boat harbour seemed well protected. And scanning out to the furthest row of yachts, sufficient space for us to swing was seen. It seemed perfect, except for the yellow oil barrier floating next to it. Searching that area we sighted three large yellow airbags bobbing beside a strange metal structure poking out the water. Perplexed, we simply got on with the job of anchoring our craft.

In a well-practised routine, we set and pulled in the anchor; it abruptly stopped us, signifying a good bottom. From the wilds of Rowley Shoals, we had travelled to a new world that after a slow, thorough scrutiny intrigued us.

In the Martian landscape, few houses were seen amongst the many facilities humming with activity. On the island directly upwind, an ore loading facility dug into a mountain of red dust, scooping it up with a rotating dredge that shifted it on conveyor belts, sending red grit flying on the breeze. Crunching it between our teeth brought a sudden realisation that we had better cover our sails and close hatches. Welcome to Dampier, the iron ore capital of Australia.

EXPORT Inc

Once snugly anchored in Dampier's Hampton Harbour, Jude was keen to go ashore straight away, but my sore back had made me cranky, and the red dust now coating our ship had me thinking of pulling the hook to find a cleaner spot amongst the islands. But needing supplies, needing fuel, and probably needing someone new to talk with, my thoughts went instead to a relaxing hot shower. After which, feeling more social, we launched Little Red and used the outboard to go ashore.

Landing at the service jetty just as a craft carrying personnel came alongside we were immediately engulfed by gruff workers in blue dungarees wearing hard hats. No one seemed to notice grandma and grandpa, so we fell in line and marched with them up the dirt track towards the two-story building we had identified as the yacht club.

First moments in a new place are often bewildering but always special. Will pre-conceived visions ring true? Will first encounters be easygoing or challenging? Walking through the yacht club's entrance, we met a cheery lady taking meal orders who straight away could not stop telling us how wonderful Dampier was. Hmm, seemed rather dusty and harsh to me, but I kept nodding as she babbled, until I realised the bar was upstairs. Two minds alike, together Jude and I climbed the simple staircase and found heaven; a near-empty bar with my favourite brew on tap and an opening onto a balcony overlooking the busy harbour now brightly lit by yellow safety lights that added extra zest to the golden-red sun bathing the islands. Sauntering out with a celebratory brew in hand, we stood a few moments to behold the beauty while savouring the success of achieving yet another safe landfall. I so dearly love this woman who makes these adventures possible that we cuddled against the setting sun until several loud wolf whistles broke us apart. Blushing crimson, we found a cosy corner only to have our solitude broken by a man in yellow dungarees wanting to shout us a beer. Unshaven, looking more like a vagabond, Peter was actually a foreign going master running a local tug. After briefly outlining our travels, we then listened to his stories of enormous riches to be made by ticketed masters. And when I couldn't help boasting that I held those qualifications, he started making a call, so I had to catch his arm.

"No, No, Peter, I'm not looking for work."

Truth is, he seemed a bit crestfallen, but covered that by telling us his life story. Hmm, wife gone, left him for another man who now rents his house, has lost touch with his kids, and has moved site to site since it all went pear-shaped. I soon formed an impression that might be ill-founded; Dampier was a man's town, a mining town, and reminiscent of my short stint at Bougainville Copper.

Peter was a magnet for loose ends, so after retelling our story to several others, we heard their confessions as if newly arrived priests. And that soon became a drone, forcing us to shift to a table with the trio off the trimaran *Fly by Night*. They had just made the journey from Darwin. Maureen had elected to fly home to Perth after a rather disastrous sail down from Broome, but her husband would go on with his father. Seems their new second-hand boat was falling apart. More beer was needed to hear about that. Then sharing a bottle of red kept Jude and I pain-free while the place filled for the night's entertainment. And by the time Gleny Rae Virus got Fiddlin', Squeezin' and Hollerin', with her great country-western voice, we were too far gone to eat dinner.

Even spread three sheets to the wind, I am still the captain and take my responsibilities seriously. With everything we do is the constant need to look out for dangers. So we got home safely through a kaleidoscope of lights. Yep, you're right. Shouldn't go beyond what is prudent. And we do not. But hey, gotta live, gotta celebrate our victories - we work so hard to achieve them.

Next morning came suddenly with a back spasm that bowled me over as I reached for the handhold to get out of bed. After breakfast, a stretching walk onshore seemed a good idea, but I couldn't pull the outboard. So Jude did the deed. Her first success! Now she was independent of me and could go where she pleased when she wanted. Walking past the scene of last night's celebration, a lush green lawn presented a somewhat bizarre oddity amongst the red dirt and rock. In fact, in a slow pan around, everything seemed out of place. Lovely white sand rimmed a harbour of aquamarine while palms dotted a shore backed by strips of healthy green grass; all of it jumbled amongst rubble piles and rocky outcrops standing boldly upon bare red earth. Rising from the harbour, the nearly deserted land had tumbleweed blowing over it while pockets of unspectacular buildings broke the monotonous, but fascinating scenery. Dampier, established in the 1960s by mining company Hamersley Iron, was a purposely built port for its iron ore project. Many of the buildings date from that time, with the rest hurriedly added during boom periods like the present.

Asking directions found the "shopping mall," and what bliss entering air-conditioned comfort where straightaway signs of the present boom were visible. Shop windows and the community board were filled with "workers wanted" notices, and throughout the open-fronted supermarket, single men filled shopping baskets. We wandered its aisles like kids in a chocolate shop. Jude's very meticulous. No dashing about grabbing just anything. The first time inside, she'll peruse each lane, studying labels as if a final exam is needed to get out; then she may or may not take a trolley to purchase the best buys. It frustrates me to the max. Fortunately, I'm not usually with her. When it comes to food, I am more the grab and get on to the next item type. So, after my quick look about, calling Jude's attention to the cart loaded with out of date specials, I did my thing by scrutinising the adjoining bottle shop. Our conclusion: Better buys here than in Darwin, with a good choice of fresh veggies; a careful selection was landing in Jude's handbasket, along with fresh bread, and a few items from the specials cart.

Long before Jude finished, I had selected my purchases, limited by our mode of travel, then I strolled through the arcade doing stretches like a gymnast. Strange, the place was nearly vacant. Just a closed-down video shop and little else but a snack bar. Outside, across an open parking lot, a country-style pub overlooked the harbour, and that naturally had my feet stepping to check it out. Just mid-morning, the covered balcony was already shoulder-to-shoulder with an all-male clientele sipping ambers and blowing columns of smoke as if the place was on fire. Pushing through the crowd brought me to a menu posted on the glass door. The prices seemed reasonable, so I mentally penciled in taking my lady out for dinner that night. And yes, to watch the Rugby League semi-final on one of the many screens around the walls. Just to be sure, I checked with a cutie attending the bar, and she confirmed that that night's match would be screened. The attire of the three chickadees serving drinks had me thinking now here's a bonus to being in a worker's town.

Jude writes: The previous night's liquid dinner left me lacking inspiration, so I was delighted when Jack suggested dining out. Saturday night at the Mermaid was a packed house affair, quite the venue for an evening out. When we got there, all men, as far as I could tell, were overflowing the balcony into the parking lot right up to the first line of cars. Tattoos glistened on hot, sweaty bodies, singlets hung limp, smoke drifted on the stifling still air in which I felt slightly out of place. A few heads turned my way, so I quick-stepped closely to Jack's heels as he weaved and shoved through the crowd. I didn't dare get too far behind and look as if alone. The door flew open and a bunch threaded out while we nudged inside to lose the cigarette smoke to a raucous crowd playing pool, in-between gulping beers and shovelling what appeared decent food into their mouths. While the heavy odour of fermentation, food, and sweat caught my breath, the sequel took me by surprise. I suppose I must have had an astonished look, my thoughts frozen in a half-smile, for here was life; working men letting off steam in an all man's world of real characters, young and old, long and short-haired, some bearded, some tattooed and pierced; and yet, when heads turned, bodies made way to let me through.

As if someone had reserved the perfect place for us, a large wooden keg standing on end had two vacant spots in front of a widescreen already displaying the opening ceremony of the rugby league match. Once perched atop the tall stool, I felt better and for a few moments kept my eyes on the Queensland Cowboys and

Manly Sea-Eagles running onto the field. That had also diverted Jack's attention from the topless barmaids waltzing about, drawing in and enticing the boys to chat; poor dears, their eyes popping out. Close to me, crowded around the next keg, workers still in painters overalls caught my attention, so while Jack watched the footy; he's been known to miss a wedding so as not to miss a finals match, I intruded upon their conversation. I had an excuse; some looked as old as me; besides I like to make the most out of life and I was curious. They were all ever so polite, not riff-raff or downers, but good blokes from all walks of life, up from the south and as far away as New Zealand, some laid off because of their age, come to make a buck while there's a big demand for workers. Through the first half of the game, I mostly talked with this chap Russell, tall and lean he made me such a grand offer that at half time, I introduced him to Jack then strolled off to the bar. I was liking this place, its colour and in no time fell into conversation with a couple. Phew, a female and pretty at that, until I did a double-take.

Jude introduced Russell telling me he owned the boat next to us in the anchorage and straightaway, we fell into chatting about his life as a mine site worker. No younger than I, he worked twelve-hour days, six days a week, four weeks on, then a week off. One day he plans to go cruising though he's done little of that.

During our mobile phone free hour, Jude went outside to wish Jerome a happy birthday, but the din from the pub forced her to walk clean across the car park to the service road which ran along the top of the slope that runs down to some wasteland. Not much is finished in this workers town. Returning with a wide grin lighting her face, she told me that a small wallaby had bounded up the slope and, startled by her presence, had stopped a few paces away to peer at her while she'd asked Jerome about his special day. The tiny marsupial stayed on while Jude next spoke with our dear friend Lottie. Chat hour over, the cute furry thing deposited a few scats then bounded back down the slope into the shadows. Inside, Manly beat the Cowboys much to my disgust. My mate Big Al would have enjoyed that.

Next morning my back was still bad, and that seemed enough of an excuse to rest at home watching the other semi-final between Parramatta and The Storm while Jude went ashore to do laundry. The Storm won easily. After which I rose from my bed to join her and visit *Slojo*, Russell's boat.

What a big boat for one bloke. Forty-five feet of steel with so much room, *Banyandah* could float inside without touching her sides. She's not been anywhere for some time and was, as is usual with stay-in-one-spot vessels, in disarray, but not as bad as some bachelor quarters. Russell's present project, hence stuff being out, was to fix his overheating genset. Then he can run his appliances to clean up the place. But for worker's digs, it seemed fine to us, and the potential as a cruising vessel was quite apparent. All she needed was more of what every boat needs; money, love, and attention. Russell proved a gracious host; amiable, chatty, and funny, and straightaway we liked him a lot. And he must have cottoned onto us too because within the first few sentences he reaffirmed his last evening's pledge to loan us his car when he flew to Perth midweek.

"Well, it's nothing special," he sort of blew out in a chuckle as if what he said had no importance. "Just a heap in fact, but she goes, don't have to worry about that."

It's the special people we meet that make the difference. They change a short stay into a never to be forgotten experience.

On Monday Jude went ashore to the club's washing machine, donating more coins to the honesty box – she must have washed every bit of clothing, every sheet on the boat, ridding us of nine weeks sweat and dust, while I lay on my back popping more aspirins. Hardly able to stand, my big plan to rip out the gearbox and find that nuisance oil leak now seemed highly unlikely. Made more unlikely when a strong wind warning whipped up wavelets and carried clouds of fine red ore across the anchorage. It would have been majestic had it not been bombarding our boat with gritty dust. While the wind had us rocking round our anchor, Jude cooked up fragrant coriander curried prawns for that night's special guest, and right on cue, Russell arrived bumping across the waves in a very large tinny that had no soft bumpers. He made such a meal of coming alongside, we were lucky to snare him even after he'd chucked us a line on his third time blown past.

Copious amounts of good Aussie red wine made Jude's lovely meal all the finer, and Russell's humorous chatter intermixed with plenty of our salty sea stories kept emptying our wine glasses. Later, when the wind howled more furiously, we told more stories, discussed future plans, and drank more wine until we all knew this had the chance of becoming a monumental session, which none of us really wanted. That's when the question of Russell going home came up and it was quickly decided it wouldn't be safe, so a forward bunk was made up.

After blowing near gale all night, the wind suddenly eased just before first light, a routine we'd later get to know very well. Thus, as the sun started to brighten the eastern hills, Russell got safely off to work. After that, Tuesday passed in something of a haze. Wednesday brought another strong wind warning from the south, but the "B" hung in tightly while I typed notes and Jude cleaned house. Staying onboard until late afternoon, Jude and I then braved a saltwater soaking to drive Russell to the airport. Climbing into a dusty old beast that some vagrant would have looked perfectly at home in, surprisingly Russell's car never missed a beat.

After waving our new mate off at the airport, we suddenly had more freedom. Thanks to Russell, we could wander the countryside at will and celebrate this, Jude drove us to the main town of Karratha twenty clicks up the road. Karratha, aboriginal for "good country," was the name of the original cattle station established there in 1860. It is now the largest city in the Pilbara. Developed along with Dampier to service Hamersley Iron, Dampier Salt, and Woodside's North West Shelf Gas Project, its size jumps during each boom until now its suburbs sprawl ten kilometres along the area's only access road.

According to Jude, all of Woolworth's layouts are the same, which makes navigation easy. Knowing just where to go, she set off filling a cart, her eyes bulging when they feasted on the massive display of produce, cheaper than anywhere else she has stored. Being a faithful puppy, I toddled alongside for a few aisles then bolted to study the boozatorium after I discovered it through a side door.

Our first excursion into the Pilbara, where it does rain but doesn't look like it ever does, was to the Burrup Peninsula that we were hearing so much about in recent news. Keen to see the site containing upwards of a million ancient Aboriginal rock art engravings that Woodside wants to shift so they can expand their LNG plant, we thought it best first to visit the present Woodside plant; and were agog at what we witnessed, a 23rd-century city complete with flaming gas flares.

During summer, temperatures soar above 45° C (113° F), but now in September, the temperature was only 40° C (104° F) in the shade. Inside the air-conditioned tourist information centre, there was a very complete display of what geological formations they try to locate, what the drill platforms look like, how they drill, even a cute cartoon film on the creation of oil that showed how Woodside harvests it, cracks it into components then liquefies the gas for transportation around the world. At present, a fifth extension is under construction, which will lift LNG production to 16.3 million metric tonnes per year, having completed the fourth in 2004. A sixth extension is already planned, the one that will require shifting the aboriginal petroglyphs.

Jude had prepared a sumptuous picnic that we enjoyed at a shady table overlooking the plant. And so while we munched our tuna sandwiches, we observed the hustle and bustle of production that was happening right alongside new construction. And this had us wondering if there had been any explosions with so much highly flammable liquids and gases around arc welders and cutting torches. So it did not surprise us when nine months later a massive explosion at another plant shut off gas to a third of WA.

Next stop; down a dusty sidetrack to Deep Gorge where we found tall runs of red rocks with worn smooth edges, all very similar in size, containing the world's largest concentration of petroglyphs. Collectively the rocks looked very pretty against their harsh surroundings, heaped up as if dumped on the desert floor by giant trucks. Individually they were just rocks, but as soon as we got out of the car, we spotted the rock art. Not deeply engraved, but created by incising, pecking, and abrading by the Jaburrara people. Not surprising us, the Jaburrara people were completely wiped out by police and settlers in 1868. The heat radiating off those rocks seemed to make them glow deep carmine red as if their prehistoric formation was still underway. Nevertheless, after changing into bush gear and bundling up our cameras, we wandered about for several hours, finding hundreds of these markings that depict marsupials, ancient folk and symbols, which until the present day, time had effected little.

Robin Chapple of The Australian Greens party says, "We face the prospect not only of bulldozing, blasting and other defacements of the rock art, but we now have evidence that acid emissions from industry will rapidly erase the greater part of the rock art province."

To shift them in total is impossible, but individual works of art could be removed for display. That, of course, would lose the spatial relationship and rob viewers of their real environment. On the other hand, few tourists can tolerate the heat of their original location, which means more will see them in museums. A typical quandary of today.

Back to reality the next day, I pumped oil out the engine tray then topped up the sump. It being too windy to chance disabling the ship by removing the gearbox, that got scratched off the worklist. Instead, we traversed the open desert to dump the old smelly oil at the tip and purchase new oil at Karratha. When examining the dozens of different oils, I noticed one by Castrol especially formulated for pre1990 engines. Hmm, I wondered if this might help cure our oil leak and decided to give it a go.

Savouring our ability to go anywhere and carry tonnes of goods in Russell's car, Jude drove us back to Woolies, where she did her first major shop since Darwin. To fill in my time, I purchased copious amounts of beer and red wine. Back in Dampier, we came unstuck. An even lower tide than the night before had Little Red sitting on the mud once she was loaded with all our goodies. It was now not possible to return home, so we hatched plan B, hurrying off to the yacht club balcony for a couple of cold beers while the sun set off another four-alarm fire behind the islands and across the harbour.

Dampier landing at low tide

When Saturday dawned hot and windless, we were off on another excursion, this time to explore further north, the historical towns of Roebourne and Cossack. But first, a quick stop at Karratha to look through their Op shop. With our limited storage, Op shops are grand places for near-new clothing more suitable to a new climate and Jude found two adorable blouses while I scored three dandy business shirts; cool, light cotton with long sleeves for keeping the sun out. But my best buy was a book for bad backs; *Callanetics*, showing loosening up moves, strengthening exercises, plus a chapter on *Emergency Relief for Spasms*. All for two bucks each.

Russell's claptrap rattled north across the flat red desert with every window open while few trees broke the sparse scrub interspersed by grey saltpans. After an hour's run, passing a sign welcoming us to Roebourne changed very little, only adding a scant line of trees that followed a turbid river to a town that is dead, but still going through the motions of life.

This area of the Pilbara has a robust European history dating back to 1699 when William Dampier sailed into the Archipelago aboard his ship the *Roebuck*. This town is not named after Dampier's ship, but in honour of John Septimus Roe, first Surveyor-General of Western Australia who earlier had served under Lieutenant King aboard the *Mermaid*.

The area was first explored by Francis Thomas Gregory in 1861, who reported upwards of 2 to 3 million acres of land suitable for grazing. He also drew attention to the possibility of a pearl oyster industry. Then two years later in 1863, the first settlers arrived, including Gregory's cousin, Emma Withnell who took up 30,000 acres along the Harding River at the foot of Mount Welcome. In common with other settlers of that time, they hired local Aborigines to work as shepherds, labourers, and shearers. Four years after first explored, the population had grown to about 200, with the Withnells' property serving as a local hub. John Withnell opened a store and provided cartage service for other settlers. The law arrived in April 1866, when Robert John Sholl was posted there straight from the failed Camden Harbour settlement, setting up camp near the Withnells' home while trying to locate a suitable townsite. Sholl eventually decided to establish the town at his camp, where, on 17 August 1866, after surveyor Charles Wedge had drawn a plan consisting of 106 lots, Roebourne became the first gazetted town in the North West.

From the top of Mount Welcome, more a pimple than a mountain, the earth ran away flat and hot like a thin vegetarian pizza while down below, a wild-west movie set stood lifeless. The only thing saving the view from wrenching a hole in our souls was the distant blue sea dancing in heatwaves. Freewheeling down the hill gave Russell's old car some chance of not boiling over in the excruciating heat, and once at the bottom Jude kept her rolling straight into the old goal that's now a museum.

Whitewashed cornerstones and window abutments decorated the red stone building which has an ornate iron gate across its entry. This led us to a small reception area and into the clutches of an extremely informative local lady. Once started, she poured out historical facts that painted a mural of hardworking pioneers seeking sustenance from a harsh land. Barely pausing for breath, she then contrasted that with present life, which she claimed was even harder, trying to merge two different cultures into one when there's no future on the land. Getting past her, we entered a circular room linking the four cellblocks that now contain exhibits of the vicious implements used in the past. In the late 1800s, Aboriginal prisoners had a chain around their neck secured by a padlock. This was linked by chains to others with upwards of ten shackled together. In 1905, there were 86 prisoners, all black, and only four guards, so chaining was seen as security against an uprising. Looking with incredulous eyes at old photographs; upon the open desert stood nine naked Aborigines chained by the neck. It was titled, "Blackbirding - the kidnapping of Aborigines for forced labour, profitable for some early settlers."

The practise of kidnapping and forced labour of Aboriginal people was known as "Blackbirding" and was a profitable business for some early settlers

Nestled at the mouth of the Harding River, some thirteen kilometres north of Roebourne, the ghost town of Cossack has experienced a somewhat chequered past to bring it to its present state. Once the gateway to northwest Australia, and once home to a pearling fleet of over 80 luggers, official records show that at its peak in 1894, 141 European and 225 Asiatic lived in Cossack, with the numbers of Japanese rising to many more during the "lay up" season from November to March when pearl divers rested. Today, only a few tourists and one policeman frequent the historic buildings.

With the cry of "Gold" in the 1880s, hundreds of prospectors streamed through the port to seek their fortunes in the Pilbara fields. But Cossack's fortunes started changing in the 1890s when silting of the harbour corresponded with a growing need for larger ships. In 1904, the port facilities were relocated to Point Samson. Hard times followed, resulting in its eventual abandonment by 1950. From then until 1979 the majestic stone buildings lay in ruins. Today Cossack offers a unique look at this region's colonial past with five of the original buildings fully restored, including the Old Post Office and Telegraph building, which now house an Art Gallery, the Old Court House containing the Social History Museum, the Customs House, now tearooms, and Galbraith's Store.

In just one short week, we'd had a wide-eyed look at this fast-growing part of Australia. We had seen first hand the largest export of raw materials in Australia's history and witnessed the enormous problems created by this boom. Nature has been given a back seat while land prices have soared. Workers are in such demand that huge pay packets are being offered to entice them to this isolated environment. And the abundance of wealth has driven up the cost of everything but basics, with the new rich spending as if the tap will never run dry. It's alarming because many are borrowing considerably more to capitalise on the opportunity. The boom times are upon them, but we wonder what will happen when the bust arrives.

Following our excursion to Roebourne and Cossack, Sunday was used to finish off last-minute chores. Jude drove to Karratha for a big shop of fresh stores because our plan was to depart just as soon as that night's Rugby League Grand Final had been played out. She returned with a dinghy filled with fruit and veg, and after stowing it, proceeded to add up all our food costs since departing Darwin. It came to just on $700 for fresh and packaged food, averaging about $65 each week. Beer and wine need to be added to that. Also, diesel fuel, plus whatever was spent in the various pubs for meals and drink to arrive at an overall cost.

Russell rang from the airport at 5 o'clock, so again Jude started the outboard and went to pick him up, and although we'd invited him over for a few coldies while watching the footy final, sorting himself out took more time than he thought because he'd picked up someone else's bag at the airport and had to go back. That left Jude barracking for Manly while I cheered on The Storm, who easily out-muscled the Sea Eagles to take this year's trophy. Russell found his way over just in time for a post-match roast chook dinner, followed by farewell drinks that went on a wee bit late considering we'd be sailing the next day.

The strong winds earlier in the week had given way to a quiet night followed by an easy morning, perfect for moving *Banyandah* alongside to take on fuel and water. Lucky that. Jude wasn't quite up to speed after the night's celebrations. The calm conditions made the fuel dock busy, so we had to wait an hour before taking on 310 litres at $1.75/litre ($543). That brought our all-up costs, complete with food and drink for eleven weeks while travelling 1300 miles, come to just under $2,000.

Russell came by to wish us a fond farewell, and we promised to stay in touch, which we still do, calling him every now and then during our free hour. Our final chore before shoving off and heading out on the next adventure was to take on nearly 700 litres of good Dampier drinking water. And now with *Banyandah* sitting low on her marks, we untied from the wharf, but had a dilly of a time getting her off as the sea breeze was jamming us against it. But away we did get, raising mainsail and using the engine to leave much the same way as we'd come in - except we were now much richer in knowledge about the fast-growing Pilbara.

SETTING THE NIGHT ON FIRE

The summer sun was nearer the horizon than its zenith by the time we had taken on fuel and water and had scrubbed off the red earth acquired during *Banyandah's* ten-day stopover in Dampier. And not wanting to wait another day and become coated with iron ore again, it was rather fortunate that an archipelago of 43 uninhabited islands began at the gates of the harbour. From the chart, I had already chosen two to check out.

With mainsail raised, we departed using the engine through the same maze we'd threaded coming in, until reaching East Intercourse Island where we altered course south around a humongous ship loading another chunk of Australia for export. From her decks high above, tiny stick figures wearing white hard hats waved farewell. So to thrill them with thoughts of faraway places, we unfurled our spotlessly white headsail to its fullest then set it smooth and taut like an upright 747 wing, sending *Banyandah* slipping silently towards floating hills with golden beaches and twisted rocks. Created only six to eight thousand years ago by rising seawater flooding coastal valleys, today twenty-five of those islands form a conservation park that features pristine beaches, superb fishing, historical shipwrecks, and Aboriginal rock engravings.

A moderate sea breeze produced such a delightfully uplifting movement of scenery that we bypassed the first anchoring spot just so we could continue to unwind from our harried time storing the boat. The second spot, Enderby Island, named by Lieutenant King in honour of his friend Samuel Enderby, was just what the doctor ordered; calm water surrounded by islands and a pair of sea kites soaring above a wide bay. Sipping a couple of coldies, we wet our fishing lines while our eyes peacefully roved over the scenery and we discussed what lay ahead. Funny, we had no plan. You'd expect the captain and master's mate to have it all mapped out, but that's just not the case. With the summer southerlies now becoming well established, all we wanted was to move south against them, down the Western Australian coast without breaking gear or hurting ourselves.

The most direct route lay along the coast in daylight hops or overnight passages between safe anchorages. This might seem the easiest way to travel the miles, but in fact, Jude and I find it easier to make longer hops with bigger breaks in-between. An important factor, the distance our chunky craft can travel in daylight hours, which is dependent on whether she's going with the wind or tacking into it. Down this coast, common sense said we'd be battling the wind. Therefore a good passage in daylight hours might only yield twenty miles; fifty or sixty overnight. And if caught out battling a powerful headwind, it's possible we'd actually be set backwards. That meant we would have to hide in anchorages and wait for just the right weather. And, according to our guidebook, many of the anchorages on this coast were marginal in strong southerlies.

On the other hand, *Banyandah* has covered vast spans of water for many years, and she is nicely set up for long hops. Therefore, we favour making longer runs between the better anchorages, and then waiting for the next weather window before blazing ahead; even if that means staying in one spot for weeks with our voyage taking several days.

Eighty miles off the Pilbara coast lay an intriguing archipelago of more than 250 low-lying islands named Montebello, Italian for Beautiful Mountain, by the French explorer Nicolas Baudin in 1801. But there's a much earlier reference to these islands from 1622. In fact, it's the earliest recorded sighting of *Terra Australis Incognita* by an English ship and happened when *HMS Tryal* was wrecked on rocks just west of those islands.

The Montebello Islands most fascinating claim to fame occurred in the 1950s when a bunch of mad scientists went looking for an out-of-the-way place to play with their new toys. They did not want anyone to see these horrible devices in case they did something naughty, so they never told their friends or neighbours. Now, these mad scientists didn't think they were doing anything bad. No, they thought they were just being very clever because if these new toys were good nasty toys, then nobody would ever bully them again. Or so they thought. So they searched the far ends of the world until they found a place that nobody wanted. What they found were islands, just ordinary flat bits of land that curled around each other like runaway vines with nothing except wild creatures that included massive white-bellied sea eagles, dugongs, ten different whales, five species of turtles, and a whole bunch of fish calling it home. And then on a quiet day when everybody else in the world was rebuilding their homes destroyed in the last war, these madmen set up their toys and pushed a big red button. Kerpow!

Extract from the FSC Guidebook:
Three nuclear weapons tests were carried out at the Montebello Islands in the 1950s:
Hurricane, a 25-kilotonne ocean surface blast aboard HMS Plym, was detonated 400 metres off Trimouille Island on October 3, 1952.
Mosaic G1, a 15-kilotonne blast from the top of a 31-metre tower on Trimouille Island on May 16, 1956.

And Mosaic G2, the largest nuclear weapon ever tested in Australia, a 98-kilotonne tower blast on Alpha Island on June 19, 1956. The fallout from this device was measured in Brisbane when it rained two days later. This test broke an assurance made personally by the British Prime Minister to Prime Minister Robert Menzies of Australia that the yield would not exceed 2.5 times that of Hurricane (thus about 62 Kt). But the true yield was concealed until 1984.

Hmm, when looking for an out of the way place, sounds like Doctor No and his gang might not have read Mark Twain, "What gets us into trouble is not what we don't know. It's what we know for sure that just ain't so."

I mean, did they know for sure that nuclear explosions were safe? Did they have the slightest inkling that radioactive sub-microscopic particles kill the chromosomes of all creatures - including man - and that they keep flying round 'n' round for something like 10,000 years?

I suppose today's scientists must know for sure that the islands are now safe. Why else would they let Jude and me, or any tourist, sail right to the very spot where an early atomic device was detonated? They must also know for sure that visitors might be tempted to touch the creatures that have lived amongst all those invisible particles for so many generations. And of course, they would know for sure that we'd be eating the seafood living amongst all that radiation. Uh-oh! That got me praying our continued survival is not something they know for sure - that just ain't so!

We lay comfortably in East Bay, Enderby Island where a mild SW wind kept us cool through the night and on waking found the low tide revealing some enchanting rocks where had been a sandy shore. My desire to explore prompted me to nudge Judith awake.

"Oi, you. Shake a leg."

But that desire was extinguished as quickly when a light northwesterly drifted in, a fair sailing wind, which instead, started us stashing stuff to get underway.

Clank-clank-clank, our chain fell into its locker, pulling the anchor up till its loud metallic clunk against the bow rollers sent me aft.

"OK love, we're away. Turn her to port and I'll ease the main."

Then with *Banyandah*'s bow tracing an arc across Enderby's grassy hills, I unleashed our headsail, which started water tinkling along our waterline. Rounding East Point, I streamed the trolling line then joined Jude amidships to enjoy what was a fantastic day to be underway looking for a new place to explore.

Three huge yellow cyclone moorings loomed ahead and peering forward to gauge if a change of course was needed, I asked, "Should I set the windvane, or are you happy on the helm?"

After Jude indicated she wanted to hand steer, "Better keep her a bit more right, Babe. I can't make out how far the lines drift off those buoys."

As Jude turned the helm, I cast a look aft and saw our trolling line stretched tight, a white splash marking its end. "Ho! Looks like lunch just arrived."

With the way forward slowly opening up and the islands growing in number behind, the increasing heat weakened our wind, shifting it from being fair to having everything cranked in tight. Forced to follow it around sent us towards a bank of submerged dangers, and eventually, we changed directions, taking the wind on the other side of the ship. It was while turning that another sail hove into view, inshore and astern, on the same tack. Just a speck nearly lost in a haze, but slowly it kept gaining, so just on twilight, I gave a call on the VHF to alert him of our presence. John aboard *Morning Flight* said his intention was to continue along the shore, lickety-split for Fremantle in quick hops. In short phrases, his hesitant voice dribbled out plans to be there before lobster season started on the 15th of November. Informing us that a massive number of lobster pots are set, even in deep water, saying there was great danger for yachts becoming fouled on their floating mooring lines.

His nervousness increased when he added, "The southerly winds will only get stronger from now."

A couple of hours later, with our two vessels within half a mile, we could just make out his ghostly black silhouette blocking out stars, so we tacked to head west for the Montebello while his stern light carried him down the coast. Ships passing in the night, sharing a prophecy of the future.

A quiet, comfortable night followed with the moon rising at midnight, revealing absolutely nothing in sight. At nine the following morning, from out this vast emptiness rose the first oilrig. Then bumps of islands popped up about eleven. By noon, we could make out their flat coralline structure that showed extensive patches of scrubby grass, but no trees.

There are just three entrances into this group of islands whose perimeter is linked by submerged coral obstructions. Approaching from Dampier put us nearest the south entrance, which is encumbered with lots of shallow undersea lumps. But not to worry, our GPS took us safely to the passage and traversing it turned out to be quite good fun.

Dot Island heralds the opening, an impressive punctuation mark of limestone eroded around its base. In good light, we passed so close our weak wash wet it as we entered a gorgeous lagoon showing a bouquet of low isles upon a taut canvas of sapphire. The higher ones to our right guarded us from the sea. The ones on our left, strung like a necklace of pearls down its middle, lead towards the long slender island of Trimouille, where at Main Bay a broad smile of white sand seemed to beckon us. As if intrigued, *Banyandah* cut the canvas of blue, until, as luck would have it, we motored directly over the blast site of the first atomic weapon detonated there exactly 55 years earlier to the day. Its location was marked by a sudden dip on our depth sounder.

As our anchor chain paid out upon the shallow bottom, we noticed that signs warning of radioactivity dotted the large crescent-shaped bay. Well, in 40 years of exploring this planet, that was a first and a rather ominous harbinger. Feeling we needed to lessen our exposure, we ducked below for a quick bite of lunch, during which Jude suggested we row in to explore. But I declined. I needed some quiet time for reflection. Within metres of us, our depth sounder had just traced an atomic bomb crater, and that had dug up emotions from my youth, which, as I ate in silence, grew in magnitude like the mushroom cloud of mankind's dilemma.

Watching Jude row off, I ended up sitting in the shade of the dodger thinking of the '50s rhetoric and our monthly classroom evacuation drills, and the abundance of backyard bomb shelters built in my L.A. neighbourhood. I also thought about how man's mentality had not changed in my lifetime. We have not found peace. On the contrary, we are further from it. And that had me thinking if I were God, I'd fire the lot of us. Here we are, with the finest home in the entire universe and we're unable to put petty matters aside. We would instead argue about which belief is correct, an unanswerable question in my opinion, or who's got the most. Of what? - Money, power, charm, manhood, breasts! All unimportant when the planet is dead.

All that really matters is to go forward as one, equal, sharing Earth with all creatures. But do we do that? Nope. The hungry ones want a bigger slice and inflame the others to fight. Well, we're getting what we deserve. Man's myopic view of who we are is destroying the planet. So, before it's too late, you young ones had better agree to put all that ancient tomfoolery in its proper place, that's the trash bin, and get on with sharing this wondrous planet with its myriad of life. We suggest you put Earth First when making decisions.

The second nation to own "the bomb" started right at this spot. Now, how many countries have it? Do you remember, like I, being told that the arms race would act as a deterrent keeping the naughty ones in line? Has it? Or has humanity evolved and adapted? Now the naughty ones use terrorism that kills the innocent. But is that so new? And with that thought came visions of a plain square building standing at the centre of Nagasaki that housed wall-sized photographs of death and destruction. A grotesque bronze statue pointing skyward from a park right in front marks ground zero. Seventy-four thousand human lives, many innocent wives and children, were vaporised there one cloudy morning, a similar number in the same instant was maimed. And that does not begin to count the other creatures that perished. I then thought of how man has yet to learn to control his aggression and greed. The answer may lie in every child studying the teachings of Buddha to dispel the "me and mine" syndrome so predominant in human life.

Jude recalls: I was facing Jack as I rowed for the shore when a sudden stomach spasm had me feeling quite spooked. Like the times when a young girl running home from my aunt's after watching an episode of Quatermass and The Pit, terrified that some aliens might attack me. Except this time, I was rowing slowly towards what I could see was a beautiful island. I suppose I was worried about becoming contaminated with radioactive particles or taking some deadly dust back to my home, while at the same time, foolishly thinking I might shrivel up like crisp bacon as soon as I stepped on the sand. I wished my man was with me.

Near halfway, I realised a fleet of green turtles was about me, perhaps ten or twelve, offering me an opportunity to drift awhile to watch. Dark outlines of some nearly as wide as the dinghy rested on the seabed, while others swam effortlessly through the water as if silent torpedoes. When they surfaced close-by, after first popping their brown scaly heads out on long leathery necks, their wet shells sparkled shades of emerald green and chocolate. And at first glance, their heads looked like button mushrooms on thick stalks, until they twisted round like periscopes. When any saw me, they suddenly dove down, their rounded shapes and paddling flippers going like the clappers against the light sand bottom.

Realising that these creatures lived near the blast site made me think that it could not be so bad; and by the time I had reached the shore, I had a strategy in mind. After my visit, I would step straight out my boots into the dinghy, and then I would clack the boots hard together to loosen any dirt, and after that, slosh the soles about in the water to be sure. What a strange precaution for an uninhabited island.

Atomic bomb site (1950s) on the nearly uninhabited Montebello Islands

When stepping out onto the coarse sand, it contained quite a lot of delightful small shells of a uniform vanilla colour that were laid out in parallel lines like a multi-strand necklace on the beach. They were so beautiful I just wanted to reach down and scoop up a handful but didn't dare. Instead, I dashed up the beach, crossing a wide span to the dreary-looking scrub while my eyes coursed along the pale uninterrupted arc to three large signs spaced at regular intervals. I knew what they said from the guidebook: "Do not handle or remove any objects as they may be radioactive. Avoid causing dust as any particles may be radioactive. Visits to test sites should be restricted to one hour per day." Thankfully, there was no wind to stir things up, although, as a precaution, I had taken a cloth to cover my face.

I guess I had been holding my breath since first landing because when I started breathing again, it seemed to hiss out, "Come on Jude, get a hold of yourself." Then when my heart stopped racing, "I've only got one hour," could be heard echoing inside my head, so I started picking a way cleanly through the shrub, stepping straight down onto the sand between the plants so as not to kick up dust. While doing this, I spotted a plastic bag resting in a hollow and to prevent it being blown into the sea and eaten mistakenly by one of those turtles who might think it a jellyfish, I pushed it under a lump of dead coral with my boot, too frightened to remove it. Doing this reminded me of sweet dear Lance Ferris, founder of Australian Seabird Rescue who would strum a little, sing a little to help pay the costs of educating Australians on the dangers of plastic bags and balloons because turtles ingest them thinking they are jellyfish. Lance's tireless campaign these past dozen years, lobbying events managers and balloon makers to either stop releasing their gaily-coloured messages of death or make them from substances that break down with sunlight will hopefully pay off.

I found nothing of exceptional interest in the bush except some sage-like green shrub in pink flower, so I wandered back down to the beach where I discovered several lengths of rusting iron lying idle. As they were adorned with marine growth obviously acquired over many years, they started me wondering whether they had been part of the ship that held the first bomb. Shuddering, I bolted back along the beach to the dinghy. My hour wasn't up, but I clacked my boots together with venom and left that place feeling cheated about not having picked up or touched one pretty shell, and angry that this beautiful island had been changed forever.

Plenty of turtles popping their heads out the baby blue water welcomed Jude back from her stroll. And that made me wonder about the wildlife. Had those turtles read the warning signs when they laboured up to deposit their eggs under the full moonlight? Oh well, me and mine. At least we had a good phone connection allowing Jude to gaily chat back home while a glorious blaze of crimson raged around the gold fire behind the western islands.

GIANT MUTANT LOBSTER

Upright on their hind flippers, emerald green turtles swishing pink light sabres marched steadily towards me up a beach glowing like a dead sun. Vainly I struggled against chains holding me to the sign's rusted stump that mysteriously rocked back and forth. Dodging their sabres slashing around my head, I suddenly awoke drenched in sweat to find a fresh southwesterly had created a chop that put *Banyandah's* bum to shore.

Forced to seek better shelter, with the tide too low and the lagoon quite shallow, we had to wait, one eye to the weather while the other watched the tide creep up the beach.

While waiting, I perused charts and read the FSC Guidebook, and ended up fancying a tiny anchorage in Champagne Bay on Delta Island that would require passing through a narrow gap between limestone cliffs.

Around noon, without incident, we traversed the lagoon, but upon spying our destination, the stone gap looked like a raptor's beak, so we baulked at going in; deciding instead to anchor outside and take Little Red through to test the waters. Sounding as we went, there was only just sufficient depth in the gap, and then good water didn't extend very far into the bay, making it so tight, both a bow and stern anchor would be required to stop us from swinging onto sand flats. Even then, we'd still be bum to shore, with the only way out back through the gap that required mid-tide or better for safe passage. In the face of so many hurdles, our passion for extreme places was thwarted. So Jude and I carried on across this captive waterway by dinghy.

Around us was low land carpeted in succulents and clumps of dry weedy grass, filled in-between with low scrub making a mottled collage that flowed down to pretty sand beaches. Each of these was separated by craggy low cliffs in shades of light pink. At the far end of this nearly enclosed lagoon, another narrow opening was blocked by three lumps sprouting sharp spikes that would stop *Banyandah*, but Little Red dodged them easily. Turning left, we entered a new channel obstructed by a maze of tiny islands in water so transparent we thought we could reach out and touch the bottom. So we continued exploring, looking for somewhere to park our special lady. And sure enough, after passing a bay loaded with nastier jagged rocks, we found a lovely one clear of dangers. Entering, we found that Delta Island blocked the wind, and onshore were three magical looking lightly tanned beaches split by more eroded walls resonating in shades of grey through pink. Entirely empty, ours for the taking, all we need do was fetch *Banyandah* and take up residence.

With her mast in sight above the low island, within minutes we were re-entering the bay and floating timelessly, first in one-half, then the other, trying on the scenery before deciding where to park. Decisions! Decisions! Deciding what part of paradise is sometimes a hard choice. After lengthy deliberations, we chose a position near a long limestone wall riddled with small caves that ignited our curiosity and had us parking so close it was doubtful we'd float after the tide took away the scant water under our keel.

With one thing or another, we hadn't swum since Rowley Shoals and could hardly wait. Walking off the middle beach into water so transparent only the cool change rising up our torsos marked its increasing depth, our feet touched limestone so smooth God must have trowelled it flat before filling the oceans. Unlike Rowley, there were no sharp corals to avoid, but there were gaily-coloured tropical fish; black and white damsels, electric blue tetras, and orange striped angelfish following behind playing hide and seek. Turning about, they'd scatter. Going forward again, they regrouped into an entourage.

Swimming past the sandy pocket, we followed weathered limestone that divided the bay, stretching muscles not used for some time. I was just beginning to savour the rhythm of thrust, pull, and breathe, when Jude swam quickly over to drag me back to a shelf sticking out half a metre above the bottom. Extending her arm, she pointed to two antennae poking out. And diving down, I saw a good-sized tropical rock lobster sitting under the shelf waving its feelers about, his black pea eyes unaware of my close inspection. Tropical rock lobsters are vegetarians and do not have large pinchers, but they are yummy food. So I was mad with myself that I had not brought along my leather gloves, or I'd have grabbed him on the spot. Back on the surface, I took shore bearings thinking I'd return later. Then I swam on a few more feet. Crikey! Another pair of antennae was sticking out. This got me thinking the place must be loaded with delicious crustaceans and my belly began to rumble with thoughts of lobster thermidor. Then just when my runaway juices had me thinking of tackling one barehanded, a tasty coral trout poked its head out and I was suddenly wishing I'd brought along my speargun too.

Returning home for glove and speargun, it was decided to first throw a baited line over the side, which, after five minutes, removed the need to get wet again when a pan-sized red emperor took the bait.

We don't just frolic and play on the good ship *Banyandah*. The next day I donned my work clothes and changed the engine oil even though I had only topped it up with six litres before leaving Dampier. Already it had haemorrhaged half of that on the run to the Montebello Islands. This big old Perkins holds thirteen litres, which first has to be drained into the drip tray then sucked out using a hand pump; all done while hunched up and twisted like Houdini. And while the cockpit floor was unbolted and up, the oil filter got changed, the injector pump received a drink of oil, and the saltwater pump was greased. Then I refilled the engine with the new "pre1990" oil purchased in Karratha.

After that, it was playtime. Jude had tickled my thoughts with several ways of cooking lobster since first spying the beasts, so I was definitely pencilled in to grab one for dinner. Having not done this for a long time, I needed to practice my technique because they are thorny devils, sheathed in something akin to a suit of armour with hundreds of daggers sticking out. Strange the way Nature works. A closer look will reveal all those daggers point the wrong direction! The beast might walk forward with those swords coming at you, but their real power is in their tail, which propels them backwards. Thus, to catch one, all that's required is a swift, sure hand grabbing its body then not letting go, keeping in mind the terrific power of their tails. They'll pull free unless ripped sharply out their cave, then up, out the water.

As if a knight getting ready for a jousting tournament, my decrepit wetsuit from yesteryear was dug out its locker. Now it's sad to report that this knight has become a bit more rotund over the years, so my gut had to be sucked in like a Sheila donning a corset before the zipper could be forced shut. Then we both prayed it wouldn't burst open. Woozy from lack of breath, the sooner I charged into battle, the better, and straight away Jude rowed me to the battle site where I wasted no time, slipping straight into the water. Then my Queen, her eyes wide in anticipation, rowed to the gallery to await the outcome. Swimming to where my landmarks lined up, I dolphin dived with a good lungful of air, gloved hand at the ready. Lobster, to my limited knowledge, always return to the same hole after their nocturnal feed, so I was sure I'd see antennae poking out. But I did not. In fact, pulling myself right up to its lair, I found it completely empty.

Up I came feeling cheated and yelled to Jude that the damn beast had fled. Then I muttered to myself, "Never worry, I'll go get the second one even though it's smaller."

Swimming over to site number two, I had to re-quell my jitters after having psyched myself up to do battle then finding no beast. So, when over the next spot, I swam round 'n' round, taking several calming breaths while searching for the telltale antennae sticking out. But I didn't see them either. Down I went. Double-damn! The word must have spread, that tasty crustacean had also fled.

All morning we had been talking of little other than fresh lobster with melted butter, so I came up feeling I'd let the team down. Jude felt the same. Her brow started to pucker when she saw me surface empty-handed, and before a tear could be shed, I quickly promised to find another. Then before she could reply, I swam off with my head looking down.

Spreading further and further out, I flippered along looking for telltale antennae amongst a shallow seabed filled with craggy lumps and cracks containing many likely hiding spots. The more promising holes and caverns I dove to peer in. And in one of these was a substitute. This one was so near its cave's entrance, I threw out my hand, grabbed it then sped for the surface before it knew what had happened. Now I had forgotten that lobsters emit a series of low frequency "creaks" when flapping their tails, and hearing these creaks reminded me that sharks home in on these sounds of distress. So, while rushing for the surface, I twirled around on the alert, more worried about snapping sharks than losing the beast. But once held aloft in the air, where its tail clacked uselessly, I relaxed seeing Jude rowing hastily over to claim our prize. Faster than, Jack grabbed a lovely lobster could be said, our dinner lay stunned on the dinghy's red floor, ready for the pot. And I felt just like a victorious knight when receiving my Queen's kiss.

Now, the last time we'd eaten rock lobster, the world had been a different place. For one thing, humanity had been at peace. Not that we were better people then. But everyone sort of tolerated the others' differences. At that idyllic time in our lives, we were at a slightly more isolated spot than the Montebello. It was a sunken reef out on its own, far away in the vast Pacific where a full moon had brought two friends and the *Four J's* into the shallows to search for night-wandering molluscs. Instead, around our feet crawled an army of armoured crustaceans, their eerie silhouettes marching across sugar-white sand under brilliant moonlight. A bright spark amongst us thought of stepping on a beast, and ho! It was pinned to the bottom without fuss. Leaning down, like picking up litter, it got unceremoniously dumped into our dinghy. We'd come for pretty shells but stumbled over so many crayfish, we felt obliged to pick them up as if clearing the site to find our actual target. In the end, we didn't find any olive shells, nor bailers, or even a spiny murex.

Instead, in two hours, our red tinny became filled with twenty-three of the critters that were kept alive by half-filling our craft with seawater.

Sally and Stu off *Suleka* were with us in the hunt. So, all up with our two sons, we had six mouths to feed, which, seeing none of the critters had red egg sachets, meant nearly four each. Too many for one feed. Neither yacht had a freezer, so what to do with the remainder posed a quandary until Judith said she would bottle the excess in preserving jars. During the following three days we ate nothing but firm white crayfish; first plain with melted butter, then in a cheese sauce, and then while Jude preserved the remaining tails in her empty Mason Jars, we munched the last meal of curried crayfish. That's when our stool turned a strange colour, and none of us ever wanted to see another thorny critter again. But know what? Not one of those animals died in vain. Each and every one went across our dinner table because they kept deliciously fresh once Jude had cooked them in sealing jars.

At the Montebello's a few days later we had a craving for another feed of those thorny devils, so I suited up to go hunting. Taking the dinghy over to the long wall, we slipped over the side into a magical kingdom of small colourful fish darting up and down and in and out a wall of Swiss cheese. Jude whipped out her trusty W20 digital camera to capture the little beauties in living colour, while I snooped about peering into holes, hoping a Moray Eel wouldn't lunge at me before I found the treat my woman wanted. Halfway along the wall, it dipped in, forming a small bay underwater, split by a vertical chasm. Into this fish swam as if on a highway leading to an unknown inner sanctum. Watching them disappear into the gloom, I could just make out the whiteness of sharp teeth and wondered if I should retrieve my speargun from the dinghy for a pot shot into the dark. But remembering my orders, I went back to snooping under rocks and soon found a lobster right out in the open. Strange, they're nocturnal feeders, and something reminded me of the time I was hunting wild pig in Indonesia. Having shot at, and missed a big boar right on sundown, I had waited up a tree all night hoping the beasts would return. A wait in vain. Buggered and weary, I had no sooner rowed home for a sleep when a village boy swam out, calling "babi" while pointing towards the gardens. Knowing wild pigs only raid crops after dark, I nevertheless rowed in with my double-barrel shotgun and trouped back into the fields to where the young lad pointed. Sure enough, there was a wild boar, a big one, lying down. And like seeing this lobster out in the day, something didn't gel. Loading my gun, I crept closer and was astounded the beast didn't move. Then the penny dropped. Taking my weapon, I strode straight up to the creature and nudged it. It was dead. Obviously hit by my previous night's wild shot.

After this flashed through my head, I boldly swam straight up to the lobster and picked up a perfectly formed moulted shell, complete with legs and antennae. Lobsters, like the other 50,000 known crustaceans, such as crabs and shrimp, cannot enlarge their exoskeletons, their hard outer shells. They are part of the phylum called Arthropoda, Greek for joint and foot, referring to their jointed feet. Land creatures in this phylum include all insects, centipedes, and spiders. Ever pick up what you thought was a dead spider and found just an empty shell? That was probably a moulted exoskeleton, composed of a tough, inflexible substance called chitin that must be moulted as the creature grows.

Knowing more rock lobsters were around, I continued snooping under every ledge, looking in every crack until I found a pair so far in I couldn't reach them. While Jude chased pretty fishes with her camera, I widened my search to the lumpy boulders surrounded by weed further away from the wall. These were a bit deeper, requiring more breath and stronger swimming to search. But nothing is too good for my lady who just that morning had gushed about delicious Lobster Mornay.

After umpteen futile looks, finding only that empty shell and two unreachable critters, I was about out of energy when I dove on a convoluted rock about the size of our dinghy. Finding it split in the middle by a fissure, as I drew near, a collage of green and white armour completely filled the crack. Aghast at such a sight, I went skyward to regain my breath and consider what to do next. Swimming above the boulder, nothing was visible. So I took a large breath and snuck slowly up to the end that contained a low opening. When a metre away, I flattened to the bottom and peered in. My God! A monster lived within. With antennae nearly my entire arm's length, the size of this mutant was hard to judge, except facing me were hundreds of sharp-pointed daggers and two beady eyes as big as black marbles. Could I get a hand round him I pondered as I again rushed for air? Whoosh, chest heaving, I swam around and round getting more uptight as images of the creature pulling me into its lair played silly buggers under my hair. Diving down to determine its actual size, I could only establish it to be nearly my body length, including its antennae. Was it possible to extract something so large from its den? And how much harm could its armour do to mere mortal skin? This had me asking, was I stupid enough to take on such a beast on its home turf?

Like all dangerous tasks, if I can come up with a reasonable plan, one that's not overly risky, I'll be more apt to take it on. Half hoping the beast had taken flight, I submerged again and circumnavigated its chamber. But I found only the one opening and narrow crack. Back up, I decided the only way was a frontal attack; grab the beast across his carapace then pull with all my might. I could always let go, or so I thought.

After steeling courage by taking several deep breaths, I surreptitiously made my assault only to find his antennae up and blocking my way to its body. Swimming about I tried to calm down by looking at other rocks, hoping to find a beast not quite so challenging. While doing this, Jude came by, wondering what all my actions were about. And when I pointed to the boulder, she stole down for a look and came up, eyes bulging, her facemask leaking from a mile-wide smile. And then before she could put the wind up me, I dolphin dived straight for the opening. I'd had enough of mamsy-pamsy thoughts, my dander was up. Me? Scared of a dumb old crustacean? Never!

Reaching its lair, I could see its arm-length antennae spread wide apart and seized the opportunity to reach in behind them up to my shoulder and grabbed hold of its hard shell. It didn't react straight away; an oldie for sure, probably snoozing as grandfathers do during the day. But as I pulled, it reacted. Its tail, now rapidly flapping, crashed my head against the roof of his den while its horribly loud creaks must have been calling a dozen white pointers to attack. Out every opening, sand billowed, shrouding me in darkness. But I wasn't about to release that giant mutant even though I now felt its spikes pierce my leather glove. Jerk, jerk, bash, bash, my head smashed against the rock again and again while I fought for better purchase with my free hand. Oxygen nearly depleted, I stretched and found a grip. Then I heaved with my entire upper body until I'm sure my eyeballs bulged out. Only then did that enormous brute come out, flapping its tail, dragging me through the water by my gloved hand.

How it never got away, beats me. I was too enraged to think past surviving until another lungful of air could be sucked in. Kicking madly I surfaced gasping and spitting out water, but instinctive behaviour had me thrust the beast high into the air. Suddenly, like wheels spinning in mud, the giant creature lost traction, its tail becoming just a noisy castanet.

Sometimes I wonder why I do such crazy things. And after each time I do, I swear never to be blinded again. My plan said I could release the beast, but I forgot my nature. Hindsight is lost and wisdom forgotten when confronted by a jumbo-sized challenge. And I suffered for it. Spidery red rivulets ran down my arm - served me right, I thought.

By the time Jude had rowed us home, the beast was dead. Perhaps through a heart attack as an old man might have when attacked. Remorse filled me. Being mature-aged myself, I appreciate how every moment of life can be cherished even though a daytime nap might be needed. But the deed was done, so I set about preparing him for dinner by first cutting his tail free so it would fit our pot.

Jude had gotten what she'd desired and cooked up a yummy Lobster Mornay that filled the cabin with its sweet cheesy aroma, enough for several meals. But it didn't taste so nice to me. Only half finishing my plate, it seems I'd had enough of that delicacy to last me the rest of my days.

STORMY WEATHER

The Montebello Islands seem to be an ancient coral reef whose skeletal deposits rose from the sea to form the present array of islands. They are limestone, uniformly flat with a vertical edge, and many, like Hermite Island, have peculiar convoluted shapes that wrap around trapping bays only accessible down long twisted passages. Other islands such as Primrose, Carnation, Gardenia, and Kingcup form a chain linked by sunken shallow ridges that also trap bodies of water, none very deep, requiring a good lookout to avoid hitting isolated coral patches. This is in contradiction to what happened close by in the Dampier Archipelago that was formed by inundation from rising seawater.

Late the day after the mutant's death, when still feeling a tad depressed, looking over the same views became too confining, so Jude and I abandoned ship for a trek on Delta Island and were surprised to find that directly behind its narrow fringe, the land did a backflip. Crossing a line, we left sand and started climbing over rough limestone, which at times was both jagged and fragile and covered in part by low spinifex grass and an unknown scrub mainly made up of sharp dry twigs. We picked our way carefully because a foot in a hole causing a fall would have been disastrous. My low spirits began to rise as we gained height, the views changing to what would be expected on an advertisement for paradise lost. After breasting a small hilltop, it all got a whole lot better when one island followed another, separated by glistening pathways reflecting the low silvery sun. No sign of manmade clutter could be seen to alter Nature's magic, and that lifted our spirits to have us soaring with the pair of juvenile sea eagles playing catch-me-if-you-can above our heads.

We traced the backbone of Delta until coming upon the restricted bay we had once hoped to enter with *Banyandah*. Fronting the bay, a field of purple Mulla Mulla shone wagging their tails. And beyond the bay's wind-ruffled fringe, other distant isles fuelled thoughts of a permanent hideaway. Over the next rise, we discovered fields of golden stemmed paper flowers whose buds were more like thousands of tiny silver hairs. And growing next to these were succulents of broad fleshy leaves tipped by flowers with pale purple fingers holding a pitcher pouring pollen into the bud. With good shelter everywhere and plenty of fish, if there had been fresh water, an artist would be happy to live here forever.

Next day, an increasing wind from the southwest persuaded us to linger longer rather than try to move further south. And having explored our Three Beach Bay to the max, we studied the chart, picked up our anchor then moseyed along under easy engine looking for another spot.

Finding a hidey-hole is our forte. One had no beach, the next cove lacked protection, and in this way, we found a cosy nick in an island boxed in by two others. And for the first time, a dozen rows of black buoys from a pearl farm spread out across the quiet enclosed waters. They were not in our way, although our keel may have brushed their mooring lines as we came in.

The wind began to moan that night heralding the onset of strong southerly winds that the bureau had warned would intensify over the next four days. We needed a secure anchorage, one without jagged rocks astern and preferably with a sandy beach to stroll when the wind eased as it often did midmorning. In this part of Western Australia, strong summer winds are generated by severe heat troughs rising from the Pilbara deserts, sucking colder air up from the south. These heat troughs are wind generators similar to those of the Red Sea, which has expansive deserts on both sides of it. Except there the winds blow from the North, straight down the middle of the Red Sea because it's in a trough that's an extension of the Rift Valley. And like here on the Pilbara Coast, the strongest winds come at night after the day's heat has gotten the wind generator going full blast.

Our chart showed good shelter just around the corner in Chartreuse Bay on Alpha Island and thinking we'd have an undemanding trip, we motored out through a gap next to Crocus Island, but straight away ran into a lumpy sea that shoaled unexpectedly. What we thought would be a fun hour wore on to nearly three before we had cleared the last obstacle and were rushing in with the tide between Bluebell and Alpha to enter Chartreuse Bay. And there to our horror, instead of clear open water were thousands upon thousands of black buoys in rows like a field of rotten cabbages. Amongst them lay a factory ship, tall and rectangular like a gigantic houseboat. Our hoped for pretty views turned out just the opposite. The shore was littered with man's discarded debris; mooring ropes, buoys, rusting oil drums and pieces of rusty red steel; every imaginable paraphernalia from an isolated operation. And where we thought we'd find shelter was filled with the company's small boats making the overall scene rather repugnant. Agog, we drifted. Jude taking photos while I studied the chart that indicated another anchorage downwind in the far corner. Alas, this too was filled with more pearl farming floats. Feeling frustrated and a bit annoyed, we dropped anchor near a yellow corner marker to study the area.

There were other islands about. But could we reach them? In addition to the buoys, the area was a minefield of shallows. I thought about asking the locals and put out a call on the VHF, but only heard silence. We were getting desperate now. Staying where we were would be inviting disaster as we were now fully exposed to the south wind where a slip in the night could mean being lost on the spiky rocks just behind us.

Away in the middle of the bay, a centre console alloy craft was touring the lines of buoys, and while we watched, a rooster tail began curling out behind it. When it cleared the farm, instead of heading for the mother ship, it turned in our general direction. As it approached, I was on the foredeck waving my arms trying to grab its attention, and when it slowed, I was surprised to see a family of four, the two children wearing life jackets and diving masks.

"Oi!" I shouted, "It's gonna blow, and I'm in a dangerous spot. Any suggestions about where to park?"

Drifting closely past our bow, a tall beefy lad in his thirties cupped his hands then called out that around the corner was another bay where we could get in close and be well protected. Pointing, he suggested we follow him through a passage found somewhere amongst those nasty rocks behind us. Nice fellow, the manager he said.

Near to where he was pointing, the water was ruffled by current passing over shallow water. Beyond that, I could not see.

"You sure? I need a couple of metres to float." I called back.

Not being positive about the depth, he offered to sound the route then call us on the VHF. A good idea as that area had lots of jagged things poking up, indicating just how suddenly the bottom changed.

Our guidebook showed this end of Alpha Island crosshatched in bright yellow, indicating it had been another nuclear weapon testing site. And although this weighed on our thoughts, the approaching storm was a more pressing worry than long-lasting Strontium 90. So, when he radioed the all clear, we came running after.

True to his word, the little bay had sufficient depth to get nicely close to a beach. Better still, the island wrapped around blocking out winds from west to east through the south, but left the pretty Montebello lagoon open at our back. Around us ran short grey walls, pockmarked and housing many small caves that made its entire surface very jagged. While directly in front lay a suntanned beach at the base of a low scruffy hill.

Before the heavy weather set in, Jude and I took the opportunity to witness the bombsite that lay just around the corner in Burgundy Bay, where our guidebook showed a bright yellow circle indicating ground zero for the most massive atomic device ever detonated in Australia. Not shown on that diagram, but immediately apparent upon rounding the corner, was another vast field of black buoys, forcing us to lift our outboard to pass over the submerged restraining ropes that ran to strong points onshore.

Up a sandy shore ran a series of rusty stumps like rotten teeth; all that is left of the pier used to transport the bomb. Trudging uphill from them, we eventually came upon a rough concrete obelisk with a spider web of hairline cracks and crude lettering on all four sides warning of radiation that made it unsafe for permanent occupation; along with details of the 1956 British detonation above this very spot. The mere reading of the words gave Jude and me the willies and had us thinking Mankind is no more intelligent than sheep. Our planet seems nearly indestructible and looking at it from space, it appears perfect. Yep, perfect for life. In fact, the only place perfect for life as far as we know. The rest of the universe is too hot, too cold, or too poisonous. Yet man dabbles with his perfect home.

Today, all the talk about global warming being the world's biggest problem isn't entirely true; it's only an indicator of humanity's devastating impact. Surely we must immediately begin to reduce our footprint and put Earth First. Otherwise, even if you do not give a damn about the other creatures, there'll be nowhere to go after we muck up the planet.

Storm winds started blowing just after we climbed back on board, and by nightfall, scudding clouds were racing overhead. Jude put together a veggie curry as we'd not been able to fish, and after finishing that, we tried to escape the shrieks and jerking on our anchor by hunkering down with our books. But there was far too much noise and commotion to get past rereading the same line again and again, so I chucked it in. And thinking of bed, I went on deck to check the chafe on our snubber.

A ship dances wildly to the wail of a storm and the constant jerking on her chain can pull an anchor out, so we use a four-metre length of stretchy nylon rope called a snubber to transfer the load of the ship to our anchor chain. This can rub on the boat and could chafe through even when protected by hose, leather, or thick cloth, so it has to be looked at and adjusted from time to time.

Trying to get forward against those blasts from the starry heavens forced me to crouch low and pull myself forward from stanchion to stanchion. A Banshee's wail surrounded me in darkness when I bent to check the wraps of cloth, then windblown spray drenched me in one of those unenviable moments rarely mentioned in glossy sailing magazines. Satisfied the snubber would not chafe through in the night, I then verified for the thousandth time that the flashes from the Northwest Island lighthouse still lined up with the shadow of Gardenia Island.

After that, I got blown back and called down to Jude, "Honey, that's all I can do. How about we go to bed?"

Getting our day clothes off in the close confines of the aft cabin, Jude had to grab onto me every time a blast hit us side on and tilted us over like on an amusement ride. The rigging shrieked, our awning flapped noisily, and the sea slapped the hull next to our heads. The resulting din kept me from falling to sleep until finally, I screamed, "Enough! It's impossible. C'mon Babe, let's get that awning down." Rising from near slumber, Jude mumbled an expletive.

House folk may need to get up to close a window in a storm, but on a boat, we are called to do battle. Clothed in little more than what Nature bestowed on us at birth while struggling to roll up an awning covering half the deck, Jude and I fought invisible forces that tried to tear it from our grip. At every fastening point, we had to shout instructions to the other or risk having the awning whipped away against the aft tower, possibly shattering the solar cells. Or worse, the awning's alloy tube could make a mess of our faces.

It seemed so much quieter after our breathing settled once back in bed that I only had to put the occasional shriek out my head to fall into a light slumber. Thankfully, Jude sleeps even lighter than I. Several times during the night, her movements roused me, and I would see her at the window with the Northwest Island light flashing across her face, checking *Banyandah's* position. Reassured that we were safe in her hands, I relaxed into a deeper sleep.

Sometime before first light, the worst had passed, and during longer quiet spells, Jude fell into a deep sleep. When shafts of a yellow sun cresting Alpha Island got me up, an immediate surge of relief ran through me. *Banyandah* had stayed anchored in the same spot. Weathering a big blow without shifting is reassuring in that we know she will take that much again, hopefully making the next time easier to relax.

And there was a next time. The storm winds from the south went on for four days. In a cycle we came to know intimately, in the mornings around nine was the best time for leaving the boat to stretch our legs. First along the shore in front of us, then the next day we chanced further afield to a hill overlooking Chartreuse Bay where peeking over the crest, battalions of white soldiers were attacking the black buoys next to our first anchorage. Quite happily, we went home to our safe little hideaway after that.

Finally, the weatherman reported a change coming on Friday, and even though it's a bad omen to sail on a Friday when the wind eased to a gentle breeze that backed round to the east, we hurriedly started packing the boat. Diving gear still lay behind the aft cabin with weight belts holding it down, and seashells sat next to the compass where we could pick them up to admire as we passed. Fishing lines rested in a pile on the starboard cockpit seat, while down below was a mess. Reference and reading books were strewn about the chart table and settee, plus the laptop, logbook and diaries stood open on the seat next to the galley.

Because everything on *Banyandah* has a storage spot, in quick time we were nearly ready for sea. Lifting the outboard, storing its fuel tank, and then hauling on board Little Red were the last chores because rolling up the awning and lashing it to the foredeck had already been done. Taking less than an hour, by the time the ship's clock struck three bells at nine-thirty, we were ready for a new destination.

Our anchorage behind Alpha lay far away from all three exits. We'd come in through South Channel, but we were going to exit through the southwest passage which is just a slight nick in the barrier reef accessed after crossing many miles of shallow flats.

No matter how many miles have passed under our keel, I sometimes get butterflies before setting off. I didn't before, at least not during the last half of our sailing life. Jude's always had nerves of steel and only gets uptight if she sees me get twitchy. So, to keep my nerves under control I follow a systematic regime of checking valves, ropes, making sure everything's secure, then start the engine. After doing this, I took a slow look round to record images that must last a lifetime, and when satisfied, I walked forward to the anchor winch and turned to Jude at the helm.

"OK Babe, let's go. Let's see how far the anchor's dug in."

Expertly Jude drove towards the anchor following my hand signals that indicate the lay of the chain as the winch hauls it in. Translucent blue sea, lightly tanned sand and blue-grey limestone seemed to jump through the sharp air now cleansed of the sea mist we'd endured during the storm. With a final grunt from the winch, our plough came up drifting a plume of sand pulled out the bottom. And once it had clanged home, I faced Jude and pointed towards ground zero bay.

"Stay in close. Let's try to sneak around that pearl lease and into the channel leading past Crocus Island."

Upon hearing this, her eyebrows shot up because she hadn't thought I'd chance to thread the reefs and buoys. And this pleased her.

Free to wander after the storm, the morning took on a sereneness like the timelessness of a photograph where everything is bright and beautiful. If we could have suspended life at that moment, be satisfied to end our days surrounded by this peace, would we? No, we would not. A new journey lay ahead, and though I was on edge, life for us is to explore and witness.

I'm not really sure how we cleared the ropes holding the nets in ground zero bay. They jumped out the murk leaving only time to pray they'd not foul our prop while twice Jude banged her out of gear to stop it turning. But once over them, it was an easy run past Crocus and through the narrow gap into the windward shallows that had caused us so much grief before the storm had struck. This time, instead of turning right, Jude took us on a bearing I'd derived off the GPS that would take us across a span of aquamarine to a distant speck near the group's southwestern exit.

Everything was going swimmingly. The widening vista had unscrambled my guts, and I was swaggering aft from my lookout when an unexpected smattering of rocks suddenly set the low water alarm screeching. Not hearing it, I was stunned to see Jude abruptly turning the wheel to go about. Oh, those devils! Popping up when we had less than a metre under our keel further whitened my beard and forced me to quickly jump back on the front rail to keep a lookout.

Passageways through outer barriers can be just about anything; deep and clear, or shallow with patches of silted sand, or they may have coral heads that become dangerous when heavy weather blows directly onto them as in this case. Approaching this one, we could see the open sea ahead, but on both sides, substantial white breakers added confusion to the wash that tossed us about like a toy boat in a bathtub. Adrenalin flowed, our heartbeats quickened, and I held my breath between each curly set, fearing what might happen if the engine should quit. Especially as there was barely enough wind for steerage now that the storm had passed. At the height of all this, our exit was further complicated by a silly ol' fish deciding our silver lure looked good for its breakfast.

"Just keep her straight and steady," I said and started aft for the taut line.

Jude glories in these moments and was utterly aglow with excitement as I rushed past. Grabbing me by my leg, she almost tripped me into the cockpit and was about to get a blast when I turned and saw her upturned lips begging a quick kiss. Beyond her, my gaze went past destructive ocean breakers to a peaceful faraway horizon, so I shrugged. Why not enjoy this wondrous life, and instead of giving her a quick peck, my arms embraced my darling wife. *Banyandah* knew the drill and kept on track while we took a few moments to savour our good life.

Then we were out, popping our headsail after hauling aboard a small Spanish mackerel that had been hoodwinked by a shiny piece of metal. As my pulse slowed, two oilrigs were sighted ahead belching fire while our spread of white sail slowly but steadily made straight for them.

Free of immediate danger, now all we had to worry about were those critters we'd dined on, and wonder if we'd set a Geiger counter clacking.

HAVE SAILS – WILL TRAVEL

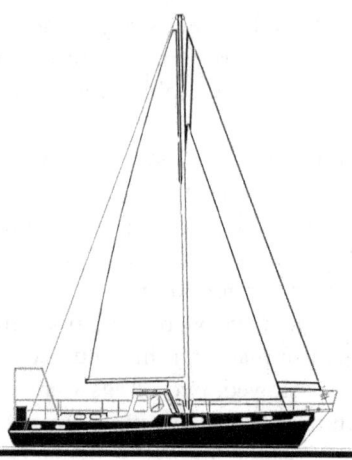

What began as a heavenly romp across a blue sea finished a real tester. We had successfully slipped out through a crack in the barrier reef guarding the Montebello Islands, in the fridge was a two meal fish, and a growing breeze was now sending us towards a God-forsaken monster standing abruptly out the sea, belching fire just a few miles ahead. Jude was in heaven. Like a magpie on a bright spring morning, she was chortling non-stop.

"How good was that! Cleared it easily. Hi-yah! Fair wind. Thanks for that, Jack. I had a wonderful time."

On and on she chirped, while I walked about trimming sails, checking gear, and looking ahead. Once Judith relinquished the wheel, I engaged Mr Aries to take over the mundane task of maintaining our course southwest towards... Well, who knew where? It would only be as far as the wind would take us. That could be Exmouth, a hundred miles ahead, or maybe one of the off-lying islands before that. But, if we got lucky, we might sail a greater distance on this fair breeze before it turned nasty. Where to? We just didn't know. But at the moment, all was bliss, except for the steel monster ahead coughing up black smoke as if clearing its throat before belching out more flames.

After passing that oilrig, in approaching darkness, a new one emerged from the sea ahead. With glaring yellow lights, from afar, it looked like a gigantic naked light bulb. Jude needed to be rested for her night watch and was getting ready for bed when our mobile phone found a tower during our free phone hour just after six. Oh, what a lovely figure she cut against the gold and crimson sunset that also played upon her animated lips as she spoke into the device. Transported by that little technological marvel from the glorious wild ocean to Jerome's living room and through his speakerphone to the grandkids, I could hear her excited voice describing the light bulb dragon, and how we had to dodge them or risk being eating by fire monsters. And I joined them in their laughter at grandma's unusual bedtime story.

The hours dragged on while the wind grew lighter, until when finally abreast the brightly lit steel-city, it died completely and left us wallowing while I watched the furious activity on the oil platform. One derrick was lifting long pipes while another unloaded a supply tender, and like an anthill that had just been given a good kick, workers were swarming on every level. A few minutes of that was enough. I would rather hear the sound of our engine than drift amongst glary yellow lights, so I hit the start button and turned *Banyandah* southwest.

By nine o'clock next morning, we had logged 100 nm in the first 24 hours and were reaching under a perfect twelve-knot wind that had me pinching myself every hour I wrote up the log. Around eleven, Jude popped out of bed into sunshine unhindered by even one speck of cloud. We shared a brewed coffee while sightseeing at not just one oilrig, but two. The first, a strange-looking contraption, was a ship with a drilling rig stuck on its nose like a dead mosquito with its proboscis pointing skyward.

Late that afternoon, I went to check the engine oil level, expecting another five litres lost as we had used the engine for six hours since topping it up. So you can imagine my glee when the dipstick came up with oil still covering the FULL mark. I almost shouted. But didn't, fearing I had missed something. Crouched over the engine with a torch, I held up the dipstick looking for water droplets thinking a blown head gasket might have let cooling water into the sump. But the oil looked clean. And shining the torch into the drip tray revealed only the small amount left from my oil change.

Sailors of wind must fill in many idle hours as their craft runs down the miles. If they can't, they will soon leave the business. But for those of us who love the unique combination of open spaces and nearness to the essential elements of life, for those who cherish having the free time to let their mind wander over thoughts too quickly stored in the past, passage making are the finest hours. Some wind sailors go around the world non-stop; some go around two and three times without ever pulling into port. They are not alone out there. Nature surrounds them everywhere they go and wildlife often accompanies them. During our afternoon hours, thick flocks of Wedge-tails chased baitfish that seemed to be following *Banyandah*, thrilling us with splendid displays of power-diving. Later, in the early evening when the sun paved a highway of molten gold from the horizon to us, we looked down that golden highway towards the land but saw nothing except blue upon blue separated by a smudge of cotton that told us the famed North West Cape lay below it.

The first recorded landing upon North West Cape happened in 1618 when the Dutch Captain Jacobsz of the *Mauritius* went ashore. When Lt. King visited in 1818, he named the large gulf to its east Exmouth after a Royal Naval Officer. Not much more happened until 1964 when an agreement between Australia and the USA created a joint naval base near the tip of the cape, which established the town of Exmouth.

Part of the phenomena surrounding this peninsula that juts out into the Indian Ocean by some thirty miles is that the continental shelf plunges into deep water quite close to its tip. The shelf becomes even narrower near Jurabi Head where the seabed drops thousands of metres just a few miles offshore. At Jurabi Head, the famous Ningaloo Reef begins; the world's largest fringing reef. It threads south close to shore for some 150 nm, protecting a ribbon of interconnected lagoons that provide a breeding ground for literally billions of fish, more than 550 species, with another 200 different types of corals.

Running south along this coast is a current of warm tropical waters called the Leeuwin Current that brings microscopic creatures known as zooplankton that attract whale sharks, the world's biggest fish that can reach 12.5 m and weight more than 21.5 tonnes. School fish also feed on the zooplankton and they, in turn, attract large numbers of pelagic fish including the larger game fish. The king of all game fish, the black marlin, and its cousin the blue marlin, roam here in the early months of the year. Other billfish like swordfish, sailfish, and broadbill also frequent these waters, as well as the good fighting mahi-mahi, wahoo, and Spanish mackerel.

What makes the wind come from one direction and not another? Meteorologists will say high-pressure systems rotate clockwise in the northern hemisphere, counter-clockwise in the southern, and that air flows outwards, towards lows pressure cells where the air spirals up into higher altitudes. But what makes one wind stop and another begin? And why, when there's a lovely breeze from the north, does it suddenly stop and be replaced a moment later by another coming from the opposite direction?

At midnight, as if Cinderella had heard the striking of the hour, our wind changed from a friendly one ushering us peacefully towards our destination, to a colder, not-so-nice southerly that forced us to harden up the sails and lay off until *Banyandah* pointed towards land. It was a gentle beast, but a beast nonetheless because we knew winds from this direction can become savage. So, after turning the watch over to Jude, I lay in my bunk listening for it to increase and sleep eluded me. Every extra puff seemed the starting signal that would send me on deck to fight the beast. Sometime during the night, I worried myself to sleep and didn't know much until a torch began flashing across my eyes. Forcing them open, I was blinded by the sun rocking across the doorway.

Rising from the cabin, instead of white soldiers rushing down upon us, *Banyandah* silently cut through a calm blue sea, her sails skin tight, reflecting the new sun's golden light. Looking towards land, I saw it clear, indisputable, though still some distance away. Jude kissed my cheek, handed me a brewed coffee and my concerns evaporated in the warm morning light.

After she slipped off to bed, conditions eased until I thought it would be foolish not to make faster miles south while we could. So I started the diesel, ran the fridge, and charged batteries while we clocked a steady five knots towards our next destination. But where was that? A bit of chart work revealed that, what at first looked a multitude of possible anchorages was in fact rather barren of safe havens for south winds until the next major port of Carnarvon, 160 nm ahead. Oh, there were numerous anchorages behind Ningaloo Reef, which in winter would have been heaven with the wind off the land. But in this season, south-westerlies whip up mighty swells making this entire west coast a lee shore. Even going close could be dangerous. However, there was one possibility according to the guidebook. A desperation anchorage hiding close under 60 m high cliffs behind Cape Cuvier, where according to the write-up, rolling swells would steal round the point to attack us. But none of this was pertinent. It was a beautiful Sunday morning.

We nearly always troll a fishing lure when sailing during daylight hours. In the past, we also dragged them through the night, but too many lures were taken by Noahs even after we devised a simple alarm, an empty tin that fell to deck whenever we had a strike.

Whether then or now our setup has always been a simple handline. Attach the lure by a few metres of stout wire trace to a swivel then 50 m of 100 kg tested mono-filament that's attached by another swivel to nearly 100 m of small-diameter braided sash cord, which makes the initial haul-in a little easier on our hands. The boat end is attached to a strong Ocky strap that's held in a bight of line that lets it stretch to its maximum length without breaking. Seeing how far it stretches is something like watching it weigh the fish. A normal-sized fish usually just takes the catenary out the line, but on this bright Sunday morn, while motoring across some of the world's best fishing ground, walking aft to our tower, I saw our Ocky strap bowstring tight and the trolling line singing.

Shocked, I jumped back shouting, "Hey Jude. Oi! Come quick. We've just hooked a monster!"

We didn't go near it. Any second the line could snap and flick back into an eye.

"It's stretched tighter than when we hooked that fertilizer sack," I said, reminding Jude of the time we hooked a big plastic fertiliser bag that nearly stopped our boat when it popped open. Just to be sure it wasn't another bag, I cautiously approached and tested its tautness, and then tiptoed back saying, "It's a real monster. Let's drag it for awhile and hope it gets free."

So we did with the white line a tightrope you could walk on. For the next couple of miles we took turns searching the sea behind us with the glasses, but the sparkling sea hid our monster. Then in the briefest second, it suddenly rose close enough to the surface for me to see a sleek dark body and long bill, which sent me racing for our video camera and calling, "It's a marlin or sailfish!"

Once when leaving Cocos Keeling with a similar fishing rig we hooked a two or three hundred kilo black marlin. In those days *Banyandah* had two masts and we used to attach the trolling line to the smaller mast's support wires, but stopped doing that after that black marlin nearly pulled it over. These days we attach the trolling gear to our new stout tower.

For a good twenty minutes, the video recorded a rather boring scene of blue sea and bowstring line, which eventually had me giving it a few serious jerks to wake the fellah up. But whoever was on the line was happy to tag-along, sometimes racing to one side or the other. Not once did it jump free of the sea, so we shut down the recorder and simply waited. And so did our monster, for another good hour. Completely bored now, I took matters in hand. Damn! I hate getting sucked into battling big fish.

Jude was assigned the all-important task of head camerawoman in addition to her regular duty, which was to keep the gathered line away from my body in case the beast makes a run I can't turn. With a serious face, she uttered a few words of encouragement then followed that up with a stern warning to be careful. Nodding I would, I took hold of the braided sash cord and started hauling. Once started, I try to keep it coming. Slacken off and the beast might turn and run. The idea is to force the creature up to the surface where its powerful tail is less efficient. Steadily, hand over hand, using the strength in my arms I pulled, all the time dreading the beast might run. But it didn't. So I kept yelling, "Come on! Tail-walk you crazy fish! Throw the hook!"

When just a boat length astern, this most magnificent creature was seen gliding effortlessly through the water with its iridescent blue sail fully extended. Only when almost close enough to touch did the creature finally jumped out the water like an excited puppy on a short leash. That's when its flashing tail splashed the sea's surface and its noble head shook in a last ditch effort to throw the hook. Oh, how we wished to see it flung free, but we did not, and the beast fell back exhausted, to be towed on its side while we wondered what to do next.

"Put that camera down! Now!" I shouted at Jude, no longer able to keep the worry out my voice. "And get the biggest pliers quick!"

Meanwhile my eyes are glued on the beast, expecting any moment to see it come alive and take a run. Instead, our eyes made contact and our minds interacted, and in my head I am sure I heard it say it would wait. Jude returned with my water pump pliers, and without hesitation, I leant over the rail and grabbed the bugger by his sword. God! He was as big as me and so much more powerful. But looking again into its eyes, I think this guy had been through this before. They were staring at me and seemed to be saying, "Okay, let's get this over. Stick your tag into me and I'll be on my way."

Fine by me. A cooperative beast. Sure made my job of reaching into its jaws and twisting out the hook a whole lot easier. After quickly checking that Jude had the camera whirling, I released its sword and was delighted to see a huge splash. And with a quick swish of its tail, the creature flashed away.

We'd had lots of excitement, plenty of photos, but no fish. So Jude convinced me to put the lure out again. I must have rocks in my head because an hour later we had the same scenario. Another taut line dragging a very boisterous tenant who might have been a bit smaller. Nevertheless, we dragged it for a half-hour because I was still recovering from my last battle. Eventually, there was another hand-over-hand tussle, this time a shiny, slippery, stinky barracuda hit the deck. It's a fish we absolutely detest. This one broke free upon hitting the deck, went berserk, snapping its dagger teeth until sent over the side.

Now Jude, she's a vixen, put on her prettiest face, cuddled me, and massaged my sagging arms, and, well, I put the lure out a third time. Fortunately, nothing happened. Not straight away. Not till about four when the sun was heading for Africa did we hear the plastic spool clunk against the tower. I let out a moan, feeling decidedly weak. I would have settled for a steaming bowl of pasta, but being a good sailor boy and a slave to my woman, I took up my station back aft and tested the line. You know, you can feel the brute shake its head when trying to throw the hook, and feeling that sent adrenalin through me. A fight hey! You want to take me on? Okay, try it. So I pulled. And it fought. And I pulled some more using my shoulders and the strength in my back, which was about all I had left. Fifteen minutes later, the bell ending round ten sounded and a 20 kg wahoo was heaved alongside where Jude ripped into it with the gaff. The two of us then struggled to bring a wiggling twitching monster up over the railing. All of a sudden, we had more fish than we could eat in a week. And that called for a cold beer before the bigger job of carving it up. No wonder I nearly dozed off on my watch.

The next day at noon, the wind found its strength. I don't know why just then, maybe it thought we'd had it too easy. Earlier that morning our log had tripped over 4000 nm since Ballina and shortly after that the wind came with a vengeance. By 3 pm, we were down to a one spot Genoa with *Banyandah* working hard on a tack back towards land. When darkness started closing in for our third night at sea, the wind increased even more, sending lines of white soldiers crashing onto our foredeck. By eight, when most folk are cuddled in front of the telly, I was urging Jude out her bed. It was time for me to brave the deck, fight the beast and reef the mainsail to prevent us spending the night watching the underwater world through our portholes. The real problem with storm winds is that they never know when to quit. Such jarring horrible motion, when I again got her out of bed at midnight, she had not slept a bit.

I was buggered. And like Jude, I couldn't sleep with such a cacophony of noise and motion that one moment buried my face, the next tossed me airborne; all the time worrying the mast would not stay up. Jude wrote at 3 am, "have only made a measly nine miles good in the last six hours." Oh, she's good at coming up with figures that inspire. Like her other note at 5 am stating we still had ten miles to go before reaching Cape Cuvier. Great! With luck, we might reach it by noon. That is unless the sails tear away!

Sailors love the rising sun. It not only brings warmth to their tired bodies, it shows them that they are still afloat, and there is hope. Hope the weather will improve. Hope they won't hit something they wouldn't have seen in the dark. And hope that they might actually survive another day at sea. So it was, with hope, that my tired body watched the porthole lighten with the first shreds of light. I hadn't slept. I may have dozed, although my mind said I'd heard every shriek, felt every wave, and worried every time *Banyandah* creaked, groaned, squealed, and shuddered.

I rose with the dawn and instantly felt reinvigorated. What a glorious sight to see shafts of yellow sun soaring above the cliffs of Australia. This last tack was taking us back towards shore and we were rewarded by spying a few miles ahead, pyramids of white salt and bright gypsum atop tangerine cliffs, a bit like carrot cake with icing. And so, after my zombie wife went to bed, I didn't hesitate, but immediately started motor sailing as straight as I could for the anchorage below Cape Cuvier.

It was bliss when the headland started offering protection. Somehow, the horrible memories of the night faded as the seas diminished while I sat spellbound on our aft box watching the cliffs rise in height. Cape Cuvier is impressive. Named by French explorer Nicolas Baudin to honour his zoologist Georges Cuvier, the cliffs are not weathered smooth but appear as if God only ripped them apart yesterday.

Jude got up after we'd motored a couple hours and together we steered past a loading structure made from welded pipe that ran out into deep water. Huge mooring buoys strategically placed around it were rising and falling with the swell. Not until close to the cliffs did we find acceptable anchoring depth, and here the swell struck us side-on before curling into foaming white combers that broke halfway to the cliffs. We were quite alone for the port was deserted except for a lone figure looking down from the cliff top, but there was one plus. We were protected from the wind.

The big swells breaking against the cliff face sent shudders up my spine. There's so much that can go wrong and hardly enough time to take action when it does. So I let us drift while Jude made a brew. Minutes later while sipping the coffee, I gazed at Jude and saw a shadow of the woman I have always had alongside and wondered if it was fair to take her out into the wild seas again. Maybe we should chance a day and night resting here.

Our limited experience with the local wind patterns said this was the start of a new system. It would stay light till noon then come in reinforced with the afternoon onshore wind and then blow heavily through the night and be worse the next day. And so, staying there hanging by the skin on our teeth, with Jude getting up every few minutes in the night to check our position by the jetty lights was an alarming prospect.

Tired decisions come reluctantly and that is when instinct takes over. Mine have served me well, so after another quick look at those cliffs and watching yet another comber crash into them, I turned to Jude. "Hey Babe, let's give this place the flick and while it's quiet, try motoring straight into the wind. We'll soon be getting some protection from Shark Bay. At worse, we can always turn back."

When older, our eyes sag from the weight of all we have seen, and when tired this drags them down even more. Yet Judith's, upon hearing my words, took on a renewed sparkle as if a challenge had been thrown down and that pert smile I love so dearly popped out.

"Okay," she said, "I'm ready. I just need to go pee."

Back up went the mainsail, which we pulled in tight. Then under engine, we drove close around the loading facility imagining the mighty seas bombarding this structure during cyclones. After rounding the point, the oncoming swells were steady, but maybe a bit calmer than before, so I opened the throttle and steered straight into them. And for a while, we went forward, albeit slowly; the sort of speed we'd be doing under sail, except now we were tracking straight towards our destination.

Ahead lay a stretch of treacherous coastline. Indian Ocean swells attack it directly and there are no chinks to seek shelter in, no headlands to hide behind. That rock coast runs twenty nautical miles south to Point Quobba and it is there that Shark Bay begins. Protected by a string of offshore islands, we hoped to see the ocean swell diminish there.

All was well for an hour then trouble came from an unexpected quarter. The engine overheated. Never had that happen before. Cooling water was still coming out the exhaust, but with a rocky lee shore close aboard this was not the time for a thorough investigation. So we shut down the engine and without much ado, unfurled the headsail, and began widening the gap between that treacherous shore and us.

An hour later, the engine now cooled, I was doing my Houdini routine squeezing into the engine room. My mission to take apart the seawater strainer. I suspected a partial blockage, but all I found were a few bits of sea grass in it. Still perplexed, I refilled the freshwater side of the heat exchanger, and started motoring again. And all was super fine for another hour, then that temperature gauge started rising again and we had to shut down once more. With cooling water hissing out the heat exchanger that meant a more serious problem; one not easily fixed while thrashing about in a nasty sea. So out came the headsail yet again, and we settled into the smash and bash, clawing our way into moderately heavy seas. No thoughts of turning back ever entered our heads.

Of course, the wind gods got angrier as the day wore on. But balancing that, with each hour we gained a little more protection from the chain of islands that lay more than 50 nm offshore on the seaward edge of Shark Bay.

Shark Bay is another world phenomenon we keenly looked forward to explore, but at that moment, its only feature interesting us was its protection. And, as the day wore on and the winds increased, the swell slamming into us lost height and power. So, by nightfall, when our GPS showed we had just sixteen miles to go to the Carnarvon fairway buoy, we knew we'd arrive there before daybreak.

When darkness had overtaken us, we were so tired, Jude crashed into bed, after which, bleary-eyed me lay down on the settee to stare into a naked light bulb to try to remain awake. In a dream like trance and no more than a dead lump of blubber rolling with the ship, a symphony of squeaks and shrills began to enter my head. I knew those sounds. But what were they. Was I asleep? No I could still hear the clock ticking. Whales! There are whales about. I bolted for the doorway and emerged into a cave like blackness to search the windy ether. Sploosh - My reward was a drenching by a white soldier crashing on deck. But there ahead I saw the faint loom of Carnarvon's town lights. Hallelujah!

At midnight, when hardly more than a walking zombie myself, Jude and I hove-to in a much calmer sea. We rolled up the headsail, lashed the helm, and sat there just five miles from our waypoint with fifteen metres under our ship. That was far enough until daylight. Carnarvon looked a small port from the chart, shallow and tricky, and not one to attempt with a flat lined brain. So I flopped down into oblivion.

A long-distance runner, when most tired at the end of his race, has only to break the tape to be a winner. An ocean-going cargo captain, after a hard passage, hands his ship over to a pilot. But wind sailors do not have it that easy. To reach safety, we must conquer all - no matter how buggered the voyage has made us. As we rounded the last corner leading into the Fascine, which is a Latin word describing bundles of sticks placed along the foreshore to help prevent erosion and the name for the bay formed by the south arm of the Gascoyne River, we saw a hodgepodge of beacons marking the narrow channel through drying sand flats that leads to Carnarvon's town centre. Some were no more than sticks, while others sprouted very fancy cardinal marks. But, they all said the same thing, go the wrong side and you will be aground.

I damn near mucked up the first mark simply by refusing to believe we could take our ship within spitting distance of such a long sand-spit. But after that, it got better. When approaching large shallow basins, sometimes it's better to arrive at low water when the majority of it is vacant dry land and only the channel has water in it. All we needed to do was keep to the centre and go slow. Then, if we hit bottom, we'd not stick.

We had been looking forward to reaching Carnarvon since first reading that 70% of Western Australia's produce grows there. Every picture we saw showed it green with wide thoroughfares, beautiful gardens, and lovely river views. Our guidebook even mentioned a special swinging basin for visiting yachts right off the clubhouse. And so, for months we had been imaging *Banyandah* swinging on the breeze, a red sunset behind her while we laughed, told stories, and soared through yachtie heaven on the yacht club balcony. The reality was quite different.

We somehow managed not to run aground traversing the several miles of shallow flats, a minor miracle that. And found the yacht club building, rather low-rent like all the rest we could see. But the real disappointment hit when we tried to find the swinging basin touted in the guidebook. But instead, we kept running aground the moment we left the channel. Hmm, that wouldn't do. Adding to our problem, there was no one in sight and the chappie at the Volunteer Coastal Patrol that I talked to on the VHF couldn't provide any clues. So we anchored right in the middle of the channel between a pair of red and green beacons, and then I set off in Little Red. First to the yacht club, where the dinghy ran aground thirty metres out. I walked around the nondescript one story building, it was locked. Opening hours: Friday night. No balcony. No bar. My dream just flew out my head. Next stop, after re-floating the dinghy, was their marina. Gosh, what a narrow channel to enter what was hardly more than a giant birdbath dug out the earth. Sighting mostly poor-man boats like mine, at last I noticed movement and raced over to a fellow climbing aboard a steel yacht of our size, and put a question to him.

"Oi! Where do visitors park round here?"

With a bemused smile, the big guy gave me a quick rundown. "It's either the marina or the Fascine."

"But I'm blocking the channel," I protested.

And his reaction was a shrug, saying, "There's no traffic."

Then he suggested we anchor off the town jetty where we'd find more swinging room. Twenty minutes later, Jude and I were sounding a basin just off a short timber jetty along the town's esplanade. With a strong wind now up our bum and water more like chocolate than Ovaltine, the task of finding sufficient swinging room without running aground had my armpits dripping. And that had me dumping the anchor thinking we'd sound more in the morning.

After killing the engine, it became so quiet and peaceful, *Banyandah* sat motionless. Until that moment, we'd not fully appreciated the strain that the noise and motion had put on us. With that huge weight lifted, we seemed to float above the deck. And everywhere seemed so fascinating now that the endless sea had been replaced by cars flashing past and little ones laughing in the park. Even a woman unloading shopping from her car proved mesmerising. For the rest of the day, we sat gobsmacked, totally absorbed by the little community our vessel had taken us to. And well before the watery sun found its way below some grey clouds, the impact of our achievement started sinking in. We had done it. We were in Carnarvon with another large chunk of Aussie coastline in our logbook. Before us was at least a month off duty touring plantations, sampling the state's finest produce, and delving further into our mysterious oil leak, and now, our overheating problems - that is if we could find a way into that marina.

It seemed fitting the celebratory cask of red wine should come out. Just a short one at first to toast our good fortune. Then another to toast our stout homemade craft. And then another top-up when our free phone hour was upon us. And a wee bit more while we boasted our good fortune to family and friends. And more had to be guzzled upon hearing their relief for our safety. And so, by dinnertime when the shore lights came on, we were well awash and feeling rather frisky. Who needed sustenance when good ol' Aussie red warms your belly, so we toddled off to bed.

We slept as if buried six feet under. Except when my wee bladder needed relief around 4 am. Even then, I was on automatic. Next I knew bright sunshine was burning holes through my eye sockets and taking out the back of me head. Oh, I groaned, and rolled over to sit up. But instead found myself wallowing on the floor. God! Maybe I shouldn't celebrate so much. The floor's tilting. Tilting! Oh, my God, we're aground!

Jumping up to the cockpit, everything was out of kilter. Christ! We had already fallen over ten degrees and the tidal stream is still going out. Uh oh, as Forrest Gump would have said, "Shit happens…"

CARNARVON DREAMING

When sailing past North West Cape, a milestone had been achieved. *Banyandah* had left behind the iron rich Pilbara district and had entered the state's agriculture heartland centred on the Gascoyne River. And how had we rewarded our stalwart craft for this achievement? Hah! By unwittingly parking her where the night breeze would set her into the shallows. Where, as we slept, she had taken the bottom while the tide ran towards another part of the planet. We had been afloat at first light when I had been on deck relieving myself, but upon waking at seven, I fell out of bed with *Banyandah* tilted over more than ten degrees and destined to fall farther.

My bleary-eyed attempt to winch her into deeper water achieved zero movement, even with the engine at full speed ahead. Sorry Miss B. Very sorry indeed when reading the next high tide would not be as high as the previous night's. Crikey! We might not float off at all!

The town was awakening to a slightly chilled dawn and a handful of early morning canine walkers and exercise aficionados had already gathered on the esplanade to discuss our predicament. There was no sniggering, no finger pointing, just a bit of chin rubbing as if they'd seen this before and were debating whether we'd fall over as much as the last foolish sailor.

Launching Little Red, Jude and I sounded the surrounding area while taking photos of course. Using a chunk of metal tied to a knotted string, we discovered the channel shelved suddenly and that a couple metres more towards the timber jetty would have saved us. But as we were nearer the other shore, our rudder and keel were well planted in mud. They didn't seem stressed, so with little else to do, we went home for a bowl of cereal, eaten while sitting on the cockpit floor leaning back as if in recliners.

About nine that morning, and now canted over twenty-five degrees, up to us putt-putted a strange looking craft, a bit like one of those small catamarans hired from a resort beach. Sitting regally at the back on what looked a park bench was an elderly man dressed in a wide open shirt, torn shorts, and a stained, rather faded blue captain's cap pulled down so hard that his bushy sideburns were forced out. Steering a tiny outboard, this aberration encircled us, much like an English Lord inspecting his serfs, then looking up, he commented dryly, "You missed the channel."

Ignoring Jude's wave and my "How you going," Captain Bill as we came to know him then turned about and chugged back to the marina.

In the first hour after noon, *Banyandah* had risen to just a five-degree list, so I again started the engine to retry getting off. Foolishly, my efforts only churned

up the bottom, and probably shortened the life of our stern bearing spinning in the silt. Counselling myself to be patient, I was rewarded half an hour later when, by just pulling in some chain our baby slid forward into deeper water.

The wind was now blowing strongly, complicating our repositioning more centrally in the channel. So to be sure we'd not ground again I rowed out a second anchor, setting it astern. After that frazzled start, we rowed to the jetty so Jude could walk to town to replenish our tucker box, which left me pacing up and down the shore, stretching my sea-legs while keeping an eye on our dinghy. Three local kids swimming off the jetty were showing a keen interest in it.

Carnarvon town did not look well to do. The houses along the esplanade were just a cut above shanties, with some newer, more deluxe houses scattered in-between. Away from the jetty, down near a park, the roads had neither curbs nor sidewalks, and outside were some rather tired looking autos.

Our second night passed with considerably less celebrations, just a lovely meal featuring fresh veggies before crashing into oblivion, and to our joy, miraculously awakening still afloat and upright. But our vision of a holiday, sipping beers on the yacht club balcony and safely leaving our vessel to tour the interior seemed very far away from us. And those thoughts took the gloss off that morning's celebration of our 39th year of marriage. In such a dubious anchorage, if the weather turned nasty, I wouldn't even be able to take my lady out for a romantic dinner.

About at my gloomiest, who should appear? Captain Bill, coming from the marina on his morning inspection. Aloof, and yet a comical figure with those runaway sideburns popping out his cap, he putt-putted once around then started back. But this time he deigned to respond when I waved him back.

"How you going?" I said after he grabbed hold of *Banyandah*. "Know anything about getting a berth in the marina? It's our anniversary and I was hoping to take my lady out to dinner."

Glancing sideways up and down my ship, he responded, "It's full." And pushed off.

Strange folk round here. One of the freedoms facilitated by having your own sailing ship is, if you do not like where you're at, you can move to another spot. So going below I started looking through the next series of charts, thinking we just needed to top up our food, fill a gas bottle, and then we could be off. My new sailing plans had just been formulated when I heard Bill's peewee outboard approaching again.

Coming alongside, abruptly he barked, "There's a berth, third from the far end – but only a week."

"Well great. How much will that be?"

I think being questioned was not to his liking as he blew out his lips and blustered, "Humph, what-ever they charge."

A week would do. We could go out tonight then have a look around tomorrow, replenish our stores, and get rested for our grand tour of Shark Bay. But the costs? Marinas on this coast are pricey and we needed to watch our budget.

So I asked him as gently as I could, "Do you have any idea on the money."

Uh oh! That really boiled him over because he savagely pulled the starter cord, pushed off, and started roaring away like a pipsqueak mouse. And then he surprised us both by shouting back over his shoulder.

"Something like a hundred dollars."

Jude and I were in the dinghy quick time and zooming off to inspect the entrance and proffered berth, taking along our knotted string with attached chunk of metal to sound the depths. Well, everything about the marina had an air of homemade do-it-yourself, starting first with the channel markers. They were just lengths of white plastic tubing shoved vertically into the muddy bottom. And the excavated basin was bare-naked earth held back by stacks of black tires that served as retaining walls. The berths themselves were formed by gal pipes hammered into the bottom and divided alternately by central catwalks decked with roughly made concrete tiles. To moor a vessel, loops of bent re-bar emerged out concrete filled tires. It was crude, albeit quite useable and well protected from the prevailing wind. And being well up the Fascine inside a shallow basin would provide excellent protection from cyclones. Our soundings revealed insufficient water for *Banyandah* to float in the berth during spring low tides, but enough for the upcoming week of neaps. So we attached two pick up lines to the outer piles then scampered back to hastily get underway before the wind started pumping.

Getting through the narrow channel was easy. But, there being no one around the quiet marina to assist us into our berth could make it tricky as the southwesterly had now returned in force. Blowing sideways across the channel, it would be up our bum after turning into the berth, so the trick would be stopping *Banyandah* before she ploughed into the wall of black tires. Luckily, her brakes worked well, churning water astern while Jude reached across for our set lines, securing us well before we hit. Once in, an hour's working-bee saw us secured at all four corners and the awning setup tautly. After which we had a scrub up then stepped off to find a celebratory lunch in the village.

Carnarvon's population of 9000 souls was first settled in 1876 and named after Lord Carnarvon, the then British Secretary of State for the Colonies. Carnarvon is 904 km north of Perth, at the mouth of the Gascoyne River and the tourist brochure claims it's a bustling tropical town, growing in stature over the years as a popular base to shop for locally grown produce. The major industries include fishing (prawns, scallops and snapper), pastoral (sheep, cattle & goats), mining (salt & gypsum) and plantations (bananas, mangoes, tropical fruits & vegetables). Over 115,000 sq kms of the Gascoyne are taken up by pastoral stations producing meat and wool. And over 70 banana plantations surround Carnarvon, covering 350 hectares; they produce over four-thousand tonnes of bananas annually. In recent years, mangoes have become equally popular. Carnarvon's weather is ideal for growing many kinds of produce. The most rainfall occurs in the cyclone season, December to February, when the average maximum temperature is 32° C, that's 90° F. In winter, June to August, the average maximum is a very comfortable 22° C or 72° F.

It felt good to have my hair slicked back, Jude dolled up by my side, walking through the yacht club grounds on a sandy track that separated the boats from several acres of disused construction litter and boating bits. At the corner turning towards the clubhouse stood an ablution block that also contained a washing machine in the back corner. Having neither coin slot nor honesty box tossed up the thought it must be free and that really pleased Jude. We strolled round the locked clubhouse once then sat in the shade of its covered area to admire the view down the Fascine. Three drooping palms and a clump of Acacias framed the drying sand flats; their brown expanse slashed by channels of lightning-blue, while overhead grey puffballs scudded.

Leaving the compound, we still had not met a soul when setting off down a residential street lacking sidewalks. During the ten minute walk to town, dogs yelped at us through picket fences and we dodged the occasional dead car on the verge. But I do not remember seeing another person. It was like landing on a parallel planet, one the residents had abandoned.

Downtown Carnarvon comprises two cross streets that contain the usual array of cafes and shops including Jude's favourite grocery store. We browsed the lot in an hour then I lashed out, buying my lady a veggie pie for her anniversary lunch. For me, a curried chicken pie from a bakery that was just closing, so we got the pies at half price then ate them sitting on the banks of the Fascine with the noise of the town at our backs. Holding hands, we chatted, first about the day's events getting into the marina, and then we started reminiscing our years together. Non-stop we nattered, just as we had thirty-nine years earlier when driving to Scotland for a honeymoon in our patched up VW van. The years may have taken their toll on our outward beauty, but they've enhanced our resolve to share life together. Two together is far more than two times one; it's a team, each strengthening the other, and we've found having challenges to conquer has helped us stay together. So, after a bit of eye-to-eye gazing, the gravity of our many years together suddenly struck and we giggled, squeezed hands then went home in a rush.

The clubhouse was still quiet when we returned and the trudge along the orange sandy track seemed to be taking us into a desolate land, when ahead in the lengthening shadows, leaning against the rickety gal-iron guardrail stood a lone figure perusing *Banyandah*. By his side, a black Labrador held its bandaged paw off the ground.

"How you going," was my standard opening.

And the fit middle-aged fellow replied, "I'm admiring your boat. She's so uncluttered and well laid out. Been far in her?"

Jude loves to hear her boat complimented so she jumped in, "You're welcome on board for a squiz if you like. I'm Jude."

The chap stuck out his hand. "I'm Murray. I own *Salad Days* berthed near the boat entrance."

Then he smiled so broadly we couldn't help but like him straight away. The first thing a yachtie does in a new place is peruse the other boats and we had noticed *Salad Days* on our way out at lunchtime. We had taken a special interest in her because she's a Wharram Cat, similar to one Jude and I had been hired to deliver down Australia's East Coast, and *Salad Days* had seemed so well cared for, one of the few in this marina that could safely go to sea.

Murray hopped down on deck, accepted the beer I offered and while Jude packed away her groceries, I gave him a cook's tour. We immediately started swapping stories, and in the few minutes it took Murray to describe his adventures in the outlying islands and the limited but very social nature of his club, my opinion of Carnarvon started doing a back flip. Before he left, it being a Friday night, we arranged to have dinner at the club.

And then Murray floored us by offering his pickup over the weekend, saying, "I don't need it, and I know you'll have lots of errands to run."

Then without hesitation he handed across a set of keys for the white ute parked in front of *Banyandah*.

Funny how your luck can change. One moment we are stranded high and dry without help in a strange town, the next we're secure in a pen with a new friend and a set of wheels to tour round in. After Murray's departure, a long cuddle ensued, followed by a quick change into party garb before traipsing back along the track to the yacht club, now gaily lit with a large crowd overflowing the covered area and out onto the lawn where the low quarter moon beautifully lit the quiet waters.

It's always a little awkward waltzing into a crowd of strangers who by their gay chatter are obviously good friends. And at first, we kept to ourselves hoping someone would jump up and introduce us. But no one did, so we migrated to the bar where we met a big lad with a larrikin smile called Hutch, who served up our drinks then introduced the club secretary, a rather solid lady named Jan. She and I had business. Yep, a hundred a week, but we couldn't stay longer than a week were her terms.

"Oh dear," I crooned. "I had hoped to fix my engine before having to move on."

Jan turned out a sweet helpful soul, just a normal harried housewife with a side job, as well as her own plantation to run, plus three kids to raise and a hubby to keep happy. The crux of the issue was the club's recent trouble with southern boats coming for a week then staying forever.

Hutch's lady, pretty Jenny, was next tending the bar and after a fresh round of coldies, I ordered our anniversary feast of two fisherman's baskets. We dined with two single teachers, Jenny and Jacki, and Joseph, aka Larry Joe, who had only recently arrived from Victoria. Our main topics of conversation were school discipline, or the lack of it, home education, and raising kids generally. Larry sadly missed his. We missed ours. No matter how you travel or where, be it the wider world or the back roads of your own neighbourhood, meeting new people brings about a common sharing of life's experiences and this generally shows the inherent kindness found in every one of us. There must have been sixty dining there that night and we would have spoken with half before I ran out of steam and begged Jude to take me to bed. Which she did. She's a good lady. Seems we're set for another 39 years of marriage.

The next day was busy. Before we could indulge ourselves with sightseeing, new supplies were first. So we loaded our empty gas cylinder in the back of Murray's ute then blazed off down the dirt track. When you're used to walking everywhere, suddenly having transport is a special treat. The day was hot and through the open windows air blew our hair while the blur of passing scenery sent my mind pleasantly wandering over some forgotten thoughts. But my simpleton's smile was short lived. Judith was driving and I, the appointed navigator, discovered that Carnarvon sprawls over a very large area. But, hey, we had wheels, and the more distance the merrier. We investigated several stores; happy to meander up and down isles ogling the wide range of goods, and while the gas bottle was being filled, purchased extra tackle to make a second trolling spool. Then from the shop next door, I bought new filters for the engine. We briefly toured the other food outlet then spent the last hour before early Saturday closing in a big hardware store looking for things we might need. All these shops were located along the road heading north towards Exmouth and Darwin, several kilometres from the town centre, so it was heaven-sent having transport. Thanks Murray, you are a kind thoughtful man.

Carnarvon is sort of desert country, flat, without much vegetation, so you can see for miles. One sight nearly always in view was a huge communications dish just like the one in the movie. In fact, I thought it was the one. But it is not, "The Dish."

Nevertheless, Carnarvon's dish had communicated with Armstrong on the moon, so we paid it a visit. We drove right through the security gate, parked under its massive tangle of steel support, and then climbed some stairs to gain a sweeping view of blue ocean, red desert, and purple mountains further inland. And not far away, a swath of green; plantations following the path of the Gascoyne River.

On Sunday, we packed the ute with a picnic and our camera gear then set off on a mystery tour. Jude was driving and her choices were south to Bush Bay, or north to the blowholes, or inland to Rocky Pool. Coming to the first junction she turned right for Rocky Pool saying she'd had enough of the wind, which had been blowing for ages, and, "It'll be a good place to skinny-dip."

Rocky Pool Gascoyne River inland of Carnarvon

Rocky Pool is lovely. From the moment we settled into a little rocky nook under a white gumtree offering cool shade, our world was an artist's palette of colours flowing smoothly, one to another. On a cliff beside the still water, Fairy Martins had fashioned bottleneck nests from orange-red earth so typical of that region. Close by them, but slightly upstream in the dry river sand, gemstones sparkled different colours in the sunshine.

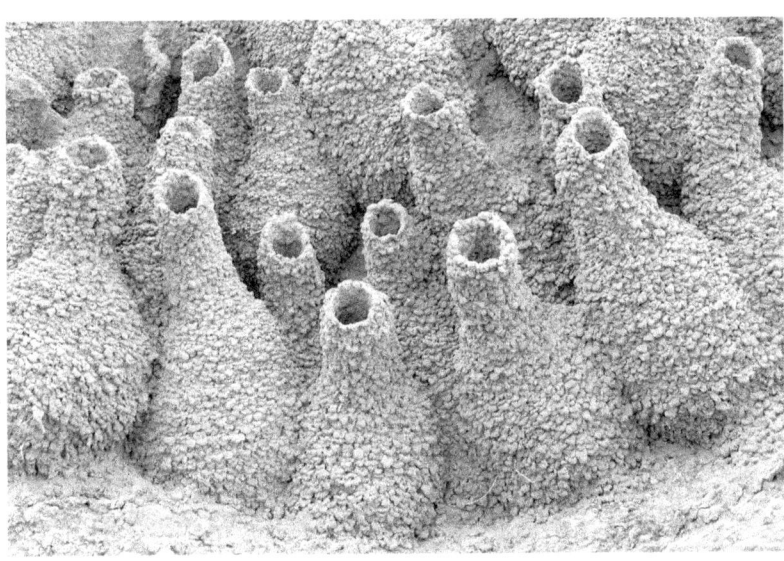

For most of its length, the Gascoyne flows underground through coarse sand and pebbles, only rising above ground in a few rock pools such as here, and Chinamen's Pool near its mouth. That changes in cyclonic deluges, when floods cut into the conglomerate rock forming its banks. Then, material deposited millenniums ago are swept away, exposing red garnets, purple amethyst, golden yellow stones, bits of petrified wood and fossils.

The following Friday, it being tax time, I mailed off my week's endeavours having just answered what felt like 23,000 questions about our modest income. Still rubbing my weary eyes, we then trudged to the club to drown the figures still running round my head. The club had just started to hum when I caught sight of a couple of hippy types sprouting dreadnoughts and gesturing wildly at the bar. Fearing they were resisting being ejected, I moseyed over to follow the action with Jude following in my shadow. At first the girl seemed skinny, until I looked closer when wiry would better describe her. Probably be victorious if wrestling any of the fellows around her. And her mate, with his wild blond hair and ready smile, was no slouch himself. Hutch was yammering at them, reading them the riot act I thought, until he beckoned Jude and me over.

"Meet Tim and Anna," Big Hutch said, indicating the two creatures washed in with the tide.

"They've just sailed in from Indonesia aboard their Wharram Cat. That's her there," and he pointed out the door to the dry bay where not more than four strides past the high tide line sat this pipsqueak catamaran hardly bigger than my son's Hobie Cat.

Their simple craft comprised two hulls with a taut trampoline between, completely open to the elements. It would float, but barely a foot above a smooth sea. That makes it rather hard to dress Manhattan style and rather than judge on dress; what we saw were two adventurous brave people aboard a demanding craft, and in awe, I grabbed Tim's hand to congratulate him,

"Quirky" - a Wharram Tiki 21

then put my arms around Anna because her tiny frame was surely filled with true grit. There is nothing more inspiring than meeting young folk looking after themselves while exploring the world and observing her creatures.

We soaked up their answers to our questions, with Jude asking how they managed their stores, the galley, medical needs, communications, clothes, washing and simply, how did they survive. Me, I was throwing in queries too, about navigation, spares, how they moved in tight spots without an engine. Compared to theirs, our modest craft provided five-star luxury. And the more we were around their bubbly personalities and infectious smiles the more we wanted to be a part of their happening. And so, with their invite to lunch came a promised tour around their six and a half metre magic carpet.

Good Murray dropped his ute off at our dockside the next morning then about midday we threw in our tucker box and drove out to Chinamen's Pool. It's the local attraction just a couple of dirt blocks out from town where wasteland edges up to mostly tall grasses, and a band of trees borders the Gascoyne River near its mouth. According to the Shire's travel guide, its trapped waters were alive with birds.

At first, we saw nothing so we ate lunch on the bank surrounded by a peaceful view of reed beds and river gums. Then we noticed a few birds down near the bend and after exchanging our tucker box for cameras, headed off in pursuit. Geez, around that bend was one of the world's greatest armadas of black swans, their red beaks looking like they were dining on red meat instead of succulent shreds of water-grass from the bottom. And around them were hoards of other critters like brown Hardhead Ducks, a few Aussie Pelicans, and Silver Gulls, plus a peppering of black and white Little Pied Cormorants, along with a number of those birds with the long curved beak, the Sacred Ibis. As if one big happy family, strutting amongst this lot were several pairs of graceful Yellow-billed Spoonbills.

We sat on the edge of the tall grass and captured all this in digital splendour, including other flocks that flew through. Curlew Sandpipers, fleet on wing, flashed erratically through the air as if dodging flak from unseen gun towers. They would suddenly alight at the water's edge where, with quick steps they attacked any tiny morsel their sharp eyes could find. Nature's so grand. Just sitting watching the other creatures going about their daily life reminded me of Tim and Anna who, like these creatures, look after themselves in a harsh demanding environment where they feel the freedom a cool breeze brings. What a shame many of today's youth appear alienated from the natural world by the unfitness of obesity, isolated from the myriad creatures sharing the planet by earphones and mobile phones.

In tune with the endless cycle of our universe, the moon had journeyed around Earth to bring the larger tides of a full moon that threatened to sit *Banyandah* on the bottom yet again. Early our second Sunday in Carnarvon, her keel grounded and as the water drained away, a gust of wind knocked us over, requiring a rapid response. Extending two halyards from the masthead and tying one to each platform on the adjacent pens, we used the mast winches to crank *Banyandah* back upright until the tide returned.

After she refloated, we took an outing up the coast to what's know as the blowholes, and now it was fortunate the wind had really piped up in the last twenty-four hours. Driving an hour north out the town, a side road took us towards Point Quobba, which had been our turning point just before the engine had overheated. After a further bit, a rough dirt track took us to the only manmade thing in sight, a red and white lighthouse. From its base came a powerful sight of relentless breakers marching across the vast Indian Ocean and crashing onto an abrupt rock shore. A cool wind rushing in from the sea sent a shiver up my spine when I recalled that just ten days ago we were out there battling those forces.

Then quite suddenly, while eying the battalions coming in, I saw a column of water suddenly shoot up. Once sighted, every few seconds a new geyser would shoot high into the sky to be blown into a shawl of spray by Nature's forces.

We had to get closer to that, so we set off in our beaut set of wheels. Just a short hop and we were halted by a huge sign, ominously stating "King Waves Kill." So simply put, it needed to be heeded.

We had to get some chores done on *Banyandah* or be stuck in Carnarvon like those southern boats. The most important was to find why the engine had overheated. That meant playing Houdini again and getting greasy. With the engine floor up, a deep cavern opens that reaches to her very bottom. You do not want to fall off a cockpit seat or miss your footing on the drainage trough around the floor opening. That's what I use to move around when the floor's up. Deep down on the right side sits the raw water pump whose rubber impellor sucks seawater in through a strainer then forces it through the engine's heat exchanger. The engine is actually cooled by fresh water like a normal car engine, but instead of having a radiator, most vessels use a contraption that has a bundle of tubes running through a closed container. Hot freshwater from the engine is pumped through those tubes where it's cooled by seawater pumped around them.

My first task was to check the saltwater pump's rubber impellor. Sometimes they lose a blade and therefore pump less. That took a day, and although it wasn't the problem, while it was out, I replaced the impellor, packing, and seals with better used spares. That left only the heat exchanger as the culprit. I'd never had one of these muck up before, although I knew their tubes can get clogged. This heat exchanger was new to *Banyandah*. When rebuilding the engine for its second life, I had removed the old faithful heat exchanger because it had become badly corroded, and replaced it with one I'd salvaged from the bottom of the Cocos Keeling lagoon, off a vessel that had burnt to the waterline then had sank in the anchorage. Guess it's obvious; I've always been a bit of a forager.

Cautiously dismantling the engine's plumbing and removing the heat exchanger, after unbolting its end covers I found our problem. Inside, the two zinc anodes protecting the metal from electrolysis had disintegrated into grey goo blocking half the tubes that were hardly larger than drinking straws. With great relief I gushed out the news to Jude, who rewarded me with quick kiss and cuddle, keeping well away from my greasy bits.

The next weekend Murray invited the four intrepid sailors home to dine with his lady Rose, and the six of us were in fine form. I often feel it's a shame we don't set up a tape recorder when a group of true-life adventurers get together. The stuff that pours out with the wine is amazing. Like Tim and Anna zipping around inside the lagoons of Ningaloo Reef with their shallow draught and nimble nature. Murray and Rose scared us by describing their encounter with a Roll Cloud.

"Like a low, horizontal tube," Murray said. It sucked a metre of seawater out their anchorage, leaving *Salad Days* high and dry with fish flopping about. Then a raging storm hit, lasting only minutes before the sea came rushing back in.

Timmy and Anna's gift of the gab and willingness to work convinced a local farmer to lend them some ground next to his shed so they could store their catamaran while they went home to South Australia for the summer. Tim had it all worked out. On the yacht club beach, he expertly undid the many lashing holding *Quirky* together, and then using a borrowed car trailer, a friend towed the hulls and rigging for storage under a big Moreton Bay Fig next to the shed. Many hands helped these young people disassemble their floating home and we had the pleasure of their company after offering them a place to sleep.

What fun having those two ragamuffins roaming round *Banyandah*. It gave Jude a good reason to whip up her special teriyaki chicken dish, and in return, next morning they treated us to a batch of little boiled eggs from Murray's battery chooks, served with neatly lined up toasted soldiers for dipping into their minute yolks.

In two quick days, they completed the disassembly and transfer, which left their dilapidated jalopy filled to the headliner with clothes, surf gear, and a strange collection of paraphernalia, the list of which would fill tens of pages.

Anna and Tim left on the Friday after a tearful last photo taken in our cockpit. Jude and I felt rather alone after they sped away, so we also said our goodbyes that night at the yacht club dinner. After nearly three weeks in Carnarvon, *Banyandah* was back in trim. We had restocked the lockers, filled the water tanks, and had chatted and chatted until our jaws ached. Now the distant horizons were calling again. Before us this time, World Heritage Shark Bay, renowned for being a warehouse for almost every sea creature. Unique because its shallow water heats up and becomes more saline. This in turn, provides a perfect environment for microscopic creatures that form the beginning of a vast food chain that reaches right up to super sized whales.

On the Saturday morning's rising tide, we reversed the task of coming in, removing the slack lines until our vessel hung on just a single taut one to an outside pylon. Waiting for a lull in the wind with our engine ticking over, when it came I gave her heaps and once again *Banyandah* set herself free. As if suddenly possessed by a spirit that needed to be unshackled, she came alive in my hands, and without fuss, made the turn for the outward channel.

Murray and Rose came by to see us off, as did a few others. We waved and immediately began to miss their companionship, but life beckoned. New sights and knowledge lay just beyond a horizon that may seem the boundary of our world, but which, in reality, only leads to new discoveries.

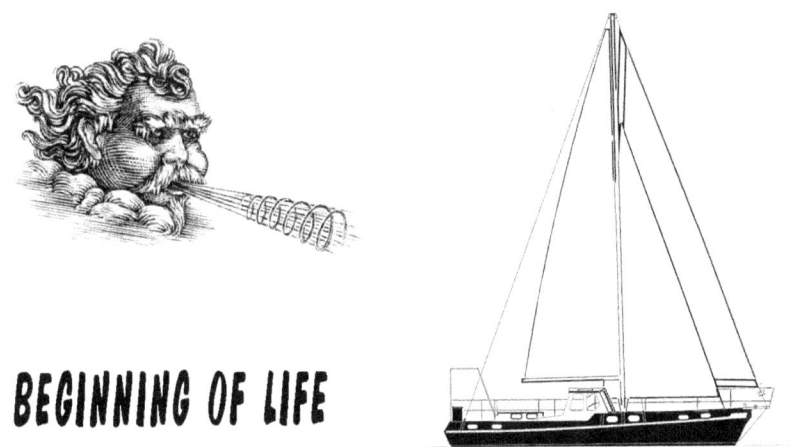

BEGINNING OF LIFE

Long before starting this voyage, there was one place other than the Kimberley and Tasmania that we knew we must see. It is a place similar to the Galapagos in that some wild animals there have no fear of humans, where each day they come with their young to interact with humans. That place is Monkey Mia in Shark Bay.

In the beginning, the first life to appear on Earth 3.5 billion years ago was minute cyanobacteria that grew in colonies that trapped sediments in a mucous they exuded. This then congealed into enormous mats called stromatolites. To you or me they might look like soft rocks, but they are living creatures, and before any other form of life developed, they were widespread in hot saline seas. But, as the Earth cooled and the waters became less saline, other creatures evolved that grazed on those minute creatures. So today, large colonies of cyanobacteria occur at only three places in the world. Two are in the Bahamas. The other is on Carnarvon's southern doorstep in Shark Bay, 800 km north of Perth. Lying between 24 and 27 degrees south of the equator, Shark Bay has the most diverse and abundant examples of living marine stromatolites on the planet.

From space, Shark Bay is split into a "W" by two peninsulas and an eastern coastal strip that makes a total shoreline exceeding 1500 km in length. Edel Land, the seaward peninsula, has three, long, thin islands extending northward from it that protects Shark Bay from the Indian Ocean. The same islands gave us protection when coming down from Cape Cuvier.

Those projections contain two large, shallow embayments where evaporation rates are very high in the hot dry climate, and this makes the shallow bays of Hamelin Pool and L'haridon Bight hyper-saline. Twice normal saltiness. Seagrass helps maintain their hyper-salinity by restricting tidal flows. They are so salty most other marine life cannot survive, resulting in few predators and few competitors for the salt-tolerant species such as tiny cockleshells and of course, Earth's first creature cyanobacteria.

I remember very well our leaving Carnarvon, almost tearfully saying goodbye to new friends before threading our way back out the maze of sand flats then raising sail upon a calm sea. As the day went on, a sea fret ate the land and hushed all sound, leaving a primeval world more suited to sea serpents with large green scales. Blindly following our compass, a blurry sun racing ahead increased our anxiety until the sun's last fire illuminated a dark irregular shape emerging from the mist ahead.

That first night in Shark Bay, the amazing desolate beauty of Red Cliffs on Bernie Island surrounded us

with smooth flowing sand drifts that rose up to a red hoodoo. Where dreaming of Murray's roll-cloud draining the bay had me rushing up into a quiet moonless night that transported me back to the beginning of time with stars so close I could have touched them.

Eager to be away next morning we motored south towards Dorre Island, planning to stop at Turtle Bay and visit Inscription Point. But when a boisterous southerly came up, we unleashed all sail and hauled them tight to cross open water for the centre of the "W" at Cape Peron. During a fast, fun sail that became more exhilarating as each mile passed, suddenly we had to dodge shoals that appeared without warning, producing heart stopping moments. And then when already high on excitement, from out the afternoon heat haze, strawberry hills greeted us. At their base, vanilla-white beaches popped out the aquamarine sea.

Our chart, now showing fast currents and more hidden obstructions, sent our hearts racing even faster. Jude was steering and I'm at the bow searching for safe water around overfalls and pale water as our taut sails pushed our speedo towards double digits. We should have reduced sail. But the sea was slight. And although dangers abound, we felt capable of harnessing those strong forces to find a way through. We love doing this. Gets the ticker going and creates memories not easily forgotten.

Thankfully our cameras were recording both the beauty and drama that soared to even greater heights after rounding the Cape. There the wind blew off the land putting our lee rail under the sea while we raced the sun to Heralds Bight. Flying into that captive bit of water in fading light got us a bit spooked when the sounder started screaming skinny water.

"Helm up," I yelled in response to Jude's cry of shallow water.

Then sails clattered down, fluttering wildly in the blasts off a vacant wild land eerily lit by a sky filled with golden mackerel scales.

Thrice we tried to get our anchor to hold and three times it came up choked with seagrass. After each failure we searched under power for a weed free spot. And eventually, on the fourth attempt, it held, although so precariously we wouldn't leave the cockpit until the windblasts subsided late that night.

Upon rising, with just a hint of leftover wind, the morning sun stole into a peach tinged sky behind Guichenault Point. Beautiful, but we both knew we'd not stay another night. The shore so distant, the holding so poor, expecting more wind we'd dare not leave the boat, even when an extensive sand spit behind us called as if a siren rising out the water.

Underway after lunch we dodged cormorants too full to fly away and saw through water so clear a stingray keeping pace. Saw turtles by the half dozen, and the dark shapes of cormorants speeding like torpedoes across the sandy bottom. Then we watched them pop up ten at a time. Some had fish in their bills, but many did not and that had us wondering how many times they have to dive for a meal.

As *Banyandah* rounded the immense sand spit, so much life held us transfixed that when a second Spanish mackerel hit the lure, Jude nearly ran us aground. While I was hauling in Mr. Fish, through the aqua veil she didn't see the pale sandy bottom suddenly turn white. My bark, and her quick reactions, saved us from grounding.

Monkey Mia appeared on a low lying point, encumbered by more shoals, which we threaded following the only thing visible, the radio tower. Our arrival did not go unnoticed. A family of dolphins were quickly upon us as we reached the first port marker. Bobbing and weaving round our bows, they escorted us to the anchorage just off the resort then headed for shore where a crowd was gathering.

In the early days, fishermen would often toss fish overboard to the congregating dolphins that followed them to shore. Then in 1964, a woman from one of the makeshift fishing camps hand fed one of the dolphins. The dolphin took the fish gracefully and returned for more over the following days. Other dolphins followed. So began a habit that continues today in what has become a ritual.

Monkey Mia is now famous of course. The main attraction; wild dolphins that come and go as they please. Everyday some swim into the clear shallows to interact with humans, delighting visitors with their grace while proudly showing off their little ones.

Our first morning off the resort was so quiet we pulled down the genoa to check it for wear and found some worn and broken stitching where the sail rubs the wires supporting the mast. Adhering to the proverb a stitch in time, Judith set to work re-stitching it using the original holes while dolphins promenaded around us on their way to shore for breakfast.

Before having lunch, we shifted closer to the beach, just off the seagrass edge, using the opportunity to change anchors from the plough to the admiralty, the traditional hook and crossbar anchor. Weighing 25 kg, it had me huffing and puffing when lugging it up from its storage spot under the saloon floor. With fingers crossed, we laid it out with every bit of our sixty metres of chain, keen to know how well it would hold in weed once the wind got up.

Now close to shore, that afternoon we snorkelled just off the beach in warm, crystal clear water, enthralled by the large numbers of sand crabs meandering across a seafloor nearly free of debris. Dinner plate sized stingrays shovelled their way through, accompanied by an entourage of tiny fish filtering out small morsels of food disturbed by them.

With the setting sun came the wind. And to our disgust, the gusty southerly immediately sent *Banyandah* sideways towards an bank, dragging the admiralty through weed with it. Jude was annoyed; dinner preparations had to be put on hold while we went through our re-anchoring routine. Yet again the anchor came up a massive ball of seagrass, which I had to clear with the boat hook before re-laying it. Then just before bedtime, during another heavy blast, it let go again and away we went, dragging our chain as though a leash on a runaway puppy. So, without much ado, we changed back to the plough then stayed up several hours to make sure it was holding.

We enjoyed a lovely week at Monkey Mia even though it was disrupted by several southerly blows that tested our tempers as well as our anchors. Neither passed the test. Although not deep water, seagrass has proved the most difficult to anchor in of all we've experienced.

We may have cursed the marine meadows of *Posidonia Australis*, known as ribbon weed, but they are an important part of the Wooramel Bank that covers approximately 1000 square kilometres of Shark Bay. Those ooid shoals contain one of the world's largest organically formed carbonate deposits and offer refuge and food for many animals ranging from tiny snails to 400 kg *wuthuga*, sometimes know as mermaids. No, not the curvaceous beauties that lured sailors off course. I mean the shy elusive dugong, one of the world's two surviving species of sea cow that are actually more closely related to elephants. Dugongs are herbivores. They feed mainly on the rhizomes of seagrasses and it's estimated that around one-eighth of the world's population live in Shark Bay. We had seen several in Heralds Bight.

Therefore, when a calm period was predicted, which coincided with a full moon that would bring the lowest tide the following night, the vast sand flat in Heralds Bight was remembered. Motoring back the twenty miles, we barely scraped in between outlying shoals then found a clear patch next to the submerged longshore drift.

When the new day came, our pre-dawn preparations disturbed some Welcome Swallows roosting along *Banyandah's* rails, and they flitted to and fro in the dim light. Then the heavy breath of dolphins sounded right beside us, and from just across the water, upon this immense slab of sand came cackles of cormorants preparing for their day's activities.

We stepped down into Little Red just as the sun's orb broke free of the night, spreading gold along the horizon and outlining the sand spit in orange-pink highlights. At that moment, seabird yammering reached a crescendo as if finalising their day's fishing expeditions. Jude rowed us in, quietly dipping oars with careful, long, steady strokes, skirting the birds without setting them to flight.

Muddy sand, rippled by the action of current, firm underfoot, shone mauve in the low morning light. And water, still draining, created intricate patterns as though a river delta seen from space. Stealthily as one can when totally exposed, we approached the massive flock of pied cormorants that numbered tens of thousands. Observing them through the video's telescopic viewfinder, the seething mass was moving synchronously, with only those craning their heads highlighted in a collage of black and white. As we approached, a few nervous terns on the outskirts took flight, accompanied by the odd silver-gull. This agitated the cormorants and they surged towards the safety of water, making those at the front swim off. At that moment, we beheld an incredible sight. As our video whirled capturing the action, they took flight. First, one clan containing a thousand, then another, until there were none left.

In seconds, the sand became barren except for some wafer-thin cone shells stuck point down, so we headed back to Little Red. Along the way, a beautiful baler shell was making a big trail and turning it over revealed intricate, pale yellow whorls on its muscular brown foot reminding us of some aboriginal paintings.

After lunch, without raising sail so the sun awning could shelter us from the hot still day, we motored back to Cape Peron, which we'd passed ten days earlier. It is around this cape that warm and cold currents converge, creating incredible diversity. The water teems with life; dugongs, dolphins, turtles, even humpback whales mingle with fish, crustaceans, and reef-building corals.

The Leeuwin current brings warm tropical water down the WA continental slope, meandering and shedding eddies along the way, dissipating some of its flow in Shark Bay, but much continues around Cape Leeuwin into the Great Australian Bight. Up from the south comes the cold Western Australian current. The resultant mixing of the two currents gives rise to layering that is vital to Shark Bay's marine ecology, with warmer, lighter water sitting on top of the colder, denser water. Warm currents provide a free ride for tropical animals, assisting their distribution down to Shark Bay and the cooler flow supports temperate species such as sharks and rays.

Approaching the terracotta hills of Cape Peron, my heart began beating crazily. Up ahead, overfalls angered the water where the two currents met, and it looked too shallow to pass through the narrow gap close inshore. It must be the adrenalin rush that endears this life to me and I felt as if in my lady's arms as *Banyandah* just squeezed through.

Anchoring just inside the current, we found little water under our keel, but nearby were abrupt, terracotta sandhills dribbling smooth runnels onto a custard coloured beach. Rowing across on the late afternoon's slack water, we pulled the dinghy way up then set the anchor for extra safety. After the muck up at Mt Casuarina, when Little Red had hung herself, we took the oars well above the high tide line rather than chance losing them with an upturned dinghy.

Atop the bluff gave a splendid view with *Banyandah* centre stage. Closer to hand, a well-presented information sign welcomed us to the Wanamalu Trail, which we read means cormorant in the Malgana aboriginal language. Further reading told us that this was the Francois Peron National Park, named after the French zoologist who arrived in Shark Bay in 1801 on the *Geographe*. That it covers the 52,000 hectares at the tip of the Peron Peninsula north of Denham, and furthermore it was Peron's observations that had added great importance to the natural history of the region.

Here is what Jude wrote in her journal:

On the top, the flies were such a nuisance we had to cover our noses and mouths with a cloth before starting along a boardwalk crossing an area of shrubby desert that had a sign indicating it went to Skipjack Point. The boardwalk ended 100 metres further on dumping us onto rouge red sand, soft and shifting underfoot, and the going got harder in the heat. Patterned with lizard tracks, our path laced its way between clumps of saltbush, spinifex, and some cotton bush. Each time our boots inadvertently kicked vegetation, swarms of flies took to the air. Crikey, they were so thick I even covered my head with my shirt, but still managed to inhale a few, swallowing one as well. It tickled wiggling down inside me until somehow it scrambled back up to my mouth where I coughed it out. Damn! To my surprise, it took flight midair. Yuk! Pissed off I smacked others against my arm, caught them then rolled them between my fingers before flicking them away. Walking alone with 'em swarming got me wondering whether they had always been here or were they introduced when the peninsula was developed as a sheep station in the late 1800s.

The cape is strangely beautiful. It's like many beaches; long, flat, barren, but with reddish dunes sculpted by the wind. My mind boggled over sweeping views of the coastline as far as Heralds Bight and the Guichenault Spit that we had explored just this morning.

From a platform built out over the sea, we saw a squadron of giant stingrays flying across pale blue, several dugongs grazing, and the strangest sight ever. Dolphins menacing cormorants that were nonchalantly preening themselves along the shoreline. While occasionally, a full-size dolphin would launch itself up the beach, creating a tidal wave of sorts. Their entertaining antics made exciting video.

Two hours later, we returned to see *Banyandah* streaming the other way in a river of liquid silver that made rowing back rather challenging. First I made ground along the shore where the current was least, until well past our vessel, when I headed out.

After a few moments, in a nervous voice, Jude urged me to row faster, saying otherwise we would miss and be swept to sea. So, I put my back into it. We got back okay, me a bit out of breath. Our speedo was out of action, jammed by weed, or we would have checked the current's speed. But when Jude slipped over the side for a quick cool off, she had to hold on tight to the ladder, saying she would never be able to swim against it.

Across the second bight and closer to the southern exit from Shark Bay is the famed Dirk Hartog Island. And there in a bay just before South Passage stands a homestead guesthouse. On the day Australia was to change its government in November 2007, we were driving our sailing-home towards a majestic, far-away vista of dunes adrift on the wind. Feathering our sails and storing them, we nosed into a superb anchorage over sand obstructed by very few patches of weed. It shelved very gently and provided lots of dragging room. Once settled, next to us on a small rock island stood a tall column of sticks as tall as us; an osprey's nest built higher over many generations and probably the one drawn by Jacques Arago during the 1818 Freycinet expedition.

Unbeknownst to us as we strolled up the pathway to the main house, we were about to meet two lovely people. Answering our cooee came a thin unshaven fellow with inquisitive eyes in a well-tanned face who said he was David, the caretaker.

In an unhurried drawl, he informed us, "The homestead has just closed for the season."

Dave and his wife Jenny, a homespun beauty who easily laughed, were cleaning up and keeping everything running. A job Dave had done many summers working for Kieran Wardle, the grandson of Sir Thomas Wardle. Over cooling drinks enjoyed in the delicious shade of the homestead's veranda, they gave us a rundown on the island's history.

In 1867, Francis Von Bibra applied for a pastoral lease over the island to farm sheep, and in early 1869, the lease was granted and the first sheep were transported to Dirk Hartog Island. A homestead was built that same year, along with five shearing sheds and a five-bedroom shearer's quarters. By the mid-1920s, the numbers of sheep had increased to approx 26,000 and the island was shipping over 450 bails of wool directly to England.

For some reason, the 1968 government decided to sell the island to the highest bidder and Sir Thomas Wardle suggested the Court Government should purchase it for its history and natural beauty. The suggestion rejected, Sir Thomas purchased the island himself.

Dirk Hartog Island then became the private retreat for Sir Thomas and Lady Wardle. They spent much of Western Australia's winter months on the island, rebuilt the shearer's kitchen, reduced the number of sheep to 6000, and shut down the northern half of the island.

When the price of wool dramatically declined in the early 1990s, Kieran Wardle, the grandson of Sir Thomas, took over to convert the island to tourism. He wanted to make its fantastic scenery and secret fishing locations available to everyone. Before Kieran took over, few people had had the opportunity to experience the island first hand because you needed a ship like *Banyandah* to make a personal visit possible.

A couple of days later we went ashore for a swim and were given a tour of the homestead. A lively discussion of life and aspirations followed while sitting on the veranda with a cooling libation. On the third day, Jenny and Dave took us inland by four-wheel drive to check and count left-behind animals as, a few months earlier, the main stock had been rounded up and shipped off in preparation for when National Parks were to take charge in 2008.

What a cracker of a day. I still shake my head. We learnt so much, saw marvellous sights, and benefited from David's knowledge and Jenny's wit. And we got a crash course on sheep farming in sparse dry conditions and heard many stories. Dave told one after we'd stopped at a large old shearing shed, of a shipwrecked sailor who had holed up inside the shed, strutting out buck-naked straight into the lens of a TV cameraman sent to find him.

In the cooler part of the day, Dave took us up into mountainous sand drifts that reminded us of our honeymoon in the Sahara. Jude's sharp eyes found a shell hundreds of metres above the sea that was thousands of years old. Reaching the crest, we leant over a cliff edge and saw powerful ocean waves and seething surf that had caused the death of many on Dutch ships.

Another day Dave and I examined the desalination plant that wasn't working, discovering choked filters and a leaky pump, which I took apart and fixed. New spares were organised, but for now, the plant made enough water for Jenny to catch up on the washing.

We found the guesthouse had a rich library and we read of Privateer William Dampier naming the area Shark Bay in 1699, obviously because of the enormous numbers of sharks and skates he encountered. But William was not the first European to step ashore. That distinction belongs to the Dutch sea captain Dirk Hartog. In October 1616, he landed at Cape Inscription, at the north end of the island that now bears his name. A copy of the pewter plate that he nailed to a post is on the wall of the library.

Even before the first Europeans landed on Terra Australis, The Malgana Aboriginal people had inhabited Shark Bay for 4000 to 5000 years. That is rather a short time in their long history. The reason being, the islands of Shark Bay were still underwater until 6000 years ago. We also read that it is thought the barrier islands of Bernier, Dorre, Faure, and Dirk Hartog were never inhabited, even though the southern one is separated from the mainland by only a narrow strait called South Passage.

Steep Point, at that southern gateway, is Australia's most westerly point, and from there the Zuytdorp Cliffs run both north and south, towering some 170 m above the sea. They have always presented a formidable obstacle to sailors and at their base lie many wrecks, where countless lives of early traders were crushed. Few escaped the mountainous waves crashing into those cliffs, and we intended to give them a very wide berth. Besides the obvious danger of running into them, there's a nasty backwash felt twenty miles.seaward.

We fell in love with Dirk Hartog, its moods and beauty, and went ashore almost daily to read more of its history that started in the early 1800s when the island's most significant industry was guano mining. Then pearls were found in the numerous sandbanks. Pastoral pursuits followed. Subsequently, fishing became the mainstay of the Shark Bay settlements and a cannery and processing works was established at Monkey Mia in 1912, then later at Herald Bight in the 1930s. Today, tourism reigns supreme. It is estimated that 150,000 tourists visit the Bay each year, to fish, holiday or just meet the dolphins.

Our stay was greatly enhanced by the adventures we had with Jenny and David, so departure day came with both nervous expectations and sadness. When we pulled our pick, Dave and Jenny ran alongside in the resort's alloy runabout to see us safely past the entrance shoals. Then with a grand wave, they turned around just as *Banyandah* spread her sails sending us towards the funnel of shallow water called South Passage.

Cape Peron

Marvellous SHARK BAY

Stealthily as one can when totally exposed we approached the massive flock of pied cormorants numbering tens of thousands

Dirk Hartog Island
once a sheep station, now National Park

Twin Ospreys at masthead

Stick nest near homestead,
possibly the one sketched
by the Freycinet expedition in 1818

TRAVELS SOUTH

We sailed away from Steep Point upon a dull-grey ocean capped by a leaden sky that seemed determined to crush us. There was little wind, and yet the sea was violent. Without a balancing force in our sails, we were forced to hang on tightly while our craft rose and fell as if our twelve tonnes was an insignificant speck of flotsam. We had escaped Shark Bay out a slit in the much-feared Zuytdorp Cliffs. Behind us, they rose in a solid curtain that seemed to have shut, forcing us to face the wild demons ahead.

Boom! - Boom! - Boom! In slow cadence like the march of death, they attacked relentlessly. Not only could we hear their awesome power reverberating off cliffs that stretched till doomsday, but we could also feel our world shudder as if God himself was reshaping Earth with leviathan hammers.

Ours is a well-equipped modern vessel with reliable diesel power. But finding ourselves between unstoppable forces and an unforgiving rock wall spooked us into imagining ourselves aboard a ship of old, engineless, drifting in windless conditions towards huge breakers crashing in majestic power. Muffled in the din, through the thin vapour, we heard faint cries of helpless men and women about to meet their maker.

That morning, *Banyandah's* engine droned on for hours, steadily putting a safe margin between destruction and us. Dreary and windless, the sky became even more threatening. Then bolts of lightning began to flash ahead. A change was coming. Something big from the south. Half our being became excited like a prizefighter waiting for the first bell. The other half trembled, fearing the unknown.

As often happens, that storm struck when the weak light of day began fading. First, a cooling breeze canted our sailing craft and increased our speed. Its first tendrils we welcomed. They broke the monotonous drone of our engine and thankfully eased our rocking. But then those puffs just kept getting stronger. Going well beyond where we hoped they'd stay until our leeward gunwale ran awash with foaming green sea.

While we loved those first easy puffs, the hearty blows that followed thrust fear through our hearts and drove us into action. Sail had to be reduced, and quickly or we would be flattened by a wind growing angrier with every blast.

This was a summer storm; blustery wind, producing a sea of limited force because its roots didn't reach up from the bottom of the world like the one encountered midwinter 1978. Then a young family with sons seven and eight, the *Four J's* had sailed from Sri Lanka bound for Fremantle; 37 wonderful days alone, surrounded by a blissfully serene Indian Ocean. But our pleasure abruptly ended the night we spotted our first shore light after 4,000 sea miles when a westerly gale attacked. Vicious and intense, it caused plenty of grief. In a night of horrors, it was the first and only time *Banyandah* has had to lay bare poles to survive. Thank goodness the blinking light on Rottnest Island kept us company because it gave us hope during a frightful night.

Even with masts bare of sail, that storm canted *Banyandah* over so far storm waves washed over her. Every second seemed our last. And the long-awaited morning's grey light brought little comfort. Clouds of spume hid all except towers of breaking white water. Only by climbing the mast could the occasional glimpse of the fast-approaching shoreline be seen.

Rottnest Island
Summertime & the living is easy

Arriving this time at Rottnest, playground for West Australia's rich - and the rest of us, it was "summertime, and the living is easy …" There was fantastically clear water, a zillion boats, and an island bus that we could hop on and off.

This lovely holiday island was first sighted by Dutch navigator Willem Vlamingh on the last day of 1696. A few days later, Willem rowed eighteen kilometres up a waterway on the mainland, which he named the Swan River.

Back in 1978, a *Banyandah* flying just a pocket hanky had surfed into Fremantle's tiny fishing boat harbour upon mountains of white water that crashed over the rock fortifications. Cowering below out the way, our sons were just young boys, while on deck trying to manage the mayhem, Jude and I were not much more than big kids ourselves. Just a short week later, in icy winter rain, *Banyandah* was on her way again; this time to cross the stormy Great Australian Bight in a race to pick up her first amateur radio charter in Sydney. That first charter set us on a new course of life, exploring the far reaches of Earth until the boys entered Ballina High School to begin their final years of school.

Arriving in Fremantle this time completed *Banyandah's* Australian circumnavigation – albeit with a thirty-year break. And the Fremantle Sailing Club applauded her efforts with a showcase berth right out front the yacht club, where friends and peers stopped to visit. One man who stopped to say hello, 20 years earlier, we had given him a lift between two Caribbean islands. Another had interviewed us in Fiji a quarter-century earlier. And another was a true legend.

I had awoken feeling a bit old this particular morning. Too much booze or one too many stories the night before had me feeling every one of my 63 years, and I was crawling rather lethargically around the cabin when I heard a rap on our railing. Coming up, my eyes clasped onto a man my age inspecting my boat.

"Bonny wee sailing ship you have laddie," were his first words and I smiled. I love people who like my boat. And replied, "She's stout and looks after you in a storm, and that's what matters, plus she's a treat to live aboard."

"Aye, I can see that," this fellow went on, his bushy eyebrows going up and down as he ran his eye over our craft.

"You're a Scots, I can tell. My wife's a Geordie," I said.

And with that disclosure, he ambled closer.

"Aye, I'm a bonny lad from the old country." He said when we were eyeball to eyeball.

"Been back lately?" I asked, thinking of our own trip to England in 1999.

"Aye, went back in 2005."

"Good flight?"

"Did nay fly, I sailed."

"You sailed to Scotland!" I exclaimed, suddenly reassessing this man.

I had been more concerned with my own problems that morning as we had been meeting so many full of dreams and claims.

Curious, I asked, "Did you do the Red Sea and canal?" Thinking what a silly question, but having twice traversed the Red Sea, thought I'd hear the latest.

But what I heard next wiped away every remaining concern for my aging.

"NO, didn't do the canal. We rounded the Horn."

"What! You went around the Horn! How big a boat?"

"Thirty-three feet."

"And how many souls on board?"

"Just me."

"Oh, you've got to be kidding. You sailed solo round the Horn, and… and you must be my age," I hesitated over the last not wanting to ruffle his feathers.

"Aye, and maybe I have a few years on you. I first rounded the Horn when I was seventy. Rounded it again when I turned seventy-five, and if my bonnie lassie lets me out again, I'll round it again in two years when I'm eighty."

Somehow I knew this man was genuine, so I said nothing but slid my hand across the rail to encompass his. Looking into those warm, gentle eyes, I felt the man's lust for life pour through me, and suddenly I was not the least concerned that I was 4,000 miles from home and about to turn a mere 64.

Later that same morning, when the club's bosun bid me a good day, I called him to the rail to disclose what I'd heard. He smirked and commented, "Oh, so you've met George. Last time he rounded the Horn, he had to go aloft to fix a parted halyard, and slipped and fell, getting his foot caught in a step loop. Ripped some tendons, but George just got himself down from the mast, wrapped the leg, and then carried on around the Horn non-stop to Scotland."

Well, since meeting George, I have never once felt the advancing years blues. And when alone on a dark watch, I feel the man beside me, and together we puff out our chests, happy to still sail the sea, and with pride look out over inky blackness to the stars.

Fremantle is jumping since the 1987 America's Cup. The shoreline is packed with new seaside flats and thousands of marina berths, all full. But the lovely old buildings around the port have been retained. There is so much to do, a month's visit was hardly enough. We rode free buses to scores of eateries, museums and galleries, the Fremantle Market, and enjoyed many social nights out.

But our sights were set on the untouched land of Southwest Tasmania. And having sailed the Great Southern Ocean once before, we knew storm cells can generate enormously powerful waves taller than many buildings. Rounding Cape Leeuwin a month later reminded us of that. A strong gale struck. Fierce winds filled our cockpit and forced us to endure a blustery, wet passage that lasted three days. Tired and wet, we arrived in Albany.

ADVENTURE BOUND

Albany, November 2008

An icy wind blowing through the companionway straight from Antarctica is chilling my neck where it juts out my knitted beanie. But if I get up to drop down the hatch, it would wake Jude. Besides, I have to get tough. Our lives could depend on it. I have to be able to think and act while my teeth chatter. Why? Because a new adventure is forming; one that will take *Banyandah* closer to the southern ice pack. And for a couple of sun-lovers - Brrr! We're not used to this.

Our six-month holiday back in our house was glorious. We slept in a bed that did not rock and let us merely turn over whenever storm winds rattled the windows. Such a comfortable life, I'm carrying an extra ten kilos. Hopefully, it will help ward off the cold.

We've come back not sure if our sons are having a competition, but every time Jerome and Julie have a child, Jason and Ally pop another one too. When we first departed, we had three, now we are up to five grandchildren, with Ally due again later this summer.

It would have been easy to have stayed home and continued racing the grandkids around the yard in a wheelbarrow or intrigue their growing minds by reading stories. But Jude and I are on a mission. While we still can, we will continue seeking notable locations to show that other creatures have a right to life and that humanity would have a better one by moderating its plunder of the planet.

Banyandah is still high and dry just where we left her, standing on her keel atop the bitumen fronting Oyster Bay near Albany, Western Australia. To reach our bed, in fact to reach anything, our galley, clothes, tools, we have to climb a basic metal ladder without guards or railing. To wee, or even empty the sink, Jude and I must use a slops bucket then trudge a football field of tarmac to a public facility that boasts a cold shower. Brrr! Got to get tough, or we'll be visiting Davy Jones' Locker and not coming back.

Between our next destination and us lies a two-week battle in the big stuff and *Banyandah* has to be in tip-top shape to tackle the Great Southern Ocean, where big seas run unimpeded around the world.

And where will that get us? Why, to the Apple Isle, Tasmania, one of the most mountainous islands in the world. But our first destination won't be her capital Hobart, or even her northern port of Devonport. Nah, that'd be too easy. Remember Matt and Gill, the young couple we met in the Berkeley River? We swapped tales of Japan for theirs of Macquarie Harbour on the west coast of Tassie. Now, like them, we want to take our sailing home up the Gordon River into thick, virgin rainforest. Little changed until recent times, some creatures have adapted, while others are endangered, and some nearly extinct. Like the Tasmania Devil, threatened by a mysterious virus.

Late Night Visitor

It's a few days before Christmas, *Banyandah* has been re-launched, and we have almost finished our re-fit. Late last night, when tied alongside the jetty abreast the Emu Point Slipway, I woke to hear my dear lady shouting. "Put that down. Get out of it."

Groggy, coming out a deep sleep, I thought she was dreaming and was about to comfort her back to sleep when I felt her crawl over me. That got me wide-awake. I sleep next to the companionway.

Rising in the dim light, I heard Jude shout that someone had been on our boat and had just gotten off. So, without a thought, I was away like a shot, over the rail, onto the dock, and off towards the empty parking lot. In the single dim lamp, a towering figure was walking off with something in his arms.

I ran after, shouting, "Put that stuff down! Walk away and nothing more will happen!"

Reaching alongside the figure, he was bigger than me, shirtless, and carrying our two green shopping bags in one hand, and in the other, swishing round 'n' round, something like a long kung fu stick, which I carefully kept out of its range.

Again I said, more calmly this time, "Now look buddy, you don't want any trouble. Just put that stuff down and there'll be no trouble."

Not a word in reply, just the swishing of that long stick. I looked about the dark marina, not a soul in sight. Looking back to the young man, the stick caught the arc of that light and became our homemade boat hook whose sharpened stainless end doubles as a gaff.

Jude now suddenly rushed up and damn near tackled the fellow, and I had to yell at her to keep away. "He's got our boat hook!"

In a shrill voice, she yelled out, "That's my dirty laundry in those bags! Just put them down and get out of here."

What was this character doing? Dead of night, stealing dirty laundry and an ancient boathook. I didn't want trouble, not for us nor this young fellow. But he would not stop shuffling towards the exit. So I began screaming out, "Help! Robber! Help!" I was so loud; someone would either come running or call the police. But the lad just kept slopping along the pavement, and no one came to our aid. Emu Point Slipway is an industrial area. There's a marina, but few live aboard.

"Look lad, my lady and I built that boat. We built every scrap, sailed her around the world, and raised our kids on her too, so she's precious to us. Won't you just put the stuff down and walk away. I promise there'll be no further trouble."

And just about when I had given up all hope, he stopped, and slowly put the hook and bags down, and then he shuddered and began to cry.

I have a love for all mankind. The world's a tough place. And having pulled myself up from a rather horrible start, I find time for lost souls wherever I encounter them.

Reaching up, putting my arm around his bare shoulder, I comforted him and asked what the matter was?

In a torrent, outpoured, "They mistreat me. Won't let me out. Don't understand."

Jude picked up her laundry and moved the boathook away from the two of us while I asked, "You talking about your family?"

"No, I've been in hospital, but the nurse abuses me, so I ran away tonight. I didn't mean any trouble. Just thought I could get some money to get to my dad."

I was still just in my nightshirt, and suddenly feeling the cold, I said, "Look, why don't we go back to the boat. Are you hungry?"

Well, of course, we did not get on the *Banyandah* but sat on the dock alongside her. And while Jude made us cups of tea and slices of bread with marmalade, I listened to this young lads outpouring.

In a nutshell, he wasn't crazy. Just knew his rights, as we all do with the telly informing us all the time that we have the right to this or that. And he had found an easy way through life as a ward of our great nation. At the present moment, he was checked into a mental ward claiming he had self-harm problems, and he had been abused.

I grew up in LA, one of the world's fiercest cities. Walk into a payphone, and the sharp edge of a knife might find your throat. Park your car on a dark street and a pistol may greet your exit. Abused? Crikey, I got touched up at thirteen and was drugged by two old farts at eighteen. So I told this young man there is no profit in looking back. Life is the future, not the past. It is tough enough without carrying extra baggage. Then thinking of our welfare system, I asked, "What's the matter, you don't like hard work?"

"No, I don't mind working. My dad and I once picked fruit, and I really enjoyed lugging 'round the bins."

"Well then, life is an opportunity. Don't waste it. The system will make you a captive. They pay you enough to survive, but not to progress. And unless you make a break, you'll be no more than you are now for the rest of your life. Look at us; we've seen the world, love all critters and still going strong because we've had dreams."

Yes, I know, won't erase a lifetime of problems in a couple of hours, so we asked if he had a family then listened to a string of woes about broken marriages and his mum's new man not wanting him around. It didn't surpass my own history.

"What about your dad?"

"Yeah, he's great. In Queensland but."

"Well, that seems the best course. Change of venues gives you a new start, and if your dad helps, you'll find some support while you get yourself moving forward again. Just find a dream."

Considering it was three in the morning, Jude then asked the most crucial question, "What are you going to do now?"

"Dunno"

Always practical, she suggested, "Why not go back to the hospital and tell them what you've done and ask them to place a telephone call to your father."

Surprising us both, he agreed. So we gave him a shirt and old jumper, exchanged my Ugg boots he'd nicked for a pair of sunny Queensland flip-flops, and he walked out our lives.

Jude called the hospital around ten, and the staff nurse exclaimed, "Oh, you're the couple." Then reported that he had told them the whole story and that they were attempting to put him in touch with his father. Do hope his life has a happy ending.

A few days later, we set sail across the Great Australian Bight.

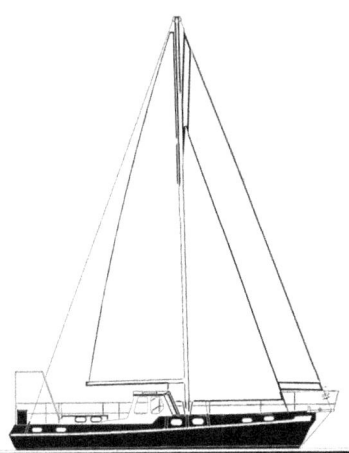

MOONLIGHT ACROSS THE SOUTHERN OCEAN

By the time the Roaring Forties pass under Australia, they have gathered energy from halfway around Earth and are either driving the sea wild or are ready to pounce when next provoked by a depression from Antarctica.

Now imagine two aging flower powers, petals shrivelling, yet with bright, strong hearts, aboard a homemade sailboat crossing this most feared stretch of water. Alone, they must look after themselves, and God forbid either be injured or suffer a body malfunction.

With my eyes aglow I have told others about the time we made a winter crossing from Albany to Wilson Promontory, me on the aft deck cudgelling the heavens trying to match Nature's fury as a black front passes overhead. With that glow replaced by humble respect, I then describe how *Banyandah* began lifting to a wave that soared high above her masthead. When its top third tumbled and turned white, froth flew from its crest, and roaring like a fast train, chased Banyandah down till it washed over us.

Eighteen months ago, with little thought of the dangers and difficulties, the *Two J's* took on this challenge once again. At that time *Banyandah* rested peacefully between the towering red cliffs of the Berkeley River gorge in a slender slit in the arid Western Australia landscape. In the shade of her awning, we were sitting listening to Matt and Gill relive their adventures aboard *Wooshee* surrounded by thick Tasmanian rainforest on the mighty Gordon River. We love those ancient silent monsters with branches dripping green mosses, so the thought of living among such grandeur had us put that destination on our must-do list while circumnavigating Australia.

But, making a promise is one thing, fulfilling it another. Especially when it involves crossing 1600 nm of the Roaring Forties and then making landfall on a lee shore that has only one safe haven, and it guarded by a narrow gap called Hells Gate.

Months of voyaging and other activities had distracted our thoughts until we began our road trip back to *Banyandah*, left in Albany during an east coast winter's break visiting family. In a lifetime of tackling challenges, we have found proper preparations lay the foundation to success. With this in mind, we had returned with two new sails and a new safety device that sounds an alarm should the watchkeeper fall overboard while the other is sleeping.

By November, we were back at Emu Point Slipway where *Banyandah* stood forlorn, like a warrior in tarnished armour awaiting some care. Here we received the best assistance from Darren Russell, a journeyman shipwright and owner of the friendliest slipway in Australia.

Six weeks of steady work had our good ship ready for sea, but we hung around for the new moon's slender face, as there's nothing quite as grand as sailing an empty sea bathed in moonlight. Two days before Christmas, we cast free our lines and sailed straight into a near gale, thinking if something's going to bust, best it happens close to facilities. Sailors don't have public holidays; everyone knows that. So while most were ripping open gifts, our Christmas Day was celebrated by having one of our loveliest sails within cooee of gigantic granite boulders, washed and weathered by white breakers off a sapphire sea.

We gunk-holed along the south coast while trying to find our sea legs again, sleeping well at Two-Peoples Bay, Waychinicup, and Cape Riche. But the night before our departure, we slept poorly. Not from nerves, but from a nasty Southern Ocean swell rolling into Bremer Bay. I swore a blue streak all that night and into the morning as we packed our disaster grab bag and lashed emergency provisions into the tinny. In a more positive note, we both slept well our first night at sea when usually it takes a few nights before we are so fatigued we don't hear the groans, clicks, and sea sounds that stops sleep coming quickly.

Leaving with no malicious weather approaching, our first challenge was finding a way through the prevailing summer high-pressure cell that contained only whispering easterly headwinds. With the rig in tight, we sailed full and by, increasing the apparent wind, which increased our speed to slightly faster than if walking upon that mirror flat ocean. Those first five days, southing came slowly while our watch keeping settled into a rhythm. Jude retired at eight, but not before seeing that I had clipped on our watch keeper's belt containing personal EPIRB, waterproof strobe, whistle, and a small transmitter that activates an onboard siren if the wearer should fall overboard.

We always post a watch. No exceptions. Dangers materialise when least expected. So, regular as clockwork, at 15 minutes past midnight I wake Jude. Then, if needed, we make any sail changes. This helps me sleep until the eastern horizon lightens. Often, I slip into a bed still warm from my lady's sleep. In the past, we have tried shifts of two, three, and four-hours. But I took so long to fall asleep that now we simply split the night in two. Jude takes a morning nap to gain extra rest.

Slow, easy miles slid past until one morning when a band of cloud wet our decks. Then presto, like an ace thumped down on a jack, the wind magically swung to the west. At last, the sails could be eased, although running from rather light winds actually slowed our progress. But, with each passing day, as the moon grew larger, so did the wind strength, until, when celebrating one week at sea, it came in strong, forcing us to reef down for the first time. Barrelling along at double pace, *Banyandah* now rolled heavily in the increased swell. Tossed one way then the other, sleeping fitfully, I cursed the sudden squeaking of a windvane block until I could stand it no more. Boldly braving a wetting, I clambered topsides, braced my bum on the wet aft deck, clamped a torch between my teeth then tried to lubricate the offending block. Alas, all in vain. Towelling the cold sea off my torso, shivering, I climbed back into bed. Moments later, I was shoving tissues into my ears in a futile effort to silence the repetitive squeal that was still driving me insane. Those 24 hours were our best run. One hundred and forty-three nautical miles logged. Not our highest ever, which is nearer two hundred, but a good day's run nonetheless.

You might think mid-ocean a boring lonely place, but it is not. A long voyage like this becomes an intimate passage through time and space filled with Nature. Seabirds kept us company, clouds whisked overhead, and sea swells passed in ever-changing patterns. Early on, flocks of brown mutton-birds swooped down behind us after we had landed a big fish. Greedily they dove deep to retrieve chunks we threw them, using their wings to fly under the sea like cormorants. And if they missed, atop the sea they'd beat their wings and paddle their feet to chase *Banyandah*.

Further south, when the breeze acquired a real bite, giant albatross soared gracefully astern, effortlessly travelling many miles without moving their three-metre wings. Surely, man's first gliders were fashioned after them. Some had black slashes like mascara running through their eyes, others had snow-white wings edged in the deepest black, and a few had patterned bodies like beautiful Italian marble. Other creatures were about too. Shearwaters soared swiftly along the swells, and tiny storm petrels no bigger than would fit in our hands, their pink legs dangling, danced from wave top to wave top searching for food among the breaking seas hundreds of miles from land. These creatures of mid-ocean survive in all winds. In fact, the more it blows, the faster they swoop and soar, seeming to enjoy the extra power and challenge as they race one another in magnificent displays of aero acrobatics.

We keep a log of our journey. Each hour of every day, we record the cumulative miles *Banyandah* has run, course steered, miles achieved, wind speed and direction, barometric pressure, plus any notes we like to make. Sound like a chore? Not a bit. In fact, when the ship's bell strikes the hour, we relish the opportunity to record our passage. It would be more than 30 years since we started with store-bought logbooks, which soon proved rather expensive. So we designed our own that also contained a form for reducing sextant sights and noon meridian passages. We recorded thousands of sea miles using photocopies of this form mounted in folders. Then we had a 300-page hardback book printed for peanuts in Sri Lanka. Today, we use lined A4 hardback notebooks obtainable from most newsagents that Jude rules into columns. She also beautifully embellishes the pages with creatures we see, while all I can muster are doodles of our sail plan. With additional comments, some humorous, some laconic, a few distressed, they form an informative record of journeys we never want to forget.

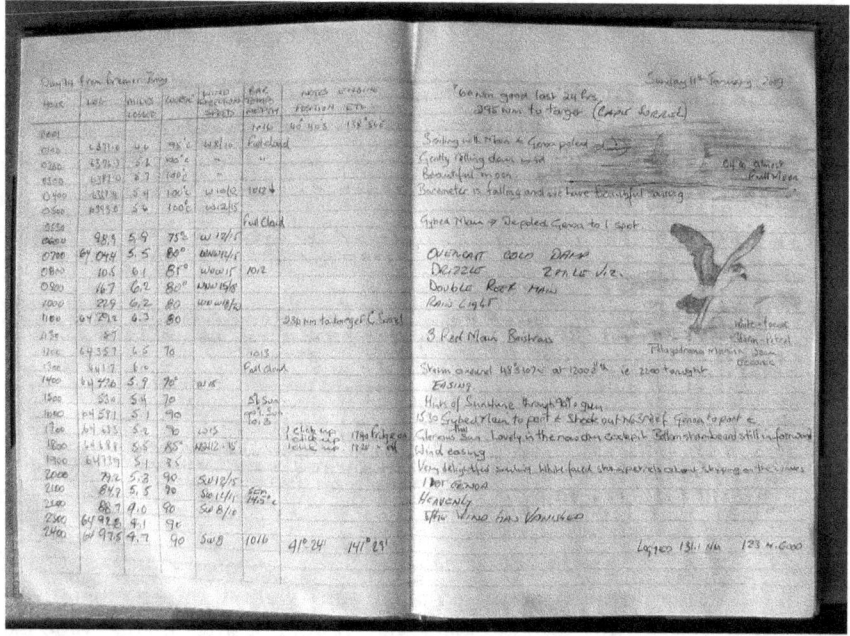

When sailing south of latitude forty, strong winds came more frequently, and we listened intently to the high seas weather forecasts issued four-hourly by the Bureau on frequency 8176. Recording the enormous amount of data first on an MP3 player, we would then replay it until we could graph the highs, fronts, and depressions. At those latitudes, the weather changes quickly. And when, just two days from landfall, a deep 970 mb low developed astern, instead of finding sleep, my mind gnawed on whether to divert to a far northern harbour or try to survive hove-to in strong gale conditions. We were checking into the Seafarer's Amateur Radio Net, reporting our position and weather, so I asked if they would check out the anchorage on King Island as an alternative. But the next day, when that depression got pushed further south and our area would receive only the cold front and 30 knots, we maintained our course.

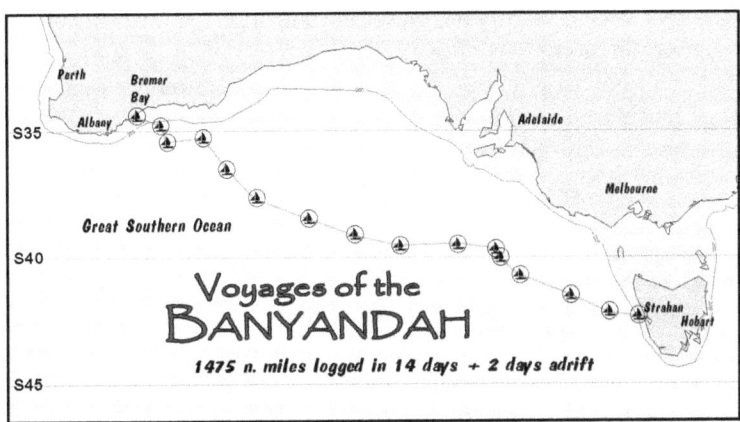

Our first sight of Tasmania came soon after that cold front had given us a kick up the backside. The mountain peaks seen between crashing waves sent our hearts soaring with pride and relief. By noon we were as close as we dare, just eight miles offshore. It was too late to attempt an entry, so we rolled up the headsail, pulled the main in tight, and hove-to. As if waiting for us to arrive, the wind eased and King Neptune's welcoming committee leapt out the sea to race past our bows in the most massive pod of dolphins seen since our earliest passages.

The lessening breeze tempted us to make a dash for the dreaded narrow gap of Hells Gate, but we resisted. Later, as the horizon darkened for yet another night at sea and the wind evaporated, I questioned if I had made the right decision. Jude bedded down, and as we were once again within mobile phone range, I settled into answering our inbox. But the wind gods weren't done with us yet. While bobbing up and down with a dark, hostile coastline now only five miles to our lee, the wind roared back with a vengeance not seen on this passage. *Banyandah* shook and she rocked. The cacophony was so deafening, Jude roared out. "What's going on?"

Vexation showing, I roared back, "Get some sleep." Though I knew she could not.

Hoping she'd find some rest, fearing she'd be clumsy if not, I tried to stay awake further into the night, but even the slatting sail and slosh of the sea couldn't hold back my weariness. Droopy eyed and unable to stay awake any longer, just as I climbed into her warm bunk, the wind ceased as if the gods had shut off a tap. Shaking my head while pulling up the doona, suddenly the wind roared back - from the opposite direction!

Exhaustion must have blocked out all noise and violent motion for I woke only when soft shadows crept into the cabin. Stumbling up, rubbing away heavy sleep, I saw Jude sitting in her chartreuse down jacket, ghostly white, staring blankly into a misty sea. The wind had gone, the sea was quiet, and a quick check of the GPS showed Cape Sorell just three miles off. Gulping down a quick coffee, I started the diesel, and through the mist, *Banyandah* went seeking her destination.

Jude didn't go back to bed. With land getting nearer, her cheeks found their usual blush as she eagerly grabbed her camera. Vapours rose like steam. First through the eerie light came the lonely white edifice of the Cape Sorell lighthouse atop ravaged rocks as *Banyandah* rode the Great Southern Ocean swells.

Not that long ago, in January 1822, two British ships set out from Hobart with orders to establish a place of banishment "to put the fear of God and Hell into the most incorrigible of Van Diemens Land prisoners." Only one, the *Sophia*, successfully navigated through the narrow gap into Macquarie Harbour. Landing at Sarah Island, Commandant Cuthbertson, his officials and a detachment of soldiers incarcerated 66 male and 8 female convicts in the most miserable place imaginable. The wretched souls passing through this narrow gap called it Hells Gate.

Free in spirit and commanding our own destinies, as we approached this treacherous gap, the sun broke through, bathing us in a warmth that added life to the vibrant colours of forest meeting the bold rocky shore. Just ahead lay an opening no larger than three house blocks abreast holding back a 50 km long body of water filled by the rivers draining southwest Tasmania. More often than not, strong currents make this gap untenable, and to enter at slack water was one reason we had waited. A strategy now paying dividends because we fought only a few knots with mild swirling eddies. While dancing around the deck recording the scenery, we thought of those poor devils who had spent their last days in this wet lonely place. But instead of leading us into misery, that narrow gap magically opened into an unbelievable expanse of smooth water where, for the first time in weeks, *Banyandah* ceased rocking. To not have to brace our every step, to not be thrown against bulkheads and doorways immediately lifted a burden that sent our spirits soaring higher still.

With seeing Strahan, a town of 800, appear around a headland came the realisation that we had achieved a dream held since that day with Matt and Gill. We had conquered the Great Southern Ocean. Before us now was the reality of a rainforest retreat. As well, another dream could now be achieved. To our south within easy reach lay the massive waterway of Port Davy; World Heritage, without tracks or roads. We'll be going there next, to explore and be amazed by the majesty of Earth.

Rottnest Island   Parker Point

Rounding Cape Leeuwin in gale
Ships came close to check on us

Leaving Albany two days before Christmas,
we sailed straight into a near gale, thinking
if something's going to bust,
best it happen close to facilities.

You might think midocean a boring lonely place
But it's not. In both strong winds and calms
across the Great Australian Bight, seabirds kept
us company, including several pairs of Albatross
And sea swells passed in ever-changing patterns

214 Two's a Crew

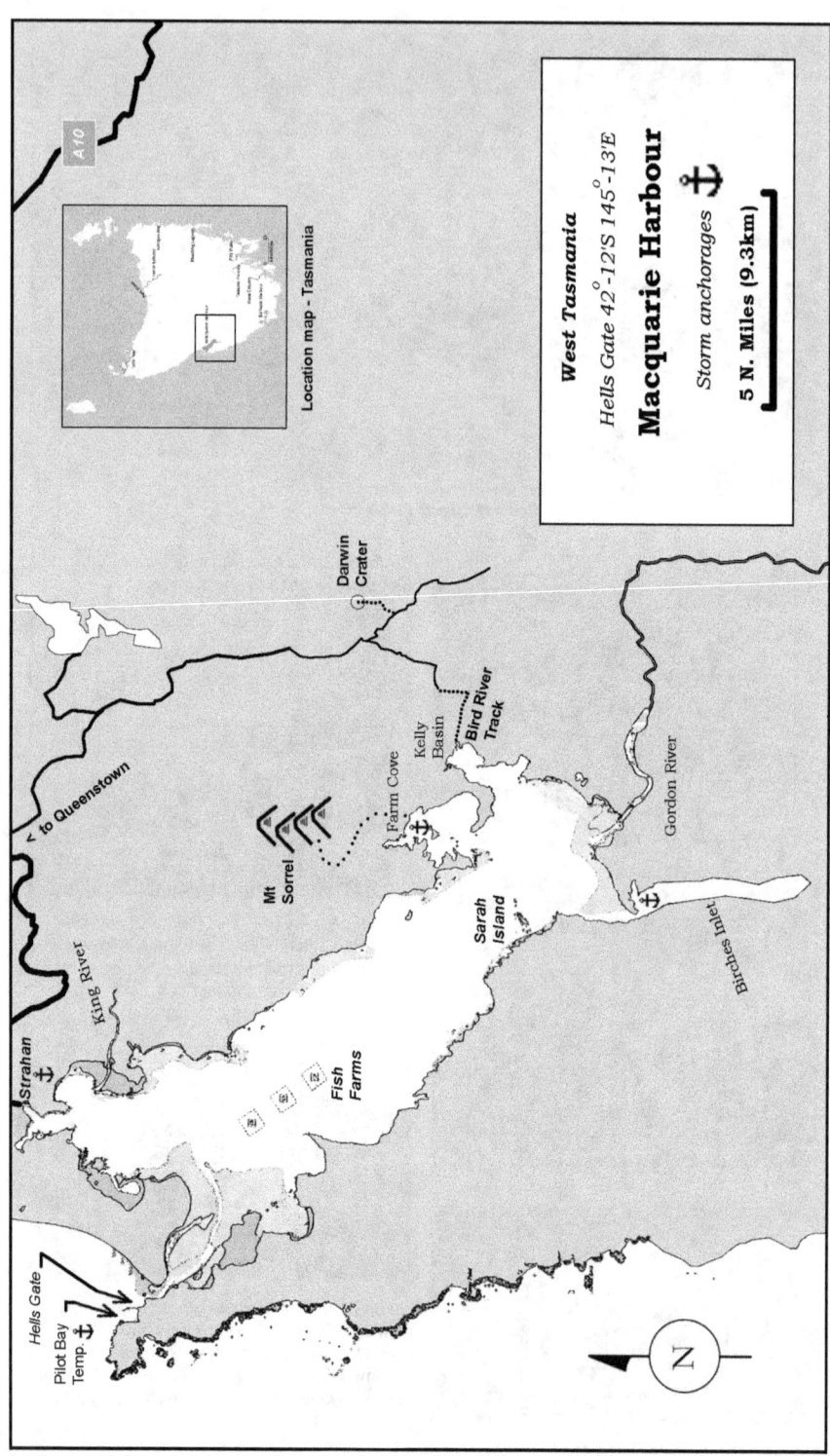

THEY CALLED IT MEEBBERLEE

When Abel Tasman became the first westerner to set eyes on Tasmania in 1642, Aborigines had inhabited the island for 35,000 years. They were the southernmost people during the Pleistocene era. During the ice age they had hunted giant marsupials on glacial plains, and then when the world warmed 9000 years ago and produced the thick rainforest typical of present-day western Tasmania, this forced them onto the coastal plains where they often travelled more than 600 kilometres each year, up and down the coast to different food sources, and to trade red ochre, which held religious significances, bonding the Aborigines with the blood of the land. They wore the red ochre on their skin and in their hair mixed with animal fat and charcoal to keep them warm and disguise their scent when hunting. Despite the cold winds and rain, this was all they wore.

Slightly more than a century after Abel Tasman, in 1770 Captain Cook claimed the entire east coast of Australia for the British Crown, and convicts were soon sent to build infrastructure. All was fine until 1798 when Matthew Flinders discovered that Tasmania was actually an island and not part of the mainland as previously thought. Worried the French might make a claim to this island and gain a foothold, Governor King, Lieutenant P P King's father, dispatched a vessel to colonise Van Diemens Land.

At that time six clans of Aborigines lived in the South West of Tasmania, and although many figures are quoted, it seems between two and eight thousand Aborigines inhabited the island. Having survived on this harsh land for longer than there had been people in the Britain Isles, with bullets and bacteria the first Europeans eradicated all but a handful of Aborigines within three decades. A "final solution" achieved, they then proceeded to rape the land of its wealth, felling 8000 trees in ten years, mostly the slow-growing Huon pine thousands of years old. They then dug gigantic holes in the earth to extract minerals, bringing thousands to the island to work while increasing the fortunes of a select few. Entire mountains were denuded to fuel the smelter fires. And the sulphur pouring out the stacks poisoned the ground, so that even today, 150 years later, Queenstown still lays a wasteland.

White man did all this in little more than 200 years of occupation. And although there may be more rules in place today, our principals haven't changed so Jude and I say, "Put Earth First," to preserve what remains.

I am no longer a city dweller needing endless comforts that Jude and I think only weakens our strain. I'm an adventurer, free-spirited, living closely with Earth, and am often affected by the hand of fate. A wind shift might take us to a new destination, or a chance encounter offer an opportunity on the other side of the world. And so it happened that as *Banyandah* cleared the sand flats held back by Hells Gate, the hand of fate guided her as she entered the deeper waters of Macquarie Harbour. A fair breeze arose, prompting Judith and me to raise sail for the final run into the settlement of Strahan. And with the engine now silent, we were free to ponder our thoughts. As we glided blissfully past the vast vacant land, we wondered how the original inhabitants had survived. They must have been cunning and robust to find food and shelter amongst the fulvous scrubby hills now flecked with white blossoms. Yet none survive here today. There were patches of green forests in the gullies of the distant mountains and we questioned whether the first settlers had cleared the woods as they had the Big Scrub that once surrounded our home port of Ballina. On the water, we spied man's hand in a multitude of large circular netted domes where Ocean Trout are bred for our tables. And as we contemplated what is better, farming fish or reducing world population, we spotted beyond the domes a smudge of white also heading for our destination.

Since olden times, whenever there are two sails, there's a race. And though the other craft was considerably larger, *Banyandah* held the lead while the lowering red sun cast long shadows upon the many peaks of Mount Sorell; its rocky ridges and verdant gullies becoming striped like a Tasmanian Tiger crouching low on the surrounding buttongrass plains. The last thylacine frozen in time? White men destroyed those shy creatures too. The larger craft gained, but we kept the lead right through the narrows leading past Regatta Point and into the harbour. Only then did we allow the larger craft right of way into a berth with signage declaring, "Stormbreaker, West Coast Yacht Charter."

Sailing oceans to distant lands, often totally surrounded by Nature, sailor's lives have threads of adventure and danger woven into a matrix of isolation and hardship that creates a strong bond between all cruising folk. We are a close-knit bunch, helping each other, because life afloat isn't easy, where first-hand advice can make the journey safer and more rewarding. Matt and Gill's recount of rainforest adventures aboard *Wooshee* had first whet our desire to come to the rarely visited west coast of Tasmania. But it was a couple we met in Albany that honed that core brilliance into the sharp points of a star adventure. Jamie, a soft-spoken Aussie with the boyish good looks typical to many veteran yachtsmen, and his English lady Niki, tall and lean, confident, oozing a zest for life shown in her grasshopper walk and bursting replies, had sailed their lovely timber craft *Siandra* around the world for 17 years by the time we first met them at the Emu Point Slipway. Hearing that they had just cruised around Tasmania for two years, I immediately invited them on board to mark up our charts. Jude and I had only just returned from five days walking in the Porongurup and my lady was away reprovisioning. So while the coffee brewed, I quickly gathered the few charts we had of the Apple Isle.

A nautical chart is much more than a roadmap. It's a guidebook of information. Where a roadmap concentrates on the more insipid details of distance and road surface, a nautical chart, when viewed by an experienced eye, creates images of adventures and dangers. It shows the contours of the seabed, whether its rock, sand, or mud, where the land is forested, where there is flatness or mountains, and where streams and rivers run. Charts were man's first guide to the unknown; they paint a picture of what the traveller can expect.

Rapid-fire, Jamie and Niki pointed to places on our charts, exploding with, "You must go here - to look for Darwin's Glass - to wander through the ruins at daybreak - hike this abandoned rail line alongside the forested Bird River - hide here and hope to see the endangered Orange-bellied Parrot." On they went for several hours, scribbling notes on our charts, marking anchorages, and imparting great chunks of knowledge that would significantly enhance our relatively short excursion through this marvellous part of the world. One note pencilled next to the town of Strahan read, "Stormbreaker Yacht Charter – say hello to Trevor and Megs from Jamie and Niki." And Jamie told me how Trevor had produced his own charts of Macquarie Harbour and the Gordon River, sounding the countless miles of shoreline for depth and dangers from his kayak.

One can read all the guidebooks, but nothing compares with local knowledge, so while *Stormbreaker* took her berth, we quickly handed the sails then putt-putted over to hail her crew, "Ahoy! Trevor about? We bring greetings from Jamie and Niki."

It rained that first night, and upon rising after a deep slumber assisted by a few celebratory red wines, I found the damp morning air had cleansed the forest and buildings of the small fishing port surrounding *Banyandah*. Sitting so incredibly quiet upon the tannin-stained waters of Risby Cove, not a ripple disturbed the reflections of the colonial buildings along the water's edge. Even the signage above them could be read upside-down. The surrounding forest-clad hills were also mirrored, creating an extraordinary vision of our vessel afloat in a bowl of tall timbers.

Dockside, activity had just begun. *Stormbreaker* lay serene in her pen, but next to her the two large power catamarans, each taking upwards of 200 tourists daily around Macquarie Harbour and up the Gordon River, busily washed their decks and took on stores. Three stories high, one gleaming white, the other burgundy red, they seemed slightly incongruous amongst the trees and colonial facades. More out of place was the seaplane whose high-pitched engine suddenly rent the air as if a starter's gun breaking the silence, and the tourist town of Strahan burst into life.

Just as suddenly now that the still waters had been broken, grey clouds stealthily crept in bringing a silent drizzle that ended my review. I went below to continue putting together a newsletter while Jude started laundering. She managed just two sheets before the black heavens turned nasty and angels wept copious cold tears. As the day progressed, the weather deteriorated. Increasing rain brought wind. By lunch, water slopped where forest reflections had been. By dinner, *Banyandah* was fighting her anchor chain, and the air whistled through the rigging and growled in the treetops. By dark, we were being thrashed about by a giant's invisible hand. Between the cacophony of scary sounds and sudden side skidding motion, sleep eluded us. Instead of counting sheep, we counted our blessings to be anchored inside, instead of at sea and took what little rest we could in between peering through portholes to verify our position had remained unchanged against the shore lights.

Many helpful folks are met by word of mouth. And so it was meeting Trevor and his lady Megs. They proved the key to our beautiful experiences in Macquarie Harbour. Here's how it came about. We had friends arriving from England and thought it would be grand if Trevor and Megs joined us on board for a dinner party. "Great," said Trevor. "First social night in months. Been that busy."

That night's conversation hardly stopped for breath; from UK weather to holidaying in Oz, childhood remembrances, charter worries, and on to places not to be missed in Macquarie Harbour, assisted by hand-drawn charts brought by Trevor. He's been chartering for 20 years, 16 of those out of Strahan. What a boon.

For three lovely days we gadabout with Doreen and Mel; one dockside chatting non-stop, one touring by car, and an overnighter at nearby Cat Island accompanied by fast sails, gunwales awash. By the time Doreen and Mel departed, all of us were smiling like Cheshire cats, although there was great sadness in our last embrace.

After they left, a high-pressure cell became fixed over the island allowing us to tackle the first excursion mentioned by Jamie and shown on Trevor's chart; the climb up that Tasmanian Tiger, the 1144 m high Mount Sorell. A note on Trevor's map indicated 15 hours return, but he also mentioned attempting the climb twice and not quite making the top, stopped once by falling snow. Jude and I weren't sure how high we'd get, but the views offered seemed worth the effort, especially as Trevor had said we would have our vessel in sight all the way up. The kick-off point was a lonely patch in Farm Cove, where convicts from the Sarah Island Penal Colony had attempted to grow crops in the early 1820s. Today it's once again just an isolated bay in the sparsely populated southwest of Tasmania.

Rain had fallen overnight, so it wasn't very pleasant dressing before dawn then rowing a wet dinghy to the forested starting point. "You'll have to bush-bash the first hundred metres, then its buttongrass," Trevor had said. I only knew that buttongrass was unique to Tasmania and imagined hillsides carpeted in something like low couch grass.

We had packed warm clothes, lunch, first aid, GPS and our personal EPIRB. Seen from the water, the mountain stood in plain view; treeless and carpeted by low vegetation, or so it looked. Therefore we did not take a topographical map. A big mistake.

It was still gloomy dark when we attempted to land and found our first obstacle; spidery trees, thick to the very edge of the water. After some minutes searching, I pointed to a spot between a tangle of roots and Jude rowed in, where grabbing a tree drenched my bush gear instantly. Oh well, I knew we'd get wet and thought the sun would eventually dry us. Standing one foot on a root with the other sinking into soft mush, through the dim light, I scanned a profusion of stunted trees interlaced with a spaghetti web of vine that blocked our passage. Pushing bodily into it, with Jude following in the tunnel I created, I immediately felt warm sticky blood. Looking at my arms, I saw green Samaria Swords slicing my skin.

"No good this way," I cried. "That stuff's razor grass."

The hundred-metre bush bash that Trevor had mentioned so lightly took an hour of torturous ploughing through bush thicker than the Big Scrub Rainforest. When we finally emerged onto the buttongrass plains, my clothes were soaked and stained watery red.

Above us, the now uninterrupted view beheld a sky turning cornflower blue with golden shafts shining through wispy clouds clinging to Sorell's peaks. Convinced we had overcome the most significant obstacle, and that the remainder would be a stroll, a quick snack of fruit renewed our flagging energy. And at first, it was a stroll. The nutrient-poor soil supported only a few stunted melaleucas, banksias, and the ubiquitous buttongrass that gets its name from a rounded seed head at the end of a long, arched, polished shaft, so thin and shiny it looks varnished. But, a smooth carpet to stroll it was not. Buttongrass grows on peat formed by sedges, in rounded clumps hiding deep-water channels.

As we began to climb higher, the peat we encountered must have contained more nutrients because the buttongrass grew taller, forcing us to raise our legs higher as if climbing a ladder. Even lightly burdened, our legs soon tired.

Climbing higher, the views over Macquarie Harbour grew more expansive. Trevor was right. *Banyandah* remained clearly in sight, dwindling in size as the day became hotter. Halfway, and gaining the first plateau, we discovered a deep chasm separated us from the main peaks. So we warmed up a cup of soup to revitalise our spirits.

Sipping the hot drink, we discussed whether to take the ridge, which was burdened with forest or drop into the chasm containing not one, but two rainforest streams. The ridge would take us up to even more forests on Sorell's side, so we chose to descend. It was steep, then very thick and as I crashed through, I was wondering how many Copperhead snakes lurked around us. Snakes and wilderness go hand and hand, and I took solace in knowing humans are not their food. I fell through branches, ripped green spaghetti vine apart, and rubbed spider webs from my eyes before we broke through into an emerald world. Mosses so thick they dripped off branches. Another variety covered the ground; pillow-like, right up to and into the babbling brook, as if God had been there with a broad green brush. The air was so fresh we glowed pink, but that pinkness soon turned red when we started struggling up the other side through the tangle.

We didn't quite make the summit before prudence sat us down for a late lunch and then turned us around for the journey home. But we did snap some fantastic photos of the wild west coast, with the expansive Macquarie Harbour and Sorell peaks forming the backdrop to quite a few. And we were enriched about the geology of the area, its plants and wildlife, being absolutely amazed to discover freshwater crayfish living in burrows on the mountainside. We recorded their mud chimneys coming out the peat and were impressed by their numbers, a dozen in a square metre. Besides the grandeur of the mountain's unrestricted views, wildflowers coloured our path. Eyebrights, which are lobelias with striated purple on their white blossoms, was my favourite. Jude's favourite, the tiny pink trumpets held between sharp, pointed, glossy leaves that pricked us through our thick trousers. So many other wildflowers attracted our camera that it became a dangerous contest balancing our time. With one eye through the shutter, the other on our GPS displaying direction and time, we only just found our dinghy as the sun started its passage around the other side of Earth. And that forced us to row home by starlight.

Don't fret my darling. Next time we'll carry a base camp and conquer the mountain over several days.

The following day we rested. I worked on our 20-year-old outboard, trying to coax it back to life after 6 months clamped to our railing exposed to the elements. Reluctantly it coughed back to life on the last pull before sundowners would have closed my shop, giving cause for celebration and solidifying our plans for a motorboat tour on the morrow.

Macquarie Harbour has several coves nipped out the land, each providing excellent protection from strong winds, and each having served a purpose in earlier times. Next to Farm Cove lies Kelly Basin, which has a most intriguing history. Whereas in 1822 Farm Cove was used to grow food for the penal colony, eight decades later Kelly Basin had an expanding community called East Pillinger serving the North Mount Lyell Copper Company. In the very early 1900s, you would have been standing amid a bustling port town of 600, with railway carriages loaded with timber, bricks, and ore shunting past, and shouted instructions ringing out, and the smell of wood-smoke hanging thickly in the air. It's an intriguing story because just a few years after the extraordinary work felling the forests to create that infrastructure, it was abandoned. The company's chief competitor bought them out and decided to use their own facilities at Strahan to ship the ore out.

Today, East Pillinger is a peaceful place, most of the town reclaimed by the forest. But from its shores, it is possible to walk along what was once the rail bed that ran alongside the Bird River, through the exquisite rainforest to the Bird River Bridge.

Our second excursion came about through another chance encounter. And this time we must have angered fate because not all of it was a grand experience. Remember Jamie had mentioned Darwin Glass. That's the pale green glass formed when a meteor strikes granite. And he had drawn a circle on our small-scale chart about where he thought Darwin Crater lay, saying they had trekked there but did not find any glass, and then added they'd seen some in Strahan that had been found in the crater.

Our recollection of Jamie's account was too vague and the terrain too thick to wander aimlessly. We needed precise coordinates. But, without an internet connection to Google them, I turned on our amateur radio to find someone who had. Surprisingly, that was easy. A fellow ham in Adelaide answered my general call of "CQ" and offered to turn his computer on even though it was 44° C in his shack. Within minutes we had the crater's coordinates, twelve kilometres beyond the Bird River Bridge, and that clinched our going.

Our walk began after spending the morning exploring the ruins left by those early pioneers. What amazing sights. Amongst mature trees stood a moss-covered rail carriage with twin fern trees intertwined around the bogies, a forlorn boiler nearly lost amongst bracken, and three collapsed brick kilns their earthen-red remains poking through a thick coating of moss and lichen.

Carrying heavy rucksacks up the Bird River gave us an excuse not to hurry along the slight gradient that featured magnificent views up and down the rainforest gorge. Upon reaching the bridge, constructed more than a hundred years earlier from local Huon pine, we found little sign of its age other than the ubiquitous green moss that covers everything not moving. Continuing along a forest drive for another five kilometres, we turned onto a gravel track that leads into the Franklin-Gordon Wild River National Park. Where, not far after saddling over a locked gate, we found a dilapidated wooden sign with an arrow declaring *Darwin Crater*.

Our worries vanished, and our weary feet lifted with a spring as we rushed forward, expecting to be at a romantic campsite overlooking a natural phenomenon by nightfall. Aah, but fate had other plans. Imagine our dismay when we found the arrow pointed away from the road and straight into a jungle. A closer examination revealed a muddy track cutting through thick undergrowth, so we dropped our loads for a confab. Sitting on the gravel road, dense forest hemmed us in and the air was heavy with the distinctive scent of leatherwood honey. Following our noses found bees droning noisily in a clearing that housed dozens of hives. The neatly stacked white boxes buzzed like a miniaturised megacity of the 23rd century.

In my mind, I still imagined a beautifully formed crater filled with exotic crystals, like the one we had visited in the Galapagos and thought that Parks must have constructed a new access road. So, leaving my rucksack behind, I searched a kilometre up the gravel road but found nothing.

"This must be it, Sweetie," I said on my return. "What do you want to do?"

Coming out the forest was a running stream, so we could have easily set up camp. We had already humped our sacks twelve kilometres from the boat, and I was fairly knackered. But Jude is the eternal optimist.

She smiled then replied, "C'mon, it'll probably open up and be easy."

So we loaded up and ducked under the green foliage.

At first, it was enchanting. Just me and my lady alone in a serene forest, where the trickle of a stream complimented the beautiful carpet of moss lying alongside the muddy track. Unsure the path was still in use, I searched for boot marks, but instead found an occasional wheel rut and central hump of what once must have been a vehicular track that now had sizable regrowth reclaiming it. As we trudged up the first hill, between heavy breaths, we fantasised a Model T Ford was clattering up behind us carrying a young buckaroo and his lady in pink gingham. Between them, she steadied a wicker picnic hamper as they bounced their way past us for a day's outing at Darwin Crater. Upon reaching the crest, and not sighting the crater or open plains in the evening's poor light, the Model T's couple bounced from our view, leaving us surrounded by a tangle of forest less than an arm's length away. Descending into head height regrowth only deepened my concern. And the relief I felt upon clearing that sank when a muddy pool replaced the scrub. Skirting around it through tangled forest proved difficult, and so our journey evolved into a mixture of pain and pleasure as, one by one, we overcame the severe conditions.

Every so often, when the heavens showed, I would activate our handheld GPS and take a fix. A little more than three kilometres from the gravel track, we came unstuck. Fallen trees blocked our way, large ones obliterating a considerable area, making it quite awkward to find a way around. In the thick gloomy forest, it became impossible to re-find the track. Close your eyes, spin around a few times, and the forest looked the same no matter which way we turned. Our route was blocked at the convergence of several gullies, so the area was a jumble of dead branches and a heavy mulch of bark and leaf matter. And although I fought a way through, it took us deeper into a darker undisturbed area with no signs of a track. White toadstools popped out the mulch and without much prompting, ogres and trolls could have jumped out the shadows next to where I sat Jude while I retraced our steps. This took more valuable time, especially as I became disorientated several times, having to call Jude to get back to the start. Eventually, an overgrown path was located under yet another fallen tree, and we trudged off feeling spooked by so easily getting lost; the GPS useless under such thick cover.

Now so late, a sense of urgency had us admitting there would be no romantic campsite overlooking a crater. A flat dry patch would suffice if we could find one. On a small mound, we investigated an area for our tent amongst a clutter of dead forest matter. Where, after chucking aside some fallen branches, we spotted the telltale movement of black critters slinking up our trousers and shuddered. We were standing in a bed of leeches! While rolling them into balls between our fingers then flicking them into the bushes, our eyes spotted several others standing erect sniffing our scent and this sent us packing. Ugh! Nature was closing in.

A few moments later, things worsened. Rain began to fall, and it got darker. Jude and I are tough. We have trekked many trails, put up with plenty of discomfort with a philosophical view that if we want to experience the real Earth, then that's the price. But that doesn't mean we have to like it. Fate finally came through in the form of a surprise opening. Within a few steps, from a dark scary forest, the heavens opened up, and between drifting rain clouds, early stars shone brightly. The only problem, the track was now a shallow stream. At first, I crashed through shoulder height growth towards what I perceived as high ground, tearing more bark from my shins in a futile effort of finding a tent site. Giving up, I took Jude's advice and started tearing out the vegetation from a small flat she had located next to the watery track. But, before starting that, I dug deep for the cask of red wine. Got to celebrate any win when the going is tough. Besides, boosts your energy is my excuse. After clinking cups, Jude hurriedly started preparing a hot dinner.

Camp made, as Jude was handing me my dinner, I felt a tingling on my eyebrow and plucked a wiggling black leech between my fingers. Yuk! Little brute. Yes, I know, he's just trying to survive too. But my worst fear is one of those devils slipping in around my eyeball.

"Enough!" I roared. "I'm eating in the tent."

Rain fell most of that night, and although Jude's feet dangled past the edge, we both arose well rested to find sunshine. Our GPS revealed the crater just a mere kilometre away and eagerly we laid out our gear to dry while we broke our fast. Then, putting on wet clothes, we set off down what was now a fast-flowing stream.

God! That morning I swore far too many times trying to follow that track to Hades. But we found the crater. Or think we did. It took two more sweaty hours of sloshing through boggy head-height bushes before our GPS started flashing *arriving destination* and a buttongrass clearing began opening up. Looking about, we could see a definite ridge surrounding us and deduced that we were smack dab in the middle of Darwin Crater.

A wry smile shaped my lips when I mentioned to Jude, "Seems we actually had our romantic campsite overlooking a natural phenomenon."

No, though we searched for hours, we did not find any meteorite glass amongst that mile-wide circle of buttongrass. We did find a two-metre-long Copperhead snakeskin, and plenty of white dolerite crystals that we choose to believe were formed by the meteor hitting this planet. But nothing else, except maybe another giant helping of true-grit and cameras filled with memories.

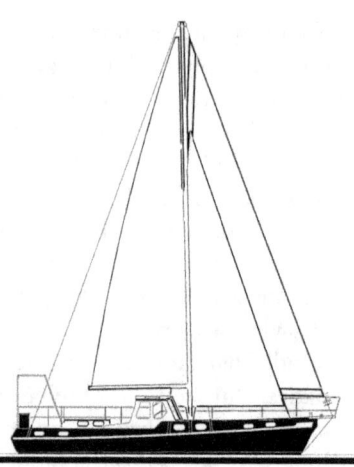

ON PAIN AND SORROW

Originally, Tasmania was called Van Diemens Land in honour of the governor-general of the Dutch East Indies who sent Abel Tasman searching for gold and silver in 1642, but its present name honours Tasman. He was the first European to sight and map its shores. When Hobart Town was founded in 1804, convict labour was sent to construct roads and buildings. To discourage escape, shipbuilding was forbidden. Some years later when the new colony needed ships, the government had to rescind this restriction, and that prompted James Kelly, a young man from Sydney who had gone to sea when a boy, to convince local merchant Thomas Birch to finance a circumnavigation of the island to locate shipbuilding resources. In particular, to find the source of massive logs sometimes found floating along the shores, which were light and strong, and seemingly indestructible. Kelly must have inherited a bit of the blarney from his Irish parents because he convinced another to lend him an 18' open whaleboat then set off late in 1815.

Nine days after leaving Hobart, 24-year-old Kelly came upon Macquarie Harbour, finding the entrance hidden amongst thick smoke from Aboriginal fires. Portentous, he told everyone. Had there not been the smoke, the Aborigines were close enough to have seen and speared him. Upon the shores of Macquarie Harbour, he found an abundance of suitable shipbuilding timbers; Huon, Celery Top and King Billy pines, as well as Blue Gum for construction, and Myrtle and Sassafras for furniture. On the 29th of December, he landed on a small island, naming it after Birch's wife Sarah. He then explored "a grand river," calling it Gordon after the owner of the whaleboat.

A year later, coal was found on Macquarie's eastern shore, and in 1819, Phillip Parker King charted its entrance in the *Mermaid*. The scene was set. Soon after, in January 1822, two British ships set out from Hobart with orders to establish a place of banishment "to put the fear of God and Hell into the most incorrigible of Van Diemens Land prisoners." The intention at the

Macquarie Harbour Settlement was clear: "Unceasing labour, total deprivation of spirits, tobacco and comforts of every kind, the sameness of occupation, the dreariness of situation must, if anything, will reform the vicious characters who are sent to you," Governor Arthur 1824.

It was said of Lt. Cuthbertson, Sarah Island's first commandant, "The most inhuman tyrant the world has known, he had neither justice nor compassion for the naked, starved and wicked; a man taken before him had no appeal. A sadistic bully of peculiar qualities." Flogging was the usual punishment, 8000 lashes dealt out in one year, administered by a heavier version of the cat of nine tails. Later, solitary confinement replaced this vile punishment. More hated, it left the men able to return to work.

And work they did, dawn to dusk, five and a half days a week no matter the weather. Timber cutters, lime burners, and work gangs camped at sites around the harbour and rejoined sawers, blacksmiths, bakers, and carpenters on Sarah Island at the weekend. Saturday afternoon was "slops"; washing and mending; Sunday the Sabbath. The prisoners provided free labour to extract high-quality shipbuilding timbers harvested from sites around the harbour and up the Gordon River, rafted them to Sarah Island, and then processed them for transport to Hobart. But, because of transport difficulties out through the narrow Hells Gate, stockpiles grew. At first, boats were built solely as a way to ship the timber out. In later years, the boats they built added value to the wood as they were sold by the Crown to finance the penal colony.

During the years 1824 through 1827, under shipwright Thomas Cole, 35 ships were constructed; "unsafe when laden; sail very indifferently." Then in 1828, David Hoy, a master shipwright trained in Dundee Scotland, took over. He had been frustrated by a lack of opportunity to build his designs in Hobart. But, under his guidance, 96 ships and boats were built with convict labour, giving the Sarah Island shipyard the highest output of any in Australia at that time. Selecting men with aptitude from the labour gangs, David Hoy trained them and used the shipyard as an experimental design station. The ships he built were praised by the surveyors.

Shipbuilding inevitably changed the character of the Settlement: "Save one venerable fern tree near the sawpits, not a vestige remained of the dense forest which once covered its surface... Captain Butler had formed, after recovering considerable area from the sea, a spacious dockyard, fronted by substantial log-built quays and protected from the northwest gales by a high lath fence."

Skilled workers were in demand: "The Settlement is badly off for a Turner... If there is a man of decided bad character, as a profligate, of this trade, let him be sent down."

Up to 385 male convicts were housed on Sarah Island and outstations at one time, and almost 2000 prisoners, military and officials passed through the Settlement during its 11 years of use. Eventually, the exceedingly dangerous entry through Hells Gate forced its closure in 1833.

On our second Sunday in Macquarie Harbour, following an enjoyable day's rest after our hard trek through the forest to Darwin Crater, with the air still and the sun bright, we took *Banyandah* out of Kelly Basin to re-enter the main harbour in search of something to do. We had quite a choice. Should we proceed up the Gordon River, or maybe we could attempt the entry into the long captive arm of Birchs Inlet, named by Kelly for his benefactor. Judith couldn't decide and given a choice, I gave *Banyandah* her freedom while I brewed a coffee. Minutes later, back on deck, I found her moving towards an ugly lone rock rising abruptly next to Sarah Island. Going to the penal colony was not an option as a tour vessel was alongside, which meant any pensive disposition would have been shattered by the hubbub and loud voices, and that just wouldn't do when trying to absorb the ambience of such an evil place. But Grummet, that lone rock looking so sinister and hostile, caught my eye, and I vividly recalled what I had read; the worst of the worst had been housed there. But how? It appeared impossible. Little more than sheer rock faces erupted out shiny black water. Recalling that the female convicts brought on the first ship had been chained inside a cave somewhere on that rock had me dashing below to search for more details.

Growing more menacing as we approached, just a few gnarled trees clung for life on its white granite faces, which looked streaked with red as if running blood. It held a fascination. Great violence had occurred on that tiny outpost, which at times can be surrounded by fierce winter storms. The exact opposite to the morning's ideal conditions that were perfect to trust the anchor and inspect a rock once home to desperate people; where men had been brutally murdered and women raped.

Stepping ashore the moment our dinghy crunched upon its pebble beach, we froze like statues, our imaginations tweaked by the silence that seemed to carry the cries of lost souls while next to our landing we envisaged the struggle of Constable Rex forcibly held underwater by nefarious convicts. In vivid images, the words we had just read leapt into life as the young married soldier vainly fought for his life. The air still reeked of fear and sweat; so much had been shed there. It drifted strongest from a cleft in the rock and investigating, we passed through a dark opening that led into the rock's heart. Where, as my eyes adjusted to the poor light, I fleetingly glimpsed eight women in rags chained to the walls, cringing more deeply and whimpering as I clattered forward upon smoothly worn stones. Through vision misted by tears, I saw soldiers brutalising those helpless waifs, taking pleasure as brutes do on those unable to defend their dignity. Escaping the cavern's close confines, I wondered if the bright sunshine was making my eyes water. Or had it been the knowledge that mankind can be twisted when absolute power manifests perversity?

I felt repulsed but turned and snapped a photo of the dark entrance, and in the camera's flash, my lady appeared prone against the wall, and my mind overlayed the previous images onto her sweet soul.

I had to dash away to lose the horror of what had occurred in the dark reaches of that cave and climbing a few feet up the rock facing Sarah Island brought me to a well-worn earthen path going up. Grummet might be called an island, but it is really little more than a large rock with soil and dead matter deposited on a flattened top that is hardly larger than a moderate garden. Today, thin, weedy gums struggle for life, along with mosses and vegetation restored by the natural wet conditions. But in its day, the rock was stripped bare and a shanty built on top that housed upwards of sixty of the worst of the worse from Sarah Island. From atop the rock's two-story height, through a spider web of branches, Hells Gate could be seen across a distance of placid reflections; so calm my rapid breathing abated, replaced by a spiritual calmness akin to entering a church. Nature enveloped me; the pale sky like the eyes of a child, undulating hills like soft toffee surrounded a shining harbour so smooth it looked perfect for a leisurely Sunday stroll.

The bushes rustled, and as Jude emerged, her hand pointed to the ground at my feet, to the oddly shaped ends of red bricks peeping out from green growth. Pushing aside clumps of moss and pepper bush heavy with purple berries exposed a jumble of other bricks that lead us past a young fern tree. Here hid the remains of a chimney. At the pinnacle of Grummet stood the remnants of what once held a meagre cooking fire, the only provider of warmth for those incarcerated.

A single leaf fluttered down, alighting on the moss-covered relics as if Nature was ashamed of what took place on her soil, hiding the remains in her own time. Another leaf twirled in front of me just as a breeze caressed my cheek. Instinctively I looked towards Hells Gate and noticed the shine had been replaced by cold steel washboard. A sudden coolness had come out of the northwest. Gales begin there. Bitter winter howlers march down this harbour, attacking with rain and sleet this exposed outpost. My heart shook when I thought of those icy blasts on men without freedom; desperate men, so tortured, death would have brought relief. No wonder so many had tried to escape. The naked rock peaks of the far distant mountains did not invite escape, nor did the tangled forests at their feet, nor the icy waters isolating Grummet. It was easy to understand why so many had perished in their attempt to gain freedom. One hundred and eighty had made an attempt in eleven years; 134 deaths recorded. Only the last 10 gained freedom, by stealing the last ship built on Sarah Island.

When a few more slender gum leaves fluttered down, *Banyandah* was pulling on her anchor against the wind chop. Our reverie was broken, and we were free to go. But to where?

Sarah Island was now available. Everyone had left. But being so satiated with human drama we could not absorb any more, we headed downwind to cross the shallow sand bar leading into the long, narrow, enclosed Birchs Inlet.

Calm, peaceful and mellow, inhabited only by sea eagles and black swans; it was a perfect place to digest all we had just experienced. For two days and three nights, we floated upon its calm waters, hoisting sail in the afternoons to take wisps of air to a new spot. Each morning, after the mist had risen, we explored our unique region. We found an abandoned sawmill, a workers' shack, and once after crossing a narrow land bridge, a harbour beach chucked high with Huon pine logs washed out the Gordon River.

That brought us to yet another calm morning, the sky still brilliant with stars. Rising before first light, I gave Jude a shake and said, "How about experiencing daybreak at the Settlement?"

It must have been the soft, moody light of the still dawn that had us slow down and pause after we climbed onto the jetty servicing Sarah Island. Both of us reached for our cameras as if compelled to record the wondrous cherub-pink lighting the peaks of Mount Sorell, perfectly reproduced on the smooth water of Macquarie Harbour, with *Banyandah* an enchanting beauty mark identifying the reflection. Behind us, birdsong enhanced the thin wash of cloud, producing a dreamlike effect. They seemed to be beckoning us hither, and reluctantly we left the jetty and took our first step upon the soil of Sarah Island.

Langerrareroune, its Palawa name, may have been a meeting place for the woman of the Perternidic, Mimegin, Lowreene, and Ninene when the clans met to gather swan eggs. Named Sarah by James Kelly, then officially known as Settlement Island during the Penal Settlement 1822 – 1833, the island of many names rose gently from under spreading shade trees to form a wide swath of grassy parkland any community would have been proud to claim. Dotted with the remnants of brick buildings, Jude read-aloud that these had been Government House; four chimneys in a row, two-roomed apartments for Commandant, Surgeon, Military Officer and Chaplain, while I gazed upon the view south to the Gordon River, entranced by such peaceful ambience.

"Each apartment had a garden plot," she read, and then turned and pointed, "and on the other side of this narrow road were the servant's quarters."

Hearing her read details of their daily life brought to my eye a melodrama; stewards in livery carried food baskets down the lane, others carried slops buckets while a well-presented military elite bowed to his lady, adjusted her shawl and touched her rosy cheek before turning abruptly to stride off in cadence towards the Settlement's Administration building just down the street. In the air, accompanying the melodious birdsong and raucous currawongs, drifted the sweetness of blossoms tainted by imaginary smoke and yeasty baking bread. A thoroughly wholesome scene of 1800s British gentry - until we strolled a few paces further on, past the foundations of the military barracks, to the narrow confines of the goal standing opposite. The cells, hardly a metre in width, were less than a man's height and windowless, making every day of solitary in darkness and silence much worse than the equivalent five lashes.

In the stillness of dawn, entirely alone on the island and able to touch these remains transferred some of the misery suffered by those entrapped between silent walls. These cells were not a virtual reality nor a movie set. Real humans had suffered greatly within the very confines surrounding us, and placing our hand on their surface seemed to act as a conduit that plunged us into a macabre fascination that forced our eyes to search for signs of human blood.

Up a hill behind the goal, through regrowth of Blackwood, Cheesewood and Celery-top pines, lightly covered in mosses adding lutescent touches to the verdant scene, a track leads to the weather side of the island. There, cliffs of rough grey rock fell straight into dark waters. And in a gully lay the base of a single-file staircase used to count the men as they moved from the muster yard up to the penitentiary, whose jagged remains still projects out the cliff top as if Frankenstein's castle.

Inside the prison, Jude and I had fun playacting; growling as if caged animals for the video camera, jumping about beating the stone walls like demented creatures. We have seen a few prisons around the world and have been impressed by their builders who had the knack of positioning them best to torment their prisoners. One atop a small Mediterranean island overlooked a vast expanse of beautiful turquoise water. Shaped like a doughnut, in the outer wall of each cell was a small window, too high up to see sky or sea. While in the wall facing inward, a window at eye level faced a central pulpit, where twice a day priests lectured the inmates on morals and civics. And here at Sarah Island, the prison sits on the brink of nearly freezing water where icy winds attack it.

During the relocation of the Aborigines, they were held on the lower level while awaiting transfer to Flinders Island, a process taking several months. "While housed on the ground floor of the Penitentiary, the prisoners did all they could to annoy them by pouring water through the boards, urinating on them and hammering on the floor." Another reason more than half of the Aborigines died in captivity on Sarah Island.

Up until now, we had only observed the punishment and hardship – "to put the fear of God and Hell into the most incorrigible of Van Diemens Land prisoners." But we had read that with the building of ships, some dignity and rehabilitation began. Men with no future were given reason to live. Under Master Shipwright David Hoy, workers were given training and rewards, for he believed "you cannot build fine ships with slave labour." The number of floggings dropped and attempts to escape much fewer. So, having seen the places of punishment, we set off to find the site of rehabilitation.

At the far western end of the island, near where the tour vessels tie-up, are what remains of the docks and shipyards. After nearly 200 years of reclamation by Nature, like that on Grummet, the remnants of the docks required a little imagination to see men at work. But, with no other tourist boat yet arrived, we snooped along the shore at will, dipping our boots in the tannin-stained water to poke at the remains of the Blue Gum skids, and to playact what it might have been like. The forges used to make iron straps and fastenings were in an adjacent clearing now taken over by bracken and mosses. Care was required to navigate around them, and then a slow meander revealed places for the fires and bellows. Helped by information signs and the guidebook we carried, the docks came to life in our minds if not through the lenses of our cameras, and we could appreciate the old adage that restoring man's self-respect allows them to respect others.

What began as a place of banishment became a place for restoring dignity, giving purpose to those who never had any. Whether they went on to a better life, we do not know nor thought about it anymore because at that moment a distant throb broke our reverie. Too early for a tour boat, I knew that sound and dashed off towards the jetty.

Van Diemens Land's most incorrigible were imprisoned on Sarah Island Macquarie Harbour, west coast of Tasmania

Across the millpond harbour, arrowhead ripples radiating from her bow came *Stormbreaker* from the Gordon. Her course was bringing her close to Sarah, and knowing Trevor, he had seen our ship lying off the island. I jumped into Little Red to intercept him. And seeing me, he diverted so that we came together just next to *Banyandah*.

As *Stormbreaker* came closer, her railing became crammed with onlookers. "Been up the Gordon?" I enquired, my gaze wandering along his passengers, none much younger than me.

"Did you enjoy your rafting trip?" I asked, standing up, reaching for the rub rail.

"No," they all laughed. "We just enjoyed a lovely night up the river."

Then Trevor leant over and handed down a brown paper bag.

"Here's your mail and yesterday's newspaper," he said with his usual exuberance.

"Ah-ha! The book about Deny King," I beamed. "*King of the Wilderness*, the amazing icon of the South West. Wonderful. Thanks." The book had been delivered to Trevor's shop.

Trevor looked across to *Banyandah*. "I was wondering when we'd meet up. How has it been?" He inquired enthusiastically.

"Oh! Just magic, Trev. We've climbed Sorell, explored East Pillinger, walked to Darwin Crater, and now we're absorbing the drama played out here on Sarah and Grummet. Next we're going up the Gordon."

His passengers' smiling faces followed my glance towards the mountain peaks that were reflected through an alabaster veil onto the mercury silver water.

"You're a lucky man, having all this on your doorstep," I said.

"Oh yeah," he smiled. "Macquarie's got everything; Nature, history, beauty, adventure. What more could anyone desire."

He raised his hand and waved goodbye.

"Must be off. Hope we share an anchorage up the Gordon."

And with that, I let go as *Stormbreaker's* engine once again shattered the silence.

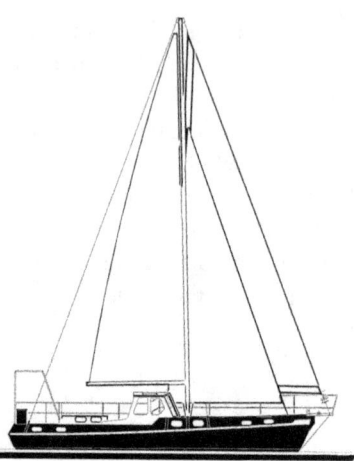

HERE COMES DESSERT

In the late 1960s and early '70s, protests over the damning of several small, naturally occurring Tasmanian lakes at the head of the Gordon River started the first rumblings of the Australian green movement as a political force. The dams, designed and constructed by Tasmania's Hydro-Electric Commission (HEC), greatly enlarged Lake Pedder to form the largest body of freshwater in Australia and provided energy for the Upper Gordon River hydroelectric generation scheme. This project created worldwide publicity and brought the environmental movement to the mainstream in Australia.

Later that decade in 1978, due in part to persistently high unemployment, the Tasmanian Government proposed a second damning of the Gordon River to help promote the electricity-intensive industry. If completed, forests that had stood since creation would have been flooded, wiped out in a blink of Earth's eye. At the time it was said the area was too mountainous and too wet for human habitation. Nevertheless, environmentally sensitive citizens protested to save Nature from destruction, while others wanting development and work rallied for it. The confrontation mushroomed into a massive demonstration centred on the tiny town of Strahan, closest to the dam site, and it became a cauldron of emotions dividing the community. A High Court battle five years later in 1983 gave the Federal Government the power to revoke the State's right to decide, and the dam was stopped.

Some thought sanity prevailed. Others rued the loss of jobs. Twenty-five years further on, many think this was a terrible outcome for the planet. Instead of creating a new source of green power, millions of litres of fossil fuels are burnt moving tourists in and out to see the river and forest. Funny how life evolves. The Gordon below Franklin Dam was never completed, yet the jobs it was meant to provide have been created by the tourist industry exploiting the same river that would have been dammed.

Being on the threshold of one of the most significant environmental campaigns in Australian history, we were definitely going to travel the 40 km up this river to the exact spot of that battle, to witness the wilderness that had been under threat; to help us decide if we thought the outcome was good for Earth and her creatures.

Sometimes when sitting down to a feast, a dessert on the sweets trolley might catch the eye. And while the dinner is being enjoyed, the brain yearns for a taste of that dessert, thinking how delicious it would be. That is how we felt as a warm zephyr softly filled our headsail, holding it full against the sliced face of Frenchman's Cap, while our eyes roamed ahead to the nick in the hills through which the Gordon River flowed. Savouring the anticipation of its exotic taste, we thought here comes dessert and wondered where else on Earth can a sailing home venture into Nature's heartland to explore virgin rainforests.

Almost every visitor to the Gordon arrives with a roar of speed and quickly changing scenery, a considerable curling wave behind. But there's another way to approach this ancient river – slow and silent - so the eye has time to scrutinise every changing nuance of the mountain peaks, to see them appear then disappear behind lush forested slopes like a big swell disappears behind an island.

We had come to live amongst its beauty, sounds, smells and creatures as well as its weather. And part of that experience would be interactive, hands-on. Not passengers looking through plate glass windows. We'd be within Nature, in the cold and heat, in the dry or wet; while navigating our craft around each bend not knowing what we'd find next.

Sarah Island was nearly out of sight when a tiny speck appeared ahead. At first, it was a log, and then it became a family of swans undisturbed by our slow approach. In the hills beyond, vibrant echoes of forest birds called and our eyes strained to pick out their movements.

The river's first marker slid past, its red top-notch badly needing a coat of paint. And automatically our eyes dropped to the water where we noted the tide assisting our entry. The bottom is rising, and entering the unknown I shivered ever so slightly wondering how far up the tide has an effect. As if demonstrating that we were indeed entering the land, a massive dead tree, with the root ball and all its branches stuck in macabre repose, passes with that family of black swans feeding next to it. Their necks gracefully extended, black majesty to beaks dipped in scarlet red. Startled into flight by the closeness of *Banyandah*, the silence is broken by splashing feet and rapidly beating wings. Heads forward, red beaks at the front, we gasp at the sudden explosion of their brilliant white markings becoming blurred motion.

After the welcoming shallow entry, low marshy land spreads on both sides, leaving a wide path of water that varies little. Ahead, the treed fringes close in before rising mountains. We are sailing smoothly, without much conscious effort, in something akin to an orchestra playing a soft prelude while the audience finds their seats. Then the fringes disappear. The mountains come together in jagged walls of grey and green separated by a slender tongue of silvery-black water. Where they met, wind roughens its surface. The conductor points to the percussions and a distant drum roll mentally prepares Jude and me for a blast from the heavens. Our pulse quickens. In a short heartbeat, our laid-back sail through forest, sky, and water turns noisy and exhilarating. The warm breeze becomes a cold blast knocking *Banyandah* off the upright and causing Jude to smile. She loves working the wheel, keeping us midway between vertical walls now whizzing past. While the Kimberley gorges were smooth red rock without vegetation, these are verdant with a lime green fondant dribbling down in places.

That first gorge ends in a left bend that takes away our last sight of open space. Now totally surrounded by land, dreamy warmth closes in. The water becomes still. The air starts buzzing with insects. All around us, forested hills are crisscrossed with shallow gullies, down which quick blasts of wind sneak, putting Jude and me to work adjusting sails to make a slow passage. Then we drift until the next explosion.

Around the next bend looms Heritage Landing, where a long queue of people is waiting for the power cat to arrive. Standing in the hot sun, they are looking bored and limp. A few swat March flies, others look furtively downriver for their ride back to town; for a shower, a change of clothes, a cold drink. We give them a wave as we sail past. Cameras flash. So we wave again then turn ahead to the approaching horseshoe bend that signals the end of commercial traffic. From this point on, for as far as *Banyandah* can go, the river will be ours. To limit the effect bow waves have on the delicate vegetation growing right to the river's edge, Tasmanian National Parks restrict commercial vessels from proceeding further than Heritage Landing. *Stormbreaker* has an exemption and picks up rafters near the end of navigable water. But Trevor wasn't due for a week. A moot point you may think. But upstream, with many tight bends, at times obscured by mist, knowing the river is ours adds to our comfort.

Our day had begun before daybreak. We'd had a rollercoaster ride of emotions when examining the ruins on Sarah Island, and these had been keenly discussed on the slow sail to the Gordon. Then everything had changed. And now late in the afternoon, after the drain of negotiating river bends under sail, coupled with the high of actually being surrounded by Gordon River forest, we were keenly looking forward to a lovely spot to rest. Our destination had already been selected on Trevor's chart, a river bend where Eagle Creek entered, and a walking track and campsite were marked.

River depths varied considerably. The bends, where a sudden change of direction has scoured the bottom, are often exceptionally deep. Our sounder was revealing a thirty-metre deep canyon as we approached our chosen spot, plummeting down from four. This was something we would get used to as we proceeded upstream, but it alarmed us that first day. So, for a half-hour we cautiously meandered about, moving *Banyandah* close towards the trees then back midstream. A bit like a dog sniffing out a comfy spot to lie down, going in circles until we found the most perfect view up a mountainside of virgin forest, where the rising sun would warm us the soonest. Down went the anchor into six metres of black water and the silencing of our engine brought a hush only broken by birds twittering, and the occasional grumbling of our chain on a rocky bottom.

We're not exactly teenage lovebirds anymore, but we kissed and cuddled on the foredeck while our eyes drifted over the natural beauty of our world. Both of us thanked the other for a job well done, for actually realising a dream that had taken determination and hard work to achieve.

Upon still waters, we slept in a cabin far colder than any other night, while waters from high mountain peaks took the warmth from our ship. Then, as the new day grew lighter, mist imprisoned us in a soothing silence, removing any reason to hurry from under the doona. We ate griddlecakes spread with jam and honey while a light drizzle, hardly more than thick mist, continued hiding the mountains right down to the water's edge. When unable to hold back our curiosity any longer, we donned rain slickers, packed our cameras, and rowed ashore to explore.

The first sight gladdened our hearts. We had not seen a single Huon pine and had become somewhat melancholy thinking the early settlers had harvested so many the slow-growing pines had become extinct. So imagine our pleasure in finding within a stone's throw, not just one, but scads of Huon pines growing with their limbs brushing the water.

Three aromatic pines grow in Tasmania; King Billy, Celery Top, and Huon. Essential oils protect their timber from rot, so they were prized by the first settlers for shipbuilding. After the convicts were removed, "piners" worked the west coast rivers, cutting out trees under challenging conditions. Once felled, the logs were manhandled to the river in wet, cold conditions then floated to log booms built downstream. Huon pines grow exceptionally slowly, less than twelve centimetres in diameter per century! But they can live for more than 3000 years. Its heartwood is light cream to yellowish with closely spaced annual rings often less than a millimetre apart. Its leaves are very distinctive, somewhat similar in appearance to a common cypress, but a brighter, light green on branches that droop.

Driving a yacht on a river is a bit like driving a car along a street in that the direction is dictated, but we could go when we liked. And as we loved being in a new spot for sundowners, we set off in long shadows to explore a few more river bends. Our wandering from one bank to the other showed we would hit the trees before the bottom. So instead of worrying, just like tourists, we searched for platypus and ducks, watched eagles soar overhead, and examined the myriad variety of trees.

The next feature on Trevor's chart was a meromictic lake held captive next to the river, where the layers of the lake had remained unmixed for years, decades, or centuries. Coming abeam of it we saw only trees but detected a hollow in the tree line about a hundred metres in, and let go the anchor though we'd hardly travelled a mile from our last anchorage.

Fisherfolk had told us in Strahan, "There are brown trout up the Gordon. Just cast a lure next to a deadhead and they'll pounce."

I tried in the last failing light, drifting through the cool air in Little Red, tossing my silver lure amongst fallen trees. All I hooked were dead branches, so I changed to bait, and then something struck. Pow! And with adrenalin pumping my arms, I hauled up dinner. What came over the side really surprised me. Not speckled like a trout, but plain brown. A slimy snake-like thing as long as my leg, it coiled around my arm the moment I touched it. Ugh, an eel. I hate slimy things and reached for my knife to set it free. Then an image came to mind of the one we had caught in a New Zealand lake that had exploded my taste buds after coming off an open fire. So, I collected deadwood from overhanging branches; and that put slimy eel to the top of the menu. Back on board, the rail-mounted BBQ was dug out, and midstream, under a blanket of stars, we cooked the critter. Know what? Jude noted in her journal, "very fatty, but delicious."

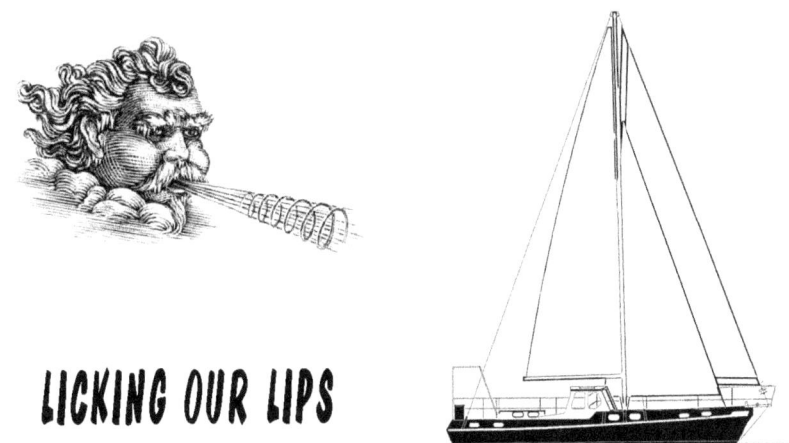

LICKING OUR LIPS

During the night following our star-filled BBQ, it rained. Not misty drizzle, but a good drink for the forest with more to come. A cold front was crossing the southwest bringing gale-force winds. Huddled aft under the doona, this caused us some concern because the Gordon was only a few lanes wide where we had parked. We could swing around on our pick, but only just. Any dragging along the rock bottom would result in us being speared by a fallen tree or becoming entangled amongst overhanging branches.

Looking out the portholes confirmed it would stay bleak, so I started forward to brew a coffee thinking it'd be a good day to catch up on some reading. But we were to do little of that.

Stepping into the cockpit, our world had been transported to the heavens. Sticky clouds drifted across diaphanous darkness that vaguely showed splotches of sage, with more transparent patches sprinkled soft white like cherry blossoms on a country path. Up around the mountain peaks, a silky mist swirled in the rose-pink morning light, sometimes obscuring the peaks, while down on quicksilver water *Banyandah* became surrounded by cotton candy shapes. One moment, a magical kingdom, the next all hidden except the silence.

Our morning brew was forgotten when Jude poked her head up, and then just as quickly ducked below to grab her cameras. Wrapped thickly like a bear in a couple of jumpers, I delighted at her glee bounding about pointing her lens at those misty creatures that consumed all in their paths.

And seeing her move within the swirls made me wonder if there could possibly be another dimension, one joining Earth to all its creatures. Not a visible one like the mist, but one beyond our senses, from where all life comes and eventually re-enters. Looking up into our kingdom of soft changing colours, its slow drifting clouds shifting the early light, my chill warmed and instilled a hope that my essence might one-day drift across the glory of Earth to mingle with all I love so dearly.

My poor brain overloaded. It had reached its limit, and my senses began droning like busy bees around spring flowers. No... That buzzing wasn't in my head. The droning came out the mist, down the hills, from upriver, and was getting louder and louder. Jude looked at me. But I shrugged and joined the search. Upstream on the bend lay Snag Point, a pale yellow sand spit we had briefly explored the day before, where for eons the Gordon has been depositing fine sand next to a wall of trees that were now thickly draped in mist. As if those trees had trapped a colony of bees, and the mist was amplifying their anger, the noise was getting much louder down there. Then as the breeze swirled the fog around us again, from around Snag Point, this noisy creature emerged, dragging a great swathe of sticky cloud with it.

Too loud for a boat, and yet it cut the water as it rushed down upon us. Then as if it had pulled free of a sticky web by snapping misty tendrils, a seaplane rose off the step and became airborne just as its wingtips rushed past our heads. Only when we saw the pilot give us a wave did we regain some control of our senses and swing round to snap photos of it labouring up into the silky mist and rose-pink light.

Conditions deteriorated. A curtain of rain began falling that kept us indoors all morning. But, by lunchtime, we had itchy feet. Donning wet weather gear, I told the rain to bugger off then marched forward to pull up the anchor. The rain had slowed sufficiently for us to see along the dull watery track, with both river edges just visible through the mist. Snuggled together, sipping mugs of hot soup we journeyed further up our river of mystery.

By the time the soup had warmed us, the rain had stopped. And now that the air was clearing, God's searchlight began probing holes in the grey blanket, producing a diffused light that turned the river into liquid metal. Then upon rounding a bend, a blinding shaft of golden sun transformed the dull forest into a Disney production bursting into life. Next to lilac-purple Sassafras and glossy Myrtles, Leatherwoods twinkled with raindrops. Then another veil descended. Stretching goblin-like, its tendrils swirled round and round, again robbing us of all vision. Popping *Banyandah* out of gear, we drifted in the thick mist. Our hearts thumped while our eyes strained, seeking dangerous shapes. Suddenly, another shaft of light lit cliff faces dead ahead that had a narrow void between them and a dagger erupting right in the middle.

"That's got to be Butler Island," I whispered with reverence, remembering the image I'd seen in Trevor's pictorial history book showing a piner's punt alongside a tall rock sprouting a lone tree.

And I could just hear Jude's high lilt of "photo opportunity," as she dashed to grab her camera.

Manoeuvring *Banyandah* into just the right camera angle, we anchored, and she became the perfect platform to witness the world around us. The air continued to brighten, turning hillsides snowy-white with Leatherwood blossoms whose large four-petal flowers sent sweetness drifting on moist air. Then Nature's show began in earnest. Within a natural open-air stadium, the greatest light show imaginable got into full swing. We'd not pre-booked, not had we to wait in long queues nor pay a scalper an exorbitant price. And this was not a once-in-a-lifetime offer. Every day, all over Earth, she shows us her grandeur. Starting with first light painting pink edges on night clouds, or wind song rustling leaves or misty rain casting rainbows over high peaks. And here in the Gordon, wispy tendrils of mist clinging valiantly to the cleft and dagger, while up a shallow valley, a silken bandage gently covered the forest. All alive, in motion, stimulating, giving purpose to life; for what can be more rewarding than to observe, and learn, and wonder.

Such lofty thoughts are allowed when alone in Nature, and they are best cherished for sometimes they are fragile moments easily broken. Our magic show was being conducted in the absence of noise akin to an empty church. So between us, few words were said; even the forest creatures were silent. But then an intrusion came through the vacuum, a slight droning. We knew that sound, and this time I had the video camera in motion and pointing towards the increasing drone coming from the mist surrounding dagger island. Quite astonishingly, whoosh, that same seaplane charged airborne through the crack, one wingtip nearly touching the cliff, the other just below the lone pine atop dagger island. In the same instant that we saw him, he must have seen us. With our mast as high as that tree, the plane jolted upwards, its pontoons bisecting our masthead as I panned and followed it skywards. Sunshine glinted off its windows as it disappeared into the mist.

Taking a deep breath, I blurted out, "What a shot!"

Our nerves were so jangled, Jude broke into hysterical giggles. "Is he allowed to do that?" Then gravity hit. "Gosh, he could have hit us!"

Late afternoon I tried fishing from the boat, but when a big blast of wind put *Banyandah* horribly close to deadheads poking up behind us, I rallied my crew, and in the last light, shifted back downstream to a wider straight run. While we lay in bed that night, *Banyandah* was buffeted by blasts that knocked us about, but we never went crunch or crashed into the forest.

Early next morning required thermals and three jumpers, plus a windcheater. But the view made up for that. Down the hillside, the treetops were swaying as a massive stadium filled with people doing a Mexican wave. While above, white cotton ball clouds be-bopped amongst blue. One moment it would be silent, the next, windblasts ruffled the water and wet us with spray. I love the power of the wind. It energises me. I see a force to be harnessed, so the thought struck of how grand it would be to sail *Banyandah* through the gap at Butler Island. Heck, if a flyboy can do it – we can too!

Jude is supremely confident in our ability, and when I outlined my plan, it didn't surprise me when she said, "What a great photo opportunity."

So we went into action. We didn't start the engine nor put up the main. We just hauled up the anchor and let the next blast start us towards the bend leading to that narrow cleft. During the next lull, we unfurled our huge headsail, and when the next blast came, I saw Jude at the helm, teeth clenched and smiling widely. Then she screamed out, "Seven knots! Wow-wee!"

Now that's a lot of speed to be moving twelve tonnes through an unknown rocky channel. But the wind was alternating between calms and gusts, so I figured we could dump sail, start the engine, and always stay in control. Besides, the dagger was not far ahead, and my hands were holding the video camera, filming from the back of the boat. So, I just yelled out encouragement and suggested she keep to the outside of the bend. But when shooting our approach, I noticed wind-blown spume filling the gap, and that is when the first touch of doubt rumbled around my empty belly.

Catastrophic moments don't always strike in an instant. Some come in waves that rush faster and faster till they become overpowering. That's pretty much what happened with us. Each blast got stronger and stronger, physically knocking us about like a demon was playing with a toy boat it hated.

The moment the clear gap changed to a wall of jagged rock charging at us, Jude's excitement turned to fear. And watching her frantic action on the wheel, it took my most calming voice, shouted above that demon wind. "You're doing great. We'll be fine. It'll be deep mid-channel."

Approaching the slit, the intensity of that demon blasted water into spume and seemed to lift our craft up like that seaplane. From the past, when scuba diving through a channel in a strong surge, I remember being warned not to put my hands out as it wasn't necessary, the water flow would keep me clear. And that's what I hoped would happen here. Standing on the aft rail, one hand gripping a backstay, my other tried to pan the camera across vertical walls as they closed in. Crikey! It was beautiful and frightening - until we were between them. That's when all the fury and shaking melted into the background and I could focus down on the little things, like wavelets slapping the base and lapping green moss, and the lone pine jutting out a crack. Butler Island was indeed a dagger-like a shard. Vertical sides only slightly tilted, and when right next to it, Jude yelled out, "Ninety feet under us."

I jumped down and hurried forward to film Jude at the helm. And with the gap disappearing astern, through the viewfinder, more great swirls of the river were being blown into spray. Then panning to my lady, her eyes were intense. She was working the wheel hard, looking side to side, and checking the depth.

So I yelled, "Turn left," thinking we'd get out the wind funnel.

Instead, that's when things started turning pear shape. Our sail reaches up fifteen metres and filled by that demon wind, it too had become a powerful monster.

Alarm bells started ringing the moment Jude yelled, "Bottom's coming up! Twenty feet – fifteen – twelve!"

Dumping the camera, I rushed to haul in the sail. Panic freezes the mind. So as calmly as I could in the noise and commotion, I told Jude, "Start the engine," and then I let fly the sheet holding the sail. Released, that sail exploded, crying out in pain while being flogged by the ferocious wind. I had to shut that out. I had to concentrate on getting the sail in, but I just did not have the strength.

Not wanting to panic, I purposely didn't look at the fast-approaching riverbank as I shoved Jude aside and engaged astern gear. Giving our 50-year-old Perkins full stick, only then did I look up and pray as the trees rushed towards us. With the engine doing all it could, Jude and I then worked together to roll up our angry sail. Poor thing, she suffered a rather nasty long tear.

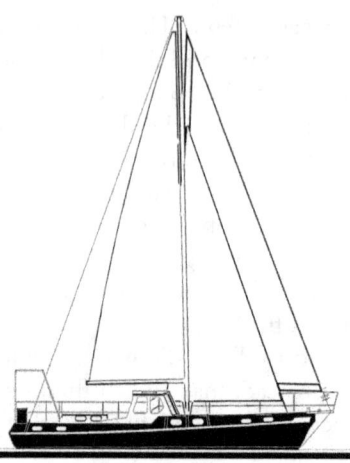

DIGESTIVE ANYONE

Soon after recovering from our little mishap, we passed around the shoal that had given us such a fright, remembering only too well Trevor's instructions to nearly touch the overhanging branches while I cursed the black water that so successfully hid everything. This brought us to yet another danger, the narrows at Sir John Falls.

Around the open basin fronting this canyon, the 1982 protestors had gathered, led by Dr Bob Brown, then the leader of the Tasmanian Wilderness Society, and soon to be a state parliamentarian then a federal senator. Announcing a blockade would begin on December 14, the same day the UNESCO committee was due to list the area as a World Heritage Site, it drew an estimated 2500 people. Not only Tasmanians but from interstate and overseas. Those against the dam camped on one side in a clearing. Those for the dam stayed on the other of the river at Warners Landing; a dock and staging area built by the Hydro-Electric Corporation to facilitate the landing of dam construction materials. The location of the dam itself was to have been a few kilometres further upstream in a rock throat just below the confluence with the smaller Franklin River.

After tying up to the run-down Warners Landing, we walked a boggy track covered in mosses to a clearing of several hectares that still contained a few bits of abandoned machinery. Both beautiful and interesting. Then Jude rowed us across to what is now the kayakers' hut – a place for those rafting down the river, where they can spend a dry night, but which in the late '70s was accommodation for Hydro-Electric employees. Along with a guestbook filled with comments on rain, rats, and snakes, two glossy posters were quoting HEC personnel: *Mr Hoyle, one of the last to leave, remembers the camp as "fairly primitive," but says morale was high amongst the workforce. "When you are under siege, morale tends to lift rather than fall."* He says the workers were interested in the history of the area, particularly after discovering the remains of an old stable. *"Far from being a pristine wilderness, we realised people had been working in this area for hundreds of years."*

The confrontation is so long in the past, and the results totally confused by the degradation caused by our extreme use of fossil fuels, I could only smirk and think, "Man will argue every point eloquently while Earth burns."

Outside, Jude found a path through a green, sweet glen that went over a creek then past the dock used by *Stormbreaker* and the seaplanes. Further ahead through more enchanting foliage, Sir John Falls roared over a sheer rock face half-hidden by luxuriant ferns.

The next morning we set off on the final leg up the Gordon, entering that narrow canyon after Jude photographed a sign declaring that seaplanes take off and land within their confines. Great! This made me even more nervous. And while I had *Banyandah* just idling along to absorb the fantastic scenery better, all my senses were on high alert for that drone. But, our worries faded before passing the first bend. The magnificent beauty captured our imaginations and we discussed how many eons it must have taken to carve out this tiny canyon. Whenever it began, it is still happening today. Jude called my attention to a landslip exposing bare earth and then pointed out a fallen grandfather tree that had collapsed a whole hillside in a tangle of dying vines that had young trees pushing through.

As we approached the end of our journey, the cold outpouring of mountain streams, down a channel now barely wide enough to turn about in, gave me goosebumps almost as big as the swirls and whirlpools sweeping us off course.

After travelling more than 40 km into World Heritage forests, on day six of our river journey, the white rapids of Big Eddy were spotted ahead, and that began our search for a place to park. At last, we were fulfilling our dream to live right amongst thick rainforest, but we had forgotten about reality; the swirls, eddies, tight confines. And now we had to use our skills to manage them, or we'd soon be in trouble. Our sounder showed a steady bottom, so I picked a marginally wider spot before dropping the anchor, first saying a short pray. As expected the bottom was rock, scoured clean by floods, so I had Jude let out the whole lot, 60 m of chain for 6 m of depth, hoping we'd snag something that would hold us, but not snag so well it wouldn't let us leave. Once settled, we watched how the whirls coming down one side then the other sent *Banyandah* towards one forested wall then sweep us towards the other. Relaxed on the aft seat with a good strong cuppa, one moment we could have plucked Leatherwood blossoms off one side, and then moments later pick another bunch from the opposite bank. Fearing the constant jerking on the chain every time we pulled up would eventually set us off downriver, a course of action was needed to remedy our meandering.

The plan we devised required lines to each shore from *Banyandah's* back corners, to hold her in a triangle midstream. While readying the lines we searched the shore for strong points but saw few amongst so many overhanging branches. As I rowed in, Jude paid out the line, but straightaway the current played the devil with the line, forcing me to put my back into the oars. This complicated a difficult process. Therefore, I was quite pleased to have successfully secured us to a log until I discovered a tick burrowing into my neck. When we found just the one line held us steady, we forego the second, which soon proved a wise decision.

A few hours later, while filming some background from Little Red, three large rubber rafts carrying nine people paddled around the upstream bend and Jude hailed them. Afterwards, she told me they had seemed exhausted, explaining they had been 12 days from Collingwood – 120 km up the Franklin. That's a lot of wet and cold; a long-distance requiring teamwork.

While at first we enjoyed scanning the forest walls finding flowers and identifying trees and searching for creatures; soon the icy mountain air started to be felt. Then as soon as the sun sank below the ridgeline, the moisture bore right into our bones and the colour left the hills. In minutes, rising mist extinguished the few stars in the overhead slot, thrusting us into bitterly cold darkness.

Big Eddy, a collection of mostly submerged rocks, creates a torrent of rapids even kayakers will not attempt. They prefer one of the channels either side whose narrowness stops access to anything larger than a tinny. A small one like ours, with several horsepower pushing it, is probably ideal. Even then, it is easy to get into serious trouble. Hitting a rock, damaging a prop is common and can lead to drifting side-on into the rapids and overturning in near-freezing water. Two weeks earlier, an overseas army officer had capsised and drowned; his body was still lodged upriver awaiting a special rescue squad.

But Jude and I had not sailed the Roaring Forties or tackled Hells Gate to be denied a visit to the famous Gordon below Franklin dam site - even though we would have to leave our cherished craft to fend for herself in a narrow rock canyon. A matter not taken lightly.

Even before the protests of 1982, the Gordon River already had its natural flow restricted by a dam. Fifteen years earlier in 1967, under the Gordon River Power Scheme, a concrete dam 140 m high was constructed across a narrow gorge in the upper Gordon. At the same time, Lake Pedder was considerably enlarged by the construction of three rock-filled dams, with the trapped water flowing through the McPartlan Pass Canal into Lake Gordon. From there water flow is controlled by demand for electricity; more flowing during working hours, even more in hot weather when air conditioners are turned on. Add to that the effect of falling rain increasing river flow; leaving *Banyandah* to the whirlpools and swirls was a significant concern. She is family, her safety foremost in our thoughts. However, at times, she is put at risk. We take all precautions, are smart and prudent, and then seize the moment to experience life. After all, the opportunity might be snuffed out tomorrow.

With this in mind, just after daybreak the next day we packed our knapsacks with food and safety gear, tossed in a bucket of tools for our cantankerous outboard then set off in Little Red. I don't think either of us looked back. Ahead was the challenge. Crikey, if a rough-tough army officer can get into trouble, then we'd have to be extra careful.

Approaching Big Eddy, creeping along the outside bend looking for snags, we took it easy up the fast flow. Smooth water runs deep and finding a path between two boiling rocks, I eased the tinny through without mishap. Jude visibly relaxed and had us laughing like kids rushing off on another adventure.

Once past that obstacle, the river was slower, and the scenery expanded into rocky slopes that wore a cap of cerulean blue, the colour of the millennium supposedly bringing peace and tranquillity. At the nose of the dinghy, Jude became our lookout, pointing out jagged lumps ahead, while I sucked in the sweet mountain air and felt the elation of an explorer. This only lasted until we rounded the next bend.

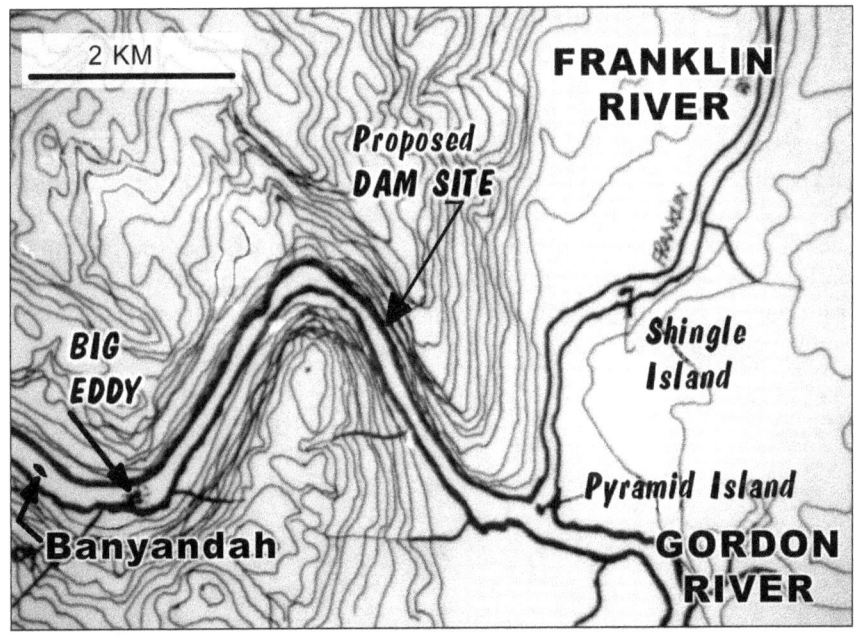

Narrowing to less than a short city block, steep faces reached for the heavens, marking the throat of the designated spot. From a practical point of view, perfect to dam. For a lover of Nature, an insane sin.

It's about 6 km to the Franklin from Big Eddy; two long straight runs and two rock obstructed bends, all littered with fallen trees; some bleached beige, others decayed, and not so many moss-covered trunks indicating a more active river. After passing the dam site, the forest spread out into big country filled with a lot more of that cerulean blue that produced a calming effect as we became nothing more than a gnat on a dinosaur's back.

A few minutes later, the famous confluence almost slipped past, lost in the grandeur. It was nothing like two powerful forces coming together. Pyramid Island at its mouth, hides the Franklin. No larger than an oddly shaped tennis court, we landed on its smooth pebbles, tramped a few steps across flood-swept tea tree and could see straight up the Franklin. Like many other forest rivers, along the edge was a mess of tree litter. Nature in action.

Jude leant down and picked up an unusual stone, and when she handed it to me, I thought it had come from someone's lunch. It looked just like manufactured meat in gelatine, globules of red amongst translucent yellow.

Taking the dinghy up the Franklin required more care, due to it being narrower, shallower, and faster, with heaps more rocky outcrops. Jude kept her usual lookout, pointing out unusual lumps of conglomerate and stratified rocks like slices of layer cake. Then when rounding a bend, we ran into a bank of milk-white rounded stones that our propeller crunched into. Jude tried to row, but, "Hey Honey, we're going backwards." So I took the oars with the same results. Ahead lay an island of those same white stones piled high. To reach it, we tried pulling ourselves against the current along the bank. But, it beat us again, so we clambered ashore for a forest wander through the thick stuff until reaching a viewpoint overlooking that polished stone island. A perfect spot for our picnic.

On the way home, we stopped to investigate various rock forms, and this took us back to Pyramid Island, where our eyes fastened onto dozens of unusual stones underfoot. It was like standing in a miner's pan trapping all the good stuff coming out the Franklin. Head down kicking stones, the slight splattering of rain carried human voices, and looking up, coming round the bend were three more rubber rafts.

I fired up the video and Jude called out, "Hope you're smiling."

And they did more than that. The rafters burst out laughing and cheered loudly, then began throwing one another into the water; telling us it is tradition to float from the slightly warmer Franklin into the colder Gordon. Brrr, you'd never get me doing that.

After they disappeared, we powered further up the Gordon, running into a set of dangerous rapids where we had a bit of fun running fast amongst the swirling water. We soon tired of the outboard's noise amongst such intense beauty, and with the river running at speed, silenced it, and started rowing home. For some of the distance, we just drifted; watching, listening, enchanted by the wonders of life as if on a Disney ride through a magical kingdom. Both of us became convinced every schoolchild should undertake just such a journey. This is Tasmania's last wild river. In fact, it is one of the world's last wild things. Here Nature reigns supreme.

The Gordon below Franklin Dam would have destroyed all the open forest around the confluence and 35 km up both rivers. Every tree, every bit of moss, every critter, every vestige of beauty, every wonder of Nature; swamped by rising waters so mankind could power up more industry and provide more jobs needed by a growing population.

A significant confrontation blocked it then, but destroying Earth's creatures and their habitat still goes on. It seems to us that humanity will continue changing Nature into suburbs until only zoos and small plots of natural Earth remain, and those will be corrupted by containment.

Impossible, many will think. A balance will be found. But when? In our time travelling the world, too much of the wild kingdom has been tamed and utilised by man. Do we still see massive numbers of creatures like those recorded by Matthew Flinders near this same location little more than two centuries earlier? "…sooty petrels as we had never seen…fifty to eighty yards in-depth, three hundred in breadth; the birds were not scattered, but flying as compactly as their wings allowed; during a full hour and a half…a number not less than a hundred million." Adding to this, wild creatures are now dying from strange afflictions; Tassie Devils, Koalas, Hairy Wombats to name a few. Even our forests are suffering from rising salt and insidious dieback. Then there's the destruction of coral reefs by global warming and phosphates.

The decision to halt the Gordon below Franklin dam was hailed as a win for the environment, but today heaps more pollution is created by the loss of the green power it would have produced. What a quandary. Humankind is an insatiable beast. And contrary to popular belief, we are not in control, but running downwind with way too much sail.

When Jude and I close our eyes at night, we dream of the world's children grasping a vision of a healthier world, with more space for her creatures and humans alike. Where less pollution would mean it's no longer a controlling factor. Where plenty of space would allow us to be more tolerant of others.

Our answer has always been to reduce humanity's footprint. Maybe a new financial model would help. The old one centred on need and greed has taken us to greater heights, but now we are on the edge of a precipice. The planet is polluted, the wild kingdom depleted, and today more humans work more hours for less contact with family and Earth and her creatures. Sorry, that just seems crazy to us.

Within an hour of reaching home, drained by our physical and emotional journey, saddened by witnessing more glorious Earth that is probably doomed, we had to leave. I rallied the crew, retrieved the shoreline, and then prepared to hightail it out of there. We had come, we'd conquered, and we had witnessed what once had been man's folly, and might be again. Now it was time to go.

When the full moon rose that night, solace would be sought anchored beside the pretty White Marble Cliffs. And as the anchor clattered aboard, I perked up imagining Jude's singsong lilt of, "Photo Opportunity."

LOST HIDEAWAY

Returning to the historic township of Strahan at the top of Macquarie Harbour was a journey back through all we had seen and done the previous three weeks, like playing a video in reverse, refreshing memories of this beautiful part of Earth. Just as we had roared out of Strahan with all sails reefed down, so our re-entry came with sails tightly stretched, showy white water at our bows. After an exhilarating romp up the harbour to the exact same spot, our anchor rattled down directly opposite the colonial buildings. Hello Strahan – *Banyandah* is back.

Over the weekend, Jude and I got down the damaged headsail then spread it on the foredeck to check the damage. Sails are more than our wind engines, they're our mates. Strong and beautifully shaped, we often look at them and know UV is a significant problem. If the headsail isn't stored tightly furled then a bit of sailcloth is left outside the UV protection strip that wraps around it last. UV sucks the strength out sailcloth, makes it limp and easily torn. This sail had been weakened by its previous owner, and we found nearly three metres of flaccid cloth adjacent to the protection strip. And in that run, a one-and-a-half metre rip. Deciding to not only repair the tear but also to beef up the weak area, we needed a three-metre patch; and knowing a sewing machine would make the job easier, went off to find Trevor. Unfortunately, he didn't have a suitable machine, but gave us some stick-on sail repair material; enough to hold the tear closed while a patch could be hand sewed to the other side.

Shortly after midday, *Stormbreaker* slipped off to pick up another group of rafters at Sir John Falls, and with Trevor's kind permission, we moved into his berth to charge batteries, fill water tanks, do laundry and be closer to the shops to start reprovisioning. For the next few days, like a yo-yo, Jude would be up and down the hill to the supermarket. Meanwhile, I used shore power to put together a video clip of *Stormbreaker* and *Banyandah* at Sarah Island. The clip also contained some lovely Gordon River scenes, the seaplane just clearing Butler Island, and plenty of local colour. When finished, I set it up on the computer in Trevor's shop so prospective customers could have a preview.

Repairing the headsail took Jude's next four mornings. The many stitches making it a long task; each stitch-hole first had to be made with an awl and hammer to pierce the many layers of heavy cloth. She spent her afternoons provisioning for a minimum of six weeks without a shop. Meanwhile, I had to get the alloy dinghy repaired. We row it everywhere, and the oarlocks were tearing out the body, requiring re-welding with a strengthening plate.

A midweek meal at Trevor and Megs' provided some respite from our hectic efforts preparing *Banyandah* for her next adventure. By late in the week, as the last supplies came on board, all we needed was the right weather. So far, there had been beautiful calm mornings with afternoon sea breezes mainly from the south, disastrous for us to sail to Port Davey.

When imagining the journey around the island of Tasmania, I saw us making this overnight journey close to shore, the mountains and beaches lit by moonlight while we conjured up bands of Aborigines hunting along the shoreline. However, when dreaming, I forgot my impatience once *Banyandah* was ready. The daily southerlies were only making me more impatient and ready to head off when anything vaguely favourable was forecast. That happened the following weekend. A cold front was approaching. We normally shelter from these, but northwest winds usually precede a cold front's icy southerly blasts, and we could get a good sail on winds from the north. However, once the front passes, we had better be well sheltered, or we'd get hammered by severe headwinds. Deciding to chance it, we enjoyed another lovely meal with Trevor and Megs, dining out on Saturday night.

Sunday was so warm and bright, gosh, I could have laid back and been caressed by Earth's goodness. Instead, we hoisted sail and got underway.

Speedboats zoomed around us, and inland there were dust clouds from local anglers heading to their sweet spots. Meanwhile on board, Jude and I were back at work, watching for shoals, trimming sails, hunkering down all loose items.

We gushed out through Hells Gate, swept along by a swift outgoing tide; hair-raising with sharp rocks flying past. That made the unencumbered open sea even more relaxing. Tell ya, nothing compares to the laid-back easiness of a clear horizon.

Our voyage south did not go exactly to plan, even though it had been well thought out. It's feast or famine, that's how we found sailing Tasmania's west coast. Clearing the lonely white structure on Cape Sorell, we turned south and straight away, we were punching into a slight headwind even though a favourable one had been forecast. The wind was not very strong, so we kept the engine ticking over and the mainsail in tight, and cruised along at between four and five knots. Good going, except for the noise.

During a real wowser of a sunset, the wind started fading. Then as darkness fell, the Met department upgraded the approaching cold front to a strong gale. And wouldn't you know, the breeze evaporated, leaving us just 24 hours to find shelter.

Jude and I often just drift when the wind subsides. The sea gets so calm, wildlife seems attracted to *Banyandah,* and for a limited time, we get to share life with the wild creatures. But we will not drift along a lee shore when the next blast will be a ripsnorter. We are adventurers, not fools. Therefore, we motored at a comfortable pace all my watch, and when it ended at midnight, miraculously we were blessed with a light, caressing breeze off the land, sufficient to haul all sail and set the windvane. That meant I got a good night's sleep, waking with first light coming up behind Low Rocky Point.

Upon a golden ocean filled with streaks of fading reds, imagine me against the rail communicating with Nature and watching the last of the moon on its side like a smile. Two bright planets above it seemed like twin beauty marks, and directly below, the Low Rocky lighthouse still casting its beam round and round through a thin mist that created an end of the world feel to the way ahead. During the next easy hour, Jude got some more sleep while the sun dissipated the mist, leaving only blue mountains touching a silver metal sea. Marring its mirror sheen, what first appeared as floating tree roots became flippers of seals basking on their backs, their flippers upright as if warning all of their presence. Their absolute ease seemed to shoo away what little breeze we had, forcing us to motor again. Straightaway we were rewarded by catching a most beautiful fish. One we had never seen before, possibly in the tuna family with large aquamarine scales. It proved a tasty lunch, especially as we had not caught a fish in weeks.

Once past midday, instead of the forecast favourable winds down the coastline, the sea became oily calm with a large flock of petrels floating on the water ahead. Dive-bombing the fringe around them were exquisite yellow-faced Australasian Gannets with sharp, arrowhead beaks in front of a glossy white missile. Above the throb of our diesel, we heard the petrels chattering. The flock was huge, maybe numbering a couple thousand, but no-where near what Flinders recorded. Nevertheless, they reminded us of earlier times when wildlife was more bountiful.

Looking to the shore also took us into the past. Dramatic rock clusters popped out of mountains smoothly coated in tawny brown buttongrass. Their tops and flanks appeared snow-capped where the white quartzite burst through. To our eyes, it seemed this isolated corner of Tasmania had changed little in thousands of years, but we knew the last two hundred had seen a total upheaval. Even before Deny King had lauded its magic to the world, tourism had discovered Port Davey.

In 1642, Abel Tasman may have been the first to sight the Port Davey inlet, but his chart shows a smooth coastline. Matthew Flinders, when just a young midshipman, along with his friend George Bass, ship's doctor turned explorer, set sail in 1798 aboard the tiny *Norfolk* to prove Tasmania was indeed an island. Approaching two rounded hills, a strengthening southwester had timber blocks groaning in tune to the flap of flaxen sails while the two lads exchanged broad smiles. The taller, his hair having pulled free from its tie lets it fly to shed droplets like those off the mane of a stallion galloping along a misty ridge. Rushing down from treeless mountains, the wind drives their frail craft further into the icy Southern Ocean while young Matthew valiantly pulls at the tiller and George tries to control the sails. Both agree the storm has yet to reach its peak and look ahead to what appears to be white teeth erupting from turbulent water. Shaped like the teeth of seals they've seen basking on the beaches, those islets rise higher than the *Norfolk's* mast, and beyond them, they perceive, "the appearance of a considerable opening."

They are wondering whether they should maintain a safe distance, or seek shelter amongst the unknown dangers of the land. "The mountains... the most stupendous works of Nature I ever beheld... are the most dismal and barren... The eye ranges over these peaks with astonishment and horror."

A quarter-century earlier, in March 1772, the French navigator Marion Du Fresne became the first European actually to record the inlet now called Port Davey. We know this because on that blustery December day when Flinders was off the southwest coast, he mentions Marion's small chart, and tries to take the *Norfolk* in closer to investigate the opening marked by the Frenchman. But it is 1798, savage times when even the mainland of Australia is little known and there is only this one vague indication for those two lads who are a world away from assistance. Wisely, they chart what they see of the inlet and around South West Cape with a rising gale at their backs.

Even today, with satellite navigation and satellite-phones reaching everywhere, anytime, with vessels of the strongest materials, and rescue helicopters that can find stricken vessels in hours; this part of the world is still very much respected. It is still a wilderness. There are no roads within hundreds of kilometres; it is a sanctuary for the other creatures.

Truthfully, there is little man wants from it. The only viable resource was its timber and minerals, which were selectively harvested by settlers. Today it is World Heritage Wilderness. The forests are regenerating, and the remainder is mainly buttongrass hemmed in by savage seas. Nothing useful to man - except that which is essential to his spirit and connection to Earth.

While the opening into Port Davey was clearly marked on the map Flinders made of Van Diemen's Land published in 1800, James Kelly is credited as the first to discover its vast protected waterways. We know Kelly would have seen Flinders' map and may have had it with him. However, there is controversy. According to an account Kelly wrote several years after the event, he states setting out on the 12th December 1815 in an open whaleboat in which he circumnavigated Van Diemen's Land. But prior to Kelly making this claim, in a letter written in April 1816, Dr Thomas Birch, Kelly's employer, claims to have discovered Port Davey on the 22nd December 1815 when sailing the *Henrietta Packet*. From there, Birch says, "Kelly proceeded along the coast and discovered Macquarie Harbour."

Sealer, pilot, harbourmaster, businessman, James Kelly appears larger than life though few know his name. According to the inscription on the Kelly family tomb in Hobart's St David's Park, he was one of the first to be born in the new colony, entering life on the 24th December 1791 at Parramatta in New South Wales. Said to have been the son of an English army officer, records show it is more probable his parents were James Kelly, a Greenwich pensioner, who held the titular post of cook in the transport ship *Queen*, and Catherine Devereaux, a convict transported for life from Dublin in the same ship. Apparently an intelligent child, Kelly was largely self-taught and had already made several voyages out of Sydney Harbour before his thirteenth birthday when he became apprenticed to Kable & Underwood to learn "the Art of a Master Mariner." Under their tutelage, he was employed as a sealer until 1807 when he sailed to Fiji for sandalwood in their ship *King George*.

His apprenticeship completed in 1809, he sailed in the *Governor Bligh*, then in April 1810 in the *Mary Anne* to India. Upon his return, aged twenty, he became chief officer of Kable & Underwood's *Campbell Macquarie* and departed for Macquarie Island on a sealing venture. On nearly the shortest day of the year, the 10th of June 1812, his ship was wrecked. Kelly, with the luck of the Irish, was one of several picked up months later by the *Perseverance*.

James Kelly died suddenly in Hobart on the 20th April 1859. He was 67. From humble beginnings, he seems to embody the fullest experiences one can have on Earth. Adventurer, explorer, shipowner and captain, farmer and "founder of whaling" in Tasmania, he was a man of greatness and his funeral was attended by numerous merchants and many others interested in shipping and the sea. Seven of his ten children predeceased him and he is remembered by Kelly's Steps in Hobart, Kelly Basin at Macquarie Harbour, Kelly Island off Forester Peninsula and Kelly Point on Bruny Island.

Young Kelly, in an open boat off one of the world's wildest coastlines, filled my thoughts as ugly blackness approached us from astern. In the stillness remaining after our weak breeze had fled, all colour seemed to intensify. Inshore, three pillars of rock descriptively called the Coffee Pots popped out the sea. Not too far from them, two others named the West Pyramids kept them company. Free of vegetation they looked stained brown by crustaceans. Beyond them, a large bay began to open.

Chased now by a rumbling wall of blackness, we went past the two small rounded hills mentioned by Flinders and saw his dilemma. A wide span of water leads straight to abrupt rock faces. There were no visible breaks. But, unlike Flinders, we had detailed charts that showed the secret opening. Blending in with the rolling hills of spinach and fetta lay Breaksea Island, a series of mountain tips rising abruptly from the sea. It hides a narrow opening leading inland.

Our view contained such sameness that even with modern charts, we could not detect Breaksea Island. Therefore, I consulted our GPS. Bass and Flinders would have loved having one of these. Almost instantly, it lit up with a basic map of Port Davey, with *Banyandah* a blinking icon clearing its northern arm.

"Change course to 125°," I called from the nav station. "Breaksea Island is 5.2 miles ahead."

A moment later, I felt *Banyandah* swing to the left, then heard Jude call out, "I don't see it."

I was about to say that we were smack on it when I heard, "Oh wait – wait – there might be something. I'm seeing a rock face shift across others."

Stepping up to the deck, I could neither pick out the island nor the passage from the orange-flecked white rock and smooth green facade. For a fleeting moment, I doubted their existence. Then I smiled. Inside my being, that young Flinders was stirring. He wants to approach but sees nothing to encourage such a rash decision. He has the wind already and it is growing in strength. As I look over my shoulder, the black overtaking us seems like the doom of Earth is coming. Spots of rain begin to splatter and a last burst of life from a rainbow ahead heralds our salvation. But where? We must first find that opening. The gods are flexing their powers and soon a colossal struggle will begin. And we do not want to be at their mercy out here.

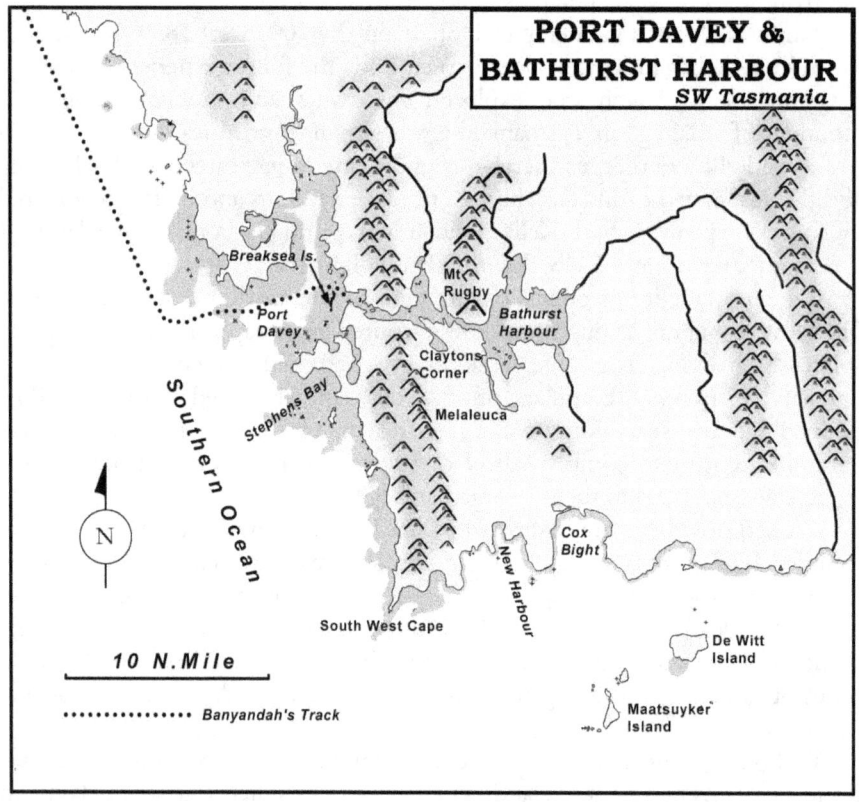

Flinders made the correct decision. Port Davey is wide open to Antarctica, only the narrow Bathurst Channel leads to safety, and it is hidden until nearly abreast Breaksea Island. By which time rock cliffs surround. There has been no escape for some. But not us. Like a magician's slight of hand, the sloping ramparts of Breaksea Island slide aside, and as the Southern Ocean swell lifts *Banyandah,* instead of driving us onto the primeval rock, she slips into the opening as if a ballerina performing Swan Lake.

Kelly named the exposed bay of Port Davey after the Tasmanian Lieutenant Governor Thomas Davey. Beyond it is Bathurst Channel; a narrow waterway that once was a valley carved by glacial ice and then drowned by rising seas after the ice age. Once past Breaksea Island, rock cliffs led us further into a smooth waterway, and like Alice tumbling down the rabbit hole, the scenery magically changes to a silent world of metallic black water contained within a crucible of ancient quartzite rock. Overhead, the sky narrows. Gone is our clear horizon and unlimited views. Then the magician performs other tricks of illusion as side pools appear. A dull white wall gives way to a quiet black inlet. Then another wall appears, droplets falling off its edge quickly become a cascade.

Darkness approaches - not with the night, but by storm. Increasingly cold drafts bring larger drops of rain. Nature claps. She's almost ready. Her next peal grabs our attention with a blinding flash of light. Luckily we're not frightened children, but still, we must find a place to hide.

While Judith drove us towards a maze of rising mountains, I studied our charts and sailing notes. The most obvious safe haven lay just a mile ahead, around a headland into Schooner Cove. The name indicates safety, but our sailing notes warn of bullets from the hilltops. Those angry ballistic blasts can sometimes charge down into bays shielded by mountains. Unlike trade winds that are steady movements of air, storms are violent blasts that when held back by mountain ridges, gain strength and strike in destructive blows. A vessel in their path can be laid on her beam-ends. Her anchors ripped free.

Across the channel from Schooner Cove, a distance no wider than a small river, lies Wombat Cove, an indentation with hardly enough room for one vessel to swing. It is open towards the channel but has vertical walls taller than *Banyandah's* mast protecting its other three sides. Recommended as a quiet, secure, parking spot, I direct Judith towards it. We had only an hour of light remaining, and see another vessel seeking shelter, then find a yacht already secured in Wombat Cove with ropes to every wall like a spider's web.

Time is running out, the light is fading. Seeking a solution, we discuss the area outside Wombat's mouth. Cliffs will protect us from north winds. Storms start there then swing to the southwest after the front passes. In that direction we would be exposed to the fetch across Bathurst Channel, so not as good. However, during the storm endured in Strahan, we survived an even greater exposure, and so I reckoned we'd weather this. Parking our baby in front of Wombat Cove, we cracked a celebratory landfall drink then ate a superb fish dinner. After that, we waited.

Slipping into bed, it was black and splattering cold raindrops, forcing us to close the cabin doors to shut out the elements. Our bodies, fatigued from the constant motion of a night at sea, fell asleep effortlessly without the need to block out our concern. And we slept in peace, totally oblivious to the storm gaining momentum until the shrieks of an angry wind woke us.

Maybe I was off being Matthew Flinders with his hair wet and flying for I awoke gripping the bed edge. In the darkness, *Banyandah* was slewing over on her side, and instantly inside my head, she and I were one. Feeling her every movement, I waited for our anchor to pull us straight. When it did, the stillness of a river anchorage returned for a moment. Then those giant thugs pounced again, this time from another direction. With each new blast came more torrential rain, isolating us further in our little cave where all we could do was wait, and pray that *Banyandah* would again regain the upright. When she did, we rested. When she did not, we wondered if her anchor had lost grip and imagined the rock face behind us and silently prayed that our keel would not crunch down on it.

When within house walls, a storm may rattle the windows and rain might drum on the roof, but the bed does not sway nor is one thrown against the bed head. Nor is sleep lost pondering where might be the rocks. That's one of the demands made on seafarer folk – it's our tithe, our dues payable to be allowed into the kingdom of Neptune. And while we pay it not gladly, we know it is balanced by hours of dreamy, free horizons ablaze in all manner of colour that sets our minds wandering.

Lying awake, waiting for the first hint of lightness to chase away the fearsome forces battering our small vessel was in its own strange way another beautiful moment of life. Each blast I wished to be the last. And though the storm abated several times, we were yet again flung about at her whim. Until grey dullness replaced the black, when the hundredth and one blast felt a bit weaker, and the next weaker still, encouraging me to rise and peek out. Sliding aside a cabin door, cold rainwater fell from the furled mainsail and splashed on my bed warm head. Not so much a repulse as a tonic that fired up my indignation. Why peek out as if a rat hiding from a cat. Was I not master of my own destiny. Chastising myself, I stood boldly to greet our first day in Bathurst Harbour, and received a bigger wetting from the same sail. Wiping water from my eyes, turning aft I discovered we had shifted.

OCHRE RED

Standing in *Banyandah's* cockpit dressed only in a wet thermal nightshirt, I stared in slight disbelief at a rock wall no more than a boat length behind us. No longer could we see into Wombat's cove, nor was the top of spider-man's mast in sight. Among these revelations, I was confronted by a world stripped of her accoutrements. Stunned by such pure beauty, I stared about forgetting our dangerous situation until the intense cold started my teeth chattering. That's when I jumped for the sounder to verify all was right. Close as we were, there were still several metres under our keel, an indication of the land's steepness.

Mist carried on the dying breeze drifted up the treeless slopes, and when a yellow-ray cracked through their greyness, a smile came to my lips. Now that the storm had passed, I yahooed my thanks to the heavens and then got on with brewing a cuppa to share with my lady who was still warm and cute snuggled in bed. Minutes later, after slipping back under the covers, her warmth chased away the chill while the ABC radio reported massive damage wrecked by our storm on the Hobart area – roofs gone, trees down, cars crushed. I could not help thanking mighty Neptune, not at their loss, but for our gain - those hundred metres - without hitting rocks.

Recalling how close destruction had come reminded me of another near-miss we survived when a storm hit Kauai, the northern island of Hawaii. On that particular night, we were bum to shore and very nervous, it was blowing so hard. Next to us was an unmanned thirty-foot plywood cruiser that at first light was seen pounding on the rocks behind us. Over several hours, the cruiser bounced on her side, making sick, crunching sounds. But there was little we could do. Around noon, a rather large track vehicle crashed through the vegetation and manoeuvred into the surf to pick up the hull with massive mechanical jaws. Understandably, an awkward job that became a disaster when during the final lift the hull cracked in two with a sickening retort heard above machinery and surf.

Our day brightened quite quickly and the landlocked waterway soon regained calmness, which encouraged the spider-man to take down his web and move out of the Wombat's lair. Seizing the opportunity, I started the engine and Jude took her place at the anchor winch. Unlike the Gordon River whose rock bottom is scoured by constant water movement, here in Bathurst Harbour, silt has been washed from peat-covered hills for eons, and digging our anchor out the ooze proved somewhat troublesome and mucky. The night's massive windstorm had ploughed it to great depths and it came out the black water as if pulled from a deep bowl of warm fudge. Jude called me forward to witness this massive blob hanging from a thickly coated chain that could have contained prehistoric crustaceans. All of which I had to scrape clean, to get it ready for its next assignment in the subterranean world.

The black waters were now mirror calm, and in detail, the three faces of Wombat Cove had been painted upon its surface. Around its edge ran a lace petticoat of quartzite weathered to a soft creamy fawn. Above this, tea tree in blossom covered the hillsides in a fluffy band of white polka dots. Above them, mild slopes of dark russet brown, much like fresh Irish potatoes with rosy hues. This exquisite scenery wrapped around, until directly off our stern stood a distant goal, a rock buttress, crudely cast in grey iron and pushing up through a mosaic of green and gold vegetation that seemed more like a net holding the rock from bursting skywards. Mist obscured its peaks, and at nearly five hundred metres, Mount Misery played hide and seek.

When it showed, Jude exclaimed, "Oh, we must climb that!"

I am not in favour of ropes tied to shore unless sheltering from a storm event with a specific wind direction. I'd instead let our baby find her own path of least resistance than have her dragged into shore if her anchor should slip. That meant finding the exact middle of the inlet, which took some time before I signalled Jude to lower the anchor. Our work concluded, we then sat amongst some of the world's best scenery to catch up our journals; but we were shortly surprised by the intensity of human activity that interrupted us. A dusky robin's beautiful song was interrupted by what sounded like a B-double truck labouring up the harbour. This mysterious annoyance was transformed into a large, modern vessel crowded with divers that anchored between Munday Island and us. Deny King called it Woody Island when he wrote of a Fairy Prion rookery on its northern end. Twin runabouts came off the stern of our noisy intruder in a show that was fun to watch. Then they sped off with six well-equipped divers, towards what our chart showed were deep holes.

Little was known of the Port Davey/Bathurst Harbour Estuary until the Hydrological and Ecological Survey of 1988 – 1989. However, even if nothing was known, this area would have been described as unique, because it is the only large estuary in southern Australia without road access or significant human impact. Apart from two small tin leases near Melaleuca Inlet, no development had occurred. At the time of the survey, the area's permanent population consisted of three tin miners, and during summer months, a daily transient population of about one hundred fishermen, bushwalkers, sailors, and airborne tourists.

The University of Tasmania conducted five field trips between October 1988 and July of the following year. They surveyed the hydrology, plankton, fish, and benthic fauna – that's the critters living in the ooze at the bottom. They found that during winter's peak freshwater outflow, a brackish surface layer extended down to about four metres, but that bottom waters were close to fully marine throughout the year. Surface waters were found to be extremely depleted in nitrates, and at the height of summer were exceptionally low in oxygen.

Marine creatures collected by gillnet were unusually dominated by sharks and skates, with the most common of the larger fish being the white-spotted dogfish, comprising 86% of the total gillnet catch. A tagging study suggested a small population of perhaps only 2500 dogfish roaming widely throughout the estuary. They also found a new species of skate whose closest relatives are in New Zealand and South America.

But by far, the most significant discovery was the abundance and variety of benthic creatures that increased westward towards the open sea. These are slow-growing sedentary animals such as sponges, lace corals, and sea squirts that are usually restricted to deeper water, but were found growing in the Channel's shallow waters. Many of them are filter feeders, and large numbers were attached to the Channel walls and floor. This was thought to occur due to the cold darkness of the tannin-stained surface water.

At that time, the forests and streams of the southwest were already protected by a conservation policy, while the marine waters of Port Davey were not. This survey eventually resulted in a World Heritage Listing that also protects the unique marine system.

Port Davey is divided into two distinct habitat zones. The tannin-stained water of the Bathurst Channel influences the eastern area behind Breaksea Island. The western area has a broader range of habitats representative of the more exposed Davey bioregion and includes a higher diversity of seaweeds including giant kelp and bull kelp. Unlike most other coastal areas of Tasmania, in this outside area, there are relatively few molluscs, crustaceans, echinoderms, and fish.

Watching the dive boat kept us entertained through a cup of tea. Then a new sound approached. From behind Munday Island came an alloy punt with a bright blue awning containing maybe six tourists and their driver. Twin outboards pushed them nicely along towards the cliffs at Schooner Cove where they set to air a pair of sea eagles, spiralling around on substantial white wings. Silencing their engines to drift under the forest, from across the harbour we could hear the eagles deep, goose-like honks, and through binoculars, photos flashed while boxed lunches were handed out.

Before the punt skedaddled, two yachts steamed in then disappeared into Schooner Cove, after that, the dive boats screamed back to their mother ship.

At the centre of so much activity, we did not need to launch our dinghy that first day.

In the stillness of the evening, with the sun just below the surrounding mountains, Jude prepared another tasty meal while I read to her another episode of Deny King's life in the Tasmanian wilderness. I hadn't heard of this fellow before Jamie mentioned the tin miner who had raised his family at Melaleuca. Jamie and Nicki had met one of his daughters during their visit there and had recommended we find *King of the Wilderness* as a primer on southwest life. And so I had ordered a copy while in Strahan and have found that the author, Christobel Mattingley let others pay tribute to this fine man and then used her perspicacious insight to add lovely touches to man, family, and Nature. Jude and I can relate to their isolated life raising children, so I hope Ms Mattingley will not mind, because here in part is what I read to Jude while steaming lentils filled our cabin with fragrance.

"The description we'd read of Port Davey had conveyed almost a sense of cosiness. Nothing could be further from reality. An eternity of ocean, an infinity of mountains …. lay between Port Davey and the rest of the world."

And this: "On a day of sparkling blue skies and bright sunshine, it was an artist's palette of colours …. But when the gales swept in ….. Mighty mountains became stark silhouettes …. a world which had lost its light."

A world which had lost its light; powerful, menacing. At times that's how it seemed to us. Being in the direct line of significant weather systems, rain overnight kept us below the next morning while pregnant clouds dropped their load on us before becoming entangled around Mount Misery.

It cleared after our simple lunch of fruit, cheese, and crackers, so we launched Little Red, and then my lady rowed me around the perimeter of our estate. Like the old Roman harbour carved from stone at Ventotene, in some places we could not touch bottom with an oar when my hand touched the wall. Before leaving the boat, we had spied an obvious path starting in the corner closest the peak. Approaching it, we found a rock shelf providing an exit for a stream that was littered with seaweed capsules. On its left side, a steep track cut up through scrub, so we landed the dinghy, secured it to fallen timber then scampered up to the first low ridge overlooking our bay. Finding *Banyandah* behaving herself created a flurry of photo opportunities before we turned to find an enchanting stroll up a buttongrass slope containing exposed patches of scree.

Proceeding from one knoll to another, each revealed expansive views like those at sea. In thirty minutes, we were a third the way up Mount Misery and could see how to conquer it. And that seemed a good turn back point. From there, another spine led westward towards a setting sun pouring liquid silver around Breaksea Island, and another half-hour walk along that ridge found us overlooking Bramble Cove, where that dazzling silver flowed round several moored yachts.

From the ridge-top above them, our jumping and hollering could not shift their attention away from the glorious sunset. Primeval in its simple appeal, with my own craft near at hand, I could see dozens of places to explore. With something like a living map spread before us, we planned little adventures; where we'd go in what weather. Straight out lay Bond Bay, a large pool of mercury protected from northerlies where a few calm days would be needed to explore the North River by dinghy and go a few miles beyond Settlement Point to the log pens that once held big Huon pines. South of Breaksea Island, which now appeared a perfectly placed natural breakwater, lay Spain Bay with good southerly protection, where we could undertake a walk across the buttongrass plain connecting it to the surf beach of Stephens Bay and the ancient middens of the Needwonnee clan.

Bramble Cove with Breaksea Island

Those plans were for another day, something to anticipate like Deny's "ta-tats" with his family. But in that midsummer twilight, we turned towards the inner harbour and started home, talking along the way about another "tats" to find the red ochre caves shown in Trevor's book.

Next morning, the clear sky and bright sun were saying get going, so Jude packed a picnic lunch into her backpack while on my back I carried water, emergency medical kit, EPRIB, and a rolled-up slicker, just in case the weather should change. On my right hip was slung the video camera in its own bag. Without needing to lock our front door, we boarded Little Red to go climb Mount Misery.

Straight away we had good fortune. During the previous day's photo opportunities, Jude had left her sunnies somewhere on the ridge, and while shooting a scene as if searching for them, by magic, through my viewfinder they suddenly came into focus atop a clump of buttongrass.

Not always able to find a track when we got near the peak, we bashed through some low stuff until large boulders started pushing through. Up close, these monoliths record the planet's journey. A very long time ago, igneous rock formed by fire was cracked and broken into very small stones that were then rolled smooth. Cataclysmic events then coated them with molten quartzite that oozed around them like fresh cement. This mass emerged as a conglomerate that was affected by the slow passage of time. Lifted above the Earth's surface, they have then cracked again, this time by ice; great chunks were then eroded by rain and wind until those smooth stones sat proudly upon its surface, where once again, across their rounded surfaces, they gained a sharp edge. Like a rough pour of concrete, today they can easily tear living flesh off hands and fingers.

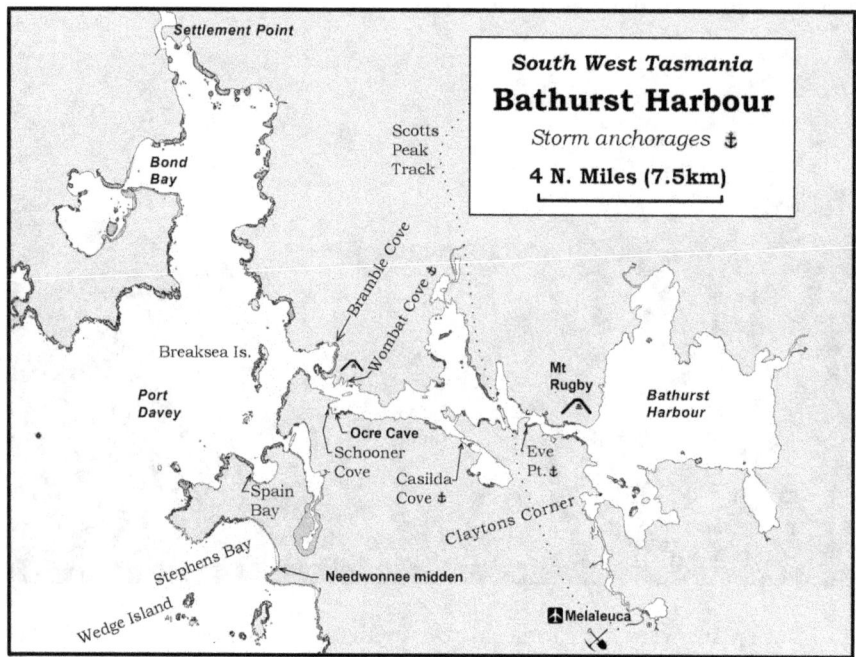

Our final approach to the peak was up the backside away from the boat. And while Jude laboured up the last steep bit, I set up the video camera to capture our successful arrival at the top. From Mount Misery's highest point, our view appeared boundless as if we were in a capsule orbiting the planet. Far away, the horizon curved away in simple blue majesty, while close around us deep valleys were dotted with white rocky peaks. To our south, across what looked like fjords, Schooner Cove lay empty, and further south lay the extensive sands of Stephen Bay, and in the far distance, Wedge Island and South West Cape. Turning north, across a connecting ridge, stood the slightly higher peak of Mount Barry. Tackling that was quickly dismissed when a convenient flat rock with a picture-perfect view towards Melaleuca enticed us to lunch. From that vantage, a treeless ridge drew a line pointing to the two narrow fingers nearly touching across Bathurst Channel. Along each finger runs the Port Davey Track from Scott's Peak to Melaleuca, and to cross the channel in-between, two dinghies are used, one stored each side.

Running rife among the larger rocks around us grew herbs with lilac flowers decorated by faint purple striations on their lower three petals. Among these Eyebrights were the ripe red cones of the Strawberry Pine, a prostrate creeper. It appears to have a square stem because the tiny, opposite leaves overlap closely, each pair fitting into notches between the previous couple as if in a square plait. I had read that male and female cones are on different plants and it is reported ripe cones are found only in January and February. Fortuitous for us to have seen them.

In the more significant gaps were Shiny Tea Tree, *Leptospermum Nitidum*, a shrub to two metres high with a multitude of finger wide, shiny dark green leaves that are elliptical and sprinkled with pink buds and white flowers up to 1.5 cm across with notable green centres.

No wonder the early botanists got so excited. Overlooking such a magical kingdom, we could easily imagine being its first explorer. But that's not what mattered. Just being there mattered; seeing, touching, learning, and most importantly, appreciating the wonders of Earth.

The first inhabitants of Tasmanian's west coast mixed animal fat with both, the red and yellow ochre, then applied that to their hair and body for decorations and warmth. Therefore, when I spied a notation in Trevor's book of an ochre cave located in Schooner Cove, my immediate reaction was to find it. My second reaction was that it would be a sacred site locked away by Parks. Maybe I'm a cynic, but my third reaction was it would be easy to find by just following the well-beaten track made by visitors before us.

Before leaving Strahan, that generous fellow Trevor Norton had loaned us two charts of the Port Davey area, meticulously marked with every anchorage he had ever visited. Along with this gold mine, he had passed across a large, blue-covered book titled, *"Maritime Tasmania – A cruising guide with historical notes."* Trevor collects fine documents, so we felt honoured to be the recipients of this first edition of what has become a classic guide, first produced in 1988 by J. Brettingham-Moore. It was on page 156, figure SW8 that the note and arrow appeared, so when entering Schooner Cove we took *Banyandah* in the general direction shown by the note and away from the normal anchorage alongside the western cliffs.

The shoreline we headed towards had a remarkable lack of variation. It may have turned in and out as if a cogged gear cut into the low bluff of peat, but it then spread inland in a featureless buttongrass plain. Therefore determining the exact spot shown in the figure was not as straight forward as we had hoped. In fact, after comparing the book's mud map with Trevor's chart, its location was so inexact, we could only plot our best guess. To help our search, our best guess was recorded into our handheld GPS just before we gleefully boarded Little Red as if two kids off on a treasure hunt.

Dark clouds shifted across the peaks, one-moment threatening rain, the next spilling bright sunlight that heated the air as Jude rowed while I sat erect searching the terrain, any moment expecting to spy a well-worn track through the buttongrass. Around us, the calm bay was deserted, and without the slightest hint of modern man in sight, it was easy to imagine being James Kelly searching for resources. Following the GPS, we crunched ashore with the device still showing thirty metres yet to go; therefore we presumed the cave must be hidden amongst the stunted trees and undergrowth at the base of the rising hillside.

Gaining the flat ground on top the low bluff wasn't easy. We groped and crashed through a tangle of Bauera and razor grass interwoven through stunted tea tree before finding the first foothold, and that took the gloss off our adventure. Though reality hurt, we persevered and eventually trudged off through knee-high grass, still following the Garmin's directions, and always looking for a track. It was when the GPS started flashing, *"arriving destination"* and finding no sign at all, we split up. Judith chose to search the rising hillside while I continued searching the plains.

Ochre cave was the notation, and the word cave meant standing height to me, but it could also be a fissure - unobtrusive, easily hidden by overgrowth. Therefore, every clump of trees and vegetation was investigated. Not by gleeful kids looking for treasure, but by grandparents, hot and sweaty under a glaring sun that had chased away the clouds. Alas, no tracks were found, no treasure, nor even a hint of a cave; but fortunately, no Copperhead snakes either.

That evening, every book, chart, and document was searched for further clues, but none was found, only confirmation in Deny King's book that the ochre cave did really exist. But not its exact location. Late that night, filled with frustration, I fell asleep hearing the rhythmic chanting of black people painted in red in my head. And during that long night, again and again, my subconscious returned to an old woman digging in darkness, scraping lumps into a leafy basket while I first cajoled then begged her to walk out into the sunlight so I could see a landmark. Awakening as first light entered our cabin, in that last second before full awareness, my subconscious shifted laterally and I awoke knowing the mud map shown on page 156 must be incorrect.

Even before the first golden rays had poured over Bathurst Mountain, I was in the cockpit with binoculars scanning the shoreline. And presto, it became so easy now that I was thinking outside the box. Thereupon an identical projection just two further up from our chosen site, a dark hole showed right at water level.

"Judith," I called, but getting no response, I dressed quickly then sped off to investigate.

What I found was far beyond the small hole imagined. In fact, it embarrassed me with its size. Our dinghy could land upon its threshold, and I could proceed into a cave that must have served for more than just a source of red ochre as masses of mussel shells littered its earthen floor and more lay exposed, embedded in a thick layer within an embankment. Like a series of snapshots, images flashed inside my head of black folk gathered together, laughing and eating under shelter while gazing upon the waters of their homeland. And it didn't take much in the morning's stillness to hear children's joyful cries as they ran headlong into the black water. Nor did it take more than a look into the darker reaches to see the old woman, one of the clan's elders, rocking on her heels, chanting to her god asking for bounty while scraping the soft red ochre from a wide vein in the earth. Climbing in beside her, I reached out and touched the vein of ochre, the blood of Earth these people believed, and that touch chased the morning chill from my soul. I ran my finger of ochre across my heart and felt the Earth's warmth. Looking out, I saw a tranquil scene of colours intermixing, running to become one encompassing all life.

Such simple folk they must have been. Many think they were ignorant, rough, and beastly; ill-equipped, cold, and continually seeking shelter. But very possibly they were happy citizens of Earth, living in harmony with the seasons and cycles of Nature. A people who enjoyed the simple pleasures of food and play—and running about naked, they must have enjoyed plenty of sex. Because of our books, our active minds, and what we call freedom, we like to think ourselves superior. But who today is free? Free of fear, free to wander with the skills and knowledge required to go anywhere and survive. How many are dogged by debt and burdened by laws that seem restrictive and contradictory, even unfathomable? And who today with our active minds can walk tall, with pride at our treatment of the planet and her creatures?

Young ones, listen to this elder who has enjoyed more freedom than most. Become one with Earth—treasure her. Put Earth First.

HUNTER GATHERER

When the world was bountiful, when fish and game roamed in vast herds, it was satisfying to use our cunning and skills to fill our table without feeling remorse for the killing. I remember.

At times, I am still a hunter-gatherer, although today I must be far more selective and sometimes feel remorse, even though I think it my right if it is a clean kill. We had been several days without fresh supplies, therefore after leaving the cave, Judith and I took our sailing home beyond Breaksea Island, back into the Southern Ocean to hunt for fish. We first trolled a shiny silver lure past rocky outcrops where we knew pelagic fish wait for prey and used our cunning to hunt the hunters, to lure them to strike, then to do battle. No fancy mechanical reels or heavy rods adorn the back of *Banyandah*. Just our simple spool and line, hand over hand, one on one, my prey in its element, against me in mine, each feeling the strength of the other, and me feeling the creature's will to live, a hefty price today. But, I think it my duty to hunt and stay connected to Earth, to experience the death fight of creatures, so that I will treasure life and the life of all animals even more.

Quite quickly we hooked a silver barracouta; called 'couta' in the fish n' chip shops, or *axe handles* to fishermen because they are long and skinny. Having hooked several on our way in, and again within moments of our lure sinking below the waves, I believe there are masses of them around these islands. But that beast regained his freedom moments after landing on our aft deck. They are not our preferred food. They smell rancid, and more often than not, they are infected with small white worms that some say are fat globules, but which we've seen wiggle. Minutes later, we suffered a repeat catch and release, which convinced us to head for Spain Bay to do some bottom fishing.

Bathurst Harbour inside Breaksea Island is World Heritage Reserve. Protected for future generations. No fishing of any kind is allowed. But, from our experiences in Macquarie Harbour, there are very few fish in the dark tannin-stained waters lacking nutrients. Outside Breaksea, the sea is blue and fresh, but again there were far fewer fish than I imagined for such isolation. Maybe we can blame modern fishing vessel with nets that lose nothing and sounders that find every creature. Inside Spain Bay, it took several hours, but enough fish was found to fill our tummies, but not more.

After a pleasant starry night, in the crisp dawn, I gave Jude a shake.

When her eyes popped open, I asked, "Fancy a walk to Stephens Bay?"

Across a mile wide plain of buttongrass, we came upon a long crescent-shaped bay wide open to the wild Southern Ocean. Just offshore, hardly more than large rocks, Wedge Island and the East Pyramids erupt from the sea. Seals bask on them in the warming sunshine. At the far southern end of this sandy beach once lived the Needwonnee clan, maybe not more than twenty souls who wandered the south coast from the Ironbound Ranges to the south shores of Bathurst Harbour. North of them were their cousins, the Ninene clan who roamed the northern shores of Bathurst Harbour to Kelly Inlet near Bond Bay. Further north, from Low Rocky Point, their distant relatives the Lowreenne hunted northwards to Macquarie Harbour. And roaming the massive waters around that harbour were the Mimegin people. Collectively these were the Toogee people of the southwest. Tasmania's northern regions, with its milder climate and better terrain, supported the highest numbers of Aborigines. It's believed that before European arrival, the Aboriginal people of Tasmania had a combined population from 4,000 to upwards of 10,000. But, from records kept to 1835, only 47 Aborigines were captured on the west and southwest coasts. Therefore, the Needwonnee clan was probably not more than one extended family. Two or three brothers and an uncle perhaps, with wives and children roaming a harsh land seeking sustenance best they could.

Upon gaining the bluff overlooking Stephens Bay, a most beautiful homeland spread before us. Surrounded by such striking colours, I immediately sucked in a lungful of saliferous air and thought it the most exquisite seascape. Aqua blue ran to eternity from white chevrons striking a curved beach the colour of ripe wheat. At its far end, that beach was terminated by a marble bookend exquisitely sculpted by the slow passage of time. Behind it, and running to the top of every mountain as if sloshed there by a broad brush, ran the ubiquitous green plains that in the low morning light seemed dusted with orange pollen from marigolds.

It is so grand to stroll upon a deserted beach. It's as if the ebb and flow of the sea suck away every care and the open space invites the mind to wander through thoughts rarely visited. Before us, the seemingly endless expanse of flat sand electrified our primeval spirits with freedom. The Needwonnee surely felt this. It could have formed the essence of their being.

Standing there alone with my woman, above the crash of surf, I imagined hearing shrieks coming from a figure running along the beach, weaving in and out the water in a playful escape from a tall, lean, muscular naked man. Alone like Judith and I, they had nothing to hide, and instead, rolled upon the other, laughing while the sea swashed over them. The image stirred something primitive within me, which I was about to put into action when "Jack!" I heard the distant call from my woman already down the bluff, staring at a giant, char-burnt sausage on the beach.

As I approached, I could see Judith pressing her woollen beanie tight against her mouth and immediately understood why. A full-sized sea lion had perished. White maggots thickly fought a battle along where the carcass touched Earth, those falling from the food line crawling over their brothers to regain a place. Ten paces on, marring the smooth expanse of sand lay a deceased dolphin, its steely grin of tiny teeth rather chilling in death. Further still, a little bundle lay. An Adelie penguin. Or I presumed it had been, not much remained.

Our information claimed there to be a midden at the far southern end of Stephen's Beach, which we presumed would be in the marble cliffs that appeared beautiful works of scrolled artwork the closer we approached. These we examined first, slipping into a visible fissure, expecting to witness the remains of long-ago feasts. Instead, it was bare, washed clean by storm-driven seas. The tide was low so we skirted the bookend around a rock shelf worn smooth by countless waves then continued our search up the other side of the rocky point. Another dark hole appeared and scrambling over what was now a field of well rounded, smooth stones we came upon a cave tall enough to enter. Again, I felt the presence of spirits but found nothing more than the dried skeletal remains of delicate, little seahorses. Upon its doorstep, we rested and ate an orange while we gazed over the waves, imagining Tasman's blunt square-rigger running for South West Cape. Fatigued, we could have lain in the sun and let its warmth renew our flagging enthusiasm, but the clock was ticking. We needed to shift *Banyandah* as a new storm was building beyond those sparkling white waves.

Back around the point, we investigated a slope carpeted with dense, tight grass, spongy but firm like bowling greens. Climbing up to a flat patch surrounded by stunted trees, we found a deserted camp festooned with flotsam, coloured ropes, and plastic buoys scratched and scuffed by their journey across the sea, but no signs of a 10,000-year feast. Crestfallen, we slowly trudged back over our footprints, wondering if our information was incorrect. Or had we just missed a clue to the midden's location. Dejected, having tried and failed, and knowing we would probably never return, took the warmth out the bright sun. Time waits for no one; we had to shift the "B" back inside Breaksea and find safety from the storm forecast to strike the next day.

At the southern end of Stephens Bay, sand is piled in a wave several stories high; clean and pure except where a trickle of water has cut a channel that discolours it. Something substantial lay next to this outpouring, bleached the same colour as the sand. Upon investigation, we found it to be the skull of a long-dead whale. "Photo opportunity," my lady called, directing me to pose alongside this relic as if I had been its hunter. As I approached, my boots crunched upon shells, and looking upon the sand drifts, I noticed the wind had blown the dune not smooth, but bumpy as if infected with mumps.

There were saucer shaped abalone amongst warrener spirals; bivalves and flat scallops also littered the dune sides. With a quickening heartbeat, I laboured up the slope, and as I progressed, the shells became thicker until breasting the ridge I beheld a small estate of flat sand thickly covered in bleached shells. Skirting this area with the highest respect, we began to notice both small and large bones amongst the shells, possibly those of swans from nearby Hannants Inlet, or wallabies from the buttongrass moorland, or seals and mutton bird from nearby islands. The sand extended inland for quite some distance until it flooded in amongst a stand of trees formed within a slight hollow. The trickle of water we had first noticed weaved through this, and standing upon a small rise, the ancient homestead of the Needwonnee people came into focus. Behind the vast sand dunes of Noyhener, the beach whose name still preserves a word of their language, they would have sheltered amongst those trees. Like standing at the doorstep of the Colosseum, here mankind had once existed for many years. Both Jude and I were overwhelmed. Were not these people as clever as the Romans, to have eked out a life in such harsh surroundings? Had they not also acquired vast knowledge? Knowledge lost by the cruel treatment of men who thought them savages. Understanding of natural cures, of Nature's movements, folklore, and living within the world's limits. Lost because the Needwonnee could not write. Sad really. But, we cannot go back in time. We can only go forward. And learn. And accept there is knowledge beyond our understanding.

Before we sneer at this comparison, it would be wise to remember the Roman Empire lasted a mere thousand years. An epoch filled with war, pillage, and slavery that in its later years the old reverence for family, state and for the gods were gone. Prosperity had brought corruption and a passion for luxurious ease, where gluttony and perversity prevailed. Contrasting sharply with that; before, during, and after the Romans, the Needwonnee had coexisted harmoniously with their world for upwards of 30,000 years. Yet, today they are gone. How did this happen?

When white man first settled on the island of Tasmania, they found plenty of wildlife for their tables. Kangaroo was the favourite and most substantial source of meat, which meant after 1803, both, Tasmanians and the newly arrived British, hunted them. With their guns, the British could hunt much more efficiently than the Tasmanians, and they pushed the animals rapidly towards extinction. Soon, the Tasmanians were starving, but the British kept shooting, sometimes for sport. This situation started violent Tasmanian resistance and escalated into the Black Wars.

Not all men of God agreed with the Wesleyan Reverend William Horton when he wrote, "I should without hesitancy affirm that they are a race of beings altogether distinct from ourselves, and class them amongst the inferior species of irrational animals." But many acted as if they did. It was the spirit of the times, and the Black Wars were fought in that spirit.

In the early days of settlement between 1808 and 1823, the small number of white females among the farmers, sealers, and whalers led to the abduction of Aboriginal women as sexual partners and Aboriginal children as labourers. These practices increased conflicts over women among Aboriginal tribes and led to a decline in the Aboriginal population.

From 1824 onwards, rapid pastoral expansion and an increase in the colony's population triggered further Aboriginal resistance. Whereas the original settlers and stock-keepers had provided rations to the Aborigines during their seasonal movements across the settled districts, as a form of payment for the settler's trespass, some say, the newly arrived were unwilling to maintain these arrangements. This resulted in Aborigines raiding settlers' huts for food. Their resistance first took shape when there were only an estimated 1000 Aborigines remaining in the settled districts.

By 1826, a pattern of guerrilla warfare by the Aborigines was identified by the colonists, some of whom acknowledged the Aborigines were fighting for their land. Relations between the Tasmanian Aborigines and the mostly British settlers had deteriorated to the point where Lt Governor Arthur had decided to use punitive measures, culminating in the declaration of martial law in 1828. From the settlers' point of view, the problem could only be solved by the extermination of the Aborigines or their removal from areas the settlers wanted.

After May 1828, a number of Aborigines were re-settled on Bruny Island near Hobart, and the authorities needed a man to supervise and if possible conciliate with the Aborigines living there. A government advertisement appeared in March 1829, for a "steady man of good character to effect an intercourse with the natives."

George Augustus Robinson, a Christian missionary, had befriended the Bruny Island Aborigine Truganini and had learned some of her language. Truganini was the daughter of Mangana, the chief of the Bruny Island clan. Her people had suffered much at the hands of sealers, whalers, and timber getters; her mother had been stabbed by whalers, her sister abducted to Bass Strait and accidentally shot dead, her uncle had been killed, and her fiancé drowned while trying to save her from timber getters. Truganini was known for her petite beauty, vivacity, intelligence, and coquettishness. During her long life, she outlived five husbands, but had no children for it is said she acquired gonorrhoea when held captive at the Adventure Bay whaling station.

It has been reported that Robinson was born in London, the youngest son of a builder. He had little formal schooling but acquired his own education by reading widely, and from an early age seems to have been interested in religion. He also had a talent for building and engineering of all kinds. In 1814, Robinson married Maria Amelia Evans in London and they had five children. Then in 1823, Robinson left England to immigrate to Tasmania, one of the empire's most obscure corners, leaving his wife and children behind. After arriving in Hobart, he set himself up as a builder and within a year was employing several men and was in profit. However, despite his success, several years went by before he could persuade his wife to join him with the children. In Hobart, Robinson seems to have been a bit of a busybody: Secretary of the Seamen's Friend and Bethel Union Society, member of a Bible Society, a visitor to prisoners and co-founder of the Mechanics' Institute.

In 1829, Robinson applied for the new government position of Conciliator and was appointed. Leaving Hobart for Bruny Island soon after, he spent his first weeks there getting to know his charges and locating a suitable place for a permanent settlement. His stated intent was to "civilise them and teach them Christian principles." A prevailing attitude among British colonisers of the day. For Robinson, a native village had to have huts, a school, and a potato garden if the Aborigines were to be persuaded to settle down and till the soil. To be "civilised", they had to adopt European dress and customs. Moreover, the aboriginal children had to learn various skills, and be trained in English, which was to be the only language of the settlement.

Very soon, however, Robinson realised that he must study the customs and language of his charges in much more detail than he had done until then. To do this, he started to travel and visited most Tasmanian clans on the coast south of Hobart. Truganini journeyed with him; she introduced him and tried to convince the Aborigines of his good intentions. In January 1830, with a party of convict porters and "friendly natives" including Truganini, he left Hobart for Port Davey where he met the Needwonnee clan. He then moved north to Macquarie Harbour. Next, Robinson travelled east to Launceston, which he reached in early October. The rest of 1830 and most of 1831 he spent in northeastern and eastern Tasmania, and on the Bass Strait islands, seeking information on the white sealers and their relationships with the Aborigines. These sealers were completely independent of the British authorities and little was known about their actions. From October to December 1831, Robinson searched central Tasmania for the feared Big River and Oyster Bay tribes. They might have been feared once, but when Robinson finally met them, disease and the settlers' rifles had reduced them to a pitiful sixteen.

From February 1832 to the end of 1834, Robinson continued his travels around the entire island, visiting all the existing tribes, acquiring a mass of geographical, ethnological, linguistic, and other data not known at that time. Robinson recorded these details minutely in journals, but these were not published and therefore the decision-makers, administrators, and geographers never read them, nor did they have any influence on later exploration or settlement.

All of Robinson's expeditions followed roughly the same pattern. There was Robinson, his two elder sons, an escort of convict porters and servants, followed by at least a dozen "friendly natives." Along the coast, boats were used. When first approaching a tribe, Robinson and other whites kept carefully in the background while Truganini and other Aborigines made contact and persuaded the tribal people to come to Robinson, who would then hand out presents and food. Initially, Robinson merely tried to establish friendly relations with the Aborigines, but soon he wanted to persuade them to come with him, promising a place where they could live unmolested by the settlers and be fed and clothed by the authorities. He also promised their customs would be respected, and that they could return to their homelands occasionally.

In the beginning, Robinson did this out of compassion. He wanted to help and improve the Aborigines, but once successful, he became less patient and more authoritarian with his charges. He also became far more interested in the financial side of his work and came to think that he alone knew what was best. Such views, all too clearly expressed towards authorities as well as Aborigines, did not win him many friends.

On his seven expeditions, Robinson collected 151 Aborigines. No force was used. His guides persuaded them that "coming in" was in their own best interest.

Later, Truganini explained why she had helped the conciliation mission. "Mr Robinson was a good man and could speak our language. I hoped he would save all my people that were left." When living near Hobart, she said, "I knew it was no use my people trying to kill the white people now, there were too many of them always coming in big boats."

The attraction of regular supplies of food and tobacco was important in persuading Aborigines to "come in." By 1833, all but a dozen Tasmanian Aborigines were on Flinders Island at the Aboriginal establishment of Wybalenna, meaning Black Men's Houses. As far as the white settlers and government were concerned, the Aboriginal problem had been solved.

Situated on Flinders Island, they were left to their own devices. Robinson left the island in February 1839, and his departure marked the end of any attempt to save the Tasmanian race. Of the 300 who had lived on Flinders, tragically 250 died in the following 14 years in what some have described as poor conditions, while other sources claim their diet, heavy with salted meat, and their refusal to tend gardens created a weakness to resist introduced diseases.

In 1847, the remaining 47 survivors at Wybalenna, including Truganini, were transferred to their final settlement at Oyster Cove, where, no longer perceived as a threat, they were often dressed up in European clothes and paraded at official engagements. In 1859, their numbers were estimated at around a dozen. The last full blood Tasmanian, Fanny Cochrane, died in 1876.

Robinson's wife passed away in 1848, and he returned to England in 1852. In 1853, he married again and had five more children by his second wife. The man who had promised to protect the Tasmanian race died at Bath, England in 1866.

No treaties were ever signed, no promises were recorded either. So very sad. Confronted by a superior force, these timid people were robbed of their freedom, and a dynasty stretching beyond the Ice Age ended. And what have we learnt from this? That all people are equal? Or, that greed, sexual appetite, ignorance, and intolerance will always see might reign supreme.

After re-crossing the buttongrass plains, leaving the Needwonnee relics to the elements, we shifted *Banyandah* back inside the safety of Bathurst Harbour as a deep depression formed off the south coast. Winds stronger than any experienced by us in Tasmania would be unleashed during the remainder of the week, and we needed a really safe place to hang out. Recalling a conversation with Jamie, in which he described a nick behind trees where he had secured *Siandra* to the shore during a seventy-knot blow, where he claimed he could have had a candle burning in the cockpit during the worst of it. That is what we needed.

Sailing in the second time past familiar sites felt good, like walking into a friend's house. Bramble Cove housed two yachts, both would be exposed. Wombat had a resident tied to its walls, and Schooner Cove was taken by two more. It was certainly busy for being so remote. As each vessel was sighted, we grew more confident that Jamie's hideaway would already be taken. And, as his description lead us to believe only one could fit in Casilda Cove, I perused the chart more seriously for a second choice.

Once beyond Schooner, we were in new territory and quite soon, a cone-shaped hill sprouted from the terrain on our right. Balmoral Hill stood like a traffic cop directing us into Horseshoe Inlet. Studying the chart, I could not imagine much protection where Jamie had indicated. In fact, firing up our laptop to review the latest nautical information on CMaps revealed a rather narrow, shallow entry, blocked mid-channel by a submerged rock, with the remainder of Horseshoe Inlet's vast expanse totally obstructed by submerged rocks. Making matters a tad bit more complicated, none of our charts showed any soundings, which meant anything could be lurking beneath those inky black waters.

Turning into the narrow entry, it seemed *Banyandah* slid into a syringe that led to a fine needle where all those obstructions lay. So, with some trepidation, we cautiously made our way towards it with Trevor's chart open next to the helm, and CMaps ticking away back aft. Just like in the game paper, rock, scissors; rock breaks cement, so we did not want to hit that silly mid-channel rock.

Of course, entering unknown waters with a savage storm about to strike pushed our heartbeats up several notches. That is part of what makes this life so exciting. But we kept it serious, playacting being very professional about running our ship while inside the racing thump grew louder as the land narrowed to a laneway and eucalypt forests closed in. Above those directly ahead, I spied something out the ordinary.

"Hey Jude," I gave her a nudge at the helm. "There's already a yacht in our spot." And I pointed to a white mast just protruding above the treetops.

As we approached the neck, our sounder started beeping at the low water under our keel, and then it hushed when the depths fell sharply after we slipped past a headland close enough to step onto. Through overhanging branches, a lovely white sloop came into view, tied close to a narrow rocky shore. Casilda Cove is just a tiny place, and I am not so brash as to squeeze in without consulting the other skipper. So we drifted about for ten minutes, hoping our engine noise would attract her crew while we visually measured the space, planning where we would drop our anchor, and to which trees we'd tie our stern. Completing that, an inflatable dinghy materialised from around another rocky point and quite soon, Rob and Kate were alongside. Without hesitation, they swept aside our concerns, saying they expected others would soon flock in.

"So grab a spot while you can. Can we help with your shorelines?"

Jude and I are quite adept at manoeuvring our vessel into awkward spots, especially in windless conditions, so we politely refused. Then professionally, we soon had *Banyandah* stern to the rocks, her bow anchor laid out with a maximum scope, and Jude scrambling up mossy slopes, lugging a couple of thick mooring lines and searching for stout trees. Within fifteen minutes, we were parked next to *Indecision* with just about a boat's width between us, and hoping no one would try to fill that buffer zone. One never knows what will happen in a fierce storm. It could quickly turn disastrous if a vessel crashes against another like dominoes on edge.

As the storm wasn't due till the morrow, once secure, we nipped over to *Indecision* for a social. Over tea and an assortment of lovely homemade bickies, Jude and I spun stories of faraway, while Rob and Kate told us about living aboard in Hobart and their plans to sail north later that year. We were especially interested to hear how they survived the harsh, Tasmanian winters, and took note when they explained about marina life, plugged into shore power with two small heaters purring and a dehumidifier going all the time. To help keep the wind and wet out, they had enclosed their entire cockpit in a clear plastic housing that acted like a greenhouse trapping the sun's heat.

Later on, when toasting each other's health with something stronger than tea, we heard another engine and soon sighted the sixty-foot ex-fishing vessel *Schouten Pass*. She looked heavily constructed from timber; probably planked with Huon or Celery Top pine as many were in these waters. Three mature couples worked her deck, wasting no time with the nicety of may we; they just threw their hook down then began backing up to the shore on the other side of *Banyandah*. Onboard *Indecision,* our four heads collectively shook disapprovingly, not enough scope we all agreed, and like a pesky mouse ruining our dessert, a bit of worry started nibbling at my subconscious. Timber sixty footers can easily weigh thirty tonnes, and I would not want that thumping down on *Banyandah* late in the night.

Ten thousand stars lit the heavens that night and not a skerrick of wind was felt, making the three vessels look rather silly with so many lines radiating in all directions. However, that was soon to pass. First light brought a zephyr that barely ruffled the waters, midmorning tea heralded the first rustling of the treetops behind us, and lunch brought to the table a low moaning as thin wispy clouds scudded overhead. By late afternoon, we knew it would be a hairy, black night because behind us the forest swayed savagely in the blasts. Down at deck level, apart from the occasional leafy twig fluttering down on us, we hardly knew a storm was raging.

The rain waited for darkness to launch its attack. In increasing waves, while snuggled up in bed, we heard the treetops roar, and Jude whispered, "Hope a tree doesn't fall onto us." That brought a new worry into my head.

Needn't have worried. The grey morning found us unhurt but chilled to the marrow. There'd be no socialising this day, only chats over our radios.

"How you guys going?" I asked Rob over the VHF.

"Catching up on my reading, Kate's baking," he replied.

At weather time, every vessel in Port Davey tuned their HF to pick up Hobart Met, where we heard that a deepening 970 mb low was forming just to our south and that things could get destructively worse. Just after this, a new yacht appeared in the opening, its blue make-do awning noisily going berserk as an orange-clad figure rushed forward. Rob had mentioned that their friends had vacated the heavy blasts in Schooner Cove. Stablemates from the marina, new to yachting, and burdened with two small children, we wondered where they'd park. And how! Where exposed, wavelets exploded into spume. Not believing our eyes, we saw Rob and Kate leave their warm, cosy home, and jump into their inflatable, now without its outboard, having been removed earlier fearing the wind might flip their dinghy. With a paddle each, sitting on the tubes, they rowed out to their friends. We feared for their safety. Rob is only a generation younger than we are, and even in calm conditions, an inflatable does not row or paddle well. In any sort of wind, they are like kites skimming across the water.

After a quick confab, lines were given across then heroically, off Rob and Kate rowed for the trees. Poor Rob slipped in the mud when trying to secure the ropes, while valiant Kate shivered in cold icy blasts. Our hearts went out to them, but we kept snugly in our companionway thinking we'd stand ready in reserve should an emergency arise.

Casilda Cove

As we watched, every newbie's nightmare was unleashed in a comedy of tragic errors. Firstly, getting the lines attached to trees was nothing short of miraculous, but then the lines proved too short to reach the yacht that had now laid out all its chain and with huge amounts of engine power had actually succeeded in backing up towards Rob and Kate. But they came up a tad short. What to do? There was no more anchor chain, and no more shore rope and a boat length separated them. Lines were heaved from the vessel, but in those winds, they all fell short. Then we watched the yacht's skipper, the children's father, remove his boots and jacket and prepare to dive in with a rope. Oh my, that seemed crazy to us. Fortunately, just as he was poised to dive, his lady rushed aft and held him back. Then while Rob and Kate dangled in icy blasts, the yacht picked up its anchor to re-position closer. That's friendship! I could never put anyone through that. After all, there were other anchorages nearby.

Alas, this tale hadn't stopped wagging. No sooner had Rob and Kate got home and put the kettle on for a hot cuppa, a savage rainsquall hit, and their friend's vessel lost grip, dragging back onto the rocks. Panic stations. The orange figure ran forward while the husband took an oar to fend off. Finding that entirely useless, he found some sense and threw off those lines so recently secured by our neighbour, and with a big blast of power, motored out. Phew! Begone, I whispered. Stop endangering the rest of us. Alas, that was not to be.

True friends, Rob and Kate, were seen diving for their clumsy inflatable and rushing again to assist. Picture heavy cold rain driving across this nightmare with bedraggled Kate and Rob, having left their wet weather gear behind, their clothing now sticking in bunches as they worked so valiantly against the windblasts. For what seemed half the afternoon they tried in vain to refasten their friends' yacht. Each time he backed up, either the shoreline was a mite short or a blast would send the yacht in some other direction. We could see that brave, wet team losing strength and kept hoping they would send their friends away, but they did not. Not until their runaway yacht nearly ploughed into *Indecision*. Now that solved the dilemma. Rob waved them off and they merely re-anchored to hang exposed to the full blasts of wind. Miraculously their anchor must have found a hole in the rocky bottom because it stuck like glue through some massive hits. And good it did. Less than half a boat length behind them, a hidden rock shelf lay ready to rip off their rudder. Now that would have given this tale an unfortunate ending.

Next morning, bright sunshine chased away the storm and trauma. And like a circus packing up, ropes were untied and coiled, engines started, and one by one, the four vessels moved off to a new venue. Rob and Kate turned *Indecision* towards the open sea to prepare for their passage back to Hobart. Their friends followed close behind. *Schouten Pass* evaporated up a nearby inlet just as we turned eastward around Balmoral Hill to line ourselves up on The Narrows; those two fingers of land that nearly touch that have deep water between them. Two inlets further on, another quiet cove lay around Eva Point just opposite Mount Rugby, the imposing guardian of Bathurst Harbour. We parked there because climbing Rugby's 731 m high peak was next on our agenda, and this well-protected cove seemed the closest anchorage to depart from.

Mt. Rugby 731 m from Eve Pt.

MELALEUCA VISIONS

There is a saying on the west coast of Tasmania that if you don't like the weather, wait thirty minutes. It might rain and blow strongly but can change to clear blue skies with the next gust of wind. Then switch back again, as it did that afternoon, obliterating our view of Mount Rugby with a misty rain. Boat bound now for several days, Judith and I were not going to let a little moisture stop us from stretching our legs, so we rowed ashore to climb the foothills behind us, hoping to see some of the track between Scott's Peak and Melaleuca that takes on average five days to walk. An easy workout to a peak unveiled part of the track and a portion of the plains near Melaleuca that was big enough to hold all of New York City. In total, those plains stretch from Horseshoe Inlet to the Great Southern Ocean and from the Bathurst Range in the east to the South West Cape Range. But we could not see the airfield, mine sites, or Park Headquarters still hidden behind Mount Beattie.

Listening to the weather forecast later that night brought resigned sighs. Another depression was forming; our third gale was on its way. Eva Point seemed to provide excellent protection and our anchor had found gooey mud, so we turned to other interests.

After a very still night, our peace was broken even before we'd had our first cuppa, not by storm winds, but by engine noise and a hearty hail of "Ahoy *Banyandah*." Sticking only my head out the hatch as I wore just a nightshirt, a massive timber-fishing vessel was right next to us with a cheerful brute leaning out the wheelhouse grinning ear to ear. On his head, a thickly woven storm-grey beanie supported by thick bushy eyebrows.

"How you going," I yelled, somewhat perplexed by such a large man and boat so close. He seemed so friendly, I wondered if I was having a senior's moment!

"Storms coming," he hollered back. Still not fully awake, I nodded. "Come over for tea and homemade scones," he yelled. Maybe he thought himself the gracious host while I'm thinking why the blazes would I chance getting wet? Black clouds were already leaking rain. But Morrie, his name we learned later, had already read my mind.

"I'll fetch you around ten."

Then he gave his vessel a burst, turning her stern towards us. *La Golondrina* appeared across her transom in fancy lettering with a pretty swallow painted in one corner.

Promptly at ten, Morrie came speeding over in a colossal alloy dinghy powered by an oversized outboard. We were ready; fenders out, cameras in hand, and wearing wet weather gear. Hearty, and quick with instructions, his helping hand quickly embarked us in the increasing slop, and then we whooshed off leaving a brilliant white wake. Alongside *La Golondrina*, Graham, a short, thickset fellow with a North County accent greeted us, followed directly by a Nordic beanpole sounding strangely American.

Morrie's vessel was a gem. Spotless and well laid out for fishing or charter work, with a substantial, spacious cabin that welcomed us with a large diesel stove purring away near the aft entry. Immediately after entering, my hand was clasped within Morrie's great paw and I felt our host's genuine warmth backing his exuberance.

Once settled in a comfy settee, a plate of scones magically appeared along with a tub of butter and a jar of homemade preserve from home-grown plums we were told. We all dug in while Morrie, seated opposite, carried on a rapid-fire discourse about his east coast property and the fruits he grows, followed by what had ripened, what's coming next, how he made scones, then a lengthy description of his wife Corrie and their extended family. All the time, the rain's slanting down outside the cabin windows. Inside, warm and cosy, with a hot drink and plenty to eat seemed so much better. So Morrie topped up the plate of scones then began telling stories of west coast fishing when a youngster. And that led him to *La Golondrina*.

"I salvaged this beautiful craft off the beach just south of Macquarie Harbour," he said to our amazement, knowing how large the seas can run there.

"Towed her back to the east coast then spent the next eight years totally rebuilding her. She's Huon on Blue Gum ribs. Had to replace the entire deck, the other got busted up by breaking waves," he said, eyes shiny with wetness. "With new machinery, she's now a beauty."

Seizing the quiet moment, I asked, "What do you do with your lovely boat? Do you fish?"

Half a scone got crammed into his great gob then ruffling through a pile of papers he handed across a pamphlet advertising his vessel for charter.

"We fish at times, but mostly transport kayakers between here and the east coast. Three should meet us here at eleven."

Just then the rain stopped, the clouds whipped off, and the beanpole jumped up to gaze at Mount Rugby now in full view. Thumbing towards the skinny American, Morrie winked. "Wants to climb the mountain."

Getting up to look, only shards of mist still clung to Rugby's slopes, and that encouraged the young sprout because he gathered up his walking gear then asked Morrie for a lift across the Channel.

My head wagged as they sped off in a creamy white wake. I was thinking it'd be wet and slippery, and the young man would be alone on a southwest peak. Still, opportunities should be seized. Jude and I had been invited, but endangering our lives with rash young ones just isn't our thing.

When Morrie returned, we discussed the danger he had allowed the young man to take.

Morrie shrugged, "Not my responsibility if the young'uns want adventure. Never do something like that?" he asked, and I just had to smile.

Deny King's World
Bathurst Harbour and Melaleuca Inlet from the top of Mount Rugby

Well, we carried on as if the young sprout had never left. Discussed overfishing, increased tourism, environmental degradation; all the things that pull at my heartstrings.

Morrie's retort, "Bring it on. It's man's destiny to shape Earth to his own liking."

That's like waving a red rag to this bull, so I got stuck into him about mankind's overpopulation at the expense of wildlife.

"Na, we'll manage," he said, handing across a new paperback titled, *The Great Controversy Between Christ and Satan*.

On the back cover, "A path is leading us into the inevitable…" Published by Harvestime Books; additional copies at low, boxful prices using the missionary order sheet.

There must be a hundred tracts following similar thoughts. Follow the faith, be it Jesus, Mohammed, Jehovah, Moses, or the prophet of your choice…. And God will prevail. Meanwhile, Earth suffers.

"Look, Morrie," I began, gently touching his elbow. "I respect your beliefs and hope you're right that God will descend from Heaven and sort this mess.

But I'd rather take a more proactive role, just in case. Mankind is clever and can do mighty things when we all pull towards a common goal. And that goal should be to get Earth back in balance, reduce degradation, and restore the wild kingdom."

Everyone has their own opinion. While most agree the planet is suffering, what we do, if anything, is where we disagree.

We stayed long enough to catch a glimpse of our young friend atop Rugby's peak then went home with a trumpeter fish and a live crayfish, compliments of our gracious Christian host. Late afternoon, after collecting his charge, *La Golondrina* shoved off with a "high ho cheerio" from Morrie, who also took the sunshine with him.

Rain returned in blasts, followed shortly by two yachts anchoring behind us. Another snuck past, parking right in front. Pee-you! He stank. Spewing whitish smoke, like burning wet newspapers it stank up my boat so I rowed against storm winds to protest.

The gale cleared off with the new morning light, and this saw our company vanish while Jude and I prepared to climb the 731 m Mt Rugby. This climb has to be a "must-do" for every visitor, the track was ground so deep. Near the top, it was far more dangerous than I had imagined, made so by numerous crevasses between rasp-sharp rocks similar to those found on Mount Misery. Nevertheless, on top, Nature in full primeval majesty reigned supreme. Melaleuca's airfield, lagoon, and mine sites, unsighted two days earlier, formed but a small part of our view that encompassed the entire southwest corner of Tasmania. Looking across the basin towards the white sands of Cox Bight, named for John Henry Cox who had anchored the British Brig *Mercury* there in 1789, had me recalling how tin was first discovered there in 1891 - alluvial tin ideally suited to recovery with pick and shovel. Deny King's father Charles had mined there after the 1930s world depression had left him unemployed. Several years later, Deny went to help and "liked the southwest straightaway. The beautiful scenery, the way the mountains slope down to the sea and the wildness of it all."

Charles mined tin there for 21 years. And Deny, who first lived with him at Cox Bight, then after marrying Margaret, they raised their family alongside Moth Creek at Melaleuca. Deny lived in the southwest for a total of 50 years. While sluicing alluvial tin out the ground, Deny raised two daughters and explored this vast, remote area. Struck by its unique beauty, he tirelessly campaigned for the area to be protected. Today's World Heritage Listing can be greatly credited to his persistent lobbying and his hospitality.

Coming down a steep mountain is sometimes harder than going up, in that it is easy to take the wrong track, and so much harder to go back up to find the correct one. Many had erred before us, leaving numerous false trails. I followed one late in the day. Then finding ourselves at a precipice, we had a frightening hour's scramble across gaps where one slip might have left us crippled. Tensions soared, and I got angry with myself, huffing and puffing from more than exertion until good fortune found the way down just before losing the light. Arriving home in darkness, ravenously we gorged on Morrie's lobster for dinner.

Over the next several days, the weather became so settled we could have been holidaying at a sunny Tahitian resort. Taking full advantage of its calmness, we toured the expansive waters of Bathurst Harbour, anchoring first behind Black Swan Island, and then a spectacular day and night at the furthest reach of the harbour, fully exposed to the weather, and the glorious reflections of Mount Rugby lit by a full moon.

Bathurst Harbour SW Tasmania
Banyandah 2009

I had been reading *King of the Wilderness* to Judith every evening, so before leaving this unique part of the world, we had to visit Melaleuca Inlet, the book's primary setting. Instead of reaching it by taking *Banyandah* down the narrow waterway encumbered with shoals, we parked her in a safe spot, and then risked travelling the five kilometres in Little Red. The age of our outboard always gives concern, but with Jude perched in the bow capturing the action on both still and video cameras, it never missed a beat, which allowed me to lie back at the controls and admire the views.

Visiting a destination one has read described in a book is a delight. The remembered words come alive and give a kick to the imagination. In this way, we were aboard *Blue Boat* with Deny and his "dorts," going home with a load of firewood after a fun "tats" to the Celery Top Islands. Halfway along the steeply sided channel, we were helping Deny and his brother-in-law Clyde heave the D2 Caterpillar off the barge, and then moments later we were with them at the scissor poles swinging the new generator onto the empty buttongrass plains.

Our journey took just an hour, but in that short time, in our minds, we were those pioneers. Everywhere we looked, we saw bleak open spaces, wet and peaty from severe weather, where travel had to be on foot, taking immense time often exposed to the cold and wet. Having raised our family in isolation too, we could more accurately imagine the difficulty of providing a safe environment for loved ones. We could easily see the fantastic opportunity for adventures, character building, and teaching of skills that were available to Deny and Margaret. Unencumbered by the hang-ups of society, with none of the restrictions placed by community living, their happiness was apparent.

My reverie got shattered when going around the last bend; warning signs were plastered on Deny's mooring poles, and looking a bit further on we saw several more along the mudflats fronting the shallow inlet. Caution! Reduce Speed! Then just where we turned off into the creek, one big-mama sign with heaps of tiny print outlined all the regulations governing a visit. Sub-section this and that, penalties apply, all the usual guff we expect.

We parked Little Red alongside a Parks and Wildlife jetty festooned with more brightly coloured warning signs and immediately looked about for the CTV camera; Jude laughingly hiding behind her sunhat. Remembering Deny's freedom, the gravity of it chilled us even though the sun shone brightly from a cloudless sky, and our enthusiasm suddenly popped like a party balloon. Still, we had come to witness and record. And so with a conscious effort, this baggage of modern life was shunted to the back of our minds, which brought forward an eagerness to glimpse Deny's airfield. Triggered by an increasing roar heralding a plane being readied for takeoff, feeling lucky we dashed along the newly constructed boardwalk, arriving just in time to see a twin-engine Caribou roar down Deny's brilliant white runway before lifting off towards bleak buttongrass hills.

As wide as a highway, as long as a shopping mall parking lot, and covered entirely with crushed white granite; this airfield had taken Deny, on his own, and at his expense, some seven years to hack from the virgin earth. It was his second airfield. The first, nearer his house, proved only sufficient for pre-war biplanes. For the majority of the year, the intense wet restricted machinery from moving on the peat. Only in January and February could Deny sit in his tiny D2 "tracla" for 12 to 16 hours each day, stripping off the metre thick spongy peat, levelling the bedrock, constructing drains, and finally covering its large surface with rock he first had to crush. This Herculean task he did for his family so that medical help would be only hours away instead of days. But the results of his hard labour have been enjoyed by thousands of bushwalkers, botanists, naturalists, photographers, painters, writers, and miners, including BHP who used Deny's airfield to fly in equipment for a competing mine.

On this day, three aircraft sat on the apron; two had brought in a dozen day-trippers from Hobart. We had passed them in the inlet going out aboard that open alloy punt we had seen the other day, as there are guided tours of Bathurst Harbour that includes lunch during summer. After traversing the full length of the field, we branched off along a track that led towards some machinery standing high above the low vegetated plains. A Quonset hut built of semicircular corrugated iron, what Deny called a Nissan Hut from his army days, invited our close inspection. It contained every manner of spare parts; Caterpillar tracks and links, an old generator, and numerous wooden boxes marked in neat lettering that included old stuff too valuable to chuck out just in case it was ever needed.

From Deny's mine, Jude and I wandered back across the airfield to a slick round building that served as a bird hide. This man of little education loved all creatures, except possibly snakes. In particular, he had a real liking for "birdies." His favourite, the Grey Shrike-thrush, he always called Richard after the singer Richard Tauber, because of its melodious voice. He also adored the Yellow-throated Honeyeaters that frequented his sugar bowl. Because of his passion and considerable work for the critically endangered Orange-bellied Parrots that numbered less than a few dozen pairs when he first moved to Melaleuca, there is now a significant recovery program. All of this was documented in photos and diagrams inside the hide that also had for visitors use a pair of binoculars to focus on a feeding platform. Strolling up to the viewing window, as the great man must have done many times, I beheld several Firetail Finches, whose crimson rumps and cherry red bills stood out gaily from their olive-brown bodies and white breasts. Focusing the binoculars, we became quite excited when seeing four feathered "birdies" with an orange circle on their underside. Cute little critters.

Finalising our visit, we took a quick peek at Deny and Margaret's house and then had a closer inspection of the hut Deny built for walkers that he dedicated to his father. Both were built in Quonset hut style with semicircular roofs and walls, so the fierce winds could not find a grip. Gosh, like I said, to touch what we'd read about sent a charge through us. Sort of electrified what can be achieved in isolated places when the mind and soul commit to a life close to Nature. I loved every moment in Deny's world. Deny King departed this life in 1991, aged 81.

Deny had two older sisters and a kid-sister by the name of Win, short for Winsome. The older sisters married and settled in town while Win followed Deny around in the bush. In the only picture we have seen, she had the same barrel chest as her brother, and the same oblong face slashed by the same loppy smile. In 1939, strong and robust aged 28, having spent her youth working the family farm and not having been anywhere, Win very much looked forward to a trip with Deny to join their father at Cox Bight. But after loading all their gear aboard Sid Dale's fishing vessel, the skipper returned with news his wife objected to a lady passenger as it was considered bad luck in those days. When Deny elected to walk the 80 km along the south coast track, Win joined him to become the first white women to accomplish that feat.

Deny remembered, "We settled down and enjoyed being there." Building a frame and sides for their tent out of flotsam, "It was like being in a little house. You could stand up in it." A fireplace with a chimney fashioned from flattened pipes "kept it lovely and warm."

After Deny came home from the war in 1946, he returned to Port Davey to hack out a homestead, and Winsome returned to help. Clyde Clayton, who had fished that coast since boyhood with his stepfather Sid Dale, brought the mail to Cox Bight on board the *Arlie D*. Taking a liking to this spirited young lady so different from town girls, they were soon married and setting up squatter's quarters outside Breaksea Island in Kelly Inlet. From that extremely remote base, Clyde fished the rough Southern Ocean, mooring his vessel in the open bay. After many years, this proved too arduous and downright dangerous with the severe winter storms. So they uprooted and shifted the lot to a new house they built just down-channel from her brother. On Claytons Corner still stands today that tribute to hard work, determination, and stamina. Boasting the only deep-water jetty in all these waters, their house had a proper hot water system and the only television to ever receive pictures from an antennae Clyde established on a nearby hilltop. Deny writes of watching Armstrong walk on the moon while a storm rattled the windows.

When I read of a TV picking up a signal in the wild South West, I shook my head in disbelief. Heck, it was hard enough to receive the weather on HF. So we just had to witness such a place. Upon returning from Melaleuca, we pulled alongside their well-constructed jetty and wandered up the earthen slope to a compact green cottage with a red tin roof set amongst rainforest littered with mosses and ferns of many shapes and colours. Entering through the laundry found a living room warmed by a massive fireplace. Absolutely astonished, commanding a corner stood a relic Kriesler television as big as a chest of drawers. How the mind works. Straightaway the screen danced with Armstrong's first step and the room came alive with Win's shrill laugh and Deny's high-pitched speech.

Having achieved all we had set out to do, from Melaleuca we slowly retraced our wake, back through Bathurst Harbour, visiting a few other bays while preparing for our next adventure - exploring Tasmania's East Coast.

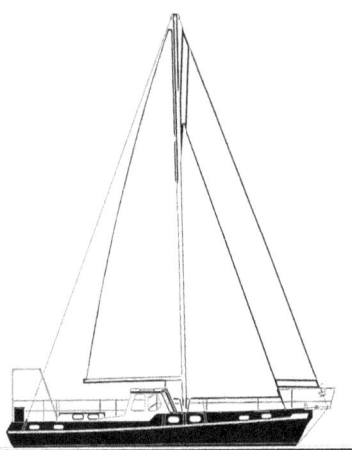

TURNING HOME

Leaving Port Davey, we fastened a shortened sail onto the tail of a gale that blew us around the sinister spires of South West Cape - then that nasty gale vanished. Lucky us. We got to explore the uninhabited south coast, now calm and serene. Yet another treat.

New Harbour is green heaven. If it wasn't open to the south, with the Maatsuyker Island lighthouse a solitary pinnacle on a wind-polished bump reminding us to expect bad weather at any moment, we would have stayed weeks to explore its wet forests and sweeping expanses of heath fully.

Any coastline exposed to the Southern Ocean is dramatic. Even after several calm days, the fractured rock headlands rising vertically out the sea still exploded in white foam. This primitive force kept us connected to Earth and caused us to wonder why man has not found a way to harness this power. It seems never-ending.

Moving closer to Hobart, Australia's second-oldest city, we watched local boaties set gill nests and knew why we'd not been catching fish! Alongside Constitution Dock, where the Sydney to Hobart racers tie-up, was a special treat. Four lanes of capital city traffic at our doorstep meant every attraction lay just footsteps away. We nearly wore out our boots visiting museums, the library, and art gallery, and a medley of historical sites. We even climbed Mount Wellington twice, once through the snow. So different from the wet west coast, brown dryness dominated the hills and

**Constitution Dock
Downtown Hobart**

everywhere were protected scenic bays and National Parks.

Rounding Tasman Island after leaving Hobart, we sailed close under Cape Pillar's grey columns of dolerite. They are Australia's highest sea cliffs - where landform, ocean, and isolation inspire reverence, respect, and fear.

Dolerite columns on Tasman Island

The Monument & Cape Pillar from Cape Hauy

Unfortunately, Tasmania, although quite delightful, is marred by stressed forests suffering root rot. That's another sad tale, like our poor Tassie Devil. Unchanged since the Ice Age, now something's amuck. Did we do that?

Feast or famine sums up sailing in Tasmania. We burnt a third of the diesel used circumnavigating Australia in Tasmania. Where frequently, we might drift or sail slowly in light winds, in Tasmania, after calm weather, the next winds will probably be destructive.

Die Back - the Greens say it's the biggest threat to biodiversity
Wineglass Bay Tasmania

HELLO FROM COFFS

Banyandah and the intrepid *Two J's* are home – almost.

Our voyage around the vast Australian continent seeking new discoveries has nearly reached its conclusion. A mere 100 miles remain. After leaving her home port 27 months ago, *Banyandah* has safely sailed 9000 nm, that's almost 18,000 kilometres through temperate, tropical, and roaring forties waters, facing strong gales and being becalmed on mirror glass seas. In the wake of such famous explorers as Cook and Flinders, she has taken us through many emotions and a great range of experiences. And yes, we do hunger for more.

On Thursday, the 28th of May, just days before the official start of winter, under scudding rain clouds and sea temps barely tipping 14° C, *Banyandah* roared out Tasmania's Wineglass Bay as soon as her anchor cleared the rippled sand bottom. A near gale stretched her triple reefed mainsail and pocket-size headsail while an army of white soldiers chased her up the coastline so fast, we damn near missed our departure point. Maybe subconsciously we feared to leave the coast. But we had to. Straight ahead in darkness awaited the notorious Banks Strait. Nasty even in calm weather.

Dinghy packed with emergency supplies water, flares, medical, fishing stored upside down

An hour before midnight, all hands manned the deck to gybe the mainsail as we turned *Banyandah* for the open sea, and then we sped off into an inky night, leaving the Eddystone lighthouse flashing a final salute.

Unable to find sleep, we were tossed about this way then that, nightmarish until the following morning's leaden sky showed confused breaking seas devoid of all life except graceful albatross aloft on hugely broad wings. Effortlessly gliding as if paper kites sent aloft from our ship, their bright white bodies ended in stout black bills lined with golden yellow along their ridge. They soared and swooped around *Banyandah* as she raced 157 nm that first 24 hours, our greatest day's run of the trip. Meanwhile, the sea temperature rose to slightly more comfortable at 16.5° C.

All that second day, we laid about seeking sleep to re-energise ourselves for the long hours of darkness so quickly approaching. As we were still below the 40th parallel, darkness outweighed daylight by quite a few hours. Its arrival even before our evening meal made watchkeeping bitterly cold, and dangerous whenever the quarter moon hid behind the cloud.

I have probably said this before, but Jude could probably sleep standing up, while I find rest with great difficulty. Therefore, after 36 hours without sleep and totally exhausted, it was a blessing that at one in the morning, I passed out in my bunk. A short four hours of oblivion passed in an eye blink, and then I was up again watching over my ship. This second 24 hours saw another 147 nm slip past while the sea temp rose to a mild 17° C. By this time, we had crossed the infamous Bass Straits that has been causing grief to shipping since being discovered by Flinders and Bass in 1798. This reduced our chance of a surprise encounter. Reducing our anxiety further, the wind gods began tempering their mood, allowing more sail to be unleashed to take us another 133 nm during our third 24-hour run.

When planning this voyage home, our primary goal was to reach Ballina in a single hop without hassles, a journey of no less than 900 nautical miles. To do this, we thought it best to avoid Australia's East Coast altogether because of several factors. Heavy coastal shipping is one. Another is the prevalence of onshore winds that makes it a lee shore with safe havens far apart. A further complication is a nasty south setting current that at times can run upwards of four knots. We have sailed this stretch of the Tasman Sea several times and have few fond memories. Quite the opposite in fact. There are several ugly ones of *Banyandah* fighting her way off towering cliffs in the dead of night while a demon wind seemed hell-bent on wrecking us.

With this in mind, I had charted a course running parallel to the coast but 100 miles seaward until nearly abeam of Ballina, where we could lay off for a final run home. Our plan was to wait for a high-pressure system to enter the Great Australian Bight, as this would generate southerly quarter winds that would tend more easterly as the high-pressure cell drifted towards New Zealand. But, we all know, when making plans, the magical forces of Nature take the commanding hand.

We started our fourth day at sea on the same latitude as Sydney and had but a few hundred miles to complete our circumnavigation. Around us, the waters had become quiet and smooth, the temperature very mild. A clear sky that night contained a dazzling moon, sending us into the heavens as if we were astronauts.

Dawn poured melted gold over the horizon then robbed us of our gentle wind. So we floundered during a lazy morning while soaking up the sun's rays, our smiles thanking King Neptune for our safe passage. Boredom set in soon after lunch, and that made us fired up the iron topsail to "charge batteries." That day we covered another 123 nm, but at a cost to our easting.

The wind returned on day six, but not a fair one, coming from north of east, and the sea temperature rose to a warm 21° C. That a bad omen.

The East Australian Current is created by trade winds that steadily push warm tropical waters towards Australia's East Coast, where striking land, they are turned south to become a river flowing unimpeded with great force.

The light headwind slowed our passage, and the higher sea temperature told us we were now within the current's grip. On day six, although we nursed 80 nm out the log, *Banyandah* only made good 40 nm on her course; the difference being our set backwards by the current.

Day seven began even worse with those headwinds gaining strength, becoming showery with occasional dark clouds passing overhead, blasting us further backwards. Being quite tired, my fuse burned short. I became irritable, biting at Judith's smallest mistakes. We tried laying a hull, thinking we could enjoy a few days rest, catch up diaries, read books, and sunbake. But the East Australian Current had other ideas, taking us back towards Tasmania at the rate of 50 miles a day!

Checking the weather ahead, there seemed no respite. So, reluctantly we swallowed the bitter pill that meant motoring for a place to bury our anchor. Pulling our sails in as tight as they'd go, we cranked up our aging diesel and steered for the mainland. Thirty hours later, land hove into view, the first since Eddystone light. Minutes later, while watching a golden sunset reach its climax over darkened land, suddenly the Smoky Cape lighthouse shone a welcoming flash.

That night a three-quarter moon lit up the smooth seas, while ahead, the loom of Coffs Harbour grew in brightness. Like a hired pony turning for its stable, *Banyandah* knew her way from there. By 2300 hours, 7½ days and 931 miles from the pink granite mountains of Wineglass Bay, *Banyandah's* anchor bit into the sand bottom of Coffs Harbour.

After a wonderful sleep, upon rising the next morning, we took a swim in 24° C water. Just one hundred miles separates us from our home on the Richmond River. But as the forecast is for more days without wind, after icy Tasmania, we'll just stay here and thaw ourselves in Coffs Harbour's warmth. Jerome, Julie, and grandkids are driving down for a weekend visit. Maybe next week, when there will be a full moon lighting our way, we can complete our dream of circumnavigating the world's fifth continent.

Coffs Harbour - almost home after 9000 n. miles

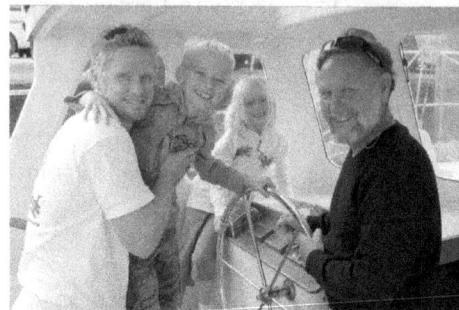

Home in time for Jack's 65th

START

Home. *Banyandah* secured to the neighbour's jetty just as though she had not faced dangers nor had adventures almost daily these past two years. And we are back in the house, looking out the same window onto a river still calmly flowing to the sea, and wondering had it all been a dream?

When I was just a young lad returning to LA from my first trip overseas, I had been amazed by how sharp and clear everything appeared. I seemed to float down the boulevard super-sensitive to the noise and mayhem, yet turned on by a new vision that had me noticing even the smallest detail.

Lots of water has passed under our keel since then, but that sharp perception has not been dulled from such extended use. If anything, it has grown more acute.

Our homecoming was grand. Jude and I are quiet folks, low profile we like to say, cruising along under everyone's radar. So only our closest friends knew we were coming in. We had a grand overnight sail up from Coffs, close to the shore with a strong, off-the-land westerly blowing across the calm water. A full moon had lit up the beaches, making it such a dreamy sail we both had stood our watch in the cockpit watching the last miles go by. Such a fast sail, we were off our beach halfway through Jude's watch, so we simply anchored off South Ballina Beach. Perfect! Just after dawn, after crossing a calm river bar, we were soon tied alongside the town jetty where our friends were waiting. Big Al rushed off, bringing back morning coffee, and then a merry band of ten spent a few pleasant hours reliving some of our finest adventures.

When the local press arrived - not for front-page news of course - I poured out my heart to a Sheila who scribbled furiously. We gave her heaps of insight into our thoughts after she mentioned she also covered environmental issues. To be frank, it resulted in very little. Her lead called us "Grey Nomads". Shock! Horror!

That weekend our growing family converged on the park next to the Missingham Bridge; a beautiful venue overlooking the river mouth with covered picnic tables, electric barbeques, and spacious grassed areas perfect for little ones to run on. Young men and boys plunged down the walls of a nearby skate park while our little ones dipped and swang in the playground.

Our noisy, happy homecoming was made even more special by the fact that I had miraculously reached the official retirement age of sixty-five. Fancy that.

Alison, Jason's lady and great mum of three of our grandchildren, is a master cake maker, and she had created magic in the shape of an admiralty anchor iced in tranquil blue like the calmest tropical anchorage.

All six little ones raced around that tropical blue longing for a taste; all except the newest, little Riley piling on weight at only five weeks new. It was delightful mayhem. To watch my oldest grandson, nine-year-old Brendan, run gleefully about, not a care dimming his bright eyes, reminded me of my long-ago childhood. Sure, he's a drama boy, but so was I. Both spoilt and demanding, but he's ever so cute, his golden locks flying when he's running about taunting, teasing, and laughing with not one hint of the road that lies ahead, as I surely did not.

In my youth, I was a lost soul in the future's department. Don't think I really cared. And why should a young person when ten, eleven, even thirteen. The road of life is long, and there is plenty of time to hone what some say is destiny.

To have raised our two sons, 24/7 was a privilege and a life-shaping experience. Countless memories forged an unbreakable bond that we don't need mention, it's just there.

While waxing fluid thoughts, we best mention something on the sailing life because a few of you might think of giving it a go. It is achievable. Many families are afloat and loving it. However, we must make this clear; it is neither easy nor always pleasant. Between the lines are hours to be filled by your own devices, maybe by reading or gazing at the horizon in contemplation. For some, this generates fear of isolation, fear of medical problems going unattended. Then there's the motion of the sea. We love being gently rocked. In fact, Jude swears it cures the joint aches she suffers on land. Nevertheless, sometimes it is downright uncomfortable even in the most beautiful surroundings. And far worse when waves tower menacingly above you.

To sail the wild parts of Earth, one must be self-reliant. A moot point because there are no corner stores, no handymen, doctors, or plumbers. A high threshold for pain and plenty of patience helps. Have we mentioned the cramped space?

Therefore, before you sell the house to buy a boat, maybe you should invest a small percentage, and rent a yacht and sail it for a week in some beautiful islands. Try before you buy is better than changing your entire life and then being disappointed. Or worse, getting divorced.

While a bit of cleverness and possessing a few skills have helped, if there is one key to our success, it is single-mindedness. Total devotion to the task at hand. For Jude and I that has been the exploration of the world together. Two are greater than one plus one. Two's a crew, a team building upon the strength of the other like a magnifying glass multiplying the power of the sun.

One of my strongest life-shaping moments was meeting Georgie Porgie. A strange little boy, he moved into the square house on the corner when I was eleven. He spoke funny, wore different clothes, and ate using his breadknife. Enchanted, I couldn't get enough of little Georgie from Bristol, the first non-American I'd ever met. In LA at that time not only had I not met someone from a different land, I had never seen a real wild creature, except maybe the brown sparrows that hopped about picking up crumbs at school. Nor had I ever seen the stars. City lights washed them away. Endless buildings, streets, cars, and stoplights were my world. To me, that was normal, the past and the future. Joining the scouts with Georgie blew that silly concept away. One moonless night, finding the ground too hard for sleep, I poked my head out the tent and was gobsmacked by an infinite black sky punctuated by trillions of twinkling stars, and that got me up, and running through shadows, suddenly aware of sweet pine aromas and strange animal sounds. It was as if my mind suddenly became fully awake.

To the youth, we say grasp life and hang on. Take pride in what you do and never give up. Brush aside failure as just one part of life. Learn what doesn't work, then get up and try again.

Above all, be fair and be smart - common sense smart. Learn to identify danger. Balance the risk with the reward, and it helps if you learn to think ahead.

As sure as I have grown to be "retired," so will you, if so blessed. In the coming tomorrows, just as Europe has united, all mankind could band together to achieve a perfect dream. One in balance and harmony with Earth.

From what Jude and I have seen, we are more than a bit out of control, and we are upsetting the equilibrium of something we do not entirely understand, or will we ever. As frequently as we congratulate ourselves for discovering something new, we find out something else has backfired with dire consequences.

The latest IUCN Red List of Threatened Species shows that 17,291 species out of the 47,677 assessed are threatened with extinction. Their results confirm that 21% of all known mammals, 30% of all known amphibians, 12% of all known birds, and 32% of all known gymnosperms (conifers and cycads) are threatened with extinction. The CSIRO *Implications of Climate Change* released in 2008 warns of substantial changes to ecosystems - human-induced and unprecedented in their nature.

Looking into the future, one must ask, do we want a world where the remaining wild creatures are caged in zoos under our protection. Many might think that OK, and many may think it will never happen, but it is where the world is heading. To live jammed together, bickering and judging our neighbours, under a book of rules so thick, our confidence is eroded, our freedom stifled. Our forefathers managed with fewer restraints. There were fewer people then, more self-reliant in a simpler world.

More space for fewer people producing less pollution would make it easy to be tolerant of others, and that should put Earth back in balance. How to achieve that dream is the big question. And, is it achievable? At this moment, most would think it is not. But, connected as we are across Earth, we believe it is time to begin discussing ways of achieving that dream.

Sir David Attenborough has said, "I've never seen a problem that wouldn't be easier to solve with fewer people, or harder - and ultimately impossible - with more."

WORLD POPULATION GROWTH

In the 50 years - 1800 to 1850 - the start of the Industrial Revolution, Migration to England more than doubled their population And the USA population more than quadrupled, 5.3 to 23.2 million.

Today the developing countries are growing world population at even faster rates.
These new world citizens will require great amounts of resources

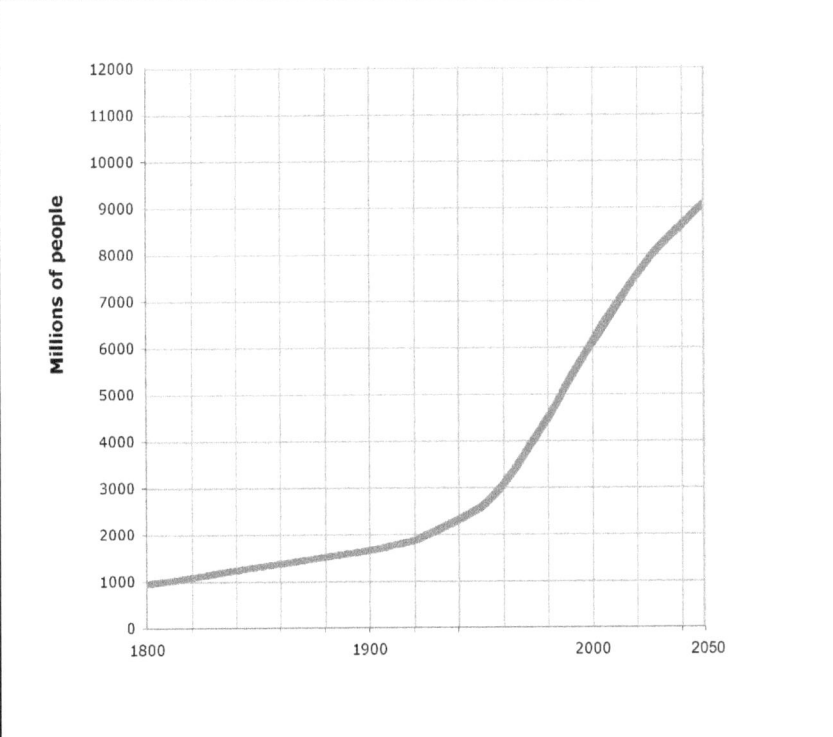

United States Census Bureau figures

SELECT BIBLIOGRAPHY

Flinders, Matthew, *A Voyage to Terra Australis*, G. and W. Nicol, 1814
Hordern, Marsden, *King of the Australian Coast*, The Miegunyah Press, 1997
Mattingley, Christobel, *King of the Wilderness*, Text Publishing Company, 2002
Hill, Ernestine, *My Love Must Wait. The Story of Matthew Flinders.* Angus and Robertson
Tyler, I, *Geology and Landforms of the Kimberley*, CALM, 2000
Brettingham-Moore, *Maritime Tasmania – A cruising guide with historical notes*, 1988
Laws, Steve, *Fremantle Sailing Club, Western Australian cruising*, 2nd edition, 1998
Edgar, Graham, *Hydrological and Ecological Survey of the Port Davey/Bathurst Harbour Estuary, University of Tasmania*, 1988 – 1989
Scott, Ernest, *The Life of Captain Matthew Flinders*, Angus & Robertson, Sydney, 1914
http://en.wikisource.org/wiki/The_Life_of_Captain_Matthew_Flinders, R.N.
Flood, Josephine, *The Original Australians: story of the Aboriginal people*, Allen & Unwin - Reference to Truganini page 87

Online sources:

The stories behind the Macquarie Harbour region
http://www.parks.tas.gov.au/file.aspx?id=6778

Brand, Ian, *Macquarie Harbour Research, Volume1, Penitentiary New,* **Department of Primary Industries, Parks, Water & Environment, Hobart**
http://www.dpipwe.tas.gov.au/library/catalogues.html

Heeres, J. E., *The Part Borne by the Dutch in the Discovery of Australia 1606-1765*
http://gutenberg.net.au/ebooks05/0501231.txt

Information on Tasmanian Aborigines, southernmost people during the Pleistocene era.
http://en.wikipedia.org/wiki/Tasmanian_Aborigines

Lake Pedder the largest freshwater lake in Australia
http://en.wikipedia.org/wiki/Lake_pedder

Photograph page 192, *Phytoplankton in Bloom.* **NASA's Terra satellite captured this image of phytoplankton in bloom in Australia's Shark Bay on November 6, 2004**
http://www.nasa.gov/images/content/121761main_image_feature_363_ys_full.jpg

Glossary

Aback: The wind is on the wrong side of the sails. Sometimes done deliberately to slow the speed.
Abeam: At right angles to the boat's centreline.
Aft: Towards or at the stern of the boat.
Antifouling: A specially formulated paint for coating a boat beneath the waterline to prevent growth of weed and barnacles.
Autopilot: An electric steering device that turns the rudder either via the steering wheel or directly.
Athwartships: Across a ship from side to side.
Beat: To sail as close as possible to the wind.
Beating to windward: Means tacking up wind.
Bilge, bilges: The lowest most internal part of the boat's hull used as a sump to drain any water which may have collected in the boat.
Bloke: a man
Bloody: very (bloody hard yakka)
Boom: Spar that runs horizontally to hold out the bottom of the mainsail.
Bow: Towards or at the front of a boat.
Bulkhead: Vertical partition usually installed to divide a vessel into cabins, and/or watertight compartments. Some bulkheads are for rigidity of construction.
Chainplates: Metal fittings on the sides and stern of a boat to which are fastened the standing rigging or shrouds.
Clew: After lower corner of a fore-and-aft sail..
Cockpit: Central lowered area between the forward living area and the aft cabin, where the helm and compass are.
Companionway: Opening and ladder leading from below decks to above decks.
Cooee: Nearby, I was within cooee of landing a big fish when the line broke.
Dodger: The solid structure over the forepart of the cockpit that protects the helmsman and companionway from the weather.
Fit-out: The built in interior of the boat.
Foredeck: The area of deck forward of the cockpit.
Forward: The front part of a vessel, at or near the bow.
Forestay: Rigging stay which runs from the stemhead on the bow to high on the mast. The headsails or jibs are set from the forestay.
Furling Headsail: Headsail set on an aluminium (foil) tube. This tube encases the forestay and the sail is stowed by rolling it around the foil.
Gooseneck fitting: Metal fitting at the forward end of the boom that attaches it to the mast, allowing the boom to turn in any direction.
Gybe: Turning a sailing vessel so that the wind passes from one side to the other across the stern.
Halyard: A rope, wire or wire-rope combination used for hoisting and lowering sails and flags on a mast.
Head: Toilet area in a vessel.

Keel: The for-and-aft protruding fin under a vessel. The keel provides stability and stops sideways drift.

Knockdown A knockdown is the term used when a yacht is rolled over with her masts and sails in the water – usually in violent squalls or huge breaking seas.

Lead: The direction taken by a rope or sheet. Lead blocks are used to alter the direction.

Log: Ship's journal, in which all references to weather, navigation, and daily happenings aboard are recorded. Also a short version of 'sumlog': the device for measuring a boat's speed and distance travelled.

Loom: To appear in view indistinctly. Loom in the clouds is light reflected from a source below.

Luff: Forward edge if a fore-and-aft sail. The luff of the mainsail is the leading edge that runs up the mast.

On the nose: The wind comes from the direction in which one wants to sail. Beating to windward when the wind is on the nose.

Portholes: The windows in a vessel.

Reach: To sail on all points of the wind except running square.

Reef: To reduce sail area by folding (slab), rolling or lashing up sections of the sails. *Banyandah* has a roller-reefing headsail on the furling foil, and a slab-reefing mainsail.

Rhumb line: A direct line between two points.

Roller furler: Rotating foil and drum, usually over a forestay, for the headsail to roll and furl around.

Rudderpost or stock: Shaft to which the rudder is attached.

Running square: Sailing with the wind directly from behind.

Running rigging: The ropes used to control the sails.

Sextant: Navigation instrument which measures the angles of heavenly bodies in relation to the horizon.

Sheets: Lines or ropes attached to and used to trim or control the sails.

Sheila: A woman

Skeg: Metal or timber support for a rudderpost.

Slipped: To slip a vessel is to haul it out of the water for repairs, modification, or antifouling treatment.

Sole: Floor of the cabin in a yacht.

Stem: The stem is the curved part of the boat at the bow into which the side parts of the boat run. The stemhead is the top of this structure at deck level.

Stern: Furthest aft part of a vessel.

Stern gland: Gland where the propeller shaft runs through the hull. The stern gland is usually packed with greasy hemp so that the shaft can turn but water cannot enter the hull.

Standing rigging: The wires supporting the masts.

Sumlog: Device to measure a vessel's speed and distance travelled.

Swages: Metal bands or collars that are slipped over two wires and then crimped with a special tool so that the wires are joined together.

Tacking: To bring vessel into wind then take wind on the other side.

Tinny: Small aluminium boat
Top End: Far north of Australia
Transom: The back of the hull, running across the stern.
Ute: Utility vehicle, pickup truck
Windvane: A mechanical device that steers a yacht in a direction in relationship to the wind. *Banyandah* has its own small rudder (servo) attached by lines to the steering tiller.
Yakka: Work (noun), as in hard yakka.

www.ingramcontent.com/pod-product-compliance
Lightning Source LLC
Chambersburg PA
CBHW050625300426
44112CB00012B/1657